Strangers in Arms

STRANGERS IN ARMS

Combat Motivation in the Canadian Army, 1943–1945

ROBERT ENGEN

McGill-Queen's University Press
Montreal & Kingston • London • Chicago

ISBN 978-0-7735-4725-4 (cloth)
ISBN 978-0-7735-9908-6 (ePDF)
ISBN 978-0-7735-9909-3 (ePUB)

Legal deposit second quarter 2016
Bibliothèque nationale du Québec

Printed in Canada on acid-free paper that is 100% ancient forest free (100% post-consumer recycled), processed chlorine free

This book has been published with the help of a grant from the Canadian Federation for the Humanities and Social Sciences, through the Awards to Scholarly Publications Program, using funds provided by the Social Sciences and Humanities Research Council of Canada.

McGill-Queen's University Press acknowledges the support of the Canada Council for the Arts for our publishing program. We also acknowledge the financial support of the Government of Canada through the Canada Book Fund for our publishing activities.

Library and Archives Canada Cataloguing in Publication

Engen, Robert C. (Robert Charles), 1983–, author
Strangers in arms : combat motivation in the Canadian Army, 1943–1945 / Robert Engen.

Includes bibliographical references and index.
Issued in print and electronic formats.
ISBN 978-0-7735-4725-4 (cloth).–ISBN 978-0-7735-9908-6 (PDF).–ISBN 978-0-7735-9909-3 (ePUB)

1. Canada. Canadian Army – History – World War, 1939–1945. 2. World War, 1939–1945 – Regimental histories – Canada. 3. World War, 1939–1945 – Participation, Canadian. 4. World War, 1939–1945 – Manpower – Canada. 5. World War, 1939–1945 – Psychological aspects. 6. Motivation (Psychology) – Canada – History – 20th century. 7. Military morale – Canada – History – 20th century. 8. Soldiers – Canada – Psychology. 9. Combat – Psychological aspects. 10. Combat sustainability (Military science). I. Title.

D768.15.E58 2016 940.53'71 C2016-900172-5
C2016-900173-3

In memory of Mark Argyle.
And for all those who have walked beside me
on the seawall over the past two decades.

Contents

APPENDICES

Figures and Tables

FIGURES

TABLES

Acknowledgments

The statement that I love writing more than just about anything else in the world will come as no revelation to my friends and family. It might, however, give some indication of the gratitude I feel, and the privilege it has been, for me to have been given the time and resources necessary to pursue a project of this scale. None of it would have been possible without a great deal of assistance.

Work on *Strangers in Arms* began almost the same day that my first book, *Canadians Under Fire*, was published in 2009, proving that there is indeed no rest for the wicked. This book's life started at Queen's University, and it benefited immensely from the sharp eyes and minds of Dr Doug Delaney, Dr Ian McKay, Dr Lisa Dufraimont, and Dr Lee Windsor. Yvonne Place, the history graduate assistant at Queen's during my time there, was also with me every step of the way through the process. The debt of gratitude that I owe to Dr Allan English, without whom neither my first major project nor this one (nor, indeed, my next one) would have ever come to light, is one I will carry for the rest of my life.

Many hands helped to build this particular house. Shen-wei Mark Lim of the Southern Alberta Institute of Technology was (once again) invaluable in helping me build the databases that allowed the tumult of my evidence to be organized into something resembling a meaningful form. Data on courts martial for sexual assault in the Canadian Army were provided by Dr Claire Cookson-Hills, based upon research she originally did for Dr Jonathan Fennell. Dr Feriel Kissoon carried out an extremely helpful reconnaissance-in-force at the National Archives in London on my behalf to fill gaps left by my initial research trip. Dr Matthew Trudgen and Dr Doug Delaney provided additional information, guidance, and support during this process. Colin McDougall's papers were acquired for me from McGill University by Pippa Cookson-Hills, whose two-hour moonlighting session was greatly appreciated, though it marked the beginning and end of her time as a historian. I lived more or less continuously in the Ottawa basement suite of Eleanor Belshaw-Hauff for the first part of 2010 while I carried out the bulk of my archival research, and haunted the abode of Dr Madelaine Morrison on many a subsequent trip; I have always been made to feel so welcome that I now think of Ottawa as a second home.

The research for this book was made possible through doctoral fellowships awarded by the Social Sciences and Humanities Research Council, as well as the Ontario Graduate Scholarship. Teaching fellowships at Queen's University also helped to make ends meet, and my students in History 476 ("Canada at War") and History 121 ("Intellectual Origins of the Contemporary West") at Queen's and History 484 ("The Stranger Arts of War") at RMC have armed me with an inspiration and confidence that I would not have thought possible. The Battle of Hill 70 Memorial Project has provided gainful and engaging employment during the preparation of this manuscript, and I owe thanks and gratitude in particular to Susan and Warren Everett and to the Hill 70 Project's Education Team. The manuscript was finalized and reviewed during my time as SSHRC postdoctoral fellow at the Royal Military College of Canada in 2015.

I would again like to thank the team at McGill-Queen's University Press for helping yet another manuscript fly through the process, starting with my editor, Kyla Madden, whose faith in my work always exceeds my own. My two anonymous readers offered extremely kind remarks and contributed their insight to the project in its late stages. For both of my books I have relied upon Jane McWhinney, whose superb copyediting elevated the manuscripts.

There is a list as long as my arm of friends and family who have contributed love, support, and assistance to me over the long years of this process. You know who you are – the Engens, Nicholbys, McNallys, Cookson-Hillses, and everyone else in Ontario, Quebec, and Alberta. Thank you to all. I would also be remiss if I did not mention the various penguins and parrots of our acquaintance. Especially Widget.

My grandfather, Robert Carl Schamuhn, passed away while this book was in press, and never got to see it on his shelf. I am left with the hope that he would have been proud.

None of this would have been possible had a brilliant, peculiar woman not sat down next to me at the University of Calgary twelve years ago and ended up staying by my side in perpetuity. Thank you, Dr Claire Cookson-Hills. I love you.

Robert Engen
12 December 2015

Strangers in Arms

Introduction

One of Canada's greatest war novels is Colin Malcolm McDougall's *Execution*. McDougall wrote the book semi-autobiographically and published it in 1958, as a "purging of the whole war experience" that he had carried back to Canada with him from the Second World War, where he had commanded an infantry company of Princess Patricia's Canadian Light Infantry (PPCLI) between 1943 and 1945.[1] *Execution* is an account of infantrymen fighting in Italy, a meditation on the existential ethics of war, and a rage against the degradation of warfare. A series of executions serve as the novel's unifying and most important theme.[2] McDougall narrates three: one is the execution of Italian prisoners by Canadian soldiers in Sicily. Another is the execution of a Canadian soldier found guilty of murder, inspired by the real-life execution of Private Harry Pringle in Italy.[3] And the last is "in the background ... the daily 'execution' of the fighting soldiers" as they are sent into battle.[4] "Execution" is the guiding metaphor for McDougall's entire experience of warfare.

Colin McDougall had waded ashore in Sicily with the Princess Pats as a platoon commander in July 1943, and fought in every subsequent action until January 1945, when a serious fever invalided him out of command of "B" Company.[5] His citation for the Distinguished Service Order describes him in glowing terms: "a most dashing and fearless officer of great skill and determination. This has been a real inspiration, an example to his men, and largely responsible for the successes of his Company."[6] During the time that McDougall served with the PPCLI, between Sicily in 1943 and the Senio River in January 1945, the regiment sustained over 1,350 battle casualties killed, wounded, and captured.[7] McDougall's unusual longevity as a junior officer meant that he would have seen hundreds of his men – whose lives were primarily his responsibility – struck down during that time, often while carrying out his orders.

It comes as no surprise, then, that McDougall's experiences coloured his novel. He remarked in his notes that one of the key themes of *Execution* is "the compassion and sacrifice of soldiers at war ... to be combined with the tragedy of survival, the dwindling of their original number."[8] Perhaps *Execution*'s most poignant scene comes in the second act, when the story's vainglorious Brigadier Ian Kildare attends a divisional meeting that sets the final plan for the Canadian attack on the Hitler/Senger Line in May 1944. The plan is a "set-piece attack," a frontal assault on an unbroken part of the line. Kildare is unimpressed with the idea, and challenges his superiors:

> Brigadier Kildare's immense figure seemed to fill the room. "I say your plan of attack is balls," he repeated. "It violates every elementary principle of war. Instead of exploiting success – over on the left where the Line is already penetrated – you're mounting a frontal attack on a position which cannot be taken by frontal attack!" ... Brigadier Kildare drew in his breath and spoke again, with a kind of measured finality. "To put my Brigade in against the strongest part of the Line – when the battle can be won elsewhere – is not war; it's a bloody execution!"[9]

McDougall believed that the real travesty was that the attack was not being launched for sound military reasons but out of administrative convenience and because: "There is something about a set-piece attack which the professional soldier finds irresistibly pleasing. The most minute detail can be provided for, each least item and contingency forecast and dovetailed into a beautifully exact operation order."[10] In the novel Kildare is right, though in reality the attack on the Hitler Line was much more successful than McDougall allows. The novel's attack ends in a shambles, leaving thousands of Canadians dead or wounded for no clear gain, as surely as if they had been executed. "The *execution* is the Evil," McDougall scrawled in his personal notebook while writing the novel; "when men consent to it they are less than themselves, they are against good, they are against God ... Man's plight is to be forced to participate in Execution."[11]

McDougall's novel had a lasting impact. *Execution* was awarded the Governor General's Prize for English language fiction in 1958 and is still regarded as a masterpiece, a key part of the Canadian canon of war writing that includes Will Bird, Timothy Findley, and Farley Mowat. In fact, Mowat, another 1939–45 war veteran, described *Execution* as "the closest approximation to the truth of the matter that I've encountered."[12] McDougall was apparently satisfied with the book, or perhaps had suffered through his experiences sufficiently during its torturous five-year writing; he never wrote another novel, and spent the rest of his life as registrar at McGill University.

Execution may have been McDougall's final word on his war experience, but it was not his first. In January 1945, after taking his Princess Pats all the way from Sicily to the Senio River, he had been struck by a serious, persistent fever, and left first his unit and then the Mediterranean theatre altogether.[13] Convalescing from his illness at No. 23 Canadian General Hospital back in the United Kingdom in April 1945, he was sent a battle experience questionnaire by Canadian Military Headquarters (CMHQ), on behalf of the British War Office's Directorate of Tactical Investigation (DTI). The questionnaire was being circulated among hundreds of Canadian junior officers who had returned from the front. It queried them about specific aspects of their war experience and invited them to offer additional personal commentary.[14] It was likely the first time McDougall put pen to paper about his war experiences, and for a much different audience. "This first-hand information regarding [your] personal experiences and the enemies' tactics and equipment," read the letter he was initially sent by DTI asking about his willingness to participate in the questionnaire, "may lead to improvement in our own technique."[15]

The novel *Execution* shows us Colin McDougall the writer, the man, and the philosopher in 1958, struggling to express to the world his "passion, and compassion, about 'execution.'"[16] The battle experience questionnaire shows us the soldier in 1945. Major McDougall gave his pro forma comments on enemy weapons usage but declined to give much information on the effectiveness of Canadian infantry weapons. He wrote at some length about the effects that German weapons had on the morale of his troops. He discussed the effectiveness of the German mortar with a note of particular dread: "its accurate sustained fire produces progressive no. of casualties, particularly in concentrated areas or where movement is not possible." He wrote about how the German mortars and self-propelled guns had a "moral effect" on Canadian infantry that increased with experience, whereas enemy machine guns and grenades were taken in stride and quickly became less terrifying. Most significantly, McDougall wrote about the factors that had the effect of raising the morale of his unit: "(1) Confidence in leaders from company level down; (2) Well planned, well fought, and successful actions; (3) Assurance that all amenities, such as leave, billets, entertainment, etc., in rest periods will be of the best. This depends on (1) of course." On the factors that lowered the morale of his unit, McDougall wrote: "(1) Lack of confidence in leaders and the resulting casualties; (2) What troops call 'being buggered about,' and regimental officers call 'poor staff work'; (3) Unfair leave or [Left out of Battle] systems."[17]

McDougall's other answers and personal remarks were entirely of a tactical nature, going into detail about German counterattacks, air support, night operations, and, at some length, anti-personnel mines, both German and Canadian.[18] Methods of crossing a minefield, he wrote in his questionnaire annexure, "depend[s], of course, on the extent of the minefield and the system of crossing. On the Gothic Line my company passed through a very thick anti-personnel minefield at night and in single file and suffered only three casualties. If forced to deploy the percentage will be considerably higher."[19]

These words were penned by the same man who, during the writing of *Execution*, would go on to ask: "Is it enough to say that execution is evil and that man is right when he struggles against it? But Faulkner said man was right when he mutinied against war. My characters, of course, do not mutiny. The 'daily' execution they accept [but] if execution is a matter of military necessity, then is military necessity wrong?" And he would end his thoughts by raging: "Damn it, there <u>is</u> betrayal! Execution betrays man!"[20] Was he remembering the minefields he had sent his men through as he wrote those words?

Perhaps McDougall's feeling of betrayal and his conflation of war with execution began during the fighting; it is unlikely that he would have expressed such sentiments on an official document such as the questionnaire while still in uniform. But the document contemporaneous to the fighting shows us a different side of his personality: that of the officer and the professional dispensing the hard lessons of his own experience at war. It is a side that likely shared many opinions with the man who struggled to write *Execution* in the 1950s. Like his fictional Brigadier Kildare, Major McDougall preferred clever "night infiltration by company groups" to set-piece assaults, and described "the feeling that an unpleasant and costly action is never going to end" as one of the most significant detriments to morale.[21] But we also see hints of McDougall as a soldier still embedded in the realities of morale, motivation, and leadership, as well as the difficulties faced by the infantrymen on the ground. The questionnaire is only a snapshot of a life, but this kind of contemporary evidence shows us a side of Major Colin M. McDougall that is different from the side we see in the pages of *Execution*.

Strangers in Arms is a study of the Canadian Second World War experience, using sources like the battle experience questionnaires, which can now provide a new and closer historical perspective than has previously been available. More specifically, it explores motivation, leadership, and morale – what Canadian infantrymen at the sharp end experienced and felt, and how these feelings guided behaviour in battle during Canada's sustained ground war against Nazi Germany.[22] In many ways it is an outgrowth of a previous book, *Canadians Under Fire: Infantry Effectiveness in the Second World War* (2009), which spoke to a single historiographical point: the claim by American writer S.L.A. Marshall that most infantrymen during the Second World War did not fire their weapons in combat.[23] This claim had been largely accepted for sixty years, but my conclusion in *Canadians Under Fire* was that the Canadian experience during the Second World War contradicted Marshall's thesis, and that subsequent works that have attempted to universalize Marshall's findings into a norm of human combat behaviour have suffered from faulty assumptions.[24] *Strangers in Arms* moves beyond questioning the Marshall thesis to explore how infantrymen actually fought on the ground, and to examine *why* they behaved in the ways they did, particularly in light of the extreme adversity they faced.

One reason why Marshall's work on combat behaviour stood largely unchallenged until the late 1980s was that historians have sometimes lacked a clear idea of how soldiers behave in combat. Many personal Canadian accounts of the Second World War, both published and unpublished, are already a part of the literature, and some go into considerable detail about the experience of battle.[25] From the perspective of this study, the problem with personal accounts is that even if postwar memories can be considered reliable, each account represents only one individual's subjective experience, with little opportunity to systematize findings. As Major W.E.C. Harrison, a member of the Canadian Army's Historical Section during the war, and afterward an historian at Queen's University, once observed about retrospective accounts: "there are few more unreliable sources of evidence than the eye-witness ... it is as difficult to read the truth through a magnifying glass as it is through a telescope."[26] And, as the great Canadian official historian C.P. Stacey was to reminisce about eye-witness accounts given in retrospect: "one scrap of paper written on the evening of the battle is worth reams of reminiscence written down or spoken into tape recorders after months or years have passed. The best historical evidence is evidence recorded *at the time*."[27] That was the reason why Marshall's work with the US Army's historical section was treated with such gravity: his interviews were supposedly carried out in close proximity to the battles he wrote about, although his actual data-collection methods were considered either flawed or nonexistent, depending upon the historian who examined them.[28] But the point is a good one: while oral histories and postwar reminiscences can play an important part in the historian's craft, they are coloured by the limits of memory and may tell us more about the recollector at the time of their recollections than about their experiences in the war. As with Colin McDougall's battle experience questionnaire *vis-à-vis* his descriptions in the novel *Execution*, we receive, at minimum, a different perspective from what he conveyed while the fighting was still happening. Individual accounts written during the war, in the form of letters, diaries, or even official documents, have the invaluable asset of proximity to events, but it is difficult to draw general conclusions from disparate individual voices, and, lacking systematization, such projects smack of the anecdotal.

A number of scholarly works in the field of Canadian military history have attempted to find solutions to the problem of how to "get at" soldiers' experiences of war. Official histories of the Second World War are unhelpful in this regard, since they are top-down histories written about (and for the benefit of) the senior officers and, in the words of historian Tim Cook, "remained focused on the generals rather than the infantrymen, and the strategic or operational picture of war rather than the experience of battle."[29] Innumerable regimental histories have been written since the end of the war, ranging wildly in quality – and most financed by regimental associations. The best of these, written by talented historians, dedicated and conscientious veterans, or both, are authoritative records of their regiment's activities and meld recollections, interviews, regimental lore, and contemporary documentation into rich historical accounts with very human protagonists.[30] Anthony Kellett's *Combat Motivation* (1982) is a major thematic study of combat behaviour through the ages, and while not solely about Canada, was written for the Operational Research and Analysis Establishment of Canada's Department of National Defence and employs many Canadian examples.[31] Kellett's work has served as a major source of inspiration for this present volume. Bill McAndrew and Terry Copp's classic *Battle Exhaustion: Soldiers and Psychiatrists in the Canadian Army, 1939–45* (1990) delved deeper into the experiences of frontline Canadian fighters than any work before or since, outlining the structure of the Canadian neuropsychiatric services.[32] Harold Margolian's *Conduct Unbecoming* (1998) is a similarly detailed – indeed, forensic – accounting of the German murder of Canadian prisoners of war in 1944 and provides key assessments of the behaviour, motivation, and disciplinary systems of the combatants.[33] Doug Delaney's biography of 5th Canadian Armoured Division's Major-General Bert Hoffmeister, *The Soldiers' General* (2005), also shows how it is possible to blend a detailed "micro-historical" biography into a more generalized exploration of the experience of war from unit command to the ranks of the general officer.[34] Terry Copp's twin books on the Canadian campaigns in Normandy and Northwest Europe, *Fields of Fire* (2003) and *Cinderella Army* (2006), draw the reader remarkably close to the firing line while still retaining a "big-picture" perspective on operations, using almost exclusively the contemporary documentary evidence.[35] Copp's earlier work on the 5th Canadian Infantry Brigade between 1939 and 1945, *The Brigade* (1992), falls into a similar category and achieves an even more specific focus.[36]

Strangers in Arms attempts to position itself among these explorations of Canadian infantry morale and motivation, primarily through the use of aggregate, systematized data sources such as battle experience questionnaires, consolidated casualty lists, offence statistics, and censorship reports, along with contemporary studies such as operational research and "lessons learned" reports.[37] British historian Jonathan Fennell has used some similar methods and sources in his recent work on the Eighth

Army in North Africa, albeit focusing on the British experience, but few if any of the equivalent Canadian sources employed in this present book have been hitherto explored.[38] This source base has allowed a wide view, permitting discussion of the infantrymen from all of Canada's battalions fighting in both the Italian and Northwest Europe campaigns. The aggregate data can answer questions applicable to how and why Canadians fought, at the same time allowing observation of the differences between the major theatres. This book is therefore something of a population study of the Canadian infantryman in the Second World War, and owes a great deal to Samuel Stouffer's social psychology study of the US Army, *The American Soldier* series (1949).[39] Many new points will be raised in the coming chapters. Some of the most important points challenge traditional ideas about primary-group cohesion and morale, and will offer some idea of how these processes may have functioned within the Canadian Infantry Corps.

A few concepts from the psychological literature require further elaboration for the sake of clarity. A good place to start is with combat motivation itself, the expression used in this book's title. As mentioned previously, Kellett's *Combat Motivation* is a skilfully written review of the topic and a classic of this field of study. As Kellett explains, motivation forms the "why" of behaviour: "the search for the determinants of human activity and for an explanation of the processes that underlie an individual's overt actions." Internal factors and external/situational factors both underlie individual actions. In *Combat Motivation* he defines motivation as follows: "conscious or unconscious calculation by the combat soldier of the material and spiritual benefits and costs likely attached to various courses of action." Combat motivation, in particular, he says, "comprises the influences that bear on a soldier's choice of, degree of commitment to, and persistence in effecting a certain course of action."[40] Israeli military psychologist Ben Shalit offers a clinical appraisal of behaviour and decision making that strikes many of the same notes. Shalit discusses motivation in terms of "the factors that build up in a person or a group to make them willing and able to engage in combat [and] how such factors can be influenced so as to make people more capable of combat."[41] Weighing upon such decisions are rewards – intrinsic and extrinsic (such as task fulfilment, duty, honour, group loyalty, pride, pay, awards) – and punishments (failure, disciplinary measures, confinement, psychiatric evaluation, possible retribution against self or family).[42] When I discuss combat motivation in this book, I treat it as the process involving a soldier's decision to fight, and to keep fighting, in combat. This makes combat motivation distinct from a soldier's motives in joining the army in the first place, and the two should not be conflated. An enthusiastic soldier rallying to the drums and trumpets may prove a great deal more reluctant once real stakes are on the table.

"Morale" is another concept that requires both explanation and definition, as it is a slippery term that usually lacks specificity. It is always agreed to be important – Napoleon famously stated: "Morale makes up three-quarters of the game [of war]; the relative balance of manpower accounts only for the remaining quarter"[43] – but a consensus on how to define it is harder to come by. In September 1945 Nigel Balchin, the British Deputy Science Advisor to the Army Council, wrote an irritated memo to the DTI telling them to "stop talking about morale as though it were a holy mystery on the one hand, or a matter of proper cattle-feeding on the other."[44] Definitions in academic studies have varied widely and changed with the times. F.C. Bartlett's interwar study, *Psychology and the Soldier* (1927), took morale to be "obedience to authority under external circumstances which impose great strain, the source of authority being within the man, or the group, that is obedient."[45] The American National Research Council's 1943 publication *Psychology for the Fighting Man*, on the other hand, defined it quite differently: "Morale is the capacity to stay on the job – especially a long, hard job – with determination and zest. It is the opposite of apathy."[46] John Baynes's excellent 1967 treatment of the Battle of Neuve Chapelle philosophically defines morale as, "in the broadest terms ... concerned with the way in which people react to the conditions of their existence."[47] Amid protestations about how imprecisely the term "morale" is used by historians, Nora Stewart, in her 1991 study of combat motivation in the Falklands War, treats morale as simply synonymous with "will-to-fight."[48] And the latest iteration of *The Oxford Handbook of Military Psychology* (2012) defines morale, a touch unhelpfully, as "the emotional bond that holds the group together."[49]

Clearly, little shared meaning is communicated when scholars use the word "morale." It is variously thought to be cheerfulness, obedience, will to fight, and simple reaction to stimuli. But given our previous definition of combat motivation, it is perhaps the National Research Council's 1943 definition that comes closest to a satisfying response in terms of associating morale with commitment to performing a job or task. In the case of this book, the jobs were those of the Canadian infantrymen of the Second World War, which were specifically detailed in the British War Office's 1935 *Field Service Regulations*: "closing with the enemy, compel[ling] his withdrawal or surrender, and holding the objectives which have been secured or the points of importance which have to be protected, as a base for further action."[50] The job of the infantry was to fight and to be able to engage directly with the enemy; all its other tasks were subordinated to the ability to fight in combat.[51] While not true of all people in all situations, when it comes to the Canadian infantrymen of 1939–45, morale is usefully viewed in the terms proposed by Shalit: "[both] the willingness to fight, and the willingness to persevere in fighting."[52] Morale goes beyond feelings of cheerfulness and comradeship. It includes those psychological forces at work within a group that compel its members to fight, and is thereby closely associated with our definition of combat motivation. This definition is also useful because it highlights the fact that, as military psychologist Frederick Manning argues, there is no such thing as "group-feeling," and morale (though susceptible to and dependent upon others) is a characteristic of individuals.[53] So morale, in this study, will be defined as the willingness on the part of infantrymen, individually and in groups, to fight and to persevere in fighting; and "high morale" will be taken to mean a high willingness to participate in combat.

What creates high morale? I will spend considerable time in each of the four campaign chapters discussing this question in the specific case of Canadian soldiers. On a more general level, however, Manning is right when he describes high morale as requiring, at minimum, three things for each individual soldier: "a *goal*, a *role*, and a *reason for self-confidence*."[54] A clear objective to fight for, an established place within a social group, and a reason to feel good about oneself and one's situation are key constituents of the willingness to fight, and of combat motivation.[55]

Closely related to the concept of morale, and sometimes used interchangeably with it, are the terms "cohesion" and "esprit de corps." The French army officer and theorist Ardant du Picq, killed in the Franco-Prussian War in 1870, was one of the first to explicitly adopt "moral cohesion" as a term and concept; du Picq defined it as that which makes a soldier capable of obedience: respect for and confidence in leaders and comrades, and fear of their reproaches and retaliation for failure.[56] Throughout the twentieth century, research has pointed to the "primary group" of ten to twelve soldiers as being the level at which cohesion is most important, while "esprit de corps" typically defines soldiers' identification with higher military formations, such as the battalion, regiment, or division. Many scholars, including Marshall and Stouffer, found that loyalty to the group was paramount in high-performing units. But the most influential study of the primary group was done by military sociologists Edgar Shils and Morris Janowitz, whose postwar work involved interviewing Wehrmacht prisoners of war to determine why some German units had fought against insurmountable odds while others surrendered easily. Shils and Janowitz found that, while Germans in effective units fought for a variety of reasons (most importantly small-group cohesion, physical proximity, devotion to National Socialism, protectiveness of NCOs and officers), those who surrendered did so because their primary-group ties had been disrupted.[57]

Shils and Janowitz effectively founded an entire field of study on cohesion. By the 1980s, when the field was dominated by soldier-scholars such as William Henderson and Charles Moskos, cohesion was freshly defined as: "the bonding together of members of an organization/unit in such a way as to sustain their will and commitment to each other, their unit, and the mission."[58] Units whose "high cohesion" could be measured were demonstrated to suffer fewer non-battle (disease and neuropsychiatric) casualties, to fight harder, to have fewer deserters, and to have fewer disciplinary problems.[59] Since the 1980s, researchers at the US Army Research Institute for the Behavioral and Social Sciences and the Walter Reed Army Institute of Research have carried out extensive research on the question of cohesion in military forces. Guy Siebold, a Walter Reed research fellow, has proffered a "standard model of cohesion" that is the end-product of decades of research, and which attempts to unify working theories on cohesion. While not uncontroversial, the standard model provides a comprehensive framework on military cohesion. It captures most aspects of military group dynamics within its structure and is useful for conceptualization.

Siebold's standard model of cohesion includes four interacting components of cohesion which are based on different structural relationships:

peer bonding ("horizontal" cohesion), leader bonding ("vertical" cohesion), institutional bonding (with the military as a whole), and organizational bonding ("esprit de corps," bonding within organizational units such as the regiment). Bonding itself refers to the creation of social relationships of changeable strength among service members and their groups, both emotional and utilitarian. In this model, peer and leader bonding together constitute "primary group cohesion," while organizational and institutional bonding constitute "secondary group cohesion."[60] "Primary group cohesion," writes Siebold, "generates the fighter, while secondary group cohesion creates the professional group member." Unlike earlier concepts of cohesion, which dwell upon friendship, comradeship, and intimate relations of masculinity, Siebold's standard model emphasizes the importance of trust among group members that they will protect one another, together with the capacity for teamwork and the ability to pull together to accomplish a task.[61] The standard model, by not fixating upon personal friendships and the "band of brothers" concept of cohesion, also allows that technical skill, proficiency with arms, and level of training (or the inverse of any of these) can be significant contributors (or barriers) to bonding and group status. As a theoretical basis for studying soldiers in battle, this model is also highly consonant with the definitions of morale that I have adopted in here. However, cohesion also remains distinct from morale in important ways. It is possible for a highly cohesive, peer-bonded group to have extremely low morale and a limited willingness to fight or to follow directions from the military institution.[62] Nevertheless, groups cohesive on all of the "sliding scales" of the standard model (horizontal, vertical, organizational, institutional) are far more likely to possess high morale, as their internal goals and experiences will align with leadership and institutional expectations.

In the standard model of cohesion, social interactions involved in both horizontal and vertical bonding among soldiers are based upon direct personal interactions and face-to-face cooperative, and holistic, supportive relationships developed over time in relatively closed groups.[63] But what takes place when the primary group is torn apart, either by casualties or by organizational imperatives?[64] In some scholarship, particularly regimental histories, it is claimed that organizational bonding, esprit de corps, and pride of unit helped to produce fighting bonds and high morale even when primary group cohesion was low or nonexistent.[65] There are other claims that ideology, nationalism, and abstract ideas of that nature can unite soldiers and function to create bonds.[66] However, as I will show in this book, such theories are at best partial answers to the challenge – and not particularly convincing ones at that – in the case of Canadian soldiers.

One of the more compelling concepts to emerge in the combat motivation literature in the last ten years is the idea of "swift trust" as an element of cohesion. Trust within peer groups, between followers and leaders, and within the organization are all bedrocks of the standard model of cohesion. However, the small but growing "swift trust" literature takes cohesion a step further and posits, supported by evidence from combat operations, that the trust predicating cohesion is not necessarily based upon extensive previous face-to-face interactions and shared experience.

An Israeli study published in 2005 by a team led by Uzi Ben-Shalom opened the discussion on swift trust. The study found that during the Al-Aqsa Intifada of 2000–01, the Israeli Defence Forces (IDF) "consciously and systematically" took apart and recombined units throughout the conflict. Under the Intifada's conditions of sudden, unpredictable, intense violence, IDF units were frequently divided into small components and assigned to other elements on short notice for specific tactical purposes and missions. What the standard model of cohesion would identify as the "primary group" was split apart and mixed with others in different geographic locations under different commanders. "Primary group cohesion could not be sustained," Ben-Shalom argues, "since the original units were under a constant process of splitting and reintegrating."[67] While these processes created uncertainty among troops, that uncertainty was not accompanied by breakdowns in troop morale and unit discipline. Instead, these new "instant units" worked very well together, although the dynamics of trust could develop along different lines. Although soldiers wanted to be back with their normal units, combat-effective temporary units could nevertheless be created on the fly. But while in regular units trust is built up organically over a span of time to create cohesive groups, teams created rapidly under tight deadlines had little opportunity for building relationships or experiencing real socialization among peers or leaders. Soldiers' opinions of one another would at first be based upon reputations, stereotypes, and cultural assumptions, but professionalism and pride would take over as motivating factors in finding ways to collaborate with complete strangers. Other factors contributing to the success of instant units included the envelopment of "guest" elements into a "host" unit (building a community through material exchange), and the creation of temporary frameworks that combined doctrine with local practices agreeable to all parties.[68] The swift trust established between strangers allowed for surprising flexibility and resilience in terms of morale and fighting efficiency in groups where primary group cohesion would normally not have existed.

Actual IDF combat operations in the field rarely corresponded with traditional understandings of bonding, particularly esprit de corps. Personnel reorganization and heavy casualties can both mean that the primary group based upon long-developed knowledge and trust among peers, shared experiences, and confidence in known leaders is a finite and expendable resource. A recent RAND report for the US Army assessed the capabilities and experiences of the French Army's expeditionary deployment to Mali in 2013. Its author, Michael Shurkin, wrote about how the small French army force, well suited to expeditionary operations and austere environments, had as its main characteristics, "modularity and scalability pushed down to the company task force," and "the ability to disaggregate and reaggregate battalions and brigades." The French *sous-groupements tactiques interarmes* ("combined-arms tactical subgroups") of approximately company size, were often task-organizing on an ad hoc basis not out of necessity, but as "a matter of doctrine, practice, and habit."[69] Through these examples, one can see potent elements of swift trust being incorporated into present-day doctrine and practice.

The Canadian Army between 1943 and 1945 was certainly not implementing swift trust among its troops by doctrine but, as will be seen as this book develops, it would have been one of the major bonds that held infantrymen together when necessary. Heavy casualties among Canadian infantry battalions (usually between 150 and 200 percent casualties per battalion and 300 percent among junior officers) as well as internal "aggregation and deaggregation" of units to fill gaps left by casualties and to create task-organized specialist teams, meant that instant and ad hoc units with unfamiliar leadership were frequently found on the ground. The processes adopted by the Canadian Army were not the same as those of the modern IDF or the French Army; however, the concept of swift trust provides considerable explanatory power as a supplement to the standard model of cohesion, and will be referred to throughout this book, even though often it must be inferred from the historical sources rather than observed directly. As such, the existence and importance of swift trust in the context of the Canadian infantry can best viewed be as a hypothesis of this study. The importance of "strangers in arms" working effectively together in combat is key to understanding Canadian military operations.

Chapter 1, "Myths and Realities of the Canadian Army," explores some of the population statistics and characteristics of the Canadian Army in the Second World War, examining who the soldiers were and why they joined the war effort. It ends with a detailed look at one particular soldier, Corporal Charles Daniel Lloyd of the Hastings and Prince Edward Regiment.

"Building the Canadian Infantry," the second chapter, gives background on the regimental system and personnel selection, and on the training provided to Canadian infantry prior to their going into combat.

Chapters 3 through 6 represent the "campaign" chapters and the core of the book's evidence. Each chapter explores one discrete time period during which Canadian forces overseas were in combat in a particular theatre. After discussing the Sicilian and Italian campaigns of 1943 in chapter 3, I proceed to examine the remainder of the Italian campaign, 1944–45, in chapter 4. Chapter 5 continues, with a study of the Canadians in Normandy in 1944, and chapter 6 follows the European war to its conclusion in Northwest Europe, 1944–45.

A series of appendices presents the data that have informed the study in more detail than the body text of the book will allow. A short treatise on methodology and sources is included as Appendix A, and a discussion of the Canadian Army's infantry organization is included as Appendix D.

1

Myths and Realities of the Canadian Army

An ancient Greek myth from the fifth century BCE tells of the Phoenician explorer Kadmos, who fought and killed a dragon at the future site of the city of Thebes. The goddess Athena told Kadmos to plant the dragon's teeth in the ground, and where he had sown the teeth a company of fully formed and armed soldiers clawed their way out of the earth to serve him. While apocryphal, the image of these "sown men" (the *spartoi*) arising from the earth imbued with a natural martial spirit, ready to fight at a moment's notice, resonates in Canadian history. Canada's soldiers are often cast in the imagination as spartoi, emerging from the land as fully constructed citizen-soldiers whenever called to arms, needing little more than a rifle and their own killer instincts.[1]

As a precursor to examining the reality of who they actually were and why they enlisted to fight, this chapter explores a few widely held assumptions about the Canadian soldiers. The Canadian soldiers were not heroes of myth, and did not spring from the soil as fully formed spartoi warriors in September of 1939. Those who were to later storm Italy and Normandy did not reach the battlefield from a void, and the way in which they were to act and behave as soldiers developed in the very specific context of interwar Canada.

WHO WERE THE SOLDIERS?

The first question in a discussion of Canada's soldiers at the time should be – though it hardly ever is – what *was* Canada then? It is frequent practice to cast nations as homogenous entities pushing together toward a common objective, if not always in harmonious lockstep. In such a framework Canada is normally identified as the "senior Dominion" of the British Empire, united with the other freedom-loving Western liberal democracies in opposition to fascism. In some political science assessments, democracy itself has been proposed as a key to combat effectiveness and as a self-evident explanation for military success.[2] And certainly in postwar rhetoric the idea that soldiers "fought for Canada" or "fought for democracy" is common enough.[3] But in the early twentieth century Canada was only partially democratic for most of its inhabitants and as a country had a dodgy relationship with the concept of "freedom." These points are often obscured because Canada stands in such sharp contrast with its enemies in Nazi Germany and Fascist Italy, with whom there was clearly no moral equivalent. However, since Canadians are our primary interest here, the concept of the nation as they experienced it deserves some scrutiny, especially since nationalism and national community are sometimes cited as major components of combat motivation.[4]

In the legal sense, Canada in the 1940s was a semi-autonomous federated state exercising power over the northern part of the continent as an outreach of the British Crown. It was called a British "Dominion," a bit of vernacular legerdemain used in 1867 because it communicated monarchical allegiance while not being as provocative to American republicanism as John A. Macdonald's favoured name, the "Kingdom of Canada."[5] With the Statute of Westminster in 1931, the Canadian state had gained some measure of control over its own foreign policy, but Canadian citizenship as a legal status was a product of the post-1945 world. It was the Canadian Citizenship At of 1946 (which came into effect in 1947) that established independent citizenship. Prior to 1947, all "Canadian citizens" and "Canadian nationals," whether native-born or naturalized, were (under the Naturalization Act of 1914) subsets of the status of "British subject."[6] British courts remained the highest judicial authority, and the source of sovereignty was situated in the British Crown. The achievement of democracy in Canada was a somewhat halting process, since representative government could be found in Parliament alongside a senate and the vice-regal delegate of a hereditary constitutional monarch. Women had been granted full federal voting rights in Canada only in 1918, and it was not until 1940 that they gained the vote in provincial elections in Quebec. Exclusions from the electoral rolls based upon racial origin remained in place until well after the Second

World War. The national voting age was twenty-one, and would not be lowered to eighteen until 1970, although special dispensations allowed that every man and woman "who being a British subject, is a member of the Naval, Military or Air Forces of Canada" was entitled to vote even if they were not yet twenty-one.[7] Although freedoms and liberties were promised to Canada's British subjects, freedoms such as expression, assembly, and conscience could often not be counted upon. As historian Ian McKay has pointed out, "in many ways such freedoms of expression were ... radically endangered in the 1910s to 1940s – with banned political parties, coerced labour camps, a massive apparatus of state surveillance, police shootings and deportations, even officially proscribed languages" – to which might be added the suppressive military "aid to the civil power" actions.[8] During the 1930s civil rights in Canada were being curtailed in ways that made leftist intellectuals believe that the country was on a trajectory toward its own brand of anti-democratic fascism.[9]

The determination of precisely who was eligible to fight for Canada, when, and why was shaped by a project of rule that was as much concerned with internal power and politics as it was with vanquishing the enemy overseas.[10] Canadian women could volunteer to join the female branches of the armed services but were under no legal compulsion to do so, and under no circumstances would they be allowed to fight as infantry – in Canada close combat remained a male domain. But certainly not all men were permitted to fight. The veterans of the Canadian Mackenzie-Papineau Battalion, who fought in the Spanish Civil War, are a good example. Despite being Canada's only soldiers with experience in modern warfare in 1939, as well as being accredited anti-fascists, the returned Mac-Pap veterans were formally barred from serving in the Canadian Army because their service in Spain had been arranged by the Communist Party of Canada (though many found ways to serve anyway).[11] And nowhere were the demands and contradictions of Canada's liberal democracy more evident than in the country's tortured relationship with voluntarism and conscription. Volunteering oneself for service became the respected mark of individualism and character, whereas those who waited to be conscripted and compelled to fight were, both officially and unofficially, portrayed as lower forms of life: passive, unstable, and irresponsible.[12]

So while my focus is "Canada" and "Canadians," it is helpful to remember that the understanding of what these concepts meant was different in the 1940s. Canada's soldiers were often motivated in combat by a sense of the grave importance and necessity of what they were doing – but at the same time, feelings of patriotism, nationalism, or of "fighting for Canada" were not prevalent among infantrymen.

What else can we establish about Canada's soldiers? In the Second World War, as in the First, Ontario was far and away the greatest contributor of fighting men and women, both in absolute terms and as a relative percentage of its population. Throughout the war 274,414 people in Ontario joined the Canadian Army, whether as General Service (GS) volunteers, National Resources Mobilization Act (NRMA) conscripts, or Canadian Women's Army Corps (CWAC), and 218,224 listed Ontario as their place of birth. Quebec came second, with 140,435 joining the army in that province and 130,711 listing Quebec as their birthplace. Beyond the two largest provinces, 92,415 men and women were drawn from the Maritimes, 15,863 from the three Prairie Provinces, 26,034 from British Columbia, and 151 from the two Territories.[13] An adjutant-general's study of October 1944 indicated that in the Canadian Army Overseas, which represented the fighting and administrative echelons in the United Kingdom and Europe, some 74 percent of soldiers were English-Canadian or British, 12 percent were French Canadian, and 12.5 percent were of other continental European extraction.[14] Indian Affairs reported that 3,090 status Indians had participated in the Second World War for Canada (2.4 percent of the 125,946 status Indians identified in the 1941 census), the majority of them in the infantry (there were no specifically Aboriginal units or sub-units, but they tended to be concentrated in the western prairie infantry regiments). The number of non-status Indians and Métis who served in the army is unknown but would have been much larger.[15]

The question of French-Canadian participation in the Second World War is a fraught topic, and the statistics lend themselves, as Yves Tremblay has put it, to prejudice against the French-Canadian war effort.[16] It is difficult to assess how many francophones volunteered because native tongue was not correlated in the war service record statistics alongside place of enrolment, and the English-speaking population of Quebec tended to volunteer in numbers out of proportion to their segment of the population.[17] Jean-Yves Gravel has estimated a total of about 55,000 French-Canadian volunteers including Acadians, Franco-Ontarians, and francophones in the rest of Canada.[18] This number is probably on the low side, however. Statistics from the Department of Veterans' Affairs indicated that, including GS volunteers, NRMA conscripts, and CWACs combined, 492,670 (67.4 percent) of Canadian Army soldiers spoke English only, 48,812 (6.7 percent) spoke French only, and 110,256 (15.3 percent) were bilingual or could communicate well in both languages.[19] According to the 1941 Census, 67.2 percent of Canadians nationwide spoke English only, 19 percent spoke French only, and 12.8 percent spoke both English and French. Unilingual French-speakers were under-represented in the army, but bilingual Canadians were in fact overrepresented.[20] As Serge Durflinger found in his wartime history of the blended anglo/franco city of Verdun, Quebec, more than half of the French-speaking Canadians who voluntarily joined the Canadian Army during the Second World War served in English-speaking regiments and units.[21]

There were both continuities and differences between the Canadian Army that went to war in 1939–45 and the one that had fought twenty-five years earlier. In 1914 approximately 70 percent (and close to 100 percent in some regiments) of other ranks (ORs) of the First Contingent overseas had been British-born, and émigrés from the British Isles remained an important source of manpower throughout the conflict, despite accounting for only 11 percent of the population in 1911.[22] It was not until 1918 and conscription that the total number of Canadian-born ORs surpassed 50 percent of the Canadian military's total manpower.[23] In contrast, about 85 percent of Canadian Army soldiers in the Second World War listed their birthplace as being in Canada, a higher rate than the general population and a reflection of the dearth of Depression immigration. Only about 67,000 – 9 percent – of all ranks in the Canadian Army between 1939 and 1945 had been born in Britain.[24]

Nonetheless, voluntarism in the Second World War remained strongest among British émigrés and social circles closely associated with British traditions. In the initial contingent of 57,722 who joined in 1939, members of the Church of England were extremely overrepresented, given their generally small distribution in the population at the time (see figure 1.1).[25]

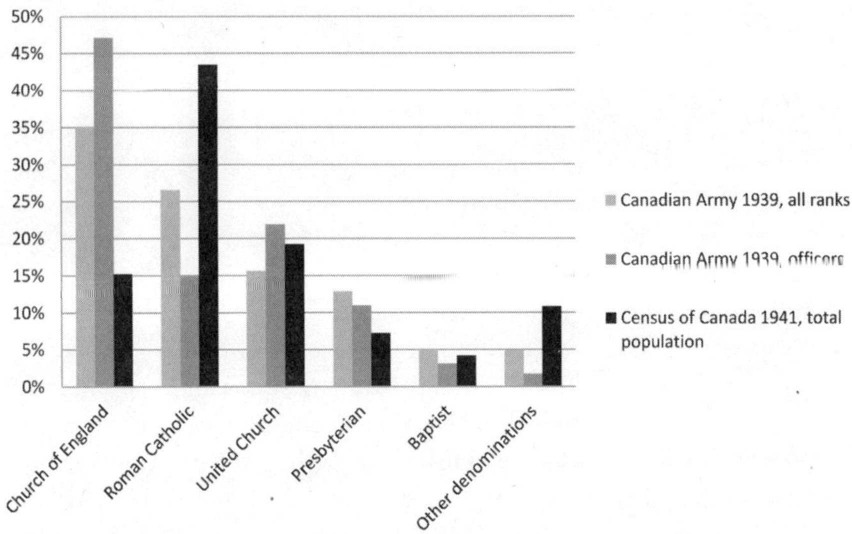

Figure 1.1: Religious denominations

At least among the 1939 recruits, professed adherents to the Church of England, who numbered only about 15 percent of the total population in 1941, had provided over one-third of all recruits, while those of the Roman Catholic faith, who were closer to half the population, provided only one-quarter. Interestingly, of the 2,947 officer appointments in September 1939, wholly half of officers identified as Anglican and only 15 percent identified as Catholic – a complete reversal of their respective national populations.[26] This comes as no surprise. The Church of England, despite being a minority religious institution, was "interwoven into the social fabric [of Canada], more so than any other denomination other than the Roman Catholic Church in Quebec."[27] The Anglican Church strongly identified with the Anglo-Canadian "establishment," and even in the 1940s there existed the sense that when it came to the Church of England, every Englishman was an Anglican, and vice versa.[28] So while the Canadian-born contingent of the Canadian Army in the Second World War was much greater than it had been in 1914–18, the minority with the strongest identification with the Anglican Church remained most eager to enlist, and received high positions within the army. These data raise questions about the social compositions of the army and which social circles the core leadership was being drawn from.

In the entire Canadian Army Overseas in Italy, Northwest Europe, and the UK, 158,000 personnel were tied up in field formations, those being the soldiers allotted to the five divisions, two independent armoured brigades, and corps and army troops. Typically, there were over 100,000 more in base and line-of-communications units, who would staff headquarters and reinforcement holding units, and meet other administrative and support needs. This distribution was the end result of a policy by which Canada, "for political reasons involving status and nationhood," insisted on having its own lines of supply and communication rather than using British sources.[29] The established strength of the five Canadian divisions combined was about 85,000 all ranks, and the total strength of all infantry battalions within those divisions was less than half that: 37,817 spread unevenly among five divisions. The number was low, considering that infantry battalions would sustain 78 percent of the army's total casualties during the fighting.[30] The Canadian Army was one in which the "tail" massively outweighed the "teeth," and skilled personnel were consistently channelled into plentiful non-combat-support, administrative, and headquarters positions.

There are two perspectives on this over-staffing. On the one hand, the Canadian Army was a fully motorized, mechanized, modern fighting force that required tremendous numbers of support personnel backing the fighting soldiers. The "teeth and tail" analogy is less useful than thinking about the army as a body consisting of complex, mutually supporting systems. The success of combatants always depended upon the good and timely work of supporting branches, and, as becomes clear in the following chapters, the excellence of Canadian logistical and support services actually firmly underlay the good morale and fighting spirit of the combat soldiers.

On the other hand, political historian Richard Walker has laid out a superb case for how the over-staffing of the Canadian Army Overseas was a deliberate policy on the part of army commanders. According to Walker this policy bordered upon conspiracy, as senior general officers, in the hopes of creating the vast postwar peacetime army of their dreams, quietly manoeuvred the Canadian government into allowing them an army so large that it could only be sustained through conscription.[31]

On the eve of its commitment to battle in Sicily in July 1943, the total size of the Canadian Army (in Canada and overseas) was 399,984 GS volunteers, plus 70,976 NRMA conscripts. By March 1945, the army had reached its peak strength of 438,744 GS and 41,700 NRMA men, most of the expansion in GS men being from conscripts who volunteered for overseas duty.[32] A total of 730,159 GS, NRMA, and CWAC personnel were appointed, enlisted, or enrolled in the army during the war – a breathtaking expansion from the small pre-war militia. This was greater than a one-hundred-fold increase in the number of full-time soldiers, and, unavoidably, resulted in a corresponding dilution of what pre-war military expertise Canada possessed.[33]

It was not surprising that very few Canadian soldiers who reached the battlefield had prewar military experience. Most of those who did had been members of the Non-Permanent Active Militia (NPAM) or the Permanent Force (PF) prior to the start of hostilities, and members of both of these peacetime services joined up almost to a man in 1939. The Permanent Force, constituting Canada's full-time, professional soldiery, was tiny; in September 1939 all 581 officers and 4,809 other ranks of the PF joined up for active service.[34] Those PF soldiers who were not dispersed to help raise and train the rest of the Canadian Active Service Force (CASF) were concentrated in the battalions of the 1st Canadian Infantry Brigade, which went overseas with 1st Division in December 1939.[35] Although the PF provided many of the senior officers who led the Canadians into battle, casualty returns indicate that there were only 104 other rank PF infantrymen who became battle casualties in the Mediterranean and Northwest Europe theatres from 1943 to 1945.[36] Recruits who attested to having experience in foreign militaries amounted to 1,252 all ranks in September 1939, and veterans of the First World War's Canadian Expeditionary Force (CEF) accounted for another 4,206, although the CEF veterans were at minimum approaching the age of forty, and hardly any would see battle in 1943–45.[37] An unknown number who enlisted during the Second World War had recently fought in the Spanish Civil War, but illegally, and veterans of that conflict's Mackenzie-Papineau Battalion were not allowed to enlist, though many did anyway.[38]

From all sources, only 4,975 men out of three-quarters of a million had listed "soldier" as their previous profession on their attestation papers.[39] Canada's army in the field was thoroughly civilian in character.

The army drew mainly, though not exclusively, upon those from working-class backgrounds. A majority came from occupations in agriculture (10%), trades such as bricklaying, carpentry, and plumbing (7%), manufacturing jobs (15%), and transportation (14%), or were listed under the category of "general labourers" (16%); those occupations alone accounted for over 62 percent of those listed by Canadian Army personnel on their attestation forms. Soldiers in white-collar occupations were in the minority: civil and municipal employees (1%), clerical workers such as accountants, clerks, and secretaries (6%), domestic and personal service (4 %), salesmen and "mercantile pursuits" (5%), students (3%), and those from the professions, including architects, teachers, engineers, lawyers, nurses, and physicians (3%). Only a little more than one percent were classified as having "ill-defined occupations," and a scant 3,774 (0.5 %) out of 730,000 Canadian Army enlistees reported "no occupation."[40] One of the views traditionally held by military historians, perhaps typified by W.A.B. Douglas and Brereton Greenhous, was that "unemployment was a form of conscription," and that a disproportionate number of General Service volunteers in the Canadian Army joined up to escape unemployment and poverty.[41] The war service records and attestation forms required self-reporting of occupations at time of enlistment, so it is likely that many enlistees who stated an occupation (particularly those involved in agriculture or "general labour") were in fact unemployed at the time. But recent studies have convincingly made the case that most Canadian soldiers were not simply volunteering for service to escape unemployment, and that the unemployed were a small minority among volunteers.[42] We do not yet have sufficient data on the occupations of those who specifically ended up in the infantry to reach any substantiated conclusions. However, given the demand for technical knowledge and managerial skills in other branches of the army, many of those with a background in agriculture or "general labour" would have ended up in the slit trenches.

The Canadian Army also had a distinctly urban background. According to a descriptive Directorate of Personnel Selection (DPS) study from 1945, 63% of Canadian soldiers came from cities, towns, and small urban communities, 20% came from farms, and the remaining 17% were originally from a rural background but had been educated in or were working in urban areas at the time of enlistment.[43] This was a marked overrepresentation of urban areas: the 1941 Census of Canada indicated that only 54 percent of Canadians were living in incorporated urban areas.[44]

As might be expected from the other demographic patterns, there was a clear educational gap in the army. Approximately 13% of soldiers had reached grades eleven or twelve, 25% grades nine or ten, 43% grades seven or eight; and 16% had completed only grades one through six or had no formal schooling at all.[45] In the 1930s and '40s education standards were still uneven in Canada: in 1941 all provinces reported on the Census that in excess of 90% of all children aged ten to fourteen were in school, but in the fifteen to nineteen age range there was considerable variation. The average level of school education across the country was grade eight, and the percentage of students above grade eight could vary wildly – from 48% in British Columbia to 20% in Military District No. 6 (Quebec City area).[46] It was estimated that the incidence of complete illiteracy in the Canadian Army Overseas in mid-1944 was about 1.3%, although a larger group was also rated functionally or semi-illiterate on the basis of intelligence testing results.[47] The Canadian Army in 1939–45 was still the best-educated force that Canada had ever put into the field. But a low level of education could also serve as a roadblock, and was sometimes used as a barrier against enlistment on the part of soldiers deemed "undesirable" by the military establishment, especially for First Nations, among whom, in the 1940s, 75% of the population had "attained a level of education equivalent to grade 1 to 3."[48]

Advanced formal education in the Canadian Army was the realm, and the main distinguishing feature, of the officer class. As historian Geoff Hayes has explored in detail, throughout the Second World War the senior army leadership privileged a system of commissioning based upon candidates' possessing some university education. The alternative, that non-commissioned officers be granted the King's Commission from the ranks, was given lip service but was never seriously implemented. This policy meant that battle-experienced other ranks with long service were typically led by young junior officers whose main qualification was a partial or full university education.[49] There was a great preference for formal higher education as a prerequisite for receiving a commission; as Hayes put it, "teachability" was valued above battle experience as a qualification for leadership positions.[50] Since a university education remained the preserve of the middle and upper classes of Canadian society during the 1930s and 1940s (the expansion of universities being largely a postwar phenomenon), entrance to the army's leadership corps was therefore carefully guarded.[51] According to the 1941 Census, only 36,863 post-secondary students were enrolled full time at universities in 1940, and 8,153 degrees were granted that year by colleges and universities nationwide.[52] The army's espoused values included selection based on merit, but merit in this case was measured as a function of education, and education in Canada in the 1930s and '40s was still usually a matter of wealth. The educational minimum presented in *King's Regulations and Orders for the Canadian Militia 1939* was for officers to have passed a provincial matriculation examination or equivalent, but for less-educated other ranks, the chances of securing a commission without any college or university schooling were small.[53] A 1944 study of the Canadian Army Overseas found that only 3 percent of other ranks had any education at the post-secondary level.[54] Officers holding degrees in technical subjects were usually snatched up by the technical branches. Those with less specifically applicable educational backgrounds in the liberal arts were often commissioned into the infantry. Of the seventy-four Queen's University graduates who died in the service of the Canadian Army during the Second World War, thirty-six held a Bachelor of Arts degree; twenty-two of those degrees were held by infantry officers.[55]

There were a number of reasons for this policy of privileging education in officer selection. Hayes argues, persuasively, that the policy had less to do with building or preserving an elite social caste than it had to do with the senior leadership building future officer candidates in their own image: as educated, technically proficient "military managers" – men whom General Andrew McNaughton perhaps typified. An Army Examiner's report from December 1942 giving detailed recommendations for officer candidates stressed intelligence and knowledge as being the basic attributes of army leadership. "In order to acquire the skills of an officer," the report read, "a man must have better than average intelligence ... Intelligence for the good officer means the ability to grasp a complex situation in its entirety, to keep in mind essentials without getting lost in irrelevant details. It means the ability to *organize* and create an effective working unit out of numerous diverse parts."[56] Higher university education was seen as the basis for synthesizing orders, communicating intentions, making decisions, and dealing with the complicated fire plans and technology around which the modern battlefield revolved. "Young educated officers may not have looked or acted like seasoned leaders of men," according to Hayes, "but the appearance of command could be learned on the job. A formal education had to be acquired beforehand."[57]

This system of privileging formal education among officers and by and large refusing to commission from the ranks may have been a strength for the Canadian Infantry Corps. The current literature on military education emphasizes a tension between institutional privileging of experience (particularly combat experience) and the privileging of education. In a recent study Bernd Horn has argued that, due to the nature of the profession of arms, the military mind tends to be conservative and functional, and utilizes personal experience as the key filter in determining what is "possible, useful, true and real." Higher education, on the other hand, is more about "the shaping of the mind" – reasoning ability, creativity, and critical thinking – and is defined by Ron Haycock as "the reasoned response to an unpredictable situation – critical thinking in the face of the unknown."[58] And as historian Randall Wakelam has proposed, "regardless of type or intensity of conflict, broad education that focuses on developing intellectual capacity to deal with complex ambiguous situations is the nexus of effective [combat] performance."[59] There is support for the idea that an educated officer corps might present more dynamic, effective leadership in complex environments than battle experienced but less-educated soldiers. This system also had the unintended side effect of concentrating battle experience and know-how among infantry non-commissioned officers. During the worst fighting, the casualty rate among platoon lieutenants could be almost double that of sergeants, while the total NCO casualty rate was usually lower than that of privates.[60] The system preserved battle knowledge and experience by concentrating it in NCOs, who were more likely to make it through an action unwounded to pass along their knowledge. While depleting the NCO corps by commissioning from the ranks may have provided more battle-experienced leaders, it would have impoverished the NCO corps in the process, and it is not clear that doing so would have provided optimal junior leadership.

WHY DID THEY JOIN?

Men and women who joined the Canadian Army during the Second World War, and the infantry in particular, came with a variety of personal motives. Historian Yves Tremblay, working with interviews of French-Canadian soldiers, has identified "les motivations plus nobles" and "les motivations plus prosaïques" as underlying the desire to enlist, and as much can be said for almost everyone who joined the Canadian military.

Some English-speaking soldiers were high-minded idealists, particularly those with family roots in the Loyalist tradition or, more commonly, in Britain itself. In the years leading up to the war there had been a renewed imperial fervour in Canada, beginning with the unveiling of the Vimy Memorial in France in 1936 and reaching fever pitch with the Royal Tour of 1939, even though politically Canada was already pulling away from the Empire.[61] The high rate of Anglican enlistment early in the war underscores these cross-Atlantic attachments. There were also family connections and pressures to serve; although no statistical studies have been done to illustrate this, many of those who served in the Second World War were, by reputation, sons and daughters of First World War veterans.[62] Previous connection with the Canadian military was also an important determinant of voluntarism. At the start of the war, 21,890 other ranks and 2,193 officers from the Non-Permanent Active Militia (NPAM) enlisted or were appointed (out of a total of roughly 51,000 in the peacetime NPAM in 1939) and, as mentioned earlier, the entire professional cadre of 4,809 other ranks and 581 officers from the Permanent Force joined the Canadian Active Service Force as well.[63] Once more spots in the CASF became available in 1940, recruitment having outstripped availability of spaces in 1939, most of the remaining pre-war NPAM militiamen would also join. The fact that voluntarism was at its highest during the periods of intense crisis indicates not only that the Canadian government "opened the floodgates" of recruiting but also that the added urgency of a dire situation could act as a motivator for enlistment. The greatest months for army recruiting during the war were those at the outbreak of hostilities in September 1939 (57,868 enlisted), and those that followed the fall of France, which inspired a grim "rush to the colours" in defence of both empire and homeland (77,770 over the months of June, July, August 1940).[64]

With Canada still emerging from an economic depression, however, “les motivations plus prosaïques” were also central to why men (and women) joined up. Unemployment was lower in 1938 and 1939 than it had been since the relatively halcyon days of the twenties, but in 1938 there remained over four hundred thousand unemployed men in the country, many on government relief.[65] The image of masses of unemployed Canadians flocking to the recruiting stations in order to get three square meals a day has been shown to give a false impression, but the prospect for other ranks of regular pay, increased social standing, and the outlandishly appealing opportunities of learning a new trade in a modern mechanized army were nonetheless major considerations for large numbers of unemployed and under-employed volunteers. “Single men who were unemployed,” writes William Weintraub in his study of Montreal, “quickly learned that in the army they could earn as much in one day as they received in a week on the dole.”[66]

The war was also a mechanism for escaping unfavourable domestic situations, sometimes even legal trouble, and many enlisted to take advantage of the fresh start that army life could offer. For men, joining up could (at least in theory) elevate one’s status with women, but it also promised a homosocial environment that could be appealing in and of itself.[67] As one soldier, interviewed some years later, put it: “You found later that the others wanted other things. Like some of the older guys just wanted to get away from a complaining wife or a lousy job or a shit of a boss, that kind of thing. One college kid wanted to impress his girl, and he was the biggest fool of all. The high school kids wanted adventure, and when all is said and done and the last dog is hung, that is probably what we was all looking for … a new life.”[68] Author Robert Collins felt similarly: “For most of us, the war was, in part, a time of discovery – of faraway places, of self, and of people unlike ourselves.”[69]

Joining the army was one thing; joining the infantry specifically was an entirely different matter. One reason that the Canadian Army suffered shortfalls in voluntary recruiting was that the government placed early emphasis on the air force and navy, which attracted 350,000 men between them, men who, according to historian J.L. Granatstein, were “the finest and most adventurous Canadians of their day … At root, the ‘old sweats’ of 1914 had told their sons that the infantry was no place to be – better join the navy or the air force, where a recruit could learn a trade, receive quicker promotion, and, with luck, not get killed."[70] As RCAF veteran Hal Sisson recollected on his decision to volunteer for the air force: "The time came, if you didn't [volunteer], the army was gonna [draft you]. I thought, 'How drunk am I gonna have to be when they yell 'Fix Bayonets!'?"[71]

At first, mobilization was done by regiment, and at that point recruits could volunteer not only for the arm of the service they preferred but also for the specific regiment they wanted to be part of, and many tens of thousands were seemingly not deterred by the thought of the bayonet. Although a few regiments had trouble meeting their initial quotas, most experienced no difficulty in bringing themselves up to full strength, as many Canadians were then interested in becoming infantrymen. However, it is possible that such men represented a finite source of volunteers that, by 1940, had largely been used up. Another reason for shortfalls as the war progressed may have been that, in contrast to the supporting branches, the infantry, although the hardest, highest-risk job in the army, provided fewer concrete skills that would be transferrable to civilian occupations after the war. After 1939, as recruiting became more centralized and rationalized, personnel selection increasingly bypassed soldiers' wishes in determining their job in the army. This change kept up the flow of recruits into the infantry,[72] but later in the war, once the fighting had intensified, fewer and fewer recruits were eager to join the infantry. When asked, volunteers from 1943 overwhelmingly expressed their desire to join the non-combat ordnance or service corps and avoid being in the direct line of fire – the infantry was by then at the bottom of every list of desired branch of service.[73] A 1945 study of the attitudes of volunteers in other branches to "remustering" as infantrymen demonstrated that there was no enthusiasm for doing so. None were eager, a bare few were willing, and most were either begrudging or actively hostile to the idea of being forced to change branches and retrain as infantry.[74] The volunteer infantryman may have been lionized by the press and by the military institution as patriotic, valorous, and manly – the "cream of the country" – but in reality many of those who volunteered for active service did not want to go into that most dangerous of combat arms, and would have avoided it had they been able to.[75] There were plenty of exceptions, of course, and mitigating circumstances, but many of the ranks who wound up in the infantry throughout the war would not have chosen it of their own accord, especially given the hundreds of other necessary non-combat jobs available within the army.

Virtually all of Canada's soldiers who served in the overseas theatres of war were volunteers, making it the second-largest all-volunteer field force in the world after the British Indian Army. The principle of voluntarism dominated Canadian political discourse: troops who were to serve outside the Western Hemisphere were to be volunteers, fighting of their own free will, and not because the government was compelling them to fight. Canada's National Resources Mobilization Act (NRMA) conscription program, instituted in 1940, was to provide for the defence of Canada itself, but conscripts could not be compelled to serve overseas, at least not until the very end of the war, when that policy was changed.

There were two reasons for a dichotomous volunteer policy. The first was nakedly political. Fierce domestic battles over conscription during the First World War had left a lasting mark on the country; as historian Jonathan Vance has said: "Rather than laying the basis for a pan-Canadian nationalism, the memory of the Great War drove the two strains of nationalism [English and French] apart ... Few French Canadians were willing to forget conscription and the rancour that characterized the last years of the war."[76] Taking Canada back into war a generation later had required finesse. Prime Minister Mackenzie King's compromise that led Canada to war in 1939, with Quebec's support, was that the country would fight for Britain, but that conscription would not be re-introduced.[77] King pledged (to the whole country explicitly, but implicitly to Quebec) in March 1939 that: "the days of great expeditionary forces of infantry crossing the oceans are not likely to recur ... Conscription of men for overseas service would not be a necessary or effective step. Let me say that so long as this government may be in power, no such measure will be enacted."[78] Although based upon too optimistic a forecast of the war's destructiveness, this compromise was necessary for national unity: while Quebec enlisted 157,000 volunteers, French Canadians by and large did not feel they could legitimately be compelled to fight overseas for a foreign cause.[79] Conscription for overseas service was political anathema, and the longer an all-volunteer force could be sustained, the less the issue would have an opportunity to poison the well of national unity.[80] As R. MacGregor Dawson put it, the fear of schism threatened to "cripple the national war effort ... set people against people, province against province, not for the duration of the war alone, but for many years to come."[81] Such were the fears of the Mackenzie King government.

The second reason for the unusual Canadian approach to conscription was the deep-seated idea in Canada that the "citizen soldier," the part-time, amateur combatant who fought of his own free will when called upon was a combatant superior both to the unmotivated conscript and to the feckless professional soldier. Historian James Wood, in his exploration of the cultural cache behind this "militia myth," argues that the myth was rooted in the early modern English military system, where citizen militias were the symbol of liberty, and regular professional soldiers were regarded with fear and mistrust.[82] While these sentiments declined in Britain itself, older traditions of the "citizen soldier" survived in the military systems of both the United States and Canada, where an adulation of the militia and a dislike of standing armies took root.[83] "The idea of the citizen soldier," according to Wood, is a concept that can be "defined as a belief in the inherent virtues of military training conducted on a part-time basis and a conviction that good citizens should provide their own defence." And a corollary to this myth was an influential belief in post-1918 Canada that the citizen volunteer made a genuinely better soldier than the conscript, a belief flushed with the CEF's triumph over the "conscripted millions of Prussian militarism": "While those who had volunteered were showered with praise and admiration upon their return, the [Canadian] conscripts of 1918 were mostly forgotten. Not only had their sacrifices been made only grudgingly, but even then their contribution was explained away with a casual reference to the fact that barely a quarter of them had ever reached the front, where they were not generally made to feel very welcome by front-line veterans until after they had proven themselves in combat."[84] Such attitudes led to Canadian policies whereby fighting for your country had to be based on the active consent and volunteering of the fighters, rather than upon their civic obligation as citizens.

The culture of voluntarism affected troops in several ways. Although there was a widespread perception in Canada that volunteers were the "cream of the country's manhood," nobly giving themselves and freely accepting unlimited liability, while the conscripts were, at best, everybody else, a reverse application of the "citizen-soldier" mentality was also at work in Canada's war effort. For political reasons conscripts would not fight, but a belief developed that conscripts *could* not fight, that they lacked the capacity, motivation, and moral fibre of the volunteer. It was the military institution itself that created and perpetuated some of the perceived differences between volunteers and conscripts.[85]

The question of whether volunteers make superior soldiers is a thorny one. Certainly a soldier who wants to be doing a task is more motivated than one who doesn't, but no simple dichotomy exists here. Soldiers often were volunteers only when it came to signing that first dotted line at enlistment; after that, the army owned them body and soul, and as the war went on it became increasingly disinterested in accommodating individual preferences for service. Many a volunteer in the Second World War proved to be an unmotivated fighter and, on the other hand, we know that many of the conscripts enlisted into infantry battalions fought hard and skilfully. One Permanent Force officer, Lieutenant-General E.L.M. Burns, remarked after the war that the voluntary system actually had the disadvantage of attracting *less desirable* recruits than could be obtained through conscription. During times of relatively high unemployment or during a long war, Burns argued, volunteers tended to come chiefly from the unemployed, the unemployable, or those dissatisfied with their employment: "By and large the ranks of the unemployed contain a large proportion of those who are economically less capable; those who have less mental and physical ability; less energy, stability, and other characteristics which render them valuable to employers," and in theory also made them less suitable as soldier material.[86] While the mass enlistment of the unemployed in 1939 has been shown to be mythical, Burns's argument about the unemployable and the dissatisfied has weight. His frank appraisal, published in the 1950s, ran contrary to the popular conception of the volunteer principle, a fact that he acknowledged: "The supposition is that all the best young men, burning with patriotic ardour, rush to the defence of the flag as soon as the call for recruits goes out. There is enough truth in this to give colour to the popular notion ... but the experience of two world wars shows that patriotism is not enough to fill the ranks of a national army."[87] In Burns's analysis, volunteers were more likely to become lower-grade soldiers and poor combatants; the conscripts, who had to be compelled to join up, were the ones most worth having. Patriotic ardour aside, intelligent, well-adjusted individuals may very well avoid non-compulsory military service in time of war, further bringing the primacy of the volunteer soldier into question.

As already mentioned, a question remains as to precisely how "voluntary" the military system in Canada was. Tremendous social and institutional pressures were brought to bear through recruiting and propaganda drives to scrounge up sufficient volunteers. Young men in Canada faced coercive peer and institutional pressure and risked severe stigmatization if they did not sign up, before or after being conscripted, to "do their bit." Recruiters would sometimes lure men with promises of being able to choose their arm of service or unit, of being able to learn a trade that would help in civil life, or of swift advancement or trades' pay.[88] Particularly later in the war, when virtually all non-tradesmen reinforcements were being channelled into the infantry, these assurances were certainly distortions.

CONCLUSION: CHARLES DANIEL LLOYD

There are as many different stories behind the Canadians who fought in the Second World War as there were individual soldiers. All were the products of difficult and uncertain times for Canada in the wake of the First World War, when notions of war and the warrior were undergoing change and when Canadian society was experiencing its greatest shifts since Confederation. I close this chapter with a reflection not on the 700,000 soldiers who passed through the Canadian Army at one time or another during the war, but on just one, who in some ways typified the trends discussed in this chapter.

Charles Daniel Lloyd, known to his family as "Chuck," was born to a large English-Canadian farming family in Picton, Ontario (not far from Kingston), in May 1921.[89] His father, William, a Great War veteran, had died suddenly in 1922, leaving behind six children. His mother passed away in 1929 of cancer, and Chuck was raised in part by older siblings and in part by Ontario Children's Aid, which placed the orphaned Lloyd children on farms around Prince Edward County. He was housed on a number of farms, few of which provided happy homes, particularly once the Depression began.[90] He did, however, get the chance to attend school on a regular basis. Toward the end of the 1930s he went to live with his older sister Eva, who had married and was working in Toronto as a hairdresser, having brought several of her siblings "to the big city" when she could afford to. In 1939 Chuck began attending a composite high school (Toronto's Central Technical School), studying air mechanics with the intention of becoming an aircraft technician. He was smart and enjoyed school – Eva believed he could easily complete his grade 12 matriculation. But he also craved an escape from the small world of rural eastern Ontario, and he became a member of the Central Tech Cadet Corps.

When war came in September 1939, the RCAF would have been the logical place for Chuck to go, given his preparatory knowledge in aircraft mechanics. But on 2 September 1939, the day after Germany's invasion of Poland and the day before even Britain or France had declared war, Chuck was in Prince Edward County visiting his older brother, Frank Lloyd, who was a peacetime militiaman with the NPAM's Hastings & Prince Edward Regiment. As an existing reservist, Frank was going to have the first, best shot at joining the Canadian Active Service Force when war was declared and mobilization began. Frank somehow convinced Chuck to join "The Regiment" as well. And so, at the age of eighteen, Chuck became an infantryman with the Hastings & Prince Edward Regiment and, sure enough, upon Canada's declaration of war a week later he successfully volunteered for active service along with most of the rest of the "Hasty Ps" militiamen. She was old enough to remember their father going to war. There is also evidence in Chuck's personal file – namely discrepancies in the attestation papers – that Frank helped him lie about his age; Frank filled out a sworn statement that Charles was nineteen, and therefore old enough to go overseas.[91] Eva, their sister, was furious, particularly at Frank for influencing their little brother to join the "damned army."[92]

We cannot know Charles's reasoning or motives for joining, but informed observations can be made. The family connection was obviously central. His father, William Lloyd, had been born in Lancashire, England, and had served in two British militia camps with the 16th Regiment prior to emigrating to Canada. Upon attestation (regimental number 636015), William listed his trade as "fireman," and joined the Canadian Expeditionary Force with the 155th (Quinte) Overseas Battalion CEF on 3 December 1915.[93] Once it reached England, his battalion was broken up to reinforce the field battalions, and William himself fought with the 21st (Eastern Ontario) Battalion in the field at Vimy Ridge, Hill 70, and at Passchendaele. William died before Chuck could know him, and never had the opportunity to pass along any sage advice about volunteering for the infantry. There was undoubtedly pressure from Frank to try to live up to their father's example once war came, and their farsightedness in joining the NPAM rather than waiting to try directly with the CASF a week later, implies considerable personal motivation for getting into the fight. Since they enlisted immediately after Germany's invasion of Poland, it seems likely that Chuck, his brother Frank, and probably both, were serious in their desire to oppose Nazi Germany, or perhaps serious about getting out of eastern Ontario. Where this sense of urgency came from – family legacy, church, or community – is difficult to say, but the result was that the Lloyd brothers were among the first in the country to volunteer.

Chuck was five foot four, and weighed 129 pounds on enlistment. He was nobody's idea of a Hector or Achilles, but he was tremendously physically fit from his years of farming. Later in the war, Charles's air mechanic training would likely have earned him reallocation to one of the army trades by personnel selection officers, but when these selection policies were being implemented Charles was already an NCO involved with physical fitness training and temporarily attached to No. 5 Canadian Infantry Reinforcement Unit in England, and he never appeared on the radar for reallocation. Although Chuck kept his nose cleaner than most Canadian soldiers once he was in England, he wound up in some trouble as well. His record shows an Absence Without Leave charge in 1943, and a case of venereal disease contracted during leave. He evidently struggled with a leadership role and twice reverted to private from his NCO rank before finally accepting that the army wanted to make him a corporal. Despite being physically very fit, he struggled with recurrent health problems. In total he spent over 1,400 days overseas.[94]

Corporal Charles Daniel Lloyd did not survive the Second World War. He died fighting in a mountaintop town called Assoro on the island of Sicily on 22 July 1943, not quite four years after he enlisted, as his "Hasty Ps" fought to break the German defensive line in Canada's first sustained campaign of the war. Despite his small stature, his death could scarcely have been more Homeric. The battle for Assoro was one of the most heroic feats of combat prowess of Canada's Second World War. Lord Tweedsmuir, the Hastings & Prince Edward Regiment's commanding officer, recited *Henry V*'s Agincourt speech before personally leading a company of hand-picked Canadian warriors – including Chuck – on a high-altitude, close-quarters assault on the mountaintop German position.[95] As the Canadians held the line atop Assoro, Chuck was hit almost square-on by a shell; his possessions were listed as being "blown to pieces," and he would have died instantly, never realizing what had happened. Because Lord Tweedsmuir was grievously wounded shortly after Assoro, the paperwork for medals and decorations was never filled out, and Chuck's sacrifice – and those of the others on Assoro – went officially unrecognized.[96]

Chuck's enlistment was exceptional in some ways, but every case was exceptional, and his shows the complicated nexus of background, circumstance, and personal motivation that existed for all Canadian soldiers. Even if his death on Assoro befitted a Homeric epic, Corporal Charles Daniel "Chuck" Lloyd was far from the image of a classical hero. But he was, perhaps, representative of the experience of myth and reality in Canada's Second World War. In many ways the senior leadership at the time looked to the infantrymen hoping to find the heroes of myth. What they found were Canada's citizen-soldiers.

2

Building the Canadian Infantry

When the Canadian Army was committed to battle in the summer of 1943, it had the peculiar distinction of being the largest formation to have been in the Second World War from the start without seeing sustained combat. With the exception of the disasters at Hong Kong and Dieppe, which produced more casualties than battle-experienced soldiers, the Canadian land forces spent four of their six war years in reserve, a component of cross-Channel defence and invasion contingents. By 1943 the soldiers of the Canadian Army were among the longest-trained combat formations in the world.

This chapter addresses the major elements that went into the "creation" of Canadian infantrymen: their system of organization and the regimental framework, the personnel selection infrastructure for choosing warriors, and key aspects of the infantry training through which the soldiers of the Canadian Army were disciplined and formed. Of these different elements, the individual training undertaken by Canadian troops has perhaps been criticized too much, and the personnel selection system too little. The idea that Canadian soldiers did not benefit as much from their extensive training as they might have has been a long-running historiographical theme, going back to C.P. Stacey and popularized further by historian John English.[1] Other more general criticisms have also been levelled at the British and Commonwealth training systems by researchers in the UK such as Max Hastings, David French, and Timothy Harrison Place.[2] In this chapter I provide background on how Canadian soldiers were prepared for war, and posit that, particularly in light of later battlefield experience, the infantry training that the Canadians received below the battalion level, even if it was not a perfect preparation for modern war, was quite effective in terms of creating combatants.

BATTALIONS AND REGIMENTS

The Canadian Army in the field in the Second World War contained, at various points, thirty-six infantry battalions and three machine-gun battalions. These battalions were all given the names of the Non-Permanent Active Militia (NPAM) regiments that initially contributed the men to their formation. Legally speaking, these battalions were separate entities from the regimental depots whose names they carried, and from which most of them had initially descended. But the idea that Canada's "regiments" fought in the war is a powerful one, possibly because those regiments have done a great deal to help shape the telling of the war's history.

The named regiments of the Canadian Army have been the organizational level at which history and ritual have been most concentrated and preserved through battle honours, mess traditions, distinctive dress, shared history, local identity, and competition with other units. The Canadian Active Service Force (CASF), raised in 1939 for overseas service, formed battalions based upon recruitment sponsored by local regiments early in the war. But in 1940 the CASF began to conduct recruitment on a more rational and centralized basis in order to provide reinforcement soldiers to those early battalions for the rest of the war. The field battalions initially took many of the soldiers, dress, and traditions from the peacetime militia regiments, as well as their names, but later in the war were not administratively linked to them.

In the British Empire and Commonwealth model of military organization, the regimental system has been both the intersection for the perpetuation of meaning and memory through regimental traditions, and the mechanism for transmitting the requirements of formal authority to lower units.[3] The origins of the modern system date from the nineteenth century. While the armies of continental Europe modernized and centralized their organizations around large formations such as brigades, divisions, and corps, each with permanent staff and regular training at the formation level, the military forces of the British Empire "resorted to such formations only on an improvised and temporary basis." The British forces were optimized not for large-scale ground wars, but with the expeditionary imperatives of colonial warfare in mind. Throughout the nineteenth century the British Army resembled "a loose federation of regiments."[4] By necessity, regiments received maximum autonomy and independence while fighting the "small wars" of empire, and as a result "the regiment" as a locus of meaning, identity, and a cause for which to fight was more comprehensible for many soldiers than the abstract ideas of crown and empire.[5] Canadian regiments were closely modelled upon the British example. As David Bercuson explains in his recent examination of the regimental system: "The main task of the regiment is to keep its history alive and guard its uniqueness. This is done to instill in its soldiers a strong belief that their particular regimental family is not only different but also superior [to all others]."[6] The militia regiments served an important social function in peacetime Canada and became a focus for provincial and regional distinctiveness.

The Canadian regimental system was geographically based, with each regiment in peacetime drawing recruits from its surrounding region. Bercuson describes the system as "the use of specific, unique regiments to recruit, train, and build cohesion inside an army that is in fact not composed of regiments as units of manoeuvre, but rather of battalions, brigades, divisions, and corps."[7] Prior to 1939, there were dozens of NPAM and a tiny handful of Permanent Force regular regiments in Canada. On the outbreak of the First World War the historical militia regiments had been cast aside as the basis for mobilization in favour of an improvised system that grouped volunteers into new numbered battalions. After that war, the Otter Committee oversaw the merger of the battle honours and traditions of the Canadian Expeditionary Force's numbered battalions with local militia regiments. During the Second World War, much to everyone's relief, regiments did indeed serve as the system of mobilization. Initially, each regimental depot contributed and reinforced one battalion of infantry for the CASF, but in July 1940 (just when the army was about to begin a major expansion) the system of direct recruitment through regimental depots was scrapped in favour of a more centralized and systematized recruiting and training apparatus.[8] Thereafter, and for the entire length of the war, references to regiments referred primarily to the named battalions serving overseas with the Canadian Army, which had initially been raised by regimental depots and took their names, and which were intended to be the bearers of the regimental traditions.

The intended effect of the Canadian regimental system was that the individual battalions raised for combat should have been regionally quite homogenous. Ideally every soldier within a regiment would at least be from the "Military District" that regiment belonged to, if not necessarily from the same city or county. This helped to establish each fighting regiment as unique, possessing a local identity that would become entwined with its formative traditions. Even after the discontinuation of the system of direct regimental reinforcement, the manpower system was supposed to function in such a way that reinforcement soldiers would be at least sent to a regiment from their own Military District, even if they possessed no prior connection to it. "Do not forget that I have placed great importance on territorial [reinforcement] of all units which have a territorial status," wrote Lieutenant-General H.D.G. Crerar when he was commander of I Canadian Corps in November 1943. "I am aware of the additional administrative burdens this places on 2nd Echelon but this will need to be accepted and the difficulties overcome."[9]

The system worked well, at least when not tested by the friction of combat. When regiments were first deployed to combat zones, they tended to be extremely regionally homogenous; in Sicily in 1943, seven of the nine infantry battalions drew over 90 percent of their soldiers from their home Military District, while the other two drew around 75 percent each.[10] The battalions deploying to Normandy in 1944 were not quite as homogenous, with most drawing somewhere between two-thirds and 85 percent of their soldiers from their own home districts.[11] However, as we shall see in the coming chapters, once the battalions were engaged in combat, the proportion of each one's soldiers drawn from their local region fell precipitously, often to below 50 percent, as reinforcements were hastily allocated on an emergency as-needed basis, with decreasing respect for regional identity or distinctiveness.

Military historians have drawn a line of demarcation between the army that volunteered in 1939 and the army that went into battle in 1943. Historian Stephen Harris, in *Canadian Brass* (1988), his classic work on military professionalism up to the Second World War, argues that, "although all the regular units saw action, and the militia served as the mobilization base for the rest of the active serve force, there was little continuity between the regiments and battalions on the order of battle on 10 September 1939 and those fighting in Europe four years later."[12] Similarly, historian Bill McAndrew has estimated that on average a Canadian infantry battalion "turned over" its personnel completely once every two years while on non-combat duty in England.[13] However, when casualty statistics from Canadian Military Headquarters (CMHQ) were analyzed for this study, it was, surprisingly, found that in the infantry battalions of 1st Canadian Division during the Sicily campaign (July–August 1943), their first sustained combat experience, almost 60 percent of private soldiers, 82 percent of corporals, and 83 percent of sergeants were "original men." They had regimental numbers that had been issued to them directly by their regiments, according to lists compiled by Clive Law.[14] Although the numbers were lower for the divisions that went into combat in 1944, significant numbers of the "original" regimental men were still fighting with the field battalions. But once the infantry battalions were committed to battle, as we shall see, the number of "original" men remaining in them declined and dwindled to almost none in the face of severe casualty rates.

During the First World War, when voluntary enlistment of Canadian-born subjects in general and French-Canadian subjects in particular was very low, only thirteen of the 258 overseas infantry battalions raised across the country were French-Canadian. Only the 22nd "Van Doos" Battalion CEF served as a field battalion, and the rest were broken up, mostly to reinforce the 22nd.[15] In the Second World War the degree of "buy-in" to the war effort by French Canada was much greater. Among the infantry, there were four French-Canadian battalions in the fighting divisions where 100 percent spoke French, and 40 to 80 percent spoke no English at all: the Royal 22e Régiment, Régiment de Maisonneuve, Fusiliers Mont-Royal, and Régiment de la Chaudière.[16] In early 1942, prior to the commitment of these units to battle, French-Canadian officers were in the minority even for French-Canadian units; and even in the four "French" battalions only one-third of officers were francophone, though all officers for these battalions were by necessity bilingual.[17] Once combat began, the proportion of French-Canadian officers would drop further. But while the French-Canadian battalions struggled desperately at times due to manpower shortages, they served well and none had to be broken up to reinforce the others.

The role of "regimental spirit" on the battlefield is a contested one. British and Canadian histories have tended to emphasize the place of the regiment in promoting bonding and esprit de corps among soldiers, while Americans, whose military has not been based upon a regimental system (and indeed, where the term "regiment" denotes a unit of manoeuvre roughly equivalent to a British brigade) have paid little attention to regimental *esprit*.[18] Soldiers will fight with or without being part of a regiment. While the regimental "family" could be a source of inspiration and pride, high casualty rates among infantrymen, coupled with a reinforcement system that was forced to send replacements to regiments with increasing disregard for regional distinctiveness, made regimental identification difficult to sustain.

SELECTING INFANTRYMEN

In the Book of Judges, the Hebrew Bible relates an apocryphal story about Gideon, a judge among the Israelites, who led his people to war against their oppressors, the Midianites. Calling upon the tribes of Israel, Gideon raised an army of 32,000 men to repel a Midianite incursion across the River Jordan. However, the Hebrew God, acting as Gideon's aide-de-camp, told Gideon he had gathered too many men – so many that, should they triumph, they would attribute the victory to themselves rather than acknowledging that God had saved them. First, God had Gideon send home those men who were afraid and wanted to leave; 22,000 returned to their homes, and 10,000 remained. But the number was still too great, so God instructed Gideon to take them down to the water, where he would test them:

> So he brought down the people unto the water: and the Lord said unto Gideon, "Every one that lappeth of the water with his tongue, as a dog lappeth, him shalt thou set by himself; likewise every one that boweth down upon his knees to drink." And the number of them that lapped, putting their hand to their mouth, were three hundred men: but all the rest of the people bowed down upon their knees to drink water. And the Lord said unto Gideon, "By the three hundred men that lapped will I save you, and deliver the Midianites into your hand: and let all the other people go, every man unto his home."[19]

It was the first, and probably the most rigorous, bout of personnel selection testing in the written record of humanity, with almost 95 percent of soldiers failing to make the cut (although, naturally, the three hundred remaining Israelites won a stunning victory). While testing would become somewhat more sophisticated than giving soldiers the hairy eyeball as they drank, the proponents of testing during the Second World War retained a sense that they were on a mission to separate the true warriors from the chaff.

The personnel selection system created by the Canadian Army for its overseas recruitment was a real source of professional pride. It was put together quickly under the stress of manpower shortages, but was seen to be of such quality that its "PULHEMS" personnel grading scheme was eventually borrowed and implemented in the British and American armies as well.[20] At the outbreak of the war, in the stampede to mobilize, arm, and expand the Canadian war machine, psychologists' ideas of allocating soldiers to particular jobs on the basis of their personal abilities and characteristics were forgotten. The slightly disconsolate members of the Canadian Psychological Association privately embarked on their own intellectual adventures to harness modern psychological occupation selection techniques in the service of the national war effort. Trials and experiments took place in 1940, and the creation of a personnel selection directorate in the British Army, combined with the enthusiasm for modern scientific systems of the Canadian Army's General Officer Commanding-in-Chief (GOC-in-C), General Andrew McNaughton, spurred the establishment of a Directorate of Personnel Selection (DPS) at Canadian Military Headquarters in July 1941.[21] A parallel organization was in place at National Defence Headquarters in Ottawa, and together they began the long processes of assessing new recruits in Canada and sifting through the immense numbers of existing army personnel overseas, using the Canadian Army's "Revised M" intelligence test and the "Q Card" for indexing and coding a soldier's records and qualifications. By May 1942 Selection of Personnel Officers (SPOs) had been established at the centralized basic training centres, and they would later be stationed at the recruiting intake depots, where they oversaw the allocation of soldiers to particular arms and branches on the basis of their personal characteristics.[22] Later in the war, the DPS began to scrutinize the suitability of the British Army's "letter" personnel categories (A1, A2, B1, B2, etc.), a relic of the First World War still in use in the Commonwealth armies.[23] The DPS designed the omnibus "PULHEMS" system whereby a seven-digit code numerically representing physique (P), upper and lower body strength (U and L), hearing (H), eyesight (E), mental ability (M), and psychological stability (S), would be assigned to every soldier.[24] By May 1943 every job and trade in the army had been assigned a "functional profile" involving the minimum PULHEMS numbers that each soldier, tradesman, or specialist had to meet or exceed in order to be allocated to it.[25]

The DPS organization was armed with two basic assumptions, as articulated by Major H.S.M. Carver, a DPS officer who wrote a monograph on the directorate in 1945. The first was the consistency of human behaviour. "This enquiry into a man's history," Carver wrote, "obviously arises from the belief that, if a record of past behaviour, attitude and performance is traced, it becomes possible to predict with some reasonable accuracy how a person will react to circumstances, jobs, and situations in the future." The second assumption was that men of a "combatant temperament" were a limited resource: "That all men do not possess to the same degree what may be described as the 'combatant temperament' and that in placing each man in an army job, limitations of this kind must be recognized ... But, although all men have not been provided with the same amount of physical courage, stamina, and aggressiveness, there is a place for most of them in the Army."[26] The goal of the DPS was therefore to build an army in which all those who would be likely to be the best warriors, categorized by a study of their innate dispositions, could be concentrated into the combat arms, and those of a softer or more timid character would be found useful work away from the action. The DPS was to be a finely tuned technical instrument for accomplishing this task, even though the reallocation policies pursued by SPOs were opposed by most field commanders and regarded with hostility by units.[27]

Both the "Revised M" intelligence test and the PULHEMS tests were administered by Army Examiners and SPOs, who ended up wielding a great deal of administrative power within the Canadian Army and whose numbers increased from zero in 1940 to 359 in April 1945. However, only one in twenty examiners and SPOs had any experience in personnel work or had specific training in applied psychology; few had any prewar military service, none were combatants, and 52 percent were brought into the army specifically to be commissioned for the Directorate of Personnel Selection. Half of the SPOs were drawn from teaching backgrounds, from the elementary to the post-secondary levels, with the balance being clerical workers, businessmen, and other professionals. All were men. Two-thirds had a university degree or partial university education, and 90 percent had at least their senior matriculation.[28] Most of their training took place on the job, in an apprenticeship model whereby examiners would work under the supervision of more experienced officers. It was not until 1944 that SPO training courses were developed. Policy for selection was determined at Directorate of Personnel Selection headquarters, and the individual examiners were confined to appraising soldiers and "making recommendations for their disposal within the framework of policies and orders provided."[29]

The medical categorization system of personnel classification, and the holistic PULHEMS system that replaced it in 1943, were in turn the gatekeepers for the selection of who would and who would not become a fighting soldier. Until 1943 infantrymen needed a medical classification of A1 or A2, had to be between eighteen and thirty-five, needed to be able to read and write, and had to score at least a D on their "M" Test for intelligence.[30] The "A" medical classification was quite broadly defined: "See to shoot or drive. Can undergo severe strain. Without defects of locomotion. With only minor non-progressive disabilities."[31] About 75 percent of the total recruit intake for the British Army, from which the system originated, were graded A1.[32] PULHEMS, once adopted, was intended to add nuance to medical classification by grading each aspect of a soldier's being separately, in a convenient seven-digit code. Each factor, or PULHEMS "letter," was assigned a grade from 1 to 5, a grade of 1 meaning that a man was fit for duty in any theatre based upon that factor; grade 2 indicating some minimally impaired capabilities; 3 indicating severe impairment; 4 indicating suitability only for home-base deployment; and 5 indicating unfitness for any army duty.[33] In May 1943 the job profile for Infantryman was given a PULHEMS number of 1111221 as the standard that each infantryman had to meet or exceed. According to CMHQ's *Physical Standards and Instructions 1943*, the infantryman would be represented as follows:

Physique (P) 1 – Fit after training, for full strain and fatigue of combatant duty. A front-line fighter.

Upper Extremities (U) 1 – Able to lift 50 lbs. up to head level. Can use rifle to shoot and for bayonetting. Can throw grenades, dig, and potentially able to drive heavy vehicles. Fit for hand-to-hand fighting.

Locomotion (L) 1 – Able to march 20 miles per day after having completed training. No disabilities of the feet or legs which would hamper the man in standing, running, climbing or digging.

Hearing (H) 1 – Able to hear normal spoken voice at 15 feet distant in one ear and 10 feet distant in other ear.

Eyesight (E) 2 – Must have 20/120 right eye, 20/200 left eye, correctable with glasses to 20/40 in both eyes. No stereoscopic vision required. Not dependent on glasses.

Mental (M) 2 – Intelligence sufficient for non-tradesman or non-specialist combatant duties or for trades requiring experience rather than ability.[34]

Stability (S) 1 – Emotionally stable – no signs of neurosis, or any serious divergence from the normal in autonomic nervous system function or stability.[35]

This, in seven digits, was the Canadian infantryman. Any man assigned a profile with a code lower than 1111221 would not be allowed to serve in the infantry – at least initially.

The PULHEMS system endured from October 1943 until the end of the war with little modification – proof of the "soundness of the system," according to Carver's monograph – but debates nevertheless ensued about the standard of infantryman within the system.[36] In 1944, at the height of the Canadian Army's manpower crisis, it was determined that there were not enough men available with PULHEMS profiles of at least 1111221 to meet manpower demands. An army examiner circular letter from 25 July 1944 highlighted the problem: "It should be noted that at present time the requirements for [infantry], [armour] and [artillery] together are higher than the total supply of personnel enlisting with PULHEMS 1111221. If current quotas are to be met, therefore, personnel with PULHEMS profiles including 2s must be allocated to those corps."[37] In November 1944 the Committee on Standards of Selection met in emergency session to consider lowering selection standards for infantrymen, to help bridge the gap between operational requirements and reinforcement availability that heavy fighting had created. The committee reluctantly approved a downgrading of the general-duty operational job profiles for infantry (and the other combat arms) to 2212221, allowing lower-graded personnel with minor "defects" in physique, the extremities, eyesight, hearing, and mental acuity into the infantry – only locomotion and psychological stability were kept at 1.[38]

One of the foremost tools at the DPS's disposal, which was used in determining the Mental "M" PULHEMS category, was the ten-page "Revised M" Test, an intelligence test with a single scale of learning ability that could "be applied both to the poorly educated or mentally dull and also the brilliant graduate of a university" and still accurately measure their innate intelligence.[39] As an army examiner circular letter put it: "Revised Examination 'M' ... has proved to be of great assistance in determining the trainability of men. It is really a test of general intelligence and learning ability and can be given to groups as large as 50 at one time."[40] "M" had been developed for military application in 1939–40 by Dr Chester E. Kellogg, then a psychologist at McGill University, but who in 1917 had been part of a staff of psychologists administering the experimental and groundbreaking US Army Alpha and Beta intelligence tests, the forerunners of all modern IQ testing.[41] The philosophies underlying American intelligence testing were reproduced in the Canadian "M" test: that "intelligence" was both reified and measurable, and that it was directly and positively correlated with combat effectiveness. Intelligence was to be measured in the following way: soldiers (or potential soldiers) were given a written Test Booklet and just over thirty minutes to complete an eight-part test. The eight parts, lifted liberally from the US Army Alpha and Beta tests, as well as from industrial aptitude tests, were: picture completion, picture absurdities (finding a deliberate error), paper form board (dividing shapes), tool recognition (drawings of thirty common tools), mechanical information (sentence completion on the use of tools), elementary arithmetic, vocabulary, and written analogies. The Non-Verbal parts were collectively scored out of 61, the Mechanical parts out of 65, and the Verbal parts out of 85, for a possible score of 211.[42] A score of less than 75 marked a soldier as "untrainable"; 100 was fairly average for a "reasonable chance of succeeding" at Basic and Advanced training centres; and 120 was seen as a minimum needed for Trades trainees.[43] During officer selection an "M" score of 160 was seen as the minimum acceptable for the granting of a commission, in combination with leadership and military qualities.[44]

The "Revised M" Test was heavily weighted toward mechanical knowledge and aptitude, with one-third of that examination devoted to tool recognition and testing familiarity with specific tools. Carver stated that a statistical correlation between success on sub-tests related to tools and success on the overall "M" Test "seem[ed] to suggest that an interest and skill in the use of tools is closely associated with the most fundamental quality of human intelligence."[45] Further, the basic working assumption of the DPS as a whole was that the "M" score was positively correlated with combat effectiveness, particularly the aggregated "M" scores of infantry battalions, and that low "M" scores and low innate intelligence were causally linked with combat ineffectiveness. A 1943 DPS report on "M" score disparities among battalions hypothesized that "variations indubitably will be found to bear a close correspondence to variations in the unit's ability to function effectively under combatant conditions."[46]

But it is doubtful whether the "M" Test was in fact measuring innate intelligence, and it is not certain whether innate intelligence even exists or can be measured. Carver and the DPS as a whole, taking what scholar Stephen Jay Gould would term a "predispositionist" position, never seriously entertained the possibility that the tests were simply measuring formal schooling. A demobilization report in November 1944 showed that "a significant positive correlation exists between school grades achieved and 'M' scores," and interpreted this to mean that "higher 'M' scores are required for success in the higher academic grades"; but somehow the report did not consider that the correlation might in fact be the other way around, with "M" scores measuring education rather than innate intelligence.[47] Success on "M" tests was also extremely language-dependent. Even though a French-language "M" Test was developed specifically for francophones, French-Canadian soldiers consistently scored drastically lower than English Canadians, to the point that examiners were quietly encouraged to uniformly and arbitrarily add fifteen points to the "M" scores of French-Canadians.[48] Only native English-speakers ever achieved the highest possible "M" scores.[49] A March 1943 DPS report studying aggregate mean "M" scores for Canadian infantry regiments showed that regiments based in urbanized, anglicized areas contained men of much greater "innate intelligence" than regiments based on rural or francophone areas. The average "M" score for the

Toronto Scottish Regiment was 140.7 for privates and 154.9 for NCOs; the average for the primarily rural Cape Breton Highlanders was 102.8 for privates, 128.2 for NCOs; and the average for the French-Canadian Régiment de la Chaudière was 94.6 for privates and 123.8 for NCOs.[50]

So what was, in fact, being measured with the "M" Test? Carver's DPS monograph gives us the answer: a table is provided in his study (reproduced as Appendix C) wherein the mean "M" scores for the military populations of entire Canadian military districts are given alongside information education, including average school grade completed and percentage with an education over eighth grade. The "M" scores for those districts correlate strongly with the average school grade achieved – from a high in Military district 11 (British Columbia) of grade 9 average school grade and a mean "M" score of 146, to a low of Military district 5 (Quebec except Montreal) of grade 6.47 average school grade and a mean "M" score of 107.[51] As with other facets of the Canadian Army, the "M" Test was really another way of measuring and privileging formal education.

The Canadian soldiers who hit the beaches of Sicily in 1943 and Normandy in 1944 were the end products of a rigorous scientific, industrial categorization and personnel selection process. Whether this process produced the very best soldiers, however, is highly questionable. The development of standardized selection procedures definitely helped to keep the support services well staffed. But they also likely screened and eliminated, for reasons of "intelligence," stability, or PULHEMS fitness, a large number of soldiers who would have made perfectly satisfactory combatants. Furthermore, the rates of neuropsychiatric casualties in the Canadian Army of the Second World War were not significantly lower than those of the Canadian Corps during the First World War, despite the introduction of rigorous personnel screening.[52] In fact, in comparison to the Canadian Corps of 1914–18, one wonders how much fitter for combat its selection and screening regimes had made the Canadian infantry of 1939–45.

INFANTRY TRAINING

The Canadian Army's infantry corps spent most of its war years, 1939 to partway through 1943, in training, interrupted only by the brief but furious actions at Hong Kong and Dieppe. The army's assumptions about how the war would be fought by its infantrymen changed several times. In 1939 and 1940 that training anticipated a return to a largely immobile trench warfare along the Western Front. It was thought that, although trench warfare would be made more exciting by the presence of armoured vehicles, the proliferation of anti-tank guns, obstacles, mines, air power would not change its fundamental character.[53] The defeat of France in May–June 1940 saw all of these assumptions upended, the Canadians evacuated from the continent, and new training begun with the aim of repelling Germans from the beaches of England. Finally, beginning in 1942, training began for a new offensive role, as the First Canadian Army was tapped as one of the major formations that would take part in the liberation (and conquest) of Europe.[54]

In terms of its content, Canadian training bore the indelible imprint of the British War Office. Throughout the war, grubby copies of the War Office's *Field Service Regulations*, *Infantry Training*, and *Section Leading* manuals could be found from British Columbia to Aldershot and from the Rhine to the Moro River, though by 1945 these documents had been heavily amended and supplemented. The Visiting Forces (British Commonwealth) Act of 1933, the lesser-known military rider to the Statute of Westminster, ensured that even if Canada was headed on its own peculiar constitutional path, its army would still operate as a subsidiary formation for the British, in combination with other imperial forces.[55] At the tactical level the Canadians remained autonomous, although they were still completely situated within the British understanding of war. During the interwar years the British updates to imperial military doctrine were debated in Canadian service journals but were treated as a *fait accompli*.[56]

How were the Canadians taught to fight? All infantry training for Canadians was bifurcated between training done in Canada and training done overseas, mostly in the UK but also closer to the front starting in 1943–45. At the onset of the war, the training of newly mobilized regiments of the Active Service Force were the responsibility of each unit's commanding officer, who was presumed to be able to develop and execute a training program adequate for the needs of new recruits and partially trained militiamen. Training began in Canada after enlistment at a district depot and focused extensively upon lower-level basic training: that of the individual and his unit, up to company strength. Collective training, done at the battalion level and higher, was conducted almost exclusively in the UK; few facilities and little suitable equipment could be found for collective training in Canada.[57] Training in Britain was normally carried out by field units, or in special "schools," and most of the collective training tended to be decentralized.[58] Field exercises at the division or corps level occurred periodically, and special assault training was undertaken prior to the invasions of Sicily and Normandy. But training in Britain still generally placed a premium upon developing the skills and training of individual infantrymen and their sub-units.[59]

As of late 1942, the infantry training method was to have soldiers spend eight weeks' training in Canada at one of the Basic Training Centres common to all arms, and then to move them for an additional eight weeks' specialty training at an advanced Infantry Training Centre.[60] The syllabus of the training centres was based on forty-five-minute periods of instruction, a nine-period day, and fifty periods in a week. Over the eight-week advanced timing, soldiers were taught parade-ground drill (8 periods); physical training including basic PT, swimming, obstacle training, and unarmed combat (40 periods); marching and long-distance route marching (53 periods); map reading (12 periods); "fundamental training," including etiquette, regimental history, and propaganda (24 periods); gas warfare training (15 periods); fire discipline (12 periods); field works, which included designing and constructing field defences, camouflage, and concealment (18 periods); and field craft, which covered movements, field signals, observation training, cover from fire, stalking, keeping direction, and advanced section and platoon training (60 periods). Sixty-three periods were also spent on the individual platoon weapons: the light machine gun, rifle, two-inch mortar, bayonet, grenades, and machine carbines, and forty additional periods allocated to Range Courses, which gave recruits the opportunity for live firing practice.[61] This eight-week infantry training course was intended to be the transformative time that turned civilians into infantrymen. Toward the end of the war, it was also administered to soldiers from other branches who were being "re-mustered" as infantrymen. For new recruits, following advanced training in Canada, the newly minted infantrymen would typically be assigned to a unit in Canada, or would proceed to a transit camp and from there overseas. In late 1943 an intermediate training step was introduced with the establishment of the No. 1 Training Brigade Group at Debert, Nova

Scotia, which gave a final four-week course to soldiers headed overseas, re-checking individual training and introducing elementary collective training for battalions.[62]

Overseas, infantrymen received more advanced training. Collective training and special tasks were the order of the day, though individual and sub-unit training remained paramount since they were easy to arrange, whereas organizing formation training exercises was a headache even when everything went right. Beginning in 1942 large-scale manoeuvres and exercises prepared the Canadian infantry brigades, divisions, corps, and, eventually, army to fight in the field – or at least they prepared the staff who managed these formations. To the infantryman on the ground, once a training exercise got beyond the company level, its ultimate size became academic, and it almost always involved trudging about from place to place according to staff instructions. But there was also an expansion of combined operations training that would allow infantry units to engage in amphibious and assault training in conjunction with artillery, air force, and naval assets.[63]

The Canadian infantry, both overseas and in Canada, became closely associated with the small-unit tactical training regime known as battle drill, a training methodology that gained prominence in 1941 and suffused infantry training thereafter. Following the Battle of France in 1940, the former commander of a British division evacuated at Dunkirk had pressed for reform of the British Army's infantry tactics. That commander was General Harold Alexander (future army group commander in Italy), who had been impressed by the infiltration tactics of the German infantry in the Low Countries: when the stress of battle had supposedly paralysed British soldiers, the Germans had practised infiltration drills dating back to the First World War, penetrating positions, cutting off British strong points, and forcing withdrawals.[64] Alexander concluded that more and different training was required to bring imperial troops to that standard of proficiency, and in a series of "Tactical Notes" issued to I Corps in October 1940 (later reissued as a supplement to the War Office's *Infantry Training* manual) he urged development of uniform drills at the platoon level and lower.[65] "It is better to know instinctively some orthodox line of conduct," Alexander wrote, "than to be paralysed by the uncertainty of what to do."[66] The drills began as demonstrations of ways in which the standard training techniques outlined by existing War Office manuals could be turned into interesting exercises accentuating basic underlying principles of tactical behaviour.[67]

The "interesting" part was key. Battle drill was first adopted by the British 47th Division, but was taken up with real enthusiasm by representatives of the 2nd Canadian Infantry Division, who were among the first to attend the 47th's battle school at Chelwood Gate in East Sussex. The Calgary Highlanders in particular were gripped by "battle drill mania," and set up their own school modelled on Chelwood. The new training techniques were a hit among Canadians, as they provided new, varied, and interesting tactical sub-unit training to troops who had been throwing stones into the English Channel for almost two years. By December 1941 all infantry units in the Canadian Corps in the UK were conducting battle drill training; by spring 1942 it was being taught in the reinforcement stream; in April 1942 a battle drill wing of the Canadian Training School was opened at Rowlands Castle in Hampshire; and by June 1942 battle drill leapt back across the Atlantic when Calgary Highlanders officers helped organize the Canadian Battle Drill School at Coldstream Ranch in Vernon, BC.[68] Battle drill swiftly became part of the standard syllabus for all Advanced Training Centres in Canada, where it was incorporated into field training.[69] Although John English claims that the battle drill "fad" had passed by 1944, battle drill was still a part of infantry training until the end of the war; Canadian Major-General P.J. Montague, visiting the School of Infantry in Durham County in November 1944, wrote that section battle drill laid down in the manuals was "NOT obsolete and is still the official doctrine for training centres in the UK."[70]

According to the parlance of the day, battle drill itself was described as the "reduction of military tactics to bare essentials which are taught to the platoon as a team drill, with clear explanations regarding the objects to be achieved, the principles involved and the individual task of each member of the team." Training for battle drill was supposed to be comprehensive, including high-standard weapons training, intensive physical fitness, field craft, battle drills, an emphasis on teamwork, and inoculation against battlefield sights and sounds.[71] Boiled down, it was about teaching teamwork and fire-and-movement procedures to infantry, who would execute swift tactical responses and be able to move aggressively forward with the weapons organic to their platoons, without reliance upon fire support generated from external sources such as the artillery.[72] Since battle drill was not taught above the company level, only weapons organic to the rifle company were incorporated, so tactics had to be based around man-portable infantry small arms. Early battle drill allotted no role to friendly tanks or artillery, which were usually attached (by doctrine) at a battalion level. "Each section," a manual from the Canadian Battle Drill School in Coldstream, BC, proclaimed, "is designed to provide its own covering fire to itself. It can, if necessary, rely on itself to get it forward."[73]

In battle drill, a basic sequence of actions was presented in response to troops coming under (simulated) fire: a section would split into constituted Rifle Group and Light Machine Gun Group, and while one group fired on the enemy location to keep them suppressed, the other group would close in, flanking the enemy left or right, switching roles back and forth until the Rifle Group was in position to make a final assault at close quarters.[74] These tactics were reproduced on a larger scale at the platoon and company levels with the core idea unchanged: find the enemy, pin them with fire from one group while one or more other groups enact a "pincer" movement to outflank, surround, and then assault the enemy position.[75] Training with battle drill was supposed to be carried out in field exercises over real terrain, but could also be done on the barracks parade square, where every movement diagrammatically represented an action on the battlefield, like a schematic. Infantrymen would first be taught the schematic, then how to use it on the ground. The idea was to develop automatic, individual responses and a comprehensive knowledge of how one's section, platoon, or company was supposed to be arrayed, which could then be projected onto the field.[76]

In practice, battle drill became inseparable from the field craft that taught soldiers how to operate and survive on the battlefield, and the more important parts of battle drill training took place under realistic conditions.[77] Courses such as the one run at the Canadian Training School emphasized physical "hardening" of soldiers to a high level of fitness, the use of movement over complex terrain, and the plentiful employment of live ammunition. Battle drill was always to be taught "on the double." "Blitz

Courses" were designed to test soldiers' capabilities and knowledge of the drill: "Built in a manner similar to an Obstacle Course, the soldier was faced with a number of tactical situations, i.e., machine-gun posts, snipers, etc., each demanding quick, decisive action," on a simulated battlefield.[78] Sections and platoons practised fire-and-movement on assault courses designed to be as harsh as possible, courses which battle-experienced soldiers would later bemoan as "an attack on our bodies."[79] Other innovations included snap-shooting ranges employing clever mechanisms to present fleeting or surprise targets.[80] Soldiers would employ their battle drill fire-and-movement tactics with blanks or live ammunition, using weapons to suppress "enemy" positions while their comrades moved to new flanking positions. The final assault would go in with machine guns providing suppressing fire while riflemen moved to close quarters with grenades, sub-machine guns, and bayonets.

Battle drill has been treated roughly in the historiography. Most famously, John English deemed it a "pedagogical dead-end" for the Canadian Army.[81] Timothy Harrison Place has also questioned the utility of this type of training, given the Anglo-Canadian propensity for blasting the Germans with artillery that supposedly left "little scope" for the actual exercise of battle drill in combat.[82] In some regards these are valid criticisms. By advocating abstract tactical ideas, battle drill sometimes subordinated terrain to manoeuvre instead of the other way around, and it constituted the continuation of some elements of parade square drill.[83] At the height of the battle drill craze Canadian units in the UK were carrying out little other infantry training besides battle drill. The fact that battle drill was taught only up to the company level was part of its appeal, since it could be arranged at low levels without the bothersome staff planning that higher battalion and formation training required (it is no coincidence that battle drill was first promulgated among regimental officers). Sometimes this problem was rationalized away with battle drill slogans such as, "Take care of the section, and the battalion will take care of itself!" which would have been useful had battalion-level command been a macrocosm of section-level command, which it was not.[84] Because of the way Anglo-Canadian divisions were structured, infantry training conducted only on the company level would never normally incorporate elements external to the company, such as tanks, engineers, and artillery. Since British doctrine placed a premium on artillery and tank support, an emphasis on low-level tactics to the exclusion of all else was potentially dangerous. Battle drill training was no substitute for combined-arms training, because unless all-arms participation in the fighting was simulated, the training would not reflect what needed to happen come the actual battle. One of the earliest critics was General Bernard Montgomery, who in March 1942 cautioned the Canadians that battle drill was not "the whole art of making war."[85]

But however "faddish" battle drill may have been, it gave the Canadian infantry a renewed enthusiasm for their training that bordered on the manic, and it armed them with small-unit tactics that, even if they were fighting an artillery-centric war, meant that they might have the confidence and ability to fight independent of support. As Terry Copp found in an exploration of the recent scholarship, in order to spare manpower and establish fire superiority against German reverse-slope defensive positions, Anglo-Canadian doctrine emphasized artillery operating in conjunction with the infantry.[86] But in terms of skill sets required by the infantryman, the fundamentals of battle drill were still necessary, and this method of training presented an excellent way to learn them. According to J.S. Edmonson of the South Saskatchewan Regiment, "Any semi-skilled soldier – if he's well-led – can line up behind a barrage and walk from A to B, but it takes more skill if he's in a dogfight in a village, in a woods, or when the situation is fluid if he's going to win it."[87]

By the end of the war, battle drill had become "the normal basic training of a soldier," the groundwork for all infantry training.[88] The development of low-level infantry skill, finesse, and ability, and the teaching of fire-and-movement tactical behaviour, were highly appropriate for modern warfare, and battle drill and the schools and units that taught it succeeded, as Timothy Harrison Place has said, in "raising the game" of the Commonwealth armies.[89] And while battle drill's vision of infantry self-reliance did not always reflect the way combat looked, it created infantrymen trained to fight as a team even when they couldn't see one another, who spoke the same tactical "language," and whose trained-for assumption was that they could fight on even bereft of all support. These traits were the basis of much of the infantry effectiveness of the Canadian Army in its coming campaigns.

As we shall see, battle drill took root. Battle experience questionnaires filled out during the fighting by over 150 junior infantry officers posed the question: "Were you able to put the tactical principles of fire and movement, taught as battle drill before going overseas, into practice?" The overwhelming answer from these infantrymen – 85 percent overall – was "yes."[90] An intelligence officer of the South Saskatchewan Regiment, G.G. Buchanan, would reflect in an interview many years later that battle drill was more useful in battle than anything else because "it was inbred into us."[91] Pedagogical dead end or not, battle drill training as a technique was put to work in combat by Canadians.

Before we leave our discussion of battle drill, a further link should be made to how Canadians were taught to fight. As mentioned earlier, Harold Alexander's earliest inspiration came from the German *Sturmtruppen* infiltration tactics: small groups acting with maximum initiative that could find weak spots in an enemy line, slip in, bypass enemy strength, and wind up in the rear lines of communication. The intention of German doctrine was to shatter morale and cohesion rather than physically destroy the enemy, since it led to the same result.[92] But battle drill was not really teaching infiltration, though the word itself was frequently used.[93] Battle drill manuals extolled how the effective leader should pursue the "DESTRUCTION of the enemy" as the primary objective. "This can only be achieved," the Coldstream manual read, "by sewing him up in the bag before the attack – by a policy of flanking movements, or if possible by encirclement."[94] But rather than really bypassing enemy units, battle drill taught soldiers to locate, fix, outflank, close with, and finally destroy enemy positions through fire and movement followed by direct assault. Methods of infiltration as laid out in battle drill manuals described the object as "not so much to capture ground as to exterminate all enemy holding the ground."[95] There was a preoccupation with direct confrontation, and with engaging and destroying the enemy in close combat. One of the foundations for early battle drill training, the War Office's 1941 *Physical and Recreational Training* manual, dealt extensively with hand-to-hand fighting and stressed ruthlessness: "Such brutal methods of attack as kicking, gouging the eyes, etc., though foreign and detestable to the Britisher, must be used without hesitation against the type of opponent we now have to face."[96] Assault practice in Canadian battle drill manuals called for combining fire-and-movement techniques with the "finishing" of the enemy by means of the bayonet, and an inordinate amount of time was spent on bayonet and melee combat training.[97] Hand-to-hand bloodletting in the assault was intended to be the final stage of offensive battle drills.

In his excellent volume on the interwar German Army, James Corum observed that the Reichswehr of the Weimar Republic, the forerunner of the Wehrmacht, was staffed primarily by officers with experience in the mobile, fluid warfare of the Great War's Eastern Front. Rommel, Kesselring, von Kleist, von Manstein, von Rundstedt, and others. These were the officers who defined German military policy and doctrine in the lead-up to the Second World War; very few "Westerners," whose primary experience was the static trench warfare of Belgium and France, rose to serious interwar prominence (excepting Hitler himself).[98] Conversely, virtually all the promulgators of Commonwealth – that is, British – military doctrine in the interwar period and the Second World War had cut their teeth in the trenches of the Western Front between 1914 and 1918. According to investigations by historian David French, British doctrine, shaped in Flanders and on the Somme, was loss-averse, firepower-heavy, and focused not on ruthless exploitation but on rapid consolidation.[99] In practice this meant seizing and holding positions and quickly shifting gears to defend them, rather than pressing forward to take advantage of enemy weakness. The British and Canadians had learned at great cost in the First World War that the German method of defence relied upon depth and immediate counterattacks that were designed to blunt infiltration. They had also learned that the best way to defeat such an enemy on a static front was by fighting conservatively. As Ian M. Brown's excellent study of the Canadian Corps in the First World War argued, German infiltration and stormtrooper tactics have won "misguided praise," whereas the Canadian system of countering German defences with firepower and "bite-and-hold" fighting has been under-appreciated.[100] The battle drill training of the Second World War, which focused upon the destruction of enemy units on the ground and then seizing and consolidating objectives, definitely took a page from the Anglo-Canadian playbook, and not the German one. But this was an entirely reasonable way to train infantrymen, given the opponent they would be facing.

Overall, the results of the training that Canadian soldiers received were quite good, with important caveats. The Canadians spent more time training than almost any other combatant army in the world, and while this was no substitute for battle experience, it gave plenty of time to develop individual skills and practice collective behaviour that emphasized teamwork, planning, winning the firefight, and destroying rather than bypassing enemy forces. Battle drill, assault landings, specialty training, and extensive weapons' handling and practice were partly responsible for the tactical skill that would distinguish Canadian infantry. Conversely, not enough pre-battle infantry training was carried out in conjunction with tanks and artillery, with the result that Canadian soldiers faced a formidable learning curve when it came to cooperating as part of a combined-arms team. As would be noted at length in Italy and Normandy, cooperation with tanks could at times be dodgy for the Canadians.[101] So, while the infantry was highly skilled at the platoon level, when the Canadians went into battle they sometimes lagged behind their enemies and perhaps even their allies in terms of integrating all arms. As the coming chapters show, some of the problems most often encountered during the campaigns involved deficiencies in combined-arms cooperation rather than deficiencies in the way the infantry were carrying out their own jobs.

CONCLUSION: OF DUBIOUS UTILITY

Selection, allocation, training, and organization were the experiences common to all of Canada's infantrymen during the Second World War, and in this chapter I have presented an overview of those elements as experienced by the Canadian soldier. My object has been to highlight some of the main characteristics of the military system that would go on to influence and shape the behaviour of soldiers in combat.

The impressive personnel selection apparatus, despite being carefully organized on an industrial-science basis, was ultimately of dubious utility in selecting for infantrymen. DPS interviewers threatened unit cohesion by causing personnel turnover, and carried assumptions about predisposition and innate intelligence that led to the discharge of many men who might have made excellent soldiers, if given the chance. While many who were obviously not cut out to be fighters were undoubtedly "weeded out" as well, it is difficult to know whether on balance the DPS did more good than harm, particularly to the infantry.

Canadian infantry training was long and comprehensive, and it generally focused on individual skills and lower-level section, platoon, and company training, since these were easy to organize and produced measurable results. Higher-level training that brought in larger formations, as well as tanks, artillery, and air power for cooperation – such as one would find on the battlefield – was less common, and the documentary evidence discussed later suggests that at least some infantrymen were insufficiently prepared for all-arms cooperation. As a consequence, the Canadian infantrymen who went into battle between 1943 and 1945 tended to be very able and capable with their own weapons, but were less familiar with combined-arms tactics. Canada was not unique in these regards; the experience of the Canadian Army was mirrored in the British Army.[102] The Americans, on the other hand, appear to have had some difficulty from the start in getting their conscript infantrymen moving aggressively in combat, but US Army combined-arms training and cooperation was a strong point of their war effort.[103] In such a context, the Canadian emphasis on training below the battalion level can be seen to have both strengths and weaknesses, which would be reflected in the coming experience of battle.

3

The Canadians in Sicily and Italy, 1943

After dinner at the Mansion House in London on 10 November 1942, Winston Churchill rose and gave one of his many memorable speeches. While praising Montgomery's victory at El Alamein and the American Operation TORCH landings in North Africa, he cautioned those present: "Now, this is not the end. It is not even the beginning of the end. But it is, perhaps, the end of the beginning."

Nine months later, on the morning of 10 July 1943, the assault battalions of 1st Canadian Infantry Division waded the final yards from landing craft to beaches on the Italian island of Sicily. It was the first commitment of Canadian troops to a sustained ground campaign in almost four years of war, and it came at a moment that Churchill might well have agreed was the beginning of the war's end: the first invasion of continental Europe by Allied forces. Canada's attachment to the Allied Central Mediterranean Forces (CMF) began portentously, with low casualties and conspicuous success. However, by the end of December 1943 only a minority of the Canadians who had landed on Sicily's Pachino Beach that day in July were still alive and unwounded.

In this chapter I explore the documentary evidence on the behaviour, motivation, and morale of the 1st Canadian Division infantrymen fighting in Sicily and Italy in the latter half of 1943. During this stage of the war the Canadian soldier was, arguably, at his strongest. Morale, cohesion, and unit *esprit* were extremely high, the troops were well trained, and throughout 1943 they consistently achieved success over the Germans and Italians. Many of the problem that were later to develop in the Canadian Army, insofar as they can be measured, were absent in 1943, but there were also struggles with inexperience and a steep learning curve to scale.

THE CAMPAIGN

Canada's war in the Mediterranean began in July 1943, when 1st Canadian Infantry Division and 1st Canadian Armoured Brigade landed in Sicily as part of Operation HUSKY, under the command of General Bernard Montgomery's British Eighth Army. The HUSKY landings involved seven Anglo-Canadian and American divisions along 150 miles of Sicilian coast, and the Canadians, combat inexperienced and fresh off the boat from England, were landed in the relatively safest area to minimize risk: the Pachino peninsula, separated from the main Axis positions by the Hyblaean mountain range.[1] It was known that the Axis would counterattack at least one of the seven Allied landing sites, the only question being *where*, not *if*, the counterattacks would fall.[2] When the Canadians first reached shore, their tactical role was beachhead consolidation. Assault brigade groups that landed included everything that would be needed to defeat an enemy counterattack on their beach: infantry, self-propelled field artillery, and anti-tank and anti-aircraft batteries.[3] As it happened, the counterattacks fell against the Americans at Gela and the British at Syracusa and Augusta, and the Canadians, unchallenged, began to push hard inland.

The Sicilian interior over which the Canadians operated is extraordinarily rugged and broken, its few metalled roads tortuously winding up switchbacks and, in short, facilitating hasty getaways.[4] Minor demolitions and small Axis delaying parties had a magnified effect and could grind Allied progress to a halt, while allowing the Axis to beat a retreat with impunity whenever they wished to avoid battle. Once the Allies were ashore the German generals on the ground knew that it was only a matter of time before Sicily fell, but their plan was to fortify a defensive line across the northeastern part of the island to hold the Allies as long as possible. This defensive line stretched from the Catania Plains on the east coast up to the north coast, the "hinge" being the fortress-towns of Assoro and Leonforte.[5] It was 1st Canadian Division that shared credit for breaking the hinge of the German defences.

The subsequent Canadian fighting in Sicily was highly successful, and not particularly costly by the later standards of the Italian campaign. The Assoro-Leonforte hinge was rapidly captured, and fierce fighting on the rugged approaches to Mount Etna obliterated the German defenders. By means of high mobility, considerable tactical skill at arms from all ranks, cooperation with allies, and a solid measure of good luck, the Canadians were one of the keys to dislodging the Axis hold on the island.[6]

Sicily then became the launching point for the Allied invasion of mainland Italy, and 1st Canadian Division was one of two Eighth Army divisions selected to cross the Messina Strait in an assault on Calabria, codenamed Operation BAYTOWN, on 3 September 1943. BAYTOWN's objectives were based upon a logistical imperative: to secure the Messina Strait for Allied shipping, which would then allow the US Fifth Army landings (codenamed AVALANCHE) to occur further north at Salerno, near Naples. After the Strait was opened, the Canadians were to advance north to engage those Germans that stood and fought, but with five hundred miles separating BAYTOWN from AVALANCHE, mutual support was not part of the original plan.[7] The Canadians landed at Reggio Calabria, this time prepared for mobility rather than for defence against a counterattack.[8] In Calabria, the Aspromonte mountain range rises to almost 1,400 metres above sea level only a few kilometres inland, limiting movement to roads. The frequent rivers and ravines necessitated innumerable bridges, which the Germans promptly demolished and booby-trapped to slow Anglo-Canadian progress. The AVALANCHE landings began on 9 September, against German opposition so strong that Fifth Army was in danger of being driven back into the sea.[9] Under orders to push harder for the north, 1st Canadian Division put together "flying columns" intended to rush north to Potenza to relieve the bridgehead, though by the time they arrived the battle at Salerno had been won. Instead, the Canadian columns assisted in the disruption of the Germans as they pulled back toward the Foggia Plain in late September.[10]

For the Canadians, the remainder of September 1943 was spent largely out of contact with the enemy, and 1st Division's general staff wrote in their war diary of "strong rumours that there is a war on."[11] By October, the Canadians were again attempting to chase down German forces, who in turn employed mobile arms, mines, demolitions, and improvised booby-traps to hold a succession of short-term positions until the Canadians would be forced to deploy in strength, and would then fall back further.[12] They were attempting to stall until a new defensive line (the "Gustav Line") could be constructed on the Sangro River further north, a line that was, according to campaign historian Eric Linklater, "the inner doors of the fortress of Italy, locked and barred."[13] The Canadians were in reserve for much of November 1943, during which time other elements of Eighth Army broke the Gustav Line on the Sangro River and inflicted considerable damage on the Germans' 76 Panzer Corps facing them.[14] Even as the weather deteriorated, plans were laid for Eighth Army to push up the Adriatic coast of Italy through the fishing town of Ortona that December, to capture the lateral highway to Rome. The Canadians were to be the spearhead.

The December 1943 campaign was a bloodbath in a mud bowl. Hampered by the weather, the ground, and the enemy – particularly the 90th Panzer Grenadier Division and the elite 1st Parachute Division – the Canadians fought across the Moro River, cleared a path through outlying objectives, and finally assaulted Ortona itself in ferocious street-to-street fighting.[15] The campaign was attritional, ugly, largely bereft of manoeuvre except at low tactical levels, and exceedingly violent, producing far more Canadian casualties than the rest of 1943 combined. Although the advance faltered beyond Ortona and had to be abandoned as an operational dead-end, the Canadians defeated some of the elite German units that had been holding the line.

FORCE STRUCTURE

From July to December 1943, 1st Canadian Infantry Division represented the Canadian contingent involved in the Italian campaign, supported by tanks of 1st Canadian Armoured Brigade. 1st Division had been mobilized for the Canadian Active Service Force (CASF) in 1939, and had been the first formation overseas; it was chosen for service in Italy because of its advanced state of training, and because its soldiers had been cooling their heels in England the longest.[16] Three of its battalions, the Royal Canadian Regiment, Princess Patricia's Canadian Light Infantry, and the Royal 22e Régiment, were Canada's Permanent Force (PF) regular units, though most of the peacetime officers and soldiers of the PF dispersed in 1939 to form training cadres.[17] All other battalions were drawn from militia regiments mobilized at the outbreak of war and supplemented by volunteers. Originally, 1st Division was to be led by Major-General Harry Salmon, but Salmon was killed in a plane crash just prior to HUSKY. When 1st Division touched Italian soil it was commanded by the icy but efficient Major-General Guy Simonds; in November 1943 Simonds was replaced by Major-General Christopher Vokes. Throughout the Italian campaign, 1st Division was part of the British Eighth Army and in 1943 belonged to several different British corps formations.

In his biography of Major Paul Triquet, VC, historian John MacFarlane refers to Triquet and his peers as the "original veterans," men who had been overseas with 1st Division since 1939.[18] This contemporary term served to divide the "original" members of the battalions from those who would join them later as replacements. Many of 1st Division's soldiers had been together since 1939, when most recruits had volunteered directly at regimental stations.[19] Beginning in June 1940, all recruitment began to take place through district depots unassociated with any particular regiment, and after 1941 all recruits were being allocated where Personnel Selection believed they would best fit.[20] Many of the "originals" had also been together as part of the Permanent Force or the Non-Permanent Active Militia (NPAM) in peacetime, and had voluntarily elected to join and stick with the infantry.

Not all of those who went to Sicily in July 1943 had been with 1st Division since 1939, but most had. Almost 60 percent of private soldiers who became casualties in Italy had been issued their regimental numbers directly at regimental stations, and over 80 percent of corporals and sergeants could say the same.[21] The "spirit of '39" ran strong in 1st Division, and no other Canadian formation first entering combat would have anywhere near this number of "originals." But they were also a finite and exhaustible resource, as figure 3.1 shows. The rapid decline in 1943 of the number of "original" soldiers in 1st Division demonstrated how fast the face of the regiment could change. By the end of December 1943 the number of "original" private soldiers in particular had declined sharply to half what it had been in July. As I show in subsequent chapters, this was only the beginning of a decline that would, before the end of the war, mark the near-extinction of "original" soldiers, at least in combat positions. These "original veterans" left in part thanks to promotion or transfer away from the front, but the diminution in their numbers was mostly the result of casualties. The long-service "originals" were a cohesive element within the division; they had lived and trained together for four years, been involved in numerous deployments, false alarms, and guard details during the war's darkest hours, and finally gone into battle together. The 1943 campaign in Sicily was their hour.

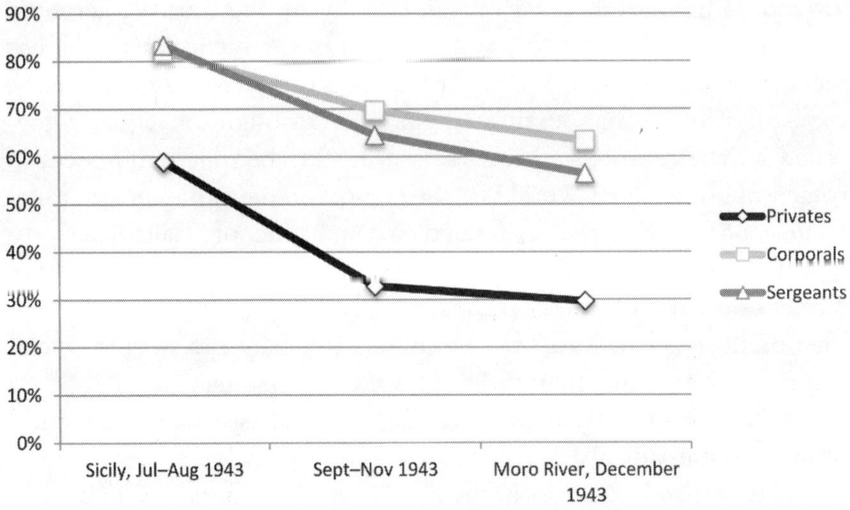

Figure 3.1: 1st Division "original" infantrymen, Italy, 1943

Although a constant stream of replacements replenished their losses from illness and combat, it was not until the grievous losses of December 1943 that the proportional number of "original veterans" began to decrease precipitously.

BEHAVIOUR IN BATTLE

The nature of Canada's Mediterranean war in 1943 was twofold: first pursuing the Axis forces; and then hard fighting once the enemy had stopped to hold its position. This pattern played out across Sicily and Italy. The pursuit battles were mobile, dispersed operations in rough terrain, and could be frustratingly slow in the face of skilful German demolitions, booby-traps, and other delaying tactics. Lieutenant-Colonel I.S. Johnston, commanding officer of the 48th Highlanders, reported that during September and October 1943: "the nature of ground in [Italy] has proved a consistently limiting factor. Consequently we have been unable to use battle drill as taught. We generally just blast the enemy off with Artillery and put in a battalion attack, adapting our movements to the ground, which governs everything. Usually by the time we get close enough to him in order to use battle drill in the tactical sense he has moved away from us."[22] Where the Germans turned to fight, conversely, the battles took on an attritional character, though one equally governed by the terrain, and the fighting quickly became reminiscent in some ways of the First World War. In a report on the battles of late 1943, Lieutenant-General H.D.G. Crerar, then commander of I Canadian Corps in Italy, observed: "In this theatre, conditions and circumstances have faced us once more with the tactical problems and conditions which typified the last Great War. The continuous trenches and wire entanglements may be missing [but] the anti-tank and -personnel mine has pretty effectively taken its place. In other and principal essentials, the tactical problem is the same."[23]

There were other echoes of the First World War in Italy. Two months prior to HUSKY, Major-General Simonds wrote a command memorandum detailing German defensive doctrine: "The enemy is quick and skilful in counter-attack, and every operation [of ours] must be launched from a firm base – a tactical feature strongly held. During advance or attack successive objectives must be firmly established." He added: "The sequence of action on reaching an objective will be: (a) Reorganize in tactical dispositions to suit the ground. (b) Patrol beyond the objective. (c) Dig in. (d) Using the objective as a firm base, seize advantageous ground beyond or to the flanks. A firm base is <u>NOT</u> established unless anti-tank guns are in position and <u>dug-in</u>."[24] Such instructions would not have been out of place at Hill 70 in the summer of 1917, because the German defensive methods, namely yielding forward positions only to wipe out exhausted attackers with an immediate counterattack, remained fundamentally unchanged. During delaying actions the Germans considered large-scale counterattacks wasteful, but even then smaller-scale local counterattacks were countenanced "to regain vital features" of the battlefield.[25] But their main defences in the Mediterranean revolved around the holding of a fixed line, and for this the Germans would position their infantry first in a forward screen of weapon pits covering a network of observation posts, disposed well in front of the line of main resistance, which was held in reserve to counterattack – a classic "elastic defence."[26] For the Canadians, plans to defeat the counterattack began before they landed in Sicily and guided their thinking thereafter.

Such tactics were undeniably conservative, but they reflected a respect for German capabilities and, most significantly, demonstrated an understanding of how to overcome them. For reasons of terrain alone, the Allies were never going to win a war of manoeuvre on the Italian peninsula, where the Germans could, with the investment of disproportionately small effort, seriously impede Allied mobility. That meant that the fighting normally had to be hard and direct, and against an enemy whose counterattacks made overreaching a hazardous proposition. Major-General Christopher Vokes, commander of 2nd Brigade and later all of 1st Division in 1943, mentioned in a battle narrative: “The immediate counterattack, at which the German is so adept, is quite ineffective against a determined defence. Time and again ‘Boche’ counterattacks of this sort were beaten off at great loss to the enemy. By our ensuring the rapid movement of tanks and [anti-tank] guns in support of consolidation, enemy armoured counter-attack was nullified.”[27] The results from battle experience questionnaires filled out by infantry officers, which specifically asked “Did you ever have to organise a rapid defence against counterattack?” were overwhelmingly answered “Yes” by respondents in the 1943 campaigns.[28] The infantry sometimes had nothing with which to confront these counterattacks except their own weapons, but they would usually be reinforced by mortars, tanks, anti-tank guns, mines, and artillery.[29]

In chapter 2, I discussed some of the potential problems inherent in the intensive focus on infantry training below the battalion level, and as early as Sicily some consequences of these problems could be observed. After the battles of Nissoria and Agira in Sicily, there were exhortations in official “lessons learned” documents for the infantry to follow more closely behind the artillery’s barrage during the advance, with the implication that failure to do so had caused the bloody repulses outside Nissoria. As 2nd Brigade assessed: “In the attack, the movement of the infantry must conform to the [artillery] fire plan and take full advantage of supporting fire. If the neutralizing effect of a concentration of fire is to be of any value, the infantry should arrive on the objective immediately after the fire lifts.”[30] The 48th Highlanders’ regimental history offered a bitter rejoinder to such remarks: “You can’t follow fire support closely while climbing a cliff!”[31] Questionnaire answers gave a different perspective: three-quarters of respondents to a question about whether their soldiers kept up with an artillery barrage effectively answered "Yes," and only three out of twenty-nine answered "No." Only half of the respondents, however, indicated that their battalions had received preliminary training in attacking beneath an artillery barrage.[32] The terrain was as great an opponent as the Axis enemy that they faced in Italy, and there was much to be learned both by the infantry and by the higher formations that attempted to coordinate all-arms cooperation. The questionnaires specify artillery barrages (designed to "cage off" an area against enemy interference or counterattack) rather than concentrations, destructive, close, or counter-battery artillery shoots, which tended to be more precise. Barrages were resource-intensive in terms of guns and ammunition expenditure and according to Canadian training literature were "not usually" practised beneath the brigade level.[33] Perhaps it is no surprise that Canadian infantrymen had not trained extensively with barrages. Artillery "stonks" and concentrations were a better adjunct to the battle drill fire-and-movement tactics, as they allowed fire to be called down at specific times and places for suppression. Nonetheless, a training deficit existed in this area.

Historian Bill McAndrew argues that Canadian tactics in Italy were too artillery-focused, and that commanders yoked operations to heavy firepower that restricted freedom of manoeuvre.[34] There were instances at Agira and again at The Gully in Italy, where artillery-based frontal-assault tactics were employed, though in both cases it is unclear what the alternative was, given enemy dispositions.[35] However, the Canadian infantry loved the artillery support available to them. Having the upper hand in firepower boosted morale tremendously, and watching the Germans "catch hell" from Canadian guns was consistently mentioned as a comfort for the infantrymen.[36] And the Canadians were not as chained to their artillery in 1943 as the historiography indicates. In Sicily they were specifically noted by the Germans for their field craft skills (*Indianerkrieg*), which a 15th Panzer Grenadier Division report noted as being "superior to our own troops. Very mobile at night, surprise break-ins, clever infiltrations at night with small groups between our strong points."[37] Fire-and-movement techniques were frequently employed, and the battle drill training had prepared the Canadians well for the fighting that they encountered in the rolling Italian terrain. The great majority of infantry officers with experience in 1943 who filled out battle questionnaires (twenty-five of twenty-nine: 86 percent) indicated that their units regularly put battle drill to use in combat.[38] Much of the success that the Canadians achieved in 1943 came about through dispersed operations and reliance on the infantry to fight forward and to hold ground against enemy counterattacks.

Another notable Canadian behaviour was the considerable "trigger-happiness" among its inexperienced soldiers, and a few officers expressed concern that proper fire discipline was not being exercised in combat. A tendency to shoot at everything that moved was particularly evident in the early going in Sicily, when the unexpectedly easy landings created a creeping anxiety about when and where the enemy would appear to put up a real fight. As Captain C.H. Pritchard of the Loyal Edmonton Regiment told 1st Division's historical officer:

> On re-entering RAGUSA [on 14 July 1943] "C" company and the platoon mounted on tanks were sniped at and the battalion suffered its first casualties, which consisted of three killed and four wounded. There has been a great deal of conjecture as to the origin of this sniping. While there is no doubt that a certain amount has been done by Fascists in civilian clothes, scraps of evidence gathered together seem to indicate that a lot of this sniping has been due to Canadian soldiers firing enemy weapons indiscriminately or firing at unseen adversaries. During the move ... a flare-up occurred on a long winding switchback road which turned out to be a general mix-up in which [Canadian] tanks at the top and bottom of the road fired at each other and [infantry battalions] joined in the fray.[39]

In the questionnaires, over half the officers indicated that their platoons and companies had been short on ammunition in battle, a greater proportion than at any other time in the Canadian campaigns.[40] As General Montgomery remarked: "A new feature of the Italian campaign was the heavy rate of ammunition expenditure ... the Battle of the Sangro was the first real warning given to us that in close and easily defended country we should expect a need for ammunition on a scale far higher than that to which we have been accustomed."[41] It was during consolidation and defence against counterattacks, when forward units were most isolated, that "rapid ammunition expenditure was the greatest worry," according to the Royal 22e Régiment's Major Henri Tellier.[42] When anxiety was running high and the enemy was close, the urge to fire and expend ammunition rapidly seemed to have been quite powerful among the well-trained but inexperienced Canadian troops. In contrast, the US Army, fighting alongside the Canadians in Sicily and Italy, indicated in their own "lessons learned" reports that they were having the opposite problem: their infantry were often making inadequate use of their own firepower.[43] Although the answer may never be fully known, it might be theorized that as a result of their battle drill training or deficiencies in combined-arms training, the soldiers of 1st Canadian Division went into battle with a greater appreciation for the need to use their own small arms than did the Americans.[44]

Few other systemic problems with infantry behaviour were reported in 1943. The Canadians achieved their greatest successes when carrying out concentric attacks that allowed their infantry the most flexibility. Their defeats came about largely when the German defensive positions became denser, the ratio of enemy soldiers on the ground increased, and opportunities for manoeuvre were reduced, creating situations where battering through the enemy with a frontal assault behind an artillery barrage became necessary.

MORALE

According to Major A.T. Sesia, 1st Division's historical officer in Sicily: "At supper tonight while speaking of today's battle [at Agira], Sprung remarked that he has never seen troops so eager to get into battle as our fellows despite the fact that they are completely [tired] out. He has seen war-weary English troops in North Africa going into battle with terror written all over their faces."[45] The Canadians' turn for war-weariness would come, but the successes achieved in an unforgiving land in the face of fierce enemy resistance gave the 1943 campaigns a much more optimistic tone, and morale was notably very high.

Battle experience questionnaires from those with experience fighting in 1943 indicate that it was the "mundane" comforts that underwrote good morale in 1st Canadian Division: mail from home, good food, rum rations (and, even more prized, Canadian beer), leave, comfortable billets, and entertainment. "Good [support and administration]," wrote Major Thompson of the Saskatoon Light Infantry, "means everything to the other ranks."[46] The only recurrent morale problem that censors' reports identified in 1943 were recorded among troops in December 1943 when mail and Christmas packages failed to arrive promptly. According to the censors' reports that month, "A very small proportion of the hoped-for Christmas mail appears to have reached the troops, particularly that destined for units in the forward areas, and complaints are found in almost every letter."[47] It is remarkable that administrative complaints were at the forefront at a time when some of the bloodiest Canadian fighting of the war – the Moro River and Ortona – was taking place. But it underscores the fundamental importance of mail to the troops on the ground. There is no direct correlation between the availability of creature comforts and the willingness of troops to fight, but as author John Steinbeck observed during his time as a war correspondent in the Mediterranean in 1943: "To the [infantryman] in the field or in barracks or on maneuver, letters are nearly the most important thing that happen or don't happen. In five minutes of talk with a soldier you know whether he has heard from home or that letters do not come. It is a constant source of conversation, of worry and of gladness."[48]

Another, more ephemeral contributor to morale, but almost as prevalent, was success in battle: "Well-planned, well-fought, successful action," "Fact of unit having beaten back a counter-attack," and "Capture of prisoners and booty" were some of the representative questionnaire replies on what contributed to positive morale.[49] Soaring morale after a particularly successful action (the Hastings & Prince Edward Regiment at Assoro being a good example) was frequently noted in the regimental histories; having a reason for pride and self-confidence was invaluable.

The Canadians liked to think about their part of the war as the "beginning of the end," and from the moment they went ashore in Sicily there was a hopeful expectation that their participation was a harbinger for the return of peace. While nobody thought that the war would be over by Christmas '43, field censors still indicated that among Canadians, "there is a general confidence prevailing that 1944 will see the end of hostilities in Western Europe. Many expect and hope that they will be home in Canada for their next Christmas."[50] Ending the war was a key motivator for soldiers, and fresh success in Italy or on any other front was discussed avidly. Knowing that they had both an attainable goal to work toward and an individual role to play in bringing about that objective was central to motivation. But there was also a tacit understanding among troops (if not among politicians) that they were fighting to end *their* war, not the entire world war. The first rumblings of discontent over the distant prospect of being sent to the Pacific to fight the Japanese after victory was attained over Germany and Italy were heard at the end of 1943.[51]

Another consideration in gauging morale is an army's mechanisms of punishment; if one accepts the assertion that good discipline is a function of good morale, then offence statistics become a potential viewport into soldiers' feelings and behaviour.[52] During active operations, harsh penalties were sometimes handed down upon Canadian soldiers in the interest of maintaining discipline, particularly for the military crimes of desertion or, much more rarely, cowardice.[53] 1st Canadian Division contained a provost (military police) company, and on average there was one provost for every 157 soldiers in the division, a high number of watchful eyes, though much of the provosts' time was spent on traffic control.[54] Discipline was a matter both for provosts and for commanding officers, and throughout the 1943 campaign quite a number of offences were tabulated by CMHQ's Discipline & Pay Section (D&PS), including both less-serious summary punishments within the unit and those offences that resulted in field general courts martial. According to D&PS records, between July and December 1943 there were 2,249 offences committed within 1st Canadian Division, 931 of them (41 percent) attributable to soldiers from the nine infantry battalions; this was very proportional, since on paper the infantry battalions made up about 42 percent of the division's total strength.[55] (Appendix E details the specifics.) The majority of offences in 1943 were for absence without leave or "conduct to the prejudice of military discipline," a catch-all disciplinary category that as often as not involved unauthorized joyriding in military vehicles.[56] Some regiments had much more notable disciplinary problems than others, although, as Robert Tooley has argued, it is probably "invidious and uninformative" to seek out associations between specific commanding officers and the number of offences in their battalions.[57] The differentials, however, indicate a range of disciplinary policies and standards at work.

Absenteeism has long been a gauge for the state of morale in armies.[58] Absence Without Leave (AWL, Army Act 15.1) was far and away the most common offence in the Mediterranean, and between July and December 1943 there were 536 charges laid under Army Act 15.1. This meant that in aggregate one in every fourteen infantrymen (about 7 percent) had an AWL charge placed against them during this campaign, though there were many repeat offenders, and irate officers could slap soldiers with an AWL charge for overstaying a leave pass by a few minutes if they felt an example needed to be made. AWL charges were a more pointed problem in some regiments than in others. The three Permanent Force battalions, including the Royal 22e, sustained the lowest rates of absenteeism in their respective brigades in the 1943 campaign, and 2nd Brigade (PPCLI, the Seaforth Highlanders, and the Loyal Edmonton Regiment) had the lowest overall rate among the infantry, according to D&PS's offence data. Desertion (Army Act 12.1), a much more serious offence, was an extremely rare charge in 1943, with only the Royal 22e, with its famously draconian disciplinary policies, laying more than a few desertion charges.[59] It is difficult in historical hindsight to know the significance of these numbers. Not every act of indiscipline resulted in a formal charge, and not every formal charge really reflected an act of indiscipline. No matter how one interprets these numbers, however, the problems of absenteeism and desertion were a minor nuisance in 1943, and most accounts noted the highly disciplined and compliant behaviour of 1st Division soldiers during this time. Soldiers were not absenting themselves from their units in any significant numbers.

Historians have dealt with the problem of neuropsychiatric (NP) casualties in 1943 at some length, but the topic should be raised here in the context of morale.[60] Firm statistics on Canadian casualties admitted into the military medical chain as "psychiatric" or "exhaustion" cases do not exist for Sicily. Reports from Canadian psychiatrists on the ground strongly indicated that there were very few of these types of casualties in Sicily, and that the same could be said for the relatively low-intensity operations in September, October, and November. 1st Division's attached neuropsychiatrist, Major A. Manning Doyle, was not able to make a complete count since not all Canadian casualties in Sicily passed through his care, but he noted that he had only treated 46 NP cases in Sicily, and by November 1943 only 190 cases had been observed among Canadian soldiers.[61] During the December battles on the Moro River and in Ortona the metaphorical dam broke, and Doyle was suddenly awash in exhaustion and "shell-shock" cases. The most serious spike in NP casualties came during the week of 12–18 December, which encompassed the time the Canadians were fighting for The Gully southwest of Ortona. Not coincidentally, this was where the fighting took on its bitterest, least successful, and most frustrating character, as repeated piecemeal frontal assaults on a powerful German position were repelled.[62]

A few patterns are observable, even though the experience of each NP casualty was deeply dependent upon individual circumstances. In 1943, NP casualties seemed strongly associated not only with the severity of the fighting but also with the relative success of operations. In comparison with the fruitless, frustrating battles in The Gully, the fight in Ortona itself produced significantly fewer NP casualties in the two battalions that took part in it: the Seaforth Highlanders and the Loyal Edmontons. The week of 19–25 December tallied about one-third the NP casualties of the previous week in The Gully, though the numbers of killed and wounded were on a similar scale.[63] Sicily likewise produced relatively few NP casualties; the battles there were quite difficult, and the Canadians at times sustained heavy casualties, but the fighting there was also very successful. These numbers suggest causal connections between NP casualties and morale, and that these kinds of casualties are correlated with more than the intensity of the fighting; the success and pace of operations, highlighted elsewhere as central to morale, also appears to be critical to the number of NP casualties. The weather, which was much more agreeable in Sicily that on the Moro River, may also have been a significant factor.

A final point related to morale is the attitude of Canadian soldiers toward the enemy. The Canadian infantrymen in closest contact with the enemy experienced a wide and vacillating range of feelings toward the Italians and Germans they fought against, from antipathy to *ennui* to respect. But from the very beginning of the Sicily campaign, some of the accounts suggest that the soldiers of 1st Canadian Division were not, on the whole, kindly disposed toward their opponents. Until that point their only real contact with the enemy had been with German bombers overhead during the Blitz in England, with German air raids on their own positions in the UK, and through seeing the bloodletting inflicted upon

2nd Canadian Division during the Dieppe Raid.[64] Once the Canadians got into the fight in Sicily, attitudes varied. There were many reports of German "dirty tricks," all of which seem to have infuriated Canadians: feigning a surrender, sending out irregular guerrilla shooters, killing prisoners, or planting improvised explosive booby-traps. All these behaviours were seen as falling outside (or in the grey area) of those normally accepted in war. As mentioned earlier, many soldiers were highly disturbed by perceived enemy "sniper" action against Canadians on Pachino Beach and the initial advance inland. Major Sesia noted: "After [1st Brigade] took Valguernera yesterday some Hastings & Prince Edward Regiment soldiers looted the shops, looking for 'vino' ... some of the drunks were wandering up and down the streets firing their rifles and Tommy-guns at civilians and houses, shouting words to the effect that these people were responsible for the deaths of their pals."[65]

But that was not the only serious incident in Sicily. "According to the information coming down to [Division HQ]," Sesia continued, "the [Canadian] troops are not bothering to take prisoners. Apparently the Hun is getting nasty and playing dirty tricks, such as giving himself up to surrender, concealing at the same time stick grenades which he throws at our troops who go forward to capture him." Grim accounts followed: "Yesterday when some Germans gave themselves up, two of them threw grenades at our fellows who went to capture them. When we finally took them they were made to dig their own graves and then were shot. This sounds rather grim and is probably untrue, but it does reflect the frame of mind that some of our troops must be in when such tricks are played on them."[66] German *Generalmajor* Eberhard Rodt of the 15th Panzer Grenadier Division alleged after the war that during the battle for Leonforte Canadians shot German POWs, athough supporting evidence is lacking.[67] Captain A.H. MacLean of the West Nova Scotia Regiment described his battalion's successful attack on Catenanuova (shortly after Leonforte) for a battle experience questionnaire: "The forward companies advanced as ordered followed by the reserve companies ... little opposition was encountered before entering the town. A German machine gun crew, having been overrun by the forward company, attempted to give themselves up to the reserve company. It was impossible to take prisoners under the circumstances, so these were disposed of."[68] One private with the Seaforth Highlanders, his opinions captured by the field censors, wrote in a letter home: "I've been in North Africa and now Sicily ... we've had some hectic times, the bullets and shrapnel come pretty thick. We took some German prisoners and they are a pretty scared lot. We captured a [sergeant] and he said the English they are good fighters, the Canadians with the red patches on their arms [1st Canadian Division's patch] are devils ... they think we don't take any prisoners, they figure we shoot them all, but they really shake in their shoes."[69] Then-Brigadier Vokes mentioned after the Sicilian campaign that while the average German soldier upheld the Conventions of War, "their paratroopers acted much differently. They seemed to shoot at anything that moved and, of course, were dealt with in the same manner."[70]

There is evidence of sustained enmity between the Canadians and Germans in the December 1943 battles as well, and a sense of hatred rather than respect prevailed among at least some combatants.[71] "Dirty tricks" and other acts of disrespect were noted in many sources. Writing home, one soldier reported: "A while back a couple of [Germans] came out with their hands up and when our boys went out to take them they dropped to the ground and the Jerries that were hidden opened up on our boys with machine guns and wiped the works out – so you can't trust the Germans."[72] Reginald Roy's history of the Seaforth Highlanders recorded an account of a burial party after Ortona: "We collected all our own dead all right, but when it came to the Jerries we made a half-hearted attempt to dig graves. But the weather was cold and the ground was frozen, so to Hell with it. We gathered them all up and heaved them down a well and heaved a hand grenade down with them. A real Vikings' funeral."[73] The feeling appears to have been mutual: "Most of the enemy fought until the last brick fell and one, taken prisoner when he was blinded but still had his weapons, said: 'I wish I could see you – I'd kill every one of you!'"[74]

It could be theorized that these attitudes might be traced to the Canadians' combat inexperience: they were stepping into a high-intensity campaign in the middle act, and alongside inexperience came fear. The American 45th Division, which like the Canadians had not seen combat before they landed in Sicily, also experienced a number of troubling incidents. The 45th had allegedly been told prior to Sicily by General George Patton to watch out for treachery when the Germans surrendered, and to "kill the [sons of bitches]" unless they were certain of their intention to surrender.[75] Several incidents followed, including the massacre of Italian POWs by 45th Division men at Biscari airfield. As historian Carlo D'Este has argued, "At Biscari, there is no doubt the 45th Division encountered examples of violations of the Geneva Convention by Axis soldiers and that their men were angry and edgy as a result."[76] Canadian attitudes and incidents may have had a similar root, though nothing as horrible as Biscari occurred in the Canadian zone. But the experiences of Italy in 1943 would be mirrored in Normandy, and again during the invasion of Germany. As historian Tim Cook has acknowledged in his study of surrender and killing of prisoners in the First World War, "it might be tempting to ascribe these unlawful actions to undisciplined or inexperienced soldiers, but they appear to have happened throughout the war, in almost every [Canadian] battle from 1915 to 1918."[77] It needs to be said that most Canadians fought hard but were happier to take prisoners than to kill them. Nonetheless, an underlying hostility and sense of personal affront seems to have at least partially characterized the conduct of operations in 1943. As historian Rick Atkinson put it, by 1943 "Rommel's genteel *Krieg ohne Hass* – 'war without hate' – was but a hazy memory from North Africa. The brutality of total war had long been felt on the Eastern Front, but as the Second World War entered its fifth year the stain spread throughout Western Europe."[78]

This was not "live and let live" warfare: fighting in Italy in 1943 could be violent and unpredictable, and, as would happen in Normandy in 1944, unlawful actions – whether taken on the spur of the moment or in retaliation for the enemy's perceived barbarities – could provoke cycles of revenge and retribution. The Canadians, newcomers to this combat environment, seem to have taken these cycles hard, and an unsanctioned culture of exacting reciprocal measures against the enemy existed at certain points. Of course, whatever illegal actions may have been taken by the Canadian soldiers were a tiny shadow of those routinely carried out by the Germans in Italy. When faced with evidence of enemy treachery or disregard for the laws of war, rage and disdain could sometimes push Canadian behaviour over acceptable wartime boundaries.

COHESION AND MOTIVATION

Documentary evidence from the 1943 campaigns provides fascinating insights into different facets of combat motivation and effectiveness. Since the 1943 battles had a number of unique characteristics that would not be replicated in the later Canadian campaigns, we need to pay careful attention to the role of esprit de corps, small group cohesion, casualties, and leadership in motivating Canadian infantrymen to fight.

Regimental histories of the Canadian Army extol the virtues of regimental pride and esprit de corps – identification with higher units and formations – and cite these as major reasons why soldiers continued to fight despite severe adversity. But really, one would expect nothing less from documents published by the regiments themselves. What do the contemporary documentary sources say? The evidence is in part ambiguous, but from what can be assessed, esprit de corps and organizational bonding with regiments and higher formations seem to have been stronger among the Canadian soldiers of the 1943 campaigns than they would be at any other point during the army's active combat operations.

Canadian soldiers took pride in belonging to their own national army, and definitely possessed a long-standing identity of being separate from the British. Insofar as Canadians in England experienced feelings of esprit de corps with higher formations, it was that national formation that they were proud to be part of. Under normal circumstances the breaking up of First Canadian Army when 1st Division went to the Mediterranean would have been extremely detrimental to morale, both for those who went into action and for those left behind. As one soldier wrote home: "I'm still here in England despite the fact that many of our boys are in Sicily and Italy … As well as the boys are doing down there in the 8th Army we still wish they would keep we Canadians [sic] as a single Army."[79]

In practice, however, most soldiers in 1st Division relished the opportunity to fight as part of the legendary British Eighth Army. The prospect of proving themselves to the battle-hardened "Desert Rats," who had driven Germany's *Afrkia Korps* from Egypt to its destruction in Tunisia, dwarfed any dissatisfaction that Canadian soldiers may have felt in leaving their national formation behind. The achievements of Eighth Army in North Africa had grown in the telling, and the name of General Bernard

Law Montgomery was gold to the soldiers of 1st Division; most of the Canadians had known "Monty" when he was GOC of South Eastern Command in England in 1941–42, which at that time had included the Canadians.[80] "What makes us mad over here," wrote one sergeant in a letter home, "is that they give the credit for [the Tunisian campaign] to [US] General Eisenhower; holy mackerel, he started in after all the rest; in our way of thinking the credit belongs entirely to the British especially the Eighth Army, and the one who should be congratulated is Montgomery, he took over at its worst time and pulled it through."[81] Once 1st Canadian Division was told (en route to Sicily) that they were to be part of Eighth Army, morale soared. The censors' report for the invasion force reads: "The fact that these troops were going to become part of the Eighth Army and be under the leadership of General Montgomery gave them tremendous confidence and writer after writer, Canadian and British, mentions it with pride. A [company sergeant-major] makes a typical remark: 'Monty says that we can do it and that is good enough for all of us.'"[82] Once the landings had commenced, an unidentified officer wrote: "Monty visited us the other day, and told us what great fighters the Canadians were. He surely has the common touch – gets in amongst the men, motions them to gather round, and then talks to them as if they were all planning together some operations and he needed their advice, and our boys have begun to speak of him in the same tones of devotion as do the boys of the Eighth [Army]. He has a touch of a 'genius' all right."[83] These favourable attitudes and feelings of reciprocal pride toward Montgomery lasted throughout the period in which he was in command in Italy – most of 1943. Farley Mowat summed up the feelings toward "Monty": "Monty plays his part in the story of the Regiment as does no other senior commander. There were those who hated him, but they were not amongst the fighting troops. There were a good many who were angered by him, but there were few men in the infantry who did not trust him, as they had never in the past, and would never in the future, trust another general officer."[84]

Canadian soldiers also felt that they benefited from Eighth Army policies under Montgomery, which magnified their organizational and institutional identification with their new formation. Many felt that they were being more fully filled-in on operational plans than they had been under First Canadian Army, something that the histories attribute largely to Montgomery's personality. "Monty had long believed that every soldier down to the rear-rank private in the last platoon should know not only every detail of his own part in the battle, but should also know the general plan," wrote Mowat. "Information that was denied to colonels in other armies, was the right of every private who served Montgomery."[85] Communicating the plans and intentions to the troops increased their investment in the higher formations under which they operated. Battle experience questionnaires routinely reported that "troops being put in the picture" was one of the most significant determinants of high morale and cohesion among Canadians.[86] The soldiers at the sharp end of combat were hesitant to place their trust in an organization that did not trust them to be able to know (and want to know) about the role they were playing.

The existence of esprit de corps and organizational bonding within regiments and battalions is harder to gauge, as these appeared far less frequently in soldiers' correspondence than did discussions of Eighth Army. Regimental pride is commonplace in postwar accounts, interviews, and histories, but little thread of it can be found in contemporary documents. This need not imply its absence, but it does highlight the problem with documenting something so ephemeral. Among officers who fought in 1943 and filled out battle experience questionnaires, none cited "regimental spirit," "regimental traditions," or anything of the like as contributors to the morale of the men.[87] Censorship reports on 1st Division mail do contain expressions of regimental pride throughout late 1943 and early 1944, but the censors infrequently commented upon them.[88] The infantry regiments certainly took on vital roles and meanings, especially for the "original veterans" of 1st Division, as their units had constituted the main social horizons of these men for years. Given that over 60 percent of the private soldiers who landed in Sicily were "originals" from 1939–40, one must appreciate that the regiment had been home for most of them for four years.

High casualty rates within 1st Canadian Division's infantry battalions would likely erode regimental *esprit* more than they would small-group cohesion (discussed later). The "original veterans" of 1st Division had volunteered directly at the regimental depot of choice, and over the next four years were steeped in the social world of their regiments. Subsequent reinforcements allocated to the infantry battalions in the intervening years to replace losses due to transfers, "defectives," sickness, and finally combat, would have had significantly less personal exposure and investment in these regiments. As MacFarlane observes, the battalion depended upon the integration of newcomers: "As new recruits were added to replace casualties, these replacements had to learn quickly, under difficult conditions, and their casualty rates were often higher. Their integration into the close-knit regiment that had trained in Britain was also difficult."[89] For reinforcement soldiers, regimental *esprit* would have to be inculcated from the time of their attachment, as they would likely have possessed little native identification with a regiment, particularly if they came from somewhere in Canada where that regiment's distinctive traditions and history were largely unknown. An analysis of the regimental numbers of Canadian casualties in Italy in 1943, discussed earlier in this chapter, shows the potential effects of casualties. The Hastings & Prince Edward Regiment had the greatest decline in "original" soldiers: 94 percent of its soldiers hailed from eastern Ontario in July 1943 and only 58 percent in December 1943. But every battalion experienced a major decline.[90] The ranks of almost all of them were replenished not only with strangers, but increasingly by strangers from completely different parts of the country. By the end of 1943 the long-serving "originals" were no longer a majority in most infantry battalions of 1st Division – a steep fall-off from their number in Sicily. Although replacement soldiers may have acquired regimental *esprit* after a short while, they could not have had the time to develop the same level of identification with their units.

So we should treat regimental *esprit* with caution as a motivating force in combat, while at the same time recognizing its importance to those who had spent years with their units. Regiments were vital social networks for infantrymen out of combat and were central to the creation of wartime memory. They provided structure and meaning. Their role in terms of combat motivation is more doubtful, however, even in 1943, when the firmest connections between the regiments and their soldiers were possible.

The issue of casualties is inseparable from cohesion and motivation. According to Canadian Military Headquarters' consolidated casualty lists, 1st Canadian Division suffered 1,016 killed, 3,289 wounded, and 224 prisoners of war from its infantry battalions between the landing in Sicily on 10 July 1943 and their withdrawal from the line after Ortona at the beginning of January 1944. These battle casualties represented over half of the establishment of approximately 7,200 for the nine infantry battalions. As a percentage of the battalions' optimal "war establishment" strength, 60 percent of private soldiers, 63 percent of non-commissioned officers, and (statistically) 100 percent of junior officers were killed, wounded, or captured during 1943.[91] Some of the wounds received were slight; many of the wounded returned to duty, and some were subsequently wounded again. The casualties arrived at different rates: Sicily and the December battles contributed most of the division's attrition, whereas fewer losses were incurrred during the mobile operations of September through November. But as a percentage of their establishment, 1st Division's infantrymen sustained over 62 percent casualties in 1943. Even these statistics underestimate the actual impact on the men at the front, because most casualties fell within the four rifle companies of each infantry battalion, and they did not make up the battalion's whole strength.

In Sicily and Italy the Canadians had mechanisms for coping with such losses. The first was a Left out of Battle (LOB) system at work in the infantry battalions, a management strategy from the First World War that would preserve part of a unit and sub-unit's core leadership against heavy casualties. (I will say more about the LOB system shortly.) Another particularly common expedient was for battalions to combine decimated companies, platoons, or sections, forming a smaller number of ad hoc sub-units, each closer to being at full strength. This is a phenomenon that characterized the Canadian infantry experience. "The average platoon (after a rest period) usually commenced a battle with 24–28 all ranks," wrote Major Henri Tellier of the Royal 22e Régiment. "After suffering say 10 casualties it was often necessary to form only TWO sections [instead of the normal three]."[92] Similarly, as Major F.J. Hammond of the Hastings & Prince Edward Regiment commented: "The 'section' was always kept as near strength as possible by robbing the other sections within the platoon. That is, [the] platoon in more cases than not worked with two sections and the company often with only two platoons, but always with sections of at least five."[93] The section, the smallest combat sub-unit, had to be kept as close to full strength as possible, though even with ad hoc improvised sub-units the section could not always be kept fully manned when combat casualties were particularly severe.[94] Ad hoc sub-units were sometimes created on an even larger scale, with entire rifle companies: at Ortona, "C" Company of the Loyal Edmonton Regiment was broken up to provide reinforcements for the platoons and sections of the other three rifle companies.[95]

Furthermore, a common practice during the campaigns in Sicily and Italy was to create task-oriented teams drawn from different groups of soldiers to complete a particular job. During the attack on Assoro in Sicily, the Hastings & Prince Edward Regiment team that scaled the cliffs and seized the heights, which included Corporal "Chuck" Lloyd (see chapter 1), was a composite "assault company" consisting of "twenty of the fittest and most active men from each of the [four] rifle companies," thrown together temporarily and sent into battle together to accomplish a seemingly impossible task.[96] Emergencies and heavy casualties could create similar situations. During the battle for Casa Berardi outside Ortona in December 1943, the junior leaders of the Royal 22e put together improvised units of all available men, "including 'B' Echelon, administrative services, maintenance, doctors, sappers, stretcher-bearers, art[iller]y [Forward Observation Officers] and so on," to fight off German counterattacks.[97] Patrolling was common in Italy, whether the positions were static or fluid, and usually preceded a major attack in order to find and fix the enemy's position.[98] Platoon- and company-mounted patrols were often mishmashes of willing or able troops drawn from lower sub-units. Reconnaissance or contact patrols were typically undertaken by platoon commanders, with a few hand-picked men from different sections.[99] Life in the rifle companies, then, involved an almost constant process of attachment, detachment, and re-attachment of personnel at very low levels. Some ad hoc sub-units were put together on a semi-permanent basis to keep units up to strength, and some groupings were temporary, assembled for a specific tactical purpose.

The other key part of the cohesion question were the replacement soldiers. They frequently came with no past regimental association and were attached to an infantry battalion as reinforcements after losses had depleted the original manpower pool. In 1943 there was no sense of crisis in Italy about the reinforcement situation, although there were often not enough replacement soldiers locally, as Allied administration and logistics struggled to keep up with losses on the ground. Particularly by December, insufficient infantry reinforcements were in the pipeline to keep the Canadian battalions up to strength during combat.[100] All the reinforcement soldiers in 1943 were "green": inexperienced in combat and in surviving life at the front, just as virtually all the "veteran" 1st Division men had been on 9 July 1943. Senior officers thought that reinforcements coming through to take the place of fallen soldiers at the front in December 1943 were "lacking the polish of trained infantry soldiers."[101] However, this may not have been a fair or accurate portrait. Most of the junior officers who fought in 1943 and who were surveyed in the battle experience questionnaires rated the standards of efficiency of their reinforcements as being at least "moderate," and only a small number (five of the twenty-nine) rated the quality of reinforcements as being "low." Almost as many (three) rated the reinforcement soldiers highly.[102] Furthermore, a recent historical study has shown that reinforcement soldiers in Italy had been trained to a good standard: all had passed Tests of Elementary Training and were fully qualified riflemen.[103] But the replacements had to learn on the spot and under fire. Some 2,400 reinforcements entered action with 1st Canadian Division throughout December 1943, and when they arrived they were usually quickly put into the line in and around Ortona, amid the fiercest fighting of the Italian campaign.[104] A reinforcement draft of Cape Breton men arrived for the Loyal Edmonton Regiment on Christmas Eve during the fight for Ortona: they were told by the Edmontons' CO: "You are 'A' Company," and were immediately put into the fight. They fought well in the last bitter days of December. Perhaps most significantly, the Edmontons thought that the untried Cape Bretoners were "tremendously good soldiers, [and] we considered them brothers-in-arms, and perhaps it was a kinship born out of the knowledge of a mutual suffering in the Depression: it is hard to say, but they were fine soldiers in every respect."[105]

The evidence indicates that at least until the end of 1943, the reinforcements were of high calibre. The complaint most often heard was that they were not battle-experienced and had not been trained by people who were battle-experienced. As 1st Brigade's Brigadier Spry remarked early in 1944: "Reinforcements have been of a very high standard both physically and mentally, but I know that they have been trained at [Canadian Base Reinforcement Depot] at [the Canadian Reinforcement Unit] and in Canada by people with no battle experience."[106] It is undoubtedly true that reinforcements lacked "polish" as riflemen, and would have benefited from the slow and incremental introduction to combat that the "original veterans" received in Sicily. But the 1943 drafts of reinforcements were well trained and became integrated very successfully, even if divisional neuropsychiatrist believed that they tended to become NP casualties at higher rates than those who had been with their regiments longer.[107]

The fighting ability of the Canadian infantry units does not appear to have been seriously diminished during 1943. Some of the fiercest and most successful close-combat situations that occurred at Ortona toward the end of December 1943 involved units that had already been heavily engaged before the battle opened.[108] It was not until 1st Division had sustained high-intensity combat for almost a month that Major-General Vokes concluded: "the troops are tired and team play within units is lacking."[109] After that month of fighting, in which one-third of the riflemen and much higher percentages of the junior leadership had been killed, wounded, or captured, and where the terrain, weather, and enemy determination retarded all forward progress, Eighth Army's entire offensive along the Adriatic coast was abandoned in favour of new engagements on the western side of the peninsula.

What was the effect of all these factors – casualties, ad hoc sub-units, and reinforcements – on cohesion? Traditionally, "small-group cohesion" has been identified with the section (10–12 soldiers at most) or the platoon (25–30 soldiers). Recombining sections, platoons, and companies – an effective way to optimize existing manpower at the "sharp end" of the infantry battalion – was employed as a response to the fact that infantry sections were regularly broken up in combat. In Sicily, before a single reinforcement was received, infantrymen were already being recombined into ad hoc sub-unit arrangements in which many of their new comrades were at best distant acquaintances from different sections, platoons, and companies. Temporary short-term units were constantly being created and taken apart for specific tactical objectives. And early in the campaign, new team members were not completely new faces: regiments brought their own "reinforcement pools" with them to Sicily. Social cohesion and regimental *esprit* were probably stronger among 1st Division's infantry battalions of July 1943 than at any subsequent point. But by December these regimental resources were long depleted, and the new men brought in as replacements were increasingly not even from the same part of the country as their new regiment. In future engagements, however, Canadians were nevertheless able to maintain high levels of effectiveness. For this to have been possible, other social forces must have been at work as well. In the coming chapters I will explore the concept of "swift trust," to show that it provides a compelling explanation for the ability of strangers and near-strangers to work together as an effective force.

Leadership was another essential dimension of motivation and cohesion. Most Canadian soldiers had little desire for heroic acts that would merit Victoria Crosses, but the great majority would follow when properly led and fight as they were trained and commanded. Leadership helped to bridge the cognitive gap between the will to survive and the ability to fight. As Captain Felix Carriere of the PPCLI put it, "It's unbelievable what people will do, and the number of casualties that can be hammered, that you can see under your eyes, and still do your work, still go, because somebody says 'Keep on going.'"[110]

Relations between officers and men tended to be quite good in the infantry battalions in 1943. Captain Carriere thought this had to do with the social climate of Canada, and, "because as soon as it was wartime any number of people would be up in the officer rank, and they were the same as the [other ranks] men that were coming in."[111] Although, as I have shown, there were educational and class dimensions in the officer/other ranks divide in Canada, most Canadian junior officers in 1943 had spent time in the ranks themselves before being commissioned, and the social distance between leaders and led was never as stark as in the more aristocratic British Army. Field censors in Italy paid a great deal of attention when criticism of officers found its way into letters home, since this could be an early sign of trouble. But in late 1943 the censors described the (perceived) attitudes expressed in most letters as confirming "a splendid spirit of cooperation existing between officers and men. Expressions of confidence recur frequently."[112] The censors' reports may have omitted a great deal; unit censorship (in which junior officers censored their own men's correspondence) was extremely unpopular with everyone involved and was usually bypassed in favour of base censorship (where mail was read and censored by strangers), but many other ranks may still have tempered any negative commentary toward officers.[113] Nonetheless, the impression gained from soldiers' correspondence indicates a great deal of confidence in their junior leadership throughout the 1943 campaigns.

Battle experience questionnaire results repeatedly stressed the relationship between leadership and morale, listing "Confidence in commanders at all levels," "Officers actually leading in attack," and "Good leadership" as positive contributors to morale, and "Apparent timidity and/or indecision on the part of commanders," "Newcomer leaders without experience," and "Lack of confidence in officers" as among the factors most detrimental to morale.[114] Leadership from the front was the most effective, and officers were expected to establish behavioural norms by example. Lieutenants commanding platoons participated in patrol actions almost to a fault in Italy, and in virtually all circumstances were the first ones "over the top" in an attack.[115] However, leading from the front came with grave risks. As Major John Dougan of the Loyal Edmonton Regiment would later reminisce, "I always felt that the job of the platoon leader was to lead, not to stay behind and to direct his section, because sometimes you're only directing 10–12 men, because platoons were never up to strength. So we had a lot of casualties among platoon commanders, and I'm certain a lot of casualties among corporals, too, and lance-corporals."[116] Captain Carriere thought similarly: "Officers and corporals were people who got hit first. Because they're leaders. An officer is supposed to lead his men, and he did. A corporal, he leads a section, he's number two, so the officer is number one, he gets it first, followed by the next guy, who is going to be the leader. And so corporals and officers had a very short lifespan."[117] Canadian officers were faulted for leading from the front too closely, especially those who, in the eyes of many, had no business at the front. "*Platoon* commanders must lead platoons into battle," a directive written at a 1st Brigade conference in December 1943 read. "*Company* commander should move up to leading elements when he must see the ground or when he is launching reserves and has no force left to commit. He should not be forward without reason and become pinned down and useless when he should be reading the battle from a point where he can affect it."[118] With casualty rates among junior officers (and sometimes even commanding officers) so high, such apprehensions were understandable.

Being an infantry platoon commander was indeed the most dangerous job in the world in 1943. Owing to the (at least perceived) need for heroic leadership by example, infantry battalion officers (lieutenants to lieutenant-colonels) in 1st Division suffered 102 percent of their war establishment strength as casualties between Sicily and the end of Ortona.

The fighting in Sicily was intense (28 percent casualty rate) but the bloodbath on the Moro River and Ortona claimed over half of those casualties (44 percent) in less than forty days.[119] The greatest burden fell on platoon commanders. During this time period, lieutenants across all nine infantry battalions suffered an average of 122 percent casualties as a function of their established strength; captains suffered 89 percent; majors 62 percent. For comparison, private soldiers in the Canadian infantry during the 1943 fighting suffered 60 percent of their war establishment strength as casualties.[120] Variations between battalions were noteworthy. During the whole of the 1943 campaigns, the Seaforth Highlanders suffered their highest casualties among lieutenants, with a staggering 194 percent of their war establishment – a proportion that cast the casualties to lieutenants in the Hastings & Prince Edward Regiment and the Royal Canadian Regiment (both at about 83 percent) in a comparatively gentle light. Curiously, the three Permanent Force battalions had the lowest casualty rates for platoon commanders specifically and for officers overall, though to attribute any particular cause to this phenomenon without a detailed and specific study would be hypothesizing.[121] (Detailed data tables on casualties are included as Appendix F.) They reflect the impressions given by the Carleton and York Regiment's official history: "casualties among infantry platoon commanders tend to be high, partly because they have to move out of cover for such necessary tasks as siting their platoon sections, checking personnel to make sure they are alright, and generally supervising their platoon sectors, to say nothing of setting an example for aggressiveness in the attack."[122]

CONCLUSION: THE CANADIAN SOLDIER AT HIS BEST

Major-General George Kitching, a general staff officer with 1st Division in 1943, wrote tellingly about the Sicilian campaign in his memoirs:

> To me, the fighting in Sicily showed the Canadian soldier at his best. All our previous training had been based on the drills learned from "battle schools" in Britain which required the initiative of each soldier to be part of the automatic deployment of sections, platoons, and companies into positions from which they could take offensive action against the enemy. These drills were based on

> a battle of movement in which the actions of every soldier were important whether carrying a rifle, a Bren Gun, a mortar, or a radio. Each was part of a team but each knew that his personal initiative in combat was a critical element. The operations in Sicily, with only one exception, gave the Canadian soldier that unrestricted use of his initiative. The exception was the first battle of Nissoria, in which the Royal Canadian Regiment attacked that town behind a timed artillery programme which, as so often happened, galloped ahead of the infantry leaving them without support at a critical time. In Italy, later in the campaign, these programmed barrages were replaced by a system that gave the infantry the fire support they needed when and where they wanted it and restored their initiative.[123]

In this chapter, in keeping with Kitching's impressions, we have looked at many ways in which the 1943 campaigns represented the Canadian infantry at the highest pitch of their morale, if not the height of their tactical skill. The soldiers of 1st Division were some of the best- and longest-trained wartime troops Canada ever put in the field; in battle they behaved aggressively and displayed tremendous low-level initiative at many points, paying a high price as a result. While the defeats and setbacks during this period have attracted historians' attention, it must be acknowledged that the Canadians in 1943 were facing elite German panzer, panzer grenadier, and parachute formations, and, as Major-General Bogert reminisced after the war, when you fought the Germans, by reputation the finest soldiers in the world, sometimes you were going to lose.[124] The Canadians fought both high-mobility and attrition-style battles in an unforgiving country that favoured the defenders. Their operations and tactics were guided by an understanding of how to defeat this enemy: consolidation rather than risky exploitation and over-reach. And 1st Canadian Division kept fighting until the end of December 1943 without a serious drop in combat effectiveness, during which time they mauled several top German divisions. There were setbacks, poor decisions, and, on the mainland, a grim strategic picture. Nonetheless, as part of Eighth Army, the Canadians chased the Germans from the base of Mount Etna to the Ortona salient before being halted by exhaustion and the weather.

What motivated soldiers during this period? Until December, infantry units were composed of men who had been operating together for a long time within their regiments. Most of the men in a battalion were from the same province or region and could draw upon a common culture and shared experiences; a very high percentage of 1st Division soldiers had been interwar NPAM or Permanent Force soldiers as well, and the regimental *esprit* and pride of peacetime service carried into 1943 as well.[125] There were many "original veterans" who had deliberately joined not only the infantry, but their specific regiments back in 1939–40, and who probably wanted to be there the most. So in terms of vertical cohesion and regimental *esprit*, 1st Division's battalions were very strong in 1943, probably stronger than those of any other Canadian units during the war. And even if what scholars have traditionally thought of as strong "small-group cohesion" was at its apogee in the 1943 campaigns, there is powerful evidence that these small groups were being constantly split up, recombined, depleted, and reinforced. So from the earliest points of their war, Canadian infantrymen were as frequently fighting beside acquaintances, near-strangers, or complete strangers as they were their "band of brothers," their close comrades. The "swift trust" that had to be established in sub-units in order for these ad hoc arrangements to be effective speaks well of the training, leadership, and "team play" within Canadian infantry units.

Strong horizontal cohesion has the potential to create behavioural problems just as easily as it can underwrite combat effectiveness. The presence of many long acquaintances, friends, and "buddies" in a unit can aggravate problems of indiscipline when leadership is lacking. While there was a tremendous spike in offences in most infantry battalions of 1st Division just prior to sailing for Sicily, it speaks well of the regimental leadership that once the troops were on the ground the number of offences, while not insignificant, was kept under control. Very few serious charges were laid against Canadian infantrymen in 1943, indicating that the leadership did not feel the need to make many examples in order to enforce discipline (with some exceptions, such as the Royal 22e in December 1943).[126] There is no indication from any documentary source that ideology, political rationale, or justifications played any significant role in motivation in 1943, although soldiers did have a fierce interest in what was happening in the broader world war on other fronts. That interest seems to have been based upon the urge of an educated citizen-soldiery to see the war ended as quickly as possible – a strong motivator. In addition, hatred and animosity toward the enemy, though not universal, appear to have been noticeable among the combat troops in 1943, and cycles of excessive, reciprocal violence are hinted at within the sources. That prevalence of ill feeling may have been connected to the stronger bonds that existed among the Canadian soldiers.

Early in 1944, more formations – 5th Canadian Armoured Division and the higher I Canadian Corps formation – joined the veterans of 1st Division in Italy, and the character of the Canadian war effort in the Mediterranean began to change. But in many ways the Canadian role in the liberation of Sicily and southern Italy was one of the greatest achievements of the war.

4

The Canadians in Italy, 1944–1945

The year 1944 saw the strengthening of Canadian commitments to the Mediterranean theatre and the continuation of a series of northward assaults upon fortified German lines and in-depth positions running across the Italian peninsula. The fighting became even more reminiscent of the First World War: fought at a slow walking pace, attritional, violent, and deadly. I Canadian Corps in Italy, now containing two Canadian divisions, was employed as an assault formation for breaking fortified German positions, a role that would have been familiar to the Canadian Corps of twenty years earlier.

If 1943 can be seen as a high watermark for motivation and effectiveness among Canadian infantrymen in Italy, then 1944 and 1945 must be viewed as a period of constant transformation, tribulation, and brutalization. Morale and motivation suffered, particularly during the long winter months. But, despite tremendous adversity and heavy casualties, Canadian soldiers continued to be aggressive, reliable, and effective. Even when morale seemed to be at a low ebb, they were capable of defeating the German military. The "original veterans" of 1939 were largely gone, and new social bonds and foundations for trust had to be established between old-timers and reinforcements. This chapter explores the documentary evidence on behaviour, motivation, and effectiveness of the infantrymen of the I Canadian Corps in Italy from January 1944 until the Corps' withdrawal to Northwest Europe in early 1945.

There is confusion over the Allied purpose in continuing the Italian campaign in 1944. Canadian historian Bill McAndrew's comments on the matter are perhaps typical: "It is not self-evident who was holding whom in Italy. Both sides had roughly comparable numbers of fighting men. Paradoxically, the operational aim of holding the Germans in Italy opposed the tactical aim of driving them out in hard fighting."[1] But "driving them out" of Italy was not the tactical aim: diverting maximum German resources to the Mediterranean front, preferably through destroying them, was. According to historian Douglas Porch: "If we add the twenty-four German divisions in Greece and the Balkans, maintained against a potential Allied landing launched from Italy, together with eight to ten German divisions in southern France, then around fifty-five German divisions – more than one-fifth of German ground forces – were tied down defending the central and Eastern Mediterranean at a time when they might have fought on other fronts."[2] German apologists, beginning with Field Marshal Albert Kesselring, the German commander-in-chief of *Oberbefehlshaber Süd* (Army Command in the South), have argued that: "The Italian theatre [also] pinned down Allied forces which, if they had been engaged on decisive fronts, might have powerfully influenced events in the east or in the west adversely for Germany."[3] But Allied logistical and shipping resources in 1944 were already stretched beyond the breaking point by attempting to stage, and then support, the invasion and build-up in Normandy. The Allies had more troops waiting in the UK than it was possible to put ashore and keep supplied just across the English Channel in Normandy; where precisely could the Allied Armies in Italy have been more usefully employed?[4] "It was not in fact [Field Marshal] Alexander's primary objective to force a major withdrawal upon Kesselring," wrote the official British historian. "The destruction of [German] Army Group C [in Italy] was more important and this he hoped to achieve south of the Po River."[5] The Allies were attempting to fight a holding battle in Italy with the possibility of annihilating the enemy, to maximize the enemy resources that could be diverted from the "main show," the invasion of Normandy.[6]

Corresponding to this objective, the role of the Canadians in Italy changed after Ortona. Gone was the fast-moving mobile warfare that had prevailed in Sicily and much of southern Italy. When the German Winter Line was finally met in late 1943, the campaign's movement slowed even as its tempo and violence increased. The weather, the geography, and the tenacity of the enemy turned central and northern Italy into a defender's paradise. During the three major operations they were committed to in 1944–45 – the Liri Valley, the Gothic Line, and the Po River valley – the Canadians became the assault force that shattered fixed defensive positions and began the consolidation and exploitation of the offensive.[7]

With Eighth Army still deployed along the Adriatic eastern coast of Italy after the Ortona fighting, and with the weather making further progress impossible, 1944 began unpromisingly for the Canadians in Italy. The momentum of the campaign swung westward toward the US Fifth Army, which made the first attempts to assault and bypass the German defences at Monte Cassino, guarding the Liri Valley on the approach to Rome. After a frustrating and demoralizing winter of endless patrols and ceaseless shellfire near Ortona, the newly activated I Canadian Corps was pulled out of the line in preparation for the big spring offensive, Operation DIADEM, the final assault on the Germans' Cassino position. The political objective was the seizure of Rome; the operational objective was the destruction of the German Tenth Army, which held the Gustav Line anchored at Cassino.[8] I Canadian Corps was initially in reserve as other formations breached the German Gustav Line, and was unleashed to break through the German failsafe position called the Hitler/Senger Line and then to exploit the rupture into the Liri Valley.

The breaking of the Hitler/Senger Line in May 1944 by 1st Canadian Division was costly but highly successful. As a I Canadian Corps after-action report summarized: "The losses inflicted on the enemy during the whole of the op[eration]s of 1 Cdn Corps, from 17 May to 3 Jun, on a conservative estimate have been considerably greater than those suffered. Casualties 1 Cdn Corps 2231 killed, wounded, missing. [German prisoners of war] taken: 1421; large numbers of enemy killed buried. The Corps advanced a distance of 64km in a straight line. The results justify the gen[eral] conduct of op[erations]."[9] But the follow-up breakthrough by 5th Canadian Armoured Division was disappointing, plagued by natural obstacles, mines and demolitions, and "faulty staff work on a high level with regard to organization of routes and traffic control."[10] In a letter to the War Office, Eighth Army's new GOC-in-C, General Oliver Leese, wrote of DIADEM: "The Canadian troops themselves have been quite excellent; their fighting has been beyond praise." The problem, however, was the leadership and staff work, for part of which Leese was to blame: "One's problem, therefore, is to train commanders and staff to make better use of the excellent material at their disposal."[11] Although the German Tenth Army was not destroyed as hoped, the nineteen enemy divisions that had defended the approaches to Rome were shattered and in full retreat, with many reduced to less than the fighting strength of a single Canadian brigade.[12]

After DIADEM, I Canadian Corps was pulled from operations for the summer; when they were next put into the line, it would be in the newly assigned role as an assault corps against the German fortified zone called the Gothic Line, which ran across northern Italy. Operation OLIVE was intended to break the Gothic Line in the Apennine Mountains and break into the Po Valley floodplains before the arrival of autumn. The two Canadian divisions attacked, in the words of historian Desmond Morton, with "hard-driving efficiency" and succeeded in "bouncing" the first zones of the Gothic Line before the Germans could properly man them.[13] Hard and protracted fighting in the hilly country was still needed before the Gothic Line defences were broken in early September 1944. Eighth Army's progress during the August–September battles was remarkable, and I Canadian Corps was the catalyst. Eleven German divisions had been defeated in sustained battle. But their army was mauled, not annihilated, and the Germans did not withdraw from Italy; after the success of OLIVE, the "breakout" of Eighth Army into the Po Valley became a mud-covered battle for a series of river lines. Throughout October and December the Canadians fought hard in mud reminiscent of Passchendaele. Local successes were achieved, and the Germans continually lost men, resources, and ground in the attritional struggle, but chances for operational-level manoeuvres that might trap and wipe out the Germans had vanished. "Some echelons of command," wrote the Royal Canadian Regiment's historian, "forget that the trapped animal often fights to the death."[14]

A second frustrating "winter of discontent" was spent in the line in 1944–45, but while morale visibly sagged the Canadians remained highly capable and combat-effective. Fighting along the Lamone River in December 1944 achieved some local success partly because of aggressive action on the part of the infantry.[15] And in early January 1945, 5th Canadian Armoured Division undertook a limited offensive to push the Germans out of a salient north of Ravenna. The attack tore apart the inexperienced German infantry division that it struck, and then, rapidly consolidating in true "bite and hold" fashion, the Canadians wiped out a counterattacking force of elite SS and Panzer-Grenadier forces.[16] The fighting near Ravenna was the last major Canadian operation in Italy before I Canadian Corps was sent to Northwest Europe to rejoin First Canadian Army.

FORCE STRUCTURE

Whereas in 1943 1st Canadian Division had been integrated into the British Eighth Army and swapped between XXX, XIII, and V Corps, the new year found the unlooked-for deployment of two new formations to Italy: 5th Canadian Armoured Division, and I Canadian Corps, beneath which both the 1st and 5th Divisions would be operating from then on.

Once I Canadian Corps was moved to the Mediterranean, Canadians were commanding their countrymen at higher levels of operations. That was the good news, if it could be construed as such. However, having a corps formation with only two divisions was unusual and potentially wasteful; deployment of three, four, or even five divisions per corps was more typical and a better use of administrative resources.[17] The other new arrival was 5th Canadian Division, an armoured formation with organic tank and infantry brigades. In late 1940, Canada had been asked to provide an armoured division for inclusion in the Canadian Corps overseas, and 5th Canadian Armoured Division had been created from mobilized militia units and supporting assets cannibalized from other Canadian divisions. It arrived in England in November 1941, two years after the 1st Division men, but still twenty-four months ahead of deployment on active operations.[18]

From the beginning, however, 5th Armoured Division was too light on infantry, as only one brigade (three battalions) was attached to it, one-third the number that 1st Division possessed. 5th Division was hard-hitting but had little durability, and with such a narrow pool of infantry to draw from, casualties were doubly felt.[19] In the summer of 1944, 5th Division's structure was amended to include a second, brand-new infantry brigade (12th Brigade, to be discussed later) of three battalions hastily improvised from existing, non-infantry assets, but between the new division and the new corps there were still only six new Canadian infantry battalions fighting on the Mediterranean front.[20] Although the two divisions would be operating alongside and under Canadian command, there was a steep price to pay in new administrative overhead.[21]

BEHAVIOUR IN BATTLE

The Canadian experience of combat in Italy would have been familiar to soldiers of the Great War's Canadian Corps, as they achieved only modestly greater mobility and power of manoeuvre in their campaign. The fighting done by Canadians was usually in the assault: slow, attritional, and focused on "breaking in" to fortified enemy positions so that subsequent formations could break through. German losses were higher than those of the Allies throughout the fighting in Italy, partly thanks to the Allies' overwhelming air superiority, but also because of a marked difference in doctrine: "the Germans favoured the sharp, fierce counter-attack which, though effective, was apt to be costly; and from El Alamein onwards the British [and Commonwealth] adopted the policy of using shells to save lives."[22] The goal of defeating the German counter-attack, preferably with as few casualties as possible, remained central to Canadian infantry doctrine in 1944–45. "Exploitation" was the Allied watchword, but after two wars spent fighting the German Army there were no illusions: any breakthrough of the German lines would be met by strong enemy counter-attacks.

Writing in 1st Canadian Division's war diary in July 1944, GOC Major-General Christopher Vokes scribbled: "I want the following simple formula rubbed home with all ranks in your units especially with [company], [platoon], and [section] leaders. They are fundamental for success." He went on to make recommendations to be followed during consolidation on an objective:

(i) Always be prepared for all-round defence.
(ii) Make full use of your automatic weapons in defence. Remember that automatic fire power is the frame-work. Conserve riflemen.

(iii) Keep a reserve in hand, mainly riflemen, suitably disposed for immediate counter-attack, for which you must be prepared in advance.
(iv) Patrol vigorously, and take advantage of opportunities. Build up a clear picture of enemy intelligence.
(v) Study the problem of attacking from your defence position. Remember that defence is only a momentary pause. Battles are won by offensive action.[23]

Most Canadian junior infantry officers who responded to battle experience questionnaires (68 percent) reported that they had repeatedly had to organize rapid defence against German counterattacks during these campaigns.[24] Sometimes the Canadians were over-eager in their preparations to meet these counterattacks. During the exploitation phase of Operation DIADEM, when 5th Canadian Division was supposed to chase down the fleeing Germans, valuable time was lost establishing "firm bases," semi-permanent defensive areas that would repel counterattacks, when they should have been moving in "bounds," consolidating rapidly on a position only long enough for other troops to take over and then moving on. A corps-level training conference in June 1944 established that firm bases were not needed in the pursuit: "The firm base is, therefore, required on [brigade] or higher level in the breakthrough battle as long as the enemy is known to have [reserves] and the threat of counter-attack is considerable. In the pursuit of a disorganized enemy, firm basis [sic] slow up the pursuit."[25] Even in a pursuit, however, an enemy counterattack could fall at any time, and a 1st Brigade "lessons learned" report from DIADEM related that during consolidation, "an [anti-tank] stop line was set up ... after each phase of the battle, and [anti-tank] vehicles were given due priority on the roads."[26] Throughout 1944 the Canadians succeeded in breaking into the German lines and inflicting grievous damage upon them through rapid consolidation, but this success came at the expense of the manoeuvre and free-wheeling exploitation that might have trapped the Germans. This experience seems to have been true on both operational and tactical levels.

For the Canadian infantry, who benefited from the British "shells save blood" axiom, attacks accompanied by artillery were almost as ubiquitous at this time as the use of small arms. Over 80 percent of surveyed infantry officers from this period indicated that they had carried out infantry attacks under an artillery barrage; and the number who had experiences with artillery support such as concentrations or counter-battery shoots would have been even higher.[27] Many Canadian infantrymen in Italy were in awe of the power of the artillery available to their side, which, from a distance, appeared to annihilate entire landscapes. "We certainly laid down a beautiful barrage on yonder Jerries," one private wrote in a letter home: "Cripes, they were smashed entirely out of control and prisoners were a bloody nuisance ... They were crying like babies, those supermen – paratroops too – but God, they were nearly mad with shellshock and nervous exhaustion from our Artillery."[28] Despite the availability of artillery, however, a lack of proper combined-arms training may have still been an Achilles heel for Canadians: an even smaller percentage of officers than in 1943 (only 38 percent) indicated that their units had received preliminary training in operating with the artillery.[29] No doubt this shortcoming resulted from the inadequacy of time for training troops at the appropriate level. Prior to Operation DIADEM, for instance, Canadian unit training in Italy had reportedly fallen into its familiar rut of focusing on the company level, neglecting the battalion and brigade levels at which cooperation and coordination with the artillery regiments took place.[30] Regardless of the training, two-thirds of surveyed officers still believed that their soldiers "kept up with the barrage effectively," but there was room for improvement.[31]

Most infantry officers had made use of the fire-and-movement tactics taught as battle drill back in England, although not every operation called for it. About three-quarters of respondents reported using battle drill tactics, and over half of those indicated that their troops used them "often" or "fairly often."[32] These results reflected the complexity of the battlefield. Fire-and-movement tactics were designed to allow infantry to work their own way forward against opposition by keeping the enemy's heads down through use of their own small arms. If brought down where it was needed, artillery could be as effective in accomplishing the task but had heightened suppressive and psychological effects, and meant less infantry exposure.[33] Artillery-based tactics, when combined with battle drill fire-and-movement, tended to work well, as a study of the Hitler/Senger Line defences by 1st Canadian Division demonstrates: "All [German] machine-gun defences were neutralized by the artillery barrage and our infantry had little difficulty getting past machine-gun positions provided the barrage was followed closely. After the barrage had passed it was found that the MGs in buildings and in earthworks were the first to come into action ... Earthworks were overcome by normal infantry platoon battle drill."[34] During the breaking of the German defensive lines, the enemy was often dense on the ground and covered by overlapping, enfilade fire positions to make infantry movement impossible without substantial artillery support, but plenty of latitude still existed for the employment of the infantry's own weapons.

Cooperation between tanks and infantry deserves special mention because armoured warfare dominated Canadian tactical thinking in Italy after the arrival of 5th Canadian Armoured Division. Of the forty-four battle experience questionnaires from this period, ten indicated that their infantry units had never previously cooperated with tanks (a surprisingly high number).[35] There was an even split among officers who said that their infantry had typically moved in front of, behind, or among the tanks, and those who claimed that the infantry moved exclusively in front of the tanks when in combat.[36] Tanks operating in front in close country were highly vulnerable to German anti-tank gun emplacements, of which there were hundreds on the Hitler/Senger and Gothic lines. As Major-General Vokes reiterated over the summer of 1944: "Don't forget the primeval formula, infantry deal with the anti-tank guns and the tanks with wire and machine guns – BUT remember always that infantry working with tanks are the eyes and close-in protection for tanks ... Never let the tanks get forward without your support close behind. You must get up to them at all costs."[37] There seems to have been little uniformity in how infantry-tank cooperation looked on the ground in practice, although most commonly, as per Vokes's instructions, the infantry were out front protecting the tanks.

Chemical warfare occurred in the Italian theatre in 1944–45 in the form of smoke and incendiary weapons, although late in the campaign and not on the same scale as later in Northwest Europe. When Canadian officers were filling out their battle experience questionnaires, few such weapons were in use. However, after the "Lifebuoy" man-portable flamethrower and the (preferred) "Wasp" tracked vehicle flamethrower were introduced to the Italian theatre in November 1944, they became favourites of the Canadians.[38] Flamethrowers were psychologically devastating weapons, and the Allies had more and better models of them than the Germans; the flame was projected in a shallow parabola like a mortar and could hit a reverse slope and seep into trenches and bunkers. The Wasp was found to be particularly effective at stopping enemy counterattacks dead in their tracks and became a useful tool in consolidation.[39] Canadians took up flame weapons so enthusiastically and successfully in the fighting west of the Lamone River in December 1944 that Eighth Army as a whole would recommend a permanent increase in their use on the Italian front. Also, while it was originally intended as a smoke grenade, the No. 77 white phosphorus grenade could have a devastating anti-personnel incendiary effect as well. Developed in September 1943, the No. 77 became increasingly common in the Italian theatre during 1944. A report from October 1944 discussed its use in house-to-house street fighting: "77 Grenades were more useful than 36s [fragmentation grenades]. If [the enemy] remained in the building, the phosphorous grenade would drive him out. In his dug-out the 36 tended to explode at the entrance and leave him intact within."[40] A 12th Brigade training memorandum told similar stories: "All who were spoken to about [the No. 77 Grenade] are very enthusiastic about it. It has a devastating effect. It is more than a smoke grenade and when thrown into enemy positions – slits or trenches – either burns or chokes the occupants into surrender or flight."[41] The human effects of flame and chemical warfare could be terrible. Farley Mowat called phosphorus "amongst the most savage weapons known."[42] The fact that the Canadians adopted flame and incendiary weapons so enthusiastically may tell us something about the nature of the fighting, and its tenor. Terror weapons that were seen to expedite the fighting without exposing Canadians to further danger were heartily embraced.

Air supremacy, which included the availability of direct air support (DAS), was another important part of the Allied campaign in Italy throughout 1944–45. By 1944, even at their weakest, the British Desert Air Force and its American counterparts massively outnumbered the Luftwaffe, to the point that there "was no anxiety among the Allied tactical air force commanders about the ability of the Luftwaffe to interfere" with operations.[43] The Desert Air Force's preferred tactical role was to interdict enemy supply lines and paralyse attempted withdrawals rather than to distribute bombs penny-packet in support of ground troops, so direct air support was not always available to the infantry. During the assault on the Gothic Line in particular, however, close support from the air was "practically constant," with over 11,500 Desert Air Force sorties being flown against the Germans overall, and 1,900 sorties being flown against targets requested by the army to the air force using "CABRANK," a system of air support featuring sequential, continuous attack upon a ground target.[44] About two-thirds of Canadian officers indicated that their units had received DAS on the battlefield, indicating that the total air supremacy translated into direct assistance for most but not all infantry units. What is more, every officer but one who reported receiving DAS for his unit commented positively upon its effectiveness in Italy.[45] Air support had a tremendous effect on morale: almost one in five Canadian officers responding to questionnaires still listed enemy "bombers and dive bombers" as the weapons that had the "greatest moral effect" upon their troops in the campaign; enemy air power left its mark on Canadian morale even when it had been swept away as an effective force.[46] The effect upon the Germans, who struggled constantly against the harsh realities of ubiquitous Allied air supremacy, would have been even more marked, and became a key moral advantage to the Canadians throughout this period.

Although the tactical methods employed by the Canadian infantry were sometimes conservative, it is difficult to see how the campaign could have been fought better or differently, given the terrain and given the enemy. Although artillery and air support were key throughout, Italy was an infantryman's war, and the success of operations depended above all upon infantry effectiveness.

MORALE

Morale among Canadian troops had been high throughout the 1943 campaigns, but they encountered serious psychological roadblocks in their fighting during 1944–45. The most influential historical works on the Canadians in Italy, books by Daniel Dancocks and particularly by Bill McAndrew, have been highly critical of the state of Canadian morale in the "forgotten theatre" of Italy, and other postwar accounts, regimental histories, and memoirs have painted a similar depressing picture of the state of Canadian morale in those years. A close analysis of the documentary evidence on Canadian morale during the Italian campaign, in the context of motivation and effectiveness, reveals a different, and perhaps more nuanced, picture of soldiers' attitudes.

The comments about Canadian infantrymen in the battle experience questionnaires give us a singular and hitherto unexplored perspective on what platoon, company, and battalion officers considered to be the main constituents of morale. (Data tables showing the percentage of officers who listed various factors that had raised and lowered morale are reproduced as Appendix G.) As with the 1943 campaigns, the questionnaires indicate that the morale of Canadian soldiers was heavily influenced by the adequate provision of basic services and creature comforts. The availability of rations (particularly hot food) and timely, regular contact with home in the form of letters and parcels were by far the greatest determinants of high morale. The importance of success in battle and of being kept "active" and on the move is also notable; inactivity and the dreariness of holding static positions were detrimental. The feeling that they were being kept "out of the picture" and were receiving bad information was the single most frequently cited detriment to morale among troops in Italy.[47] With General Montgomery gone on to a new command in Normandy, Eighth Army's "open book" policy in terms of keeping troops in the loop about operations may not have been sustained, and there seem to have been more feelings among Canadian infantrymen that they were being kept in the dark.

Curiously, religion does not show up anywhere in the questionnaires, and was almost entirely absent from the letters cited by the field censors as well (with the important exception of when Catholicism was shown to be an aspect of French-Canadian distinctiveness, as discussed later in this chapter). Religion was nevertheless in some ways omnipresent, with church parades being a compulsory feature of Sunday mornings in most regiments.[48] Chaplains were attached to each infantry battalion and, aside from attending to spiritual welfare, carried out a wide range of helpful "morale officer" duties, providing aid, comfort, and conversation wherever needed.[49] No doubt religion provided redoubt for many, but it was not a value that inspired soldiers to fight. Nothing in the censorship reports suggested any mention on the part of the soldiers of crusades or doing God's work, and the questionnaires give no indication that any officers thought that religious conviction was a significant source of soldiers' willingness to fight.

While the questionnaires do an excellent job of giving the top-down officer perspective on the state of morale, censorship reports from throughout 1944–45 allow for the articulation of the vacillations of morale affecting I Canadian Corps from the bottom up. According to the censors, 1944 began on a high note following Ortona: "There is every evidence that morale remains at the same high pitch. Those who have experienced battle conditions are eager to go on and finish the war, while others moving forward are equally anxious to see an end to it all. There is a certain war weariness apparent in some letters but without exception, all ranks are determined to carry on in the knowledge that a victorious conclusion can be seen this year."[50] By March of that year, however, the situation was deteriorating: "Bad weather during the past month has continued to make life uncomfortable for many," the censors wrote in early March. "Front line troops and others under canvas write long descriptions of the rain and snow and the appalling mud which has impeded operations. In spite of these hardships, morale has remained generally high, and men are awaiting the first opportunities to continue the fight."[51] But as March dragged on the situation became worse: "Continued bad weather and the resulting inactivity appear to be affecting morale ... Many [soldiers] declare that they are definitely 'browned off' and the question of leave is mentioned constantly ... The best morale is found in the regiments and among troops who have been engaged in a certain amount of activity."[52]

By the next cycle of censorship reports, the worst of these complaints had disappeared. In April the censors could say: "Morale is generally high. The greatest single factor affecting it adversely is the lack of letters ... The return of the weather has helped considerably in brightening the general outlook of the soldier. The endless complaints regarding the mud and wet which were so apparent before, have largely disappeared. Men are writing in a much happier strain and are presenting a pleasant picture of army life generally."[53] After the passing of the winter, morale improved considerably ahead of and during the fighting on the Gustav and Hitler/Senger Lines. "There is an air of great expectancy in men's letters which indicates a spirit of real hope and optimism regarding the coming struggle," the censors remarked in early May. "Men reflect a feeling of genuine confidence respecting their own fighting abilities and the quality of the equipment they are using. Morale is high."[54] "The outbreak of the present campaign in Italy has given great impetus to the already high morale of the troops," they wrote in late May at the beginning of the Liri Valley campaign. "Confidence in victory, in most cases, is expressed in sure but steady terms."[55] After the victory at the Hitler/Senger Line, morale apparently remained buoyant in spite of the grievous casualties: "The morale of the troops has never been higher," the censors wrote in June 1944. "Recent successes in Italy and especially the breaching of the so-called Gustav and Hitler Lines have inspired all ranks. The troops are 'on their toes,' full of optimism, proud of their past exploits and supremely confident of their ability to play a prominent part in the final defeat of the enemy. 'Now that Jerry is on the run, nothing will hold us,' is the universal attitude."[56] By July, morale among the troops was still running at fever pitch despite their being out of the line, and one report could not resist remarking: "the mail reflects a degree of confidence and optimism that has not been equalled at any time during the present campaign."[57]

The heavy and bloody fighting on the Gothic Line that began in late August and spilled into September again seemed to have the curious effect of lifting morale. "The heavy fighting in which they have recently been engaged does not appear to have affected the morale of the troops in any way," one censor wrote. "Indeed, if anything, it would seem to have raised rather than lowered the spirit of those directly involved in the operations. From all ranks come cheerful letters radiating confidence and optimism, and making light of personal hardships – even though the majority frankly state that the present battle is particularly grim, and indicate that they are meeting the stiffest opposition they have so far encountered in the Italian campaign."[58] The feeling that Italy was the "forgotten theatre" was not evident even after D-Day in Normandy, and may reflect a postwar value judgment. At the height of the fighting, the views of soldiers seemed to reflect recent scholarship that indicates that the fighters in Italy viewed themselves as a "southern front" of the Normandy campaign.[59] Nevertheless, the optimism generated by the Gothic Line offensive, the Canadians' most successful fight in Italy, took a hit in September and October when, contrary to prior expectations, fierce

German resistance persisted: "All ranks now feel that they are likely to spend a second winter in Italy – a prospect that has revived most unpleasant memories of mud and cold and that is therefore viewed with some dismay."[60]

The transition into the second winter of the Italian campaign was indeed a difficult one. By early October: "This realisation [of a second winter campaign in Italy] would appear to have had a certain sobering effect on [soldiers'] spirits, and a slight feeling of war-weariness is evident as a result. All ranks continue to stress in their letters the exceptional ferocity of the fighting in which they have recently been engaged."[61] When the weather turned truly horrid in November 1944 and the Canadians were again withdrawn from active operations, despite their being out of the line the tone of their letters became even uglier: "Much space was devoted in the mail examined to the weather conditions, and it would seem that the continuous rain and ever-present mud have had a certain damping effect on the men's spirits. It is evident that the prospect of another winter campaign in Italy is regarded with some apprehension." One NCO's comment, was cited as typical: "It looks as though we are going to spend another confounded winter here in the mud and corruption. The weather is hopeless, I never thought that so much water could come out of the sky. We are still in the line and everybody is really browned off. My God how we looked forward to getting home for Xmas."[62] The weather and the mud also featured prominently in the morale reports for the rest of November and December, and in the very last report of 1944 the censors admitted that morale was beginning to crack: "A new note of battle strain is discernible in a number of letters, and there are many references from fighting units to the difficulties encountered in recent operations and to the grim nature of the fighting in which they have been engaged."[63] The fatigue and exhaustion of troops spilled into the new year. "Evidence of a certain degree of battle weariness continues to appear in the mail. There is constant reference to the savage nature of the fighting encountered, and numbers of men frankly confess that they will be glad to be withdrawn from the line for a rest."[64] By the beginning of February, as the weather improved, the malaise had passed even as the Canadians began to move out of the Italian theatre: "Spectacular news from other fronts has done much to raise the general level of morale, and the mail reflects a considerably more cheerful and optimistic outlook than was recently the case."[65]

Interestingly, overall drops in morale as reflected in the censorship reports bear no correlation to battle casualties; nor were heavy casualties among the main sources of low morale in responses to the questionnaires (see Appendix G). The attitudes of Canadian soldiers, as reflected in their mail, remained surprisingly positive during the brutal fighting on the Hitler/Senger and Gothic Lines in 1944, despite the fact that these were the periods when significant percentages of the infantrymen were being killed every week. The impact of casualties upon morale cannot be discounted, of course, but casualties alone did not seem to lower morale. Being actively engaged on the offensive and in direct contact with the enemy, and achieving progress and success, appear to have encouraged fighting spirit rather than to have diminished it.

In contrast, the darkest periods in terms of morale seemed to have occurred post-Ortona in the first three months of 1944, and again in the last three months of 1944 and the beginning of 1945. Despite comparatively low casualties during this time, the fighting had a static, immobile, frustrating character to it, and less was achieved in terms of tangible success or victory. As Acting Major T.M. Lowe of the Cape Bretons remarked in a questionnaire, "[the] incidence of physical and mental strain was very marked under conditions where men remained static under mortar and shell fire in slit trenches."[66] Some of the bitterest and most impatient comments quoted in the censorship reports came from officers and other ranks stuck in the reinforcement depots waiting to be taken on strength.[67] Few things eroded morale like inaction and a perceived lack of progress.

Equally important is the under-appreciated relationship between morale and the weather.[68] When the weather turned rainy and cold and the Italian topsoil turned to mud, morale plummeted. This drop came partly from the memory of fighting in the muddy Ortona salient in 1943, partly from a recognition that poor weather acted as a defensive multiplier for the Germans, and partly from basic human reaction. As an OR soldier commented in October 1944: "There is so much mud here now that I doubt if we will drive Jerry out for weeks. It sure is hard on the morale to think we will be here for another winter."[69] Even Lieutenant-General E.L.M. Burns, commander of I Canadian Corps, recalling his experiences in two world wars in his memoirs, bridged them with a commentary that spanned both Passchendaele and Italy:

> It seems improbable that against such a courageous, skilful and determined enemy as the Germans any magic formula of generalship, or any innovation in strategy or tactics could have brought quick victory, victory unaccompanied by horrifying losses on both sides. But when all is said, recognizing that victory over such opponents as the Germans could only come through offensive action and wearing down their capacity to resist, the object was not likely to be attained through prolonged offensive operations in bad weather, where mud is the ally of the defenders and the enemy of the attackers.[70]

Poor weather also had deleterious psychological effects on soldiers. The physical environment was inescapable and uncontrollable, and could make lives unbearable. Weather ranked highly as a complaint among battle questionnaire respondents even if it was never the foremost complaint, and is best thought of as an insidious endemic influence upon morale rather than an acute one.[71]

One key difference between the 1943 and the 1944–45 campaigns was that, in 1943 there had been no real expectation of ultimate victory over the Axis. With the new year, this changed, and the first nine months of 1944 were full of optimism and the anticipation that the war would be won. Particularly during the late summer, the breakout from Normandy engendered notable "Home for Christmas" forecasts in Italy, and the initial success of the offensive against the Gothic Line reinforced the impression that 1944 would see a final end to hostilities.[72] Action was an important constituent to morale, but success was absolutely necessary. The hope for a swift end to the war – indeed, fighting in order to stop the fighting and allow everyone to go home – was central to motivation in 1944–45. When the end of the war looked imminent, Canadians' spirits were extraordinarily high; when continued German resistance and the beginning of foul weather spoiled those hopes, spirits came crashing down.

The state of infantry morale in I Canadian Corps can also be assessed in part through offence statistics. (The total number of offences for 1st

Canadian Infantry Division and its infantry battalions is reproduced in Appendix E.) As the Italian campaigns wore on, the percentage of soldiers who incurred disciplinary action rose sharply. This may have been because discipline itself became increasing problematic, or else because military authorities were introducing harsher disciplinary regimes. During the 1943 campaigns, according to the Discipline & Pay Section, there had been on average 375 offences per month in 1st Canadian Division, and on average 155 of those (41 percent) were from infantry battalions – that is, a percentage roughly proportional to the whole, given that the division was 42 percent infantrymen.[73] Between February and December 1944, there were on average 444 offences per month in 1st Division, of which 247 (56 percent) were from the infantry battalions. Offences were both on the rise and increasingly laid against infantrymen. In October and November 1944, the percentage of offences in the infantry battalions skyrocketed to 73 and 74 percent respectively (although the overall number of offences had declined sharply from early 1944).[74] The infantry battalions were normally far below strength during 1944, so even these percentages, which are necessarily calculated using peak war establishment numbers, are an under-representation. Most charges in Italy were still for absence without leave and, increasingly, for outright desertion. Both AWL and desertion were serious problems throughout the Commonwealth Eighth Army in 1944–45, and the Canadians do not seem to have been disproportionately affected.[75]

The most likely explanation is that the twin circumstances of the arrival of the new Canadian brass in the form of I Canadian Corps and the sharp decline in overall Canadian morale in early 1944 led new commanders to seek harsher and more frequent disciplinary measures in an attempt to remedy low morale and misbehaviour. Because the infantry were at the "sharp end," they were increasingly targeted in order to remedy the problem of absence, desertion, and other forms of combat refusal by making an example of offenders. It is difficult to make distinctions with this much historical distance. But it is an established fact that, in comparison to the 1943 fighting in Italy, the mechanisms of disciplinary coercion were working harder in 1944–45.

In addition to absenteeism and desertion, high numbers of soldiers taken prisoner by the enemy could be an indicator of wavering morale, as soldiers could use surrender as a (hazardous) form of desertion. This was certainly the most expedient way out of combat for Germans. However, only a very small number of Canadian losses were prisoners of war (POWs), and most of these had been captured in combat rather than taken as deserters; far fewer Canadians wanted to surrender to the Germans to escape the war than vice versa. The official history of the Italian campaign lists the total number of POWs from I Canadian Corps as 1,004; consolidated casualty lists indicate that 886 of these were from the infantry battalions throughout the entire campaign, exactly 5 percent of total infantry casualties in the theatre.[76] The British official historian believed that this low percentage bore an inverse relationship to morale: "The remarkably low figure for prisoners is a reflection of the high morale and fighting spirit of the Canadian Corps."[77]

In perspective, troops lost as prisoners were a grievous problem for the Germans in Italy. As early as January 1944, the commander of the German Tenth Army was attempting to stem the tide of surrender-desertions with stern orders: "In the event of a soldier being so devoid of honour as to desert to the enemy, in future the most severe measures against his family will be taken."[78] During the period from 1 December 1944 to 5 January 1945, in the midst of the river line fighting that has been treated in the historiography as highly unsuccessful and demoralizing for the Canadians, I Canadian Corps captured 2,223 German prisoners, while only 260 Canadian infantrymen became POWs.[79] From September 1943 until the Canadian withdrawal from Italy in early 1945 the Commonwealth forces in Italy were responsible for capturing some 48,400 German prisoners of war, most of them from the fighting branches; if the prisoners taken by the US Fifth Army are included, the number was over 110,000.[80] The British official history lists the German forces in Italy as sustaining 295,650 casualties between September 1943 and the end of January 1945, so somewhere in the range of 35 percent of German casualties were POW captures during that time, and 16.5 percent of all German casualties in-theatre were POWs captured by Eighth Army alone. The 5 percent of Canadian infantry casualties who were made prisoner compares favourably.[81] Whatever problems of absenteeism and desertion I Canadian Corps faced seem trivial in comparison to the haemorrhage of soldiers departing from the German Army at the same time.

The morale of Canadian soldiers in the Mediterranean theatre was complex and variable throughout 1944–45. Individuals experienced both definitive lows and jubilant highs, but insofar as we can speak of an aggregate impression of morale, these highs and lows seem to have been closely correlated with success in battle and with the weather. Creature comforts such as food, mail, and the availability of leave were among the most important factors in keeping spirits up, and the administrative arrangements of I Canadian Corps were generally up to the task of providing them. As it happened, the "tail" was vital in keeping the "teeth" supplied and motivated to fight, and there were no significant administrative breakdowns throughout 1944–45, aside from a shortage of shells over that winter.[82] As long as support elements held up their end and maintained a sense that the front-line troops were being well looked after, the army would not come close to breaking.

Canadian morale and willingness to fight wavered at several points in Italy, but at no point did low morale appear to seriously compromise fighting effectiveness. The historiography has emphasized the alienation of Canadians from the war in Italy, undoubtedly reflecting the feelings of many individual veterans. But, by the measures examined here, the crisis was not as acute as is portrayed. Early in 1944 the months of (perceived) meaningless patrolling and raids to capture prisoners and "dominate no-man's land" on the Ortona front wore down morale. However, when major operations resumed, Canadians fought – and did so very effectively – in the face of adversity. Even when desertion, absenteeism, and other offences were at their worst, only a small minority of soldiers were "voting with their feet" or otherwise causing trouble. Morale remained quite high throughout the campaign, and as a result the Canadians overall remained disciplined and achieved conspicuous successes despite fighting a gruelling, attritional war in difficult terrain and abominable environmental conditions.

COHESION AND MOTIVATION

The observations of censors and the questionnaire comments that morale was not tied directly to casualties make a significant statement, given that the casualties inflicted upon the Canadian infantry in Italy in 1944–45

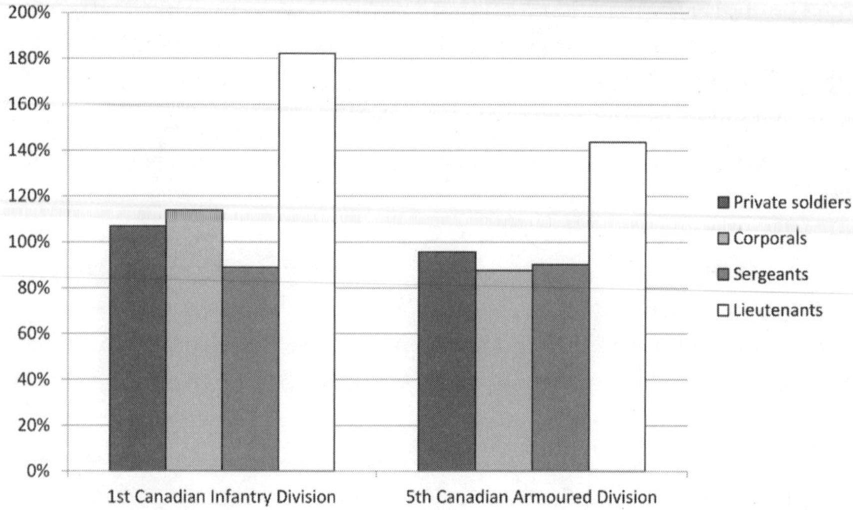

Figure 4.1: Cumulative infantry casualties, 1944–45

were extremely high. Between January 1944 and January 1945, 1st Canadian Division suffered cumulative losses to all infantry battalions equal to 107 percent of its private soldiers, 114 percent of its corporals, 88 percent of its sergeants, and 182 percent of its lieutenants. 5th Division's infantry battalions were almost equally depleted: 96 percent of its private soldiers, 88 percent of its corporals, 90 percent of its sergeants, and 144 percent of its lieutenants became casualties over the course of the fighting. Figure 4.1 shows the cumulative casualties and gives a sense of the scale involved.[83] (Complete casualty statistics for the infantry are available in a table in Appendix F.)

Since the consolidated casualty lists do not differentiate casualties at any level lower than the battalion, some nuance is lost, and so these numbers continue to be under-estimations of the effect of casualties on rifle companies. As a British V Corps report from Italy in 1944 pointed out: "If a battalion loses 12 officers, it is very probable that 10 of these will come from the rifle companies. This means that when the battalion as a whole has lost 12 out of 36 of its officers, the rifle companies have [actually] lost 10 out of 20."[84] While support companies and other elements of Canadian infantry battalions could take heavy casualties, most casualties were concentrated in the four companies of the battalion, which, according to war establishment, made up 436 all ranks out of a total of 822.[85] When the casualties for 1st Canadian Division are combined with the totals from the 1943 campaigns, the numbers become even more disquieting: lieutenants in infantry battalions suffered on average a casualty rate of 304 percent of their war establishment between July 1943 and January 1944. Private soldiers lost 167 percent to killed, wounded, and prisoners. The human cost of the Italian campaign, sometimes eclipsed by the bloodletting in Normandy, was staggering.[86]

What sustained Canadians during this brutalizing Mediterranean year, and what kept them connected to those around them? Throughout 1944–45 the Canadian connection to Eighth Army remained strong, even though the army had become unrecognizable from the force that had stormed Sicily. By August 1944 1st Canadian Infantry Division was the only Commonwealth division left in Eighth Army that had once been part of the Operation HUSKY landings thirteen months earlier.[87] 1st Division soldiers had something of a swagger in Eighth Army on account of their seniority. Ironically, though, the British managed to rotate almost every other veteran unit out of the Mediterranean theatre, whereas the Canadians – who had initially sent 1st Division to Sicily explicitly to gain combat experience to bring back to First Canadian Army prior to OVERLORD – ended up not only "holding the fort" in the Mediterranean but being significantly reinforced.

After General Montgomery's departure from the Mediterranean in December 1943, no senior commander was held in such reverential high regard again, and new commanders suffered from the comparison. General Oliver Leese, Monty's successor and the former commander of the British XXX Corps (under which the Canadians had served in Sicily) was certainly respected and could stir the troops, but he could not cultivate the same magic as Montgomery and was not loved in the same way. "Our General Leese is very highly thought of out here," one Canadian soldier wrote home, but "he is much more reserved and not the showman that Monty is."[88] Commentary on the senior Canadian leadership in the Mediterranean, including Corps Commanders E.L.M. Burns and Charles Foulkes, were never frequent enough to warrant even the barest mention in the censorship reports. Under Montgomery the Canadians had experienced an ironclad belief in success. Afterward, particularly during the winter of 1944, that certainty had waned and become infected with suspicion about high command's conduct of the war.[89] Actually being under Canadian command for the first time generated, unfortunately, few good feelings among the troops, particularly those of 1st Canadian Division, who felt they had thrived under British command in 1943. "General Crerar's I Canadian Corps had now taken over command of 1st Division," writes Farley Mowat, "and a reluctant 1st Division it was. The Corps personnel – most of whom had never heard a shot fired in anger – at once tried to make their weight felt. A deluge of trivial commands poured down on the fighting troops."[90] The corps headquarters felt the need to impose disciplinary routines on the front-line soldiers, which did little to endear the infantry to their new command structure or leadership.[91]

Regimental esprit de corps was still in evidence. "The Seaforth Highlanders were always tops in the last war," wrote one Seaforth officer in a letter home at the end of the Italian campaign: "I think we have kept up the reputation in this war. The 1st Canadian Division is considered among the finest troops in the world and the Seaforths second to none."[92] Special pride was generated when prisoners of war reported that certain units were named and feared by the Germans: "You remember the great prestige created by the S.S. Germans. They are supposed to be the elite troops of the Boche Army. I can tell you that the reputation of the [Royal 22e Régiment] among [the Germans] is far greater [than their reputation among us]."[93] Regimental *esprit* seems to have been particularly important and noticeable in the primary sources of the Royal 22e, the only French-Canadian battalion in the Italian theatre that made race and religion a real part of its identity. On 3 July, a month after the Germans were chased from Rome, the "Van Doos" were granted a private audience with Pope Pius XII followed by a special mass at St Peter's, at which Major-General Georges Vanier was in attendance alongside his former regiment.[94] When Cardinal Villeneuve, archbishop of Quebec, visited the troops in October 1944, his presence brought an outpouring of appreciation among the French-Canadian contingent in Italy. As one "Van Doo" private wrote: "One of the most beautiful, most touching ceremonies that I have yet seen took place at the time of the visit of Cardinal Villeneuve, who sang a service for the lads of my Regiment who lost their lives in the last action. After Mass he spoke of the devotion shown by the Regiment

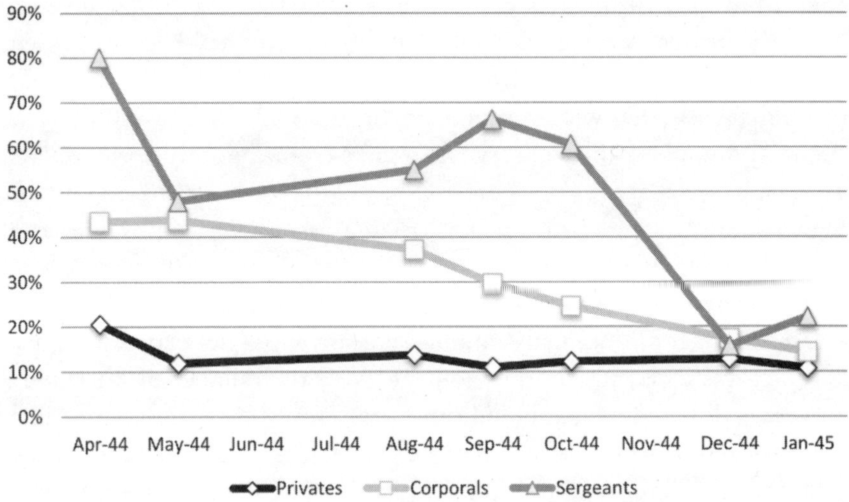

Figure 4.2: "Originals" among 1st Division casualties, Italy 1944–45

from the beginning of the conflict. After he finished, the guns fired [in salute] for nearly half an hour and several from among us who were in the fight could not keep back a few tears because the Regiment is like a great family and when someone goes from it forever, one is greatly moved."[95] Religion fused with regimental and Québécois tradition to create a unique identity in the 22e. But while the Royal 22e Régiment had a strong esprit de corps, this regiment also had by far the highest offence rate in the I Canadian Corps when it came to desertion and absenteeism throughout 1944, and the highest rate of courts martial held for its soldiers.[96] The strong shared identity did not always translate into commitment to regimental values, and could find expression in disciplinary problems (though it is worth noting that the Van Doos were known for draconian enforcement of discipline, and may have been punishing offences that went unremarked in other regiments).

Esprit de corps, or regimental spirit, was only infrequently mentioned in the censorship reports as being in particular evidence in soldiers' letters home, and was not mentioned in a single battle experience questionnaire from Italy as being one of the bedrocks of morale among infantrymen.

Data from the consolidated casualty lists show that the "original veterans," the longest-serving volunteers and those who had been with their regiments for years, were a dying breed. Figure 4.2 shows the percentage of combat casualties with "original" regimental numbers by month. The decline in numbers of long-serving soldiers from the start of the Italian campaign (see chapter 3) was precipitous, particularly among privates. A higher percentage of NCOs were "original" soldiers, but by the later stages of the campaign they too were vanishing. Many of them were promoted or moved to non-combat positions within the battalions (the increased number of "originals" among sergeant casualties between August and October 1944 just at the moment when the number of "original" corporals declined probably indicates promotions) but they were still a diminishing presence within the rifle companies. The character of the infantry regiments was altering throughout 1944–45, and by the end of the campaign the "originals" were all but extinct on the battlefield, representing only 10 percent of privates, 15 percent of corporals, and 20 percent of sergeants.[97] It may not be a coincidence that the final drop in "original" NCOs, from October to December 1944, represented one of the low points in Canadian morale, but the data only allow speculation on that point for now.

A standard policy in infantry battalions was for reinforcements arriving from their depots to be kept at battalion HQ for several days, if possible, during which time they would be "receiving instruction from experienced officers and NCOs and generally be absorbed." This briefing included receiving "an essential lecture ... by an officer on Regimental History and Tradition." However, the instructions for these policies had to be issued forcefully by headquarters because in practice reinforcements were all too often put into the front line with little chance to acclimatize to their new surroundings.[98] Mowat captured the essence of the issue as it affected the Hastings & Prince Edward Regiment: "There was but one criterion for acceptance – that the stranger be a man. And if he was, then he was accepted without question, without reservation. Negroes, Jews, Indians, Ukrainians, Germans, even Italians, they came and they were taken in ... so it was that the human face of the Regiment was constantly changing."[99] The distinctiveness of individual regiments became one of the casualties, as the bureaucratic nature of the reinforcement system tended to homogenize them over time. Only a few battalions in Italy were able to maintain any semblance of regional distinctiveness among infantrymen during 1944–45. The Royal 22e was most obvious, but since anglophone soldiers could not be easily placed into that regiment, and since unilingual francophone infantrymen could not be placed anywhere else, it is no surprise that the Van Doos retained an overwhelmingly French-Canadian (and québécois) character throughout the campaign. By contrast, in some battalions, such as the Hasty P's and the Perth Regiment, only a minority of men in the ranks were drawn from their regiment's part of the country. The average for I Canadian Corps' infantry battalions hovered at two-thirds, with significant variation, signifying that only 60 percent of a regiment's casualties in any given month had enlisted in that regiment's home Military District.[100] Recall that in the infantry battalions that went ashore in Sicily in 1943 an average of 90 percent of soldiers were from their regiment's home military district.

Although Canadian casualties had been heavy in Sicily and Ortona, the fourteen months of Italian operations that followed were the true test of cohesion, motivation, and effectiveness, as I Canadian Corps was engaged in several equally destructive battles over sustained periods of time. Despite serious losses, Canadian formations had become increasingly combat-capable during 1944–45, and had achieved a high degree of fighting proficiency by the September–October 1944 battles. Much of this had to do with a greater synergy between the fighting soldier and the staff officers, as the staff grew in experience, maturity, and organizational capability between the start of 1944 and the Gothic Line battles. The Canadians were consistently able to outfight the Germans, particularly given their advantages in firepower and air support; even if manoeuvre operations were limited, the hard fighting almost always went in the Canadians' favour. But while the staff officers were mastering the learning curve behind the front lines, the high infantry casualties direct us toward a different question: how did the Canadian infantry remain combat-effective and motivated to fight, given the casualties that they sustained?

Most postwar accounts of the Italian campaign mention the problem of reinforcements, and there are anecdotal accounts of Canadian reinforcements arriving in the theatre by the midpoint of the campaign completely untrained. Documentary sources from the time, however, indicate that there was no general sense that the reinforcements were particularly inadequate. Junior officers filling out battle experience questionnaires were queried about the "standard of efficiency" of reinforcement soldiers; they indicated overwhelmingly that the reinforcements were at least of "moderate" efficiency, and only a handful rated them "low" or "poor."[101] In addition, not a single officer respondent from the 1944–45 Italian campaigns mentioned "reinforcements" or "untrained troops" or any variation thereof as being a factor that was detrimental to the morale of their soldiers.[102]

Beginning in the summer of 1944, the fact that many of the "replacement" soldiers were combat veterans may have had an impact on how officers rated their efficiency. Due to the diversion of Allied reinforcement streams to Normandy, few completely new faces appeared in the Italian theatre between about May and September 1944.[103] Wounded soldiers were put back into the line after (and, allegedly, sometimes before) convalescence was complete. It took an extremely serious wound or amputation to get out of Italy, and the arrival of penicillin in the theatre in 1944 helped to increase the number of soldiers who could be returned to their units. Many of the infantrymen in the consolidated casualty lists for the Italian campaign had been wounded many times. Such a policy at least had the benefit of putting veterans experienced in combat back into the reinforcement streams for infantry battalions, although it is difficult to say how many wounded men returned to full service, and of those how many returned to their original regiments. The returning wounded seemed most concerned with ensuring that they made it back to their buddies, but reinforcements were allocated on the basis of need, so this did not always happen.[104]

Another policy unique to the Mediterranean was the "reallocation" or "conversion" to infantry of personnel from other branches that had a manpower surplus. The War Office had ordered the Allied Force Headquarters (AFHQ) in the Mediterranean to "live off its hump" until after the invasion of Normandy; that is, to fashion new infantry reinforcements from soldiers already in-theatre, rather than expect fresh reinforcements from England or Canada. Drastic steps were taken to ensure that no deficiency in reinforcements would occur. Anti-aircraft artillery gunners (whom Allied air supremacy had made redundant) were retrained as infantrymen and became the main source of infantry reinforcements and new infantry units. After a while, converted anti-aircraft gunners were in the reinforcement stream for every regiment, but there was an entire new brigade, the 12th Canadian Infantry Brigade, in which one battalion was composed wholly of repurposed armoured reconnaissance troopers, and another entirely of converted gunners. These converted soldiers were regarded, in the words of Farley Mowat, as "the flesh of an army that was being forced to practise self-cannibalism in order to keep the fighting units in existence."[105] Although reallocated troops had usually been soldiers for a while, they were "green" as infantrymen. Their retraining regimes during the summer of 1944 attempted to instil in them the essentials of infantry work, with a strong emphasis on small arms training, battle drill, and infantry/tank cooperative training both at an individual and a collective level.[106] Enthusiasm seemed low. Despite the fact that stern I Canadian Corps orders specifically banned the term, 12th Brigade officers maintained a running joke in their war diary about calling themselves the "12th Canadian LIGHT BRIGADE," in apparent anticipation of re-enacting Tennyson's poem on the battlefield. And, in a less subtle variation on the same joke, the battalion of reallocated anti-aircraft gunners, the Lanark and Renfrew Scottish, blackly called themselves the "slaughterhouse battalion."[107]

It is difficult to address the question of how reallocated soldiers fared in battle. Few historians treat the capabilities of reallocated soldiers with anything more than contempt, and most firmly believe, anecdotally, that reallocated troops were far more likely to become casualties. While we cannot discern with certainty the proportion of casualties in most battalions who were reallocated troops, we can at least form a snapshot of the battalion composed almost entirely of reallocated soldiers: 12th Brigade's Lanark and Renfrew Scottish Regiment. The Lanarks suffered virtually the same casualty rate among private soldiers and corporals as 1st Division's average. The unit was often 12th Brigade's reserve, but particularly during the post–Gothic Line battles in northern Italy, they carried out infiltration and set-piece attacks, complex river assault crossings in conjunction with engineers, and operations in cooperation with armoured regiments, all against elements of the elite German 1st Parachute and 29th Panzer Grenadier divisions. They did not win these battles alone, but fought with a level of effectiveness that impressed the 12th Brigade staff officers.[108] Another 12th Brigade battalion, the 4 Princess Louise Dragoon Guards (4 PLDG), fully reallocated to the infantry from their previous role as armoured reconnaissance troopers, distinguished themselves in breaking the Gothic Line and earned a personal message of congratulation from General Leese.[109] Their conspicuous success, surprising effectiveness, and, more grimly, the fact that their casualties were not significantly higher than those of other battalions all suggest that historiographical condemnations of the quality of reallocated troops needs to be revisited. They may have been unhappy in their new roles, but these fledgling infantrymen were well enough prepared to successfully engage the Germans.

To ensure that military disaster would not leave a unit unable to rebuild, Left out of Battle (LOB) personnel continued in the late Italian campaigns to be detached regularly from infantry companies and platoons. The "LOB system" was vital to maintaining continuity on the ground despite devastating casualties. Virtually all the officers who filled out a battle experience questionnaire noted that they always detached "LOB" personnel before going into battle (the one contrary opinion coming from Lieutenant-Colonel T.P. Gilday of the First Special Service Force, which as an elite unit operated according to different rules, and which ultimately had to be disbanded in the face of unsustainable casualty rates).[110] Historian Reginald Roy described the system: "Supposing a platoon to have a strength of about 33 all ranks, some six or seven men would be kept in the rear when the battle commenced. If the platoon officer took in the group, then his sergeant remained behind and vice versa. The same thing was true on the company level. If, therefore, the company commander was killed or wounded, his second in command would be called forward to take his place [from being LOB]."[111] Operational instructions from 5th Canadian Armoured Division in July 1944 standardized which personnel should be LOB for every battalion: either the battalion CO or his second-in-command: from each rifle company either the company commander or his second-in-command; a total of four platoon commanders per battalion, a total of four platoon sergeants, and twenty-four NCOs or "potential NCOs" from the rank and file per battalion. The divisional instructions read: "The purpose of leaving key personnel detailed below out of battle is to have a cadre available for reforming the unit in case of *heavy* casualties to officers and NCOs. This reforming will normally be done during a pause in the operations, or when the unit is in reserve, and the 'bulk' of the reinforcements come forward … 'left out of battle' personnel will NOT be called forward until the unit has completed a phase of offensive ops, and has time to re-organize." Control of when and where to bring forward LOB personnel was actually assigned to the brigade commander, and so, after a battle, the LOB leadership core was allocated as needed within the battalion, and officers and NCOs did not always make it back to the same company or platoon.[112]

As might be expected, ad hoc infantry sub-units continued to characterize life in 1944–45. The combination of heavy casualties, a needs-based LOB system, and a reinforcement chain that fed individual replacements or small groups into field units rather than replace those units with new ones resulted in drastic internal reorganizations, sometimes on the fly and sometimes during pauses. Platoons and companies were split apart and recombined in order to achieve balance between newcomers and the veterans who would teach them how to survive in combat.[113] The Hastings & Prince Edward Regiment temporarily broke up one of their rifle companies in 1944 to keep the others reinforced, while the Support and Headquarters companies retrained drivers, mechanics, runners, and administrative personnel to form a new improvised rifle company.[114] As Reginald Roy wrote in his history of the Seaforths: "After the Gothic Line, reinforcements arrived. Care was taken that no one platoon received a majority of reinforcements, and consequently there was some shuffling within the battalion to strike a nice balance of veterans and recruits ... [a] reason for scattering the recruits was to enable them to absorb quickly something of the deeply engrained *esprit de corps* of the Seaforths. If they remained together it took longer for them to lose their former attachments and identities."[115] Even if reinforcements had some sort of social bond among them in advance, that cohesion was discarded to help rebuild regimental identities. High casualties meant that platoons and their sections were never up to strength anyway, so the reinforcements were badly needed. Major John Clarke of the 48th Highlanders mentioned in a questionnaire that platoons were often being reconstituted, with two recombined sections being made up of surviving soldiers from three shattered sections.[116] The "primary group" was constantly being torn apart and reconstituted in different configurations. This process was particularly prevalent in Italy during 1944–45, and desperate measures were employed to keep the infantry up to minimum effective fighting strength. Universal adherence to divisional LOB policies allowed a leadership core to always be available within the battalion to rebuild and re-socialize troops, but the configuration of the sub-units was in constant flux.

It was a common expedient among the Allied Armies in Italy to recombine and reorganize units to make good on deficiencies, and the Canadians were actually quite fortunate in this respect. Although there was constant personnel turmoil among them, it never reached above the company level (save for the expedient of creating the new 12th Brigade and its battalions from existing assets). The British, on the other hand, rather than add to their fighting strength, had to permanently reduce the war establishment of all their infantry battalions from four to three rifle companies apiece, sacrificing one company per battalion to keep the others fighting. In British Guards and Rifle brigades, one battalion per brigade was disbanded to serve as reinforcements for the others. As of early 1945 four divisions in Eighth Army (two Polish, one New Zealand, and one British) all possessed only two infantry brigades instead of the normal three, a whole brigade having been broken up for reinforcements. And in October 1944 the British were reduced to completely disbanding their 1st Armoured Division and making 56th Division non-operational in order to feed the soldiers from those formations into the reinforcement streams of others.[117] The Canadians were better able to make good on their losses than most other national contingents under Allied command, and ad hoc organization was the order of the day at all levels of command in the Mediterranean.

But even though the Canadians avoided breaking up battalions, brigades, or divisions, high casualties among the infantry meant that their units were constantly operating below strength, and it was rare for a company, platoon, or section to be at its full war establishment once the fighting started.[118] Questionnaire responses on the average number of other ranks per infantry section numbered them in a range from three to eight, with an average of five and a half and a median of six.[119] Chances were good that, during active operations, any infantry section that was near full strength was composed of many men who were at best acquaintances and not infrequently strangers to one another, but whom soldiers had to nonetheless rely upon throughout 1944–45.

It is here that we see the process of "swift trust" at work. How effective was it as a cohesive force? Even with no fresh infantry replacements coming into the theatre, the unpredictability of casualty rates, the frequency of reallocation, and the constant personnel turmoil previously described would have made it difficult to establish tight social cohesion. Fewer and fewer soldiers were even from the same regions of Canada, leaving limited basis for shared identity between newcomers and veterans. Even so, it is possible that esprit de corps and regimental spirit may have been cultivated, but the extent to which soldiers – particularly reinforcements – really identified with their regiments is uncertain. In spite of the dissolution of so many social bonds, however, it is remarkable how effectively the soldiers generally fought. Junior officers were quite satisfied that even their depleted, reorganized sections could carry out aggressive close-quarters fighting in battle, with about 75 percent indicating on questionnaires that this was the case.[120] There was a general consensus among questionnaire responders that even at severely reduced strengths, Canadian infantry in Italy were combat-effective with or without the full support of heavy weapons.[121] It is unfortunate that the data only allow a generalization for the complete time period, but they support other observations that the Canadians in Italy remained quite combat-capable throughout. Not every operation went well, or was successful, but when Canadians were stopped, it was by exhaustion or especially adverse environmental conditions, not by breakdowns in cohesion. One can only say that theories of accelerated "swift trust" provide a more compelling explanation for these facts than traditional models that focus on the primacy of small-group cohesion.

Trends in leadership that were mentioned in chapter 3 continued during the fighting of 1944–45. Fully one-third of junior officers cited good leadership on questionnaires as being the top factor involved in raising morale, and poor leadership was cited by almost as many as being one of the foremost detriments to morale.[122] And as in 1943, throughout the later stages of the war in Italy, casualties to leadership cadres disproportionately affected platoon commanders, while platoon NCOs consistently suffered casualties at a much lower rate across all infantry battalions.[123] "It was probably in the NCOs," wrote Kim Beattie in the regimental history of the 48th Highlanders, "where you saw most clearly that the Regiment's business was fighting ... They were wary, tough, and alert. They had the force of the fighter. They could be ruthless and sentimental, hard-minded and gentle by turns. They had the unshakable resolution, the scorn of showing fear, the rough sense of justice, the instinctive, paternal impulse to look out for their men, which are qualities and instincts a good fighting leader must have to survive."[124] NCOs of all levels provided comparative continuity and stability (relative to junior officers, whose casualty rates were stratospheric) and were a consistent source of battle experience and cohesion within units. Although they were often shuffled around in the creation of ad hoc sub-units and the LOB system, they still provided a framework of cohesion that supplemented the highly dangerous, heroic leadership provided by officers.

CONCLUSION: TO WITHIN A STROKE OF VICTORY

Many accounts of the Italian campaign portray it as a wasted effort, a secondary and forgotten theatre of war from which, given the cost, little was gained. But as historians have more recently argued, Italy in 1944 was the "southern flank" of the Allied Western Front and served an important role as an adjunct to the Normandy campaign. The successful breaking of a German army in Italy after the breach of the Hitler/Senger Line corresponded with D-Day for Operation OVERLORD, and the OLIVE offensive in late August likewise mirrored the destruction and routing of the German army group in Normandy. Canadian soldiers in Italy were keenly aware of the strategic picture and worked it into the complex matrix of context and meaning that underlay their motivations. The war in Italy was hell: brutalizing, dehumanizing, fought under awful conditions and in forbidding terrain, against an enemy widely regarded as the best in the world. Morale sometimes cracked during the periods of static warfare and cold, wet weather. But the successes achieved – even costly, attritional successes – were seen by soldiers to be materially affecting and shortening the war, and this knowledge buoyed and sustained the morale of Canadian soldiers throughout the campaign.

Despite many setbacks, local defeats, and discouraging results, the combat effectiveness of Canadian infantrymen in Italy was maintained at a high level. Much of the fighting was characterized by close combat in the complex Italian terrain. Morale certainly declined at times, and absenteeism, desertion, and other crimes (or at least the prosecutions for these crimes) rose significantly in 1944–45 from their 1943 benchmarks, but in aggregate good morale seems, notably, to have been a function of success and activity. The worst parts of the campaigns in Italy were the static periods during the two winters that the Canadians spent on the front, when progress had to be made through sucking mud and was measured in yards. Periods of much higher-casualty fighting were indexed with periods of exceptionally high morale among the troops as long as success and forward motion toward their goal was being materially achieved, particularly during the Hitler/Senger Line and Gothic Line battles.

The mooted crisis of low-quality reinforcements seems to have been at least partially manufactured by postwar accounts and is not borne out by contemporary documentary evidence.[125] However, sub-units were constantly being torn apart by casualties, reorganized, and put back together again in different configurations, so that even those sections, platoons, and companies that were not destroyed by losses were often rearranged into new improvised forms. During periods of fighting, the "small groups" within units were often strangers or acquaintances, but swift trust and the continuity of cadres helped to maintain both cohesion and effectiveness in battle, in spite of the human misery that necessitated such ad hoc arrangements. The fact that the Canadians were constantly on the offensive, and that these offensives were seen, in conjunction with the fighting in Normandy and Northwest Europe, to be bringing the war to within a stroke of victory, was a powerful source of strength and motivation to those on the ground.

5

The Canadians in Normandy, 1944

Eleven months after 1st Canadian Infantry Division had stormed ashore on Pachino Beach in Sicily, the end of the war in Europe began with the long-awaited invasion of France. Operation OVERLORD, the Allied invasion of Normandy, marked the beginning of the three bloodiest months in Canadian history. The Normandy killing fields inflicted damage on the same scale as those of the First World War.[1] After only a few months of fighting, the infantry rifle companies of 2nd, 3rd, and 4th Canadian divisions had sustained casualties in numbers very close to those suffered in all the fighting in Italy throughout fourteen months of the campaign in 1944–45.

The Battle of Normandy involved the most difficult and ambitious military operation ever conceived: retaking France, from the sea, while opposed by some of Germany's best Wehrmacht and SS formations. From the beginning OVERLORD was treated as the "main event," the decisive theatre in which the Western Allies had to contend against Nazi Germany if they wished to contribute meaningfully to its defeat; the campaign in France was thought of as "the big push" by Allied soldiers and was viewed in apocalyptic terms by the Germans.[2]

Operation OVERLORD commenced on 6 June 1944, but was the culmination of planning and preparation that dated back to the US entry into the Second World War. Taking lessons from both Operation JUBILEE (Dieppe) and Operation HUSKY (Sicily), OVERLORD was above all a phenomenal logistical achievement: an opposed landing and sustainment on a coastline by five divisions, plus three airborne divisions in support, and thereafter the build-up to two million soldiers across those beaches. The Canadians, led by 3rd Canadian Infantry Division and 2nd Canadian

Armoured Brigade, landed at Juno Beach under cover of an overwhelming naval and air bombardment of the beach defences.[3] Rather than build up a thick anti-tank "shell" the way they had in Sicily, in Normandy the invaders opted for mobility, pushing rapidly inland with tank support in order to secure depth and keep the enemy away from the fragile logistical infrastructure on the beach.[4] Recent Canadian scholarship has demonstrated that 3rd Canadian Infantry Division's placement in the British I Corps line, astride the Meu River west of Caen, was precisely where the D-Day planners expected the strongest German counterattack against the entire Allied beachhead to fall.[5] 3rd Division achieved most of its D-Day objectives and established fortress positions just before the expected hammer descended and SS Panzer divisions counterattacked the Canadian beachhead.[6] The Canadian casualties were high, but they fought the tenacious troops of the 1st SS Panzer Corps to a standstill and, despite local setbacks, achieved their objective of gaining and defending the beach.[7]

When 3rd Division was put back into the fight two weeks later, their objective was the French town of Caen, an original D-Day objective for the British, a task that embroiled the Canadians in fighting against the Germans' armoured reserves. The town was obliterated by bombing and eventually captured, at great cost. When 2nd Canadian Division was landed in France in mid-July, both Canadian divisions were employed in fighting for the tactically important high ground south of Caen in what would turn out to be the bloodiest fighting of the entire war for Canada. The objective had both tactical and strategic dimensions: seizing the ground was important, but a greater imperative was to tie down the best German armoured units in the eastern end of the bridgehead, while the Americans prepared for a breakout in the west.[8]

The Canadians' own breakout battle was ultimately a success, although according to the historiography it did not accomplish everything it might have.[9] With the Americans pouring around the Germans' flank in the west and threatening to encircle the enemy, the newly activated First Canadian Army tried to punch its way through fresh German divisions to reach the town of Falaise, which might have allowed them to cut off the enemy retreat. With several formations under command, including the newly deployed 4th Canadian Armoured Division, the Canadians fought tooth and nail to secure the encirclement. Some 200,000 Germans were ensnared by the Allies on 12 August 1944, of whom at least 20,000 escaped before the Falaise Gap was finally closed on 21 August. Some twenty-seven German infantry divisions and a dozen armoured divisions were destroyed or captured.[10] Despite the number of Germans who managed to escape, it was a decisive victory, and the liberation of the rest of France swiftly followed from the success achieved in Normandy.

FORCE STRUCTURE

Two Canadian infantry divisions (the 2nd and 3rd), one armoured division (the 4th), plus an independent tank brigade landed in Normandy between June and August 1944, as well as one corps-level formation (II Canadian Corps) and one army-level formation (First Canadian Army). Several battalions of 2nd Canadian Division had spent a single day being mauled at Dieppe two years earlier, which had necessitated an extensive rebuilding of manpower, equipment, and confidence; it also represented the only battle experience prior to D-Day that any of these Canadian formations possessed. Partly because of 2nd Division's rebuilding process, Major-General Rod Keller's 3rd Canadian Infantry Division was chosen as Canada's assault force for the OVERLORD landings in Normandy, and the twelve months of amphibious assault training that the 3rd Division received earned them the nickname "The Water Rats."[11] Major-General Charles Foulkes's 2nd Canadian Division landed in Normandy after a few weeks, and Major-General George Kitching's 4th Canadian Armoured Division arrived even later and saw action during the August "breakout" battles. A handful of experienced officers had returned from fighting in the Mediterranean, chief among them Lieutenant-General Guy Simonds, who commanded II Canadian Corps, under which all these divisions served.[12]

The Canadian infantry divisions in Normandy were patterned on the same structure as the 1st Division.[13] 4th Armoured Division was a product of older policies than 5th Armoured Division; as discussed in chapter 4, 5th Division had doubled its complement of infantry in the summer of 1944 to make it better suited for Italian-style fighting. 4th Division operated throughout the war with a single brigade of three infantry battalions. For the landing stage of Normandy, 3rd Division was part of I British Corps but command migrated to Simonds's II Canadian

Corps when that formation was activated in July 1944. All Canadian formations in Normandy fell under the command of General H.D.G. Crerar's First Canadian Army once it became operational on 23 July 1944, just in time to stage-manage the breakout battle. All the Canadian and British formations fell under the command of 21st Army Group, led by the well-loved (by the fighting troops, at any rate) General Bernard Law Montgomery.

As mentioned, the only combat experience any of the Canadian formations possessed in 1944 were the few hours of fighting at Dieppe in August 1942. At Dieppe, 5,000 2nd Division troops, about 4,500 of them infantrymen, had put ashore as part of a "smash and grab" raid, and nine hours later only 2,200 returned to England.[14] Only one 2nd Division infantry battalion (the Calgary Highlanders) did not suffer serious casualties at Dieppe; the rest required extensive rebuilding from the leadership down to the private soldiers. The long-term effects on 2nd Division are difficult to quantify. Historian Jonathan Vance has emphasized that Canadian morale, as it could be measured, actually rose in the aftermath of the Dieppe disaster, and that the weekend-warrior peacetime mentality under which the Canadians had been operating in England was dispelled in favour of getting down to the serious business of invading the continent.[15] Most soldiers, according to the field censors assessments in a special post-Dieppe report, "are now firmly convinced that the Canadians are superior fighters to the Germans, who they consider are 'yellow' when faced with the bayonet."[16] Others, including Lieutenant-General E.L.M. Burns, who commanded 2nd Division in England for a time after Dieppe, thought that the division never fully recovered from its ordeal; it took months to "rebuild" the manpower alone and Burns perceived there to be serious leadership problems in the division stemming from resentment over Dieppe.[17] In Normandy, 2nd Division sustained grievous damage in July and August 1944, taking almost as many casualties as 3rd Division had since the start of operations in June. There were a small number of incidents in which 2nd Division units "broke" in combat in Normandy, and in the aftermath of the campaign their desertion and AWL rates (or at least the rates of prosecution of these offences) were higher than in 3rd Division.[18] It is difficult to tell whether these problems were entirely circumstantial, or if they were related to the division's character.

BEHAVIOUR IN BATTLE

The campaign plan for Normandy has been argued over and refought relentlessly in the historiography. The basic intention involved the Anglo-Canadian forces on the eastern end of the Normandy beachhead locking down and fighting, head-on, the majority of the Germans' mobile armoured forces in the theatre, while the Americans built up and launched a killing blow from the less defended west.[19] Aside from the opposed amphibious landing, it was not dissimilar from some of the campaign plans behind major battles late in the First World War: attempt to blunt Germany's excellent mobile warfare by defeating counterattacks with firepower, dissipate their concentrated strength by forcing them to deploy everywhere at once, and then strike the breakthrough blow unexpectedly.[20] In Normandy the plan worked. From D+1 onward the Canadians were opposed by formations of the Waffen-SS and Wehrmacht, many of which were closer to their full complement of infantry manpower than were the Canadians.[21] John English has estimated that the German troop-to-space density in Normandy was two and a half times that of the Russian front, so the sweeping armoured thrusts characteristic of the war on other fronts would run into problems.[22] Because of the troop density, the paucity of open flanks, and the nature of the countryside, not to mention the campaign plan itself, the Battle of Normandy bore more than a passing resemblance to the conflict of twenty years earlier for the infantrymen who had to fight it. The new technologies of military hardware, however, and the absence of permanent static trenches made the Normandy battlefields much more lethal than the Great War had been.[23]

In Italy the terrain had limited the role that armoured vehicles could play. The flat, open country to the south of Caen where the Canadians fought was, on the other hand, textbook "tank country." In Normandy the only static defences were those on the beaches; German inland defensive policy involved thinly held defensive lines and a hard-hitting mobile reserve of Panzers and infantry that would assault any Allied forces that seized an objective. The preponderance of the German armour in the theatre was arrayed against the British and Canadians on the east flank, so Anglo-Canadian advances were always met with prompt German counterattacks snapping back on their positions like elastic bands.[24] Even before he assumed command of II Canadian Corps in early

1944, Lieutenant-General Simonds, on the basis of his experiences in Sicily and Italy, had foreseen the need to prepare for counterattacks:

> As long as fresh reserves are available the Germans will counter-attack heavily and continuously ... The success of the offensive battle hinges on the defeat of the German counter-attacks, with sufficient of our own reserves in hand to launch a new phase as soon as the enemy strength has spent itself. The defeat of these counter-attacks must form part of the original plan of attack which must include arrangements for artillery support and the forward moves of infantry supporting weapons – including tanks – on the objective.[25]

General Crerar, addressing his officers a month before D-Day, similarly warned: "The German is very prone to initiate local counter-attacks, and very quick and good at doing them. It follows that Canadian unit and sub-unit Commands must be thoroughly imbued with the necessity of the speediest possible organization and consolidation of any objective which has been secured and which it is intended should be held."[26]

This was not prescience; the German approach to defence had not changed radically since the First World War, in which Crerar had fought. Battle experience questionnaires indicated that organizing defence against rapid counterattack was typical in Normandy: 71 percent, including virtually all the infantrymen who served in rifle companies, indicated that they had had to defend against German counterattacks.[27] "The counter-attack came so quickly that we had no time to ever dig in," reported Major G.E. Colgate of the South Saskatchewan Regiment. "Tanks, mortars, and machine guns were used against us within ten minutes of our gaining the objective."[28] A rifle company commander with the Royal Hamilton Light Infantry reported similar experiences: "Possibly the most difficult phase of battle is the consolidation and the repelling of enemy counter-attacks, especially if the enemy is supported by tanks."[29] Captain Sinkewicz, an intelligence officer, likewise noted: "Immediately after our troops had taken a position a counter-attack was launched by 3 to 5 [German] tanks and probably a platoon of infantry ... doing speculative shooting, spraying the ground in all directions [with fire]."[30] This knee-jerk counterattack response from the Germans was effective in preventing Anglo-Canadian breakthroughs on their front, but was very costly in manpower and resources, and was one of the key mechanisms by which the Canadians and their Allies were able to progressively grind the Germans down through attrition.

Aggregate data from the battle experience questionnaires indicate that an even higher proportion of officers in Normandy than in Italy – about 82 percent – reported putting their battle drill training into practice as fire-and-movement tactics in Normandy, with about two-thirds of these indicating that they used these tactics "often" or "fairly often."[31] Major Crummer reported that his troops did "fire and movement on almost every operation," and Major R.D. Redland, a rifle company commander with the Queen's Own Rifles, wrote in his questionnaire: "battle drill is only a form, a good one, of expressing and explaining fire and movement ... careful recce, repetition, over and over, of plans and orders, then the employment of fire and movement, are a firm guarantee to success."[32]

Canadians may have been over-enthusiastic when carrying out fire-and-movement. A Regina Rifle Regiment "combat lessons" assessment issued on 3 August 1944 mentioned that, "It was found that fire control on the sec[tion] level during an attack was weak," meaning that soldiers were making too much uncontrolled use of their personal weapons; however, the report noted that, "After the first day or so [in combat], fire discipline in the defence was good."[33] The Stormont, Dundas and Glengarry Highlanders issued a similar "lessons learned" report in mid-July: "The important point is to impress all to cover their sector and task, and not to open fire frontally and indiscriminately on any slight alarm. Withholding fire until enemy is at close range is very effective and really does break up the attack. This applies to both infantry and armour ... Enemy counter-attacks by infantry and armour can be broken up if fire is withheld."[34] The fire discipline of the Germans was frequently admired. An account by Sergeant Benson of the Black Watch emphasized one example: "[German] fire control, even with foreign-born [troops], must be extraordinarily good. He permitted us to walk all the way through May-sur-Orne where he must have had at least two companies hidden, and held the fire of all these men while we marched through ... Although he did not fire we afterwards found that May-sur-Orne was completely prepared," a ploy that helped to almost wipe out the Black Watch in that fight.[35]

There were concerns about burning through ammunition too quickly, such as in an account of Operation ATLANTIC by Lieutenant J.A.C. Auld of the Queen's Own Rifles, wherein he noted that in a fight in the town of Giberville there was a serious depletion of ammunition: "the co[mpan]y had been firing constantly and much am[munitio]n had been expended already in giving covering fire. The failure of the 18 [wireless] set made immediate replenishment impossible." Enemy fire was "replied to with what small arms remained, use being made even of German weapons."[36] Major Crummer noted with concern that his company engaged in "indiscriminate, very inaccurate firing of inf[antry] weapons to impress large number of enemy troops opposing using tracer at night, bouncing off roads, etc., hoping to lower morale."[37] Commanders wanted soldiers to make "every bullet count" in order to conserve ammunition, but on the ground – particularly among nervous and inexperienced troops – behaviour did not always match expectations. A former platoon commander with the Algonquins wrote: "I found that the men have the utmost faith in the Bren gun and were willing to carry it at any time, even to carry extra ammunition, and to the point of wanting to have the Bren rather than a rifle at any time. I saw one platoon carrying four [Bren] guns and the required ammo for each even though it was understrength by seven men."[38]

Particularly interesting is that more Canadian junior officers from Normandy reported their units employing fire-and-movement tactics in battle (82 percent) than reported that their units had attacked beneath an artillery barrage (only 70 percent).[39] In comparison to Italy, in Normandy a much higher ratio of officers indicated that their units had received preliminary training with the artillery barrage shoots, though the rate was still only about half. A notably greater proportion of officers than in Italy also believed that their troops kept up with the barrage effectively.[40] But while linear barrages were more common in Normandy, Canadian infantry were not always yoked to these shoots, and they found ways to turn concentrated artillery fire into a flexible tool. An 8th Brigade "lessons" report from early August 1944 was instructive: "the opinion is that, although it is desirable to have a barrage leading the infantry (and tanks) onto the objective [in the attack], it is of even greater importance [for the artillery] to deal with the probable enemy interference from the flanks of the advance and from behind the objective." The report continued: "The ideal plan would appear to be one that: (a) Deceives the enemy as to position of our infantry; (b) Boxes-in the enemy troops in the area of the objective with the dual purpose of destroying them there and also preventing them withdrawing to a forming-up point from which to launch counter-attack; (c) Neutralizes 'possible' enemy positions outside the path of barrage that could affect the advance or the holding of the objective." 8th Brigade planners decided that three-quarters of the artillery in any attack should be employed on alternate supporting fire tasks and should not simply be used as a barrage to shepherd infantry onto their objective.[41] 7th Brigade "lessons learned" spoke further on the same subject: "The battalion or the companies can make their way forward by use of their own fire power, but it is usual also to have the assistance of artillery to take on targets that cannot be reached by the battalion weapons or can best be seen from an observation post by an Artillery Forward Observation Officer."[42]

Heavy bombardments were never as accurate as hoped. In a "lessons learned" memo (circulated prior to II Canadian Corps being activated in the field) Lieutenant-General Simonds wrote: "[The effect of artillery bombardment] is 90% moral. The actual casualties to the defenders inflicted by covering fire is always a very small proportion of their total numbers."[43] Junior officers knew this. As Captain F.T. Rea wrote about his experience in Normandy: "From personal observation of operations in vicinity of St. André-sur-Orne … even the heaviest arty barrages and bombs cannot take out well dug-in weapons."[44] Artillery could provide excellent covering and neutralizing fire, and its effect on the enemy could, according to one German source, be "soul-shattering" for morale, but a tremendous weight of artillery fire (bringing in guns from the corps or army) or else direct observation or good spotting was needed for it to have a destructive or direct killing effect.[45] Operational research carried out after the D-Day landings found that the pre-invasion bombardment neutralized the enemy only a little and caused even less actual destruction: only an estimated 10 to 20 percent of enemy weapon positions were destroyed by the bombardment, although these studies did not account for the neutralization effect.[46] Artillery support was definitely an asset, but it was never decisive in and of itself and needed to work as an intelligent and flexible adjunct to infantry movement to be most effective.[47]

Overwhelming air power continued to work in the Allies' favour. "No single factor," claims the British official history, "did so much to assist the Allied armies' victory as the sustained air attack which seldom ceased and which rose at times to almost unbearable intensity ... the German air force could neither hit back ... nor defend itself effectively."[48] During and after the war the Germans certainly identified the Allies' air supremacy as the major key to their undoing in Normandy, usually to absolve themselves of failures on the ground.[49] The Allied air forces certainly did achieve complete air supremacy over the German Luftwaffe in Normandy.[50] Evidence indicates that direct air support was often available to infantry units, even if it was not omnipresent: precisely two-thirds of officer respondents from Normandy indicated on their questionnaires that they had received direct air support in combat.[51] When asked about the effectiveness of that support, only one single officer from the Normandy campaign rated it ineffective, and two-thirds indicated that the air support they received was "effective."[52] Air support was also ranked on the questionnaires as the third-highest factor "which had the effect of raising morale" behind rations and mail (see Appendix G).[53]

But was there a difference between the *actual* effectiveness of air support and its *perceived* effectiveness on the part of infantrymen? Two-thirds of respondents rated the air support effective, and virtually none rated it ineffective, but the one-third who responded with "Not Known" is conspicuously large, and indicates that the effects of air power may not always have been visible or perceptible by the infantry. Certainly the Allied air forces kept the air swept clean of German planes – which was indispensable. But operational research studies carried out in Normandy indicate that tactical air force pilots did not do as much damage to the enemy on the ground as they claimed: one report from August 1944 stated that pilots claimed to have destroyed about four times as many German vehicles as researchers actually confirmed destroyed on the ground.[54] A different study carried out on ground-support Typhoon aircraft concluded that anything except the largest immobile targets were very difficult for aircraft to hit, and that dozens of sorties and hundreds of rockets would be needed, on average, for just a 50 percent chance of successfully hitting a single tank or small gun position.[55] On the other hand, close air support was similar to artillery in that a "near-hit" sortie causing a tank column to scatter or the enemy in a bunker to keep their heads down could neutralize the enemy nearly as efficiently as a direct hit, and would certainly keep eyes pinned skyward. Regina Rifles combat lessons mention that even against static defences "air bombardment does not appear to be particularly effective but the effect on personnel is demoralizing. Infantry attacking immediately after can subdue the defenders quite easily."[56] The "moral power" of close air support was extremely potent, and the sight of Allied planes overhead was a tremendous morale-builder for the Canadians in Normandy.

Infantry-tank interaction and cooperation were ubiquitous in Normandy. Fully 75 percent of officer respondents from this campaign indicated that their units had worked in close cooperation with tanks.[57] To a much higher degree than in Italy, however, the tanks had a (perceived) tendency to operate well behind the infantry rather than lead the way.[58] When characterizing the Normandy battlefield, John English observed that the best armoured country was that with the fewest anti-tank guns, the sentiment with which a 7th Brigade combat lessons report from Normandy would have agreed: "The co-operation of infantry and armour envisaged as being a wall of steel followed by a wall of flesh does NOT in fact exist. The armour in this flat country cannot possibly go flat out to the objective and survive against the well-placed and -concealed enemy anti-tank guns. Therefore, they work their way forward on a flank, usually supporting the infantry by fire."[59] As Captain Harry Blanshard of the Fort Garry Horse wrote in his (armoured corps) battle questionnaire: "Practically all our work has been in support of Infantry with Sherman tank equipment. The Sherman is vulnerable to enemy anti-tank equipment, particularly at short range."[60] The vulnerability of Allied armoured fighting vehicles had been demonstrated in Italy, but the dense Normandy battlefields and the proliferation of armoured divisions in the beachhead produced new tactical problems. Tanks rarely operated in front of their supporting infantry, as the Allies' Sherman tanks were easy prey for German armoured vehicles and anti-tank guns. As a result, many infantrymen, who also understandably felt that they were easy prey, complained that the tank crews supporting them were too reluctant to behave aggressively, and refused to support the infantry closely if there was even the possibility of coming under enemy fire.[61] However, officers also noted that tank support provided a major boost to morale regardless of its relative disadvantages, and the consensus was that tanks could still play an effective role, even if tank crews' apprehension of their own vulnerability prevented them from supporting the infantry in the direct, omnipresent way that the infantry would have preferred.[62]

Flame and incendiary weapons became available much earlier in Normandy than in Italy, but difficulties with waterproofing flame weapons meant that they were not used extensively in the initial D-Day assaulting landings or the beachhead battles but became more prevalent during the inland push.[63] Captain Reginald Smith of the Stormont, Dundas and Glengarry Highlanders wrote the following about the vehicle-mounted Wasp flamethrower: "This weapon is extremely effective and a great morale builder in the battalion. The enemy dislike it intensely and we use it whenever possible. We found that the enemy was quick to surrender after seeing some of their men burned with the Flame. We had very good results from the use of Flame in our battalion."[64] Captain Guy Levesque of the Fusiliers Mont-Royal referred to the flamethrower as "the weapon that the Germans didn't fight back [against]."[65] Other infantrymen had similar comments on how flame weapons boosted morale among Canadians, usually because of the terror they inflicted upon the Germans.[66] A mid-August 1944 evaluation by the S.D.&G. Highlanders, who were on the cutting edge of employing flame weaponry, described the dramatic effect of the Wasp flamethrower: "The main feature of this weapon is that it is totally demoralizing. The enemy withdraws whether burned or not. The enemy, when engaged, ran <u>SCREAMING</u>." The report also concluded that flame weapons should not be treated as a panacea: "As the fuel capacity is most limited ... the Wasp is useless in a War of Movement."[67] On the Canadian front in Normandy, however, war was usually fought at a walking pace, and by the end of the campaign flame weapons were being prized for both efficacy and terror effect. There were reports of German soldiers abandoning all equipment to flee a position under attack by flame-throwing tanks (designated "Crocodiles").[68] Flame weapons would find much greater application later in the Northwest Europe campaign, but as early as Normandy they were seeing widespread use and their effect was considerable: of the twenty-six battle experience questionnaire respondents from Normandy who indicated having seen flame weapons used in battle, over half listed them as "outstandingly effective."[69]

The Canadian infantry in Normandy enjoyed the advantage in materiel and wanted to put it to work in extricating themselves from their unhappy situation at the sharp end whenever possible, whether that meant employing artillery, air power, automatic fire, or incendiary flame weapons. Infantry riflemen could partially compensate for the extraordinarily heavy casualties they faced by multiplying the firepower they carried. Officers in Normandy expressed a notable faith in the training regimes that had prepared them for combat. Although some elements were lacking, the Canadians believed in general that they had been well prepared for combat in Normandy. As Brigadier K.G. Blackader, commander of the 8th Canadian Infantry Brigade, which assaulted Juno Beach, commented to a historical officer in July 1944: "All the special training of the previous eight months had been carried out along thoroughly sound lines and had very well fitted the division for its task."[70] There seems to have been little perception that the Canadians' infantry training left them ill-prepared for the fighting in Normandy, and it provided an important basis for the swift trust that would prove to be so important to small-group cohesion.

MORALE

Even more so than in Italy, the battle experience questionnaires provide a look at what junior officers fighting in Normandy considered to be the main determinants of morale in their units and sub-units. (The full data tables are replicated as Appendix G.) Just as in Italy, junior officers in Normandy viewed creature comforts and contact with home as the main determinants of Canadian morale. However, the role of receiving good information and keeping knowledge flowing between high command and the man on the ground was also crucial. Keeping soldiers connected to the "bigger picture" of their actions filled a much-needed void; and correspondingly, nothing depressed morale more than the sense that soldiers were out of the information loop. A staple of the discussion of the Canadians in Normandy has been the affirmation that, to quote historian Brian Reid, "for the most part the [Canadian] soldiers were fighting for themselves and their buddies and the reputation of their unit, not for any inspirational theme or national goal," in contrast to a perception among historians that the Germans held a fanatical belief in regime and leader.[71]

The questionnaire evidence suggests, however, that the Canadian soldier had a broad vision and investment in the war effort. A contemporary report from the 7th Brigade corroborated:

> The morale of all troops is greatly affected by knowing "what is going on." This is particularly so of Canadian troops whose mental horizon stretches well beyond the edge of a slit trench. The role of the British Army in this campaign has necessitated the individual soldiers spending a lot of time sitting in his slit trench without much apparent happening around him. "What's new?" is a query heard a hundred times a day. If it is possible to get down to the soldier in his slit trench up-to-date news of what is happening by other attacking formations, he keeps his morale up with the knowledge that someone else is doing the damage. If a "Situation Report for the Soldier" was instituted and sent out frequently containing up-to-date news then he will sit and take it with a smile, whether "it" be boredom or mortaring.[72]

The average Canadian soldier also remained well connected to Canadian life and culture back home. Particularly in Normandy, on a crammed foothold on a continent, the postal corps did a heroic job of keeping the mail moving. According to the questionnaires, the availability of mail and parcels was a prime determinant of soldiers' morale in Normandy; trans-Atlantic connections to home and family played a tremendous and largely unacknowledged part in supporting the war effort. As the Calgary Highlanders' battalion war diary of mid-July 1944 related: "A large mail arrived today including parcels and much belated letters plus some new letters. Mail is a very important item in our life and the Quartermaster is simply besieged when he brings up our mail."[73] In the entire time they spent abroad, for most Canadians fighting overseas the ties to home had never been closer.

We can learn as much from messages the troops were sending back as from what they were receiving. Censorship reports paint a broader picture of the state of Canadian morale in Normandy. Letters home from the period indicated that soldiers had been plagued by anxious expectation in the months leading up to the invasion, but: "On 6 June 1944 the tone of the mail underwent a complete change … the high morale crystallized and relief that the long period of waiting is over is apparent."[74] Back in England, the soldiers of 2nd and 4th Divisions, who would not make it to Normandy until July, wrote home about the effect of 3rd Division's invasion on their mentality. One unnamed 2nd Division sergeant wrote: "It's hard by day or by night to take one's mind off those boys on the beaches ... The effect on the younger fellows (I mean those who ... expect to cross the Channel themselves in a short time) is truly electric. There's a new seriousness, less talk about wanting to go back to Canada on the basis of a discharge, because deep down in everyone's heart and conscience is the realisation that our place is right here."[75] Among those embroiled in the actual fighting, the censors reported: "Morale was excellent. Troops who had been in action were confident of their superiority to the enemy. Troops waiting to go into action were equally confident, both of their ability to give a good account of themselves, and of the quality of their equipment. Even when weary after battle, troops showed no inclination to avoid further action."[76] As far as censors' reports could tell, there was little decline in overall morale or fighting spirit throughout the Normandy battles, athough one censor mentioned reading, "Signs of weariness and nerves were observed in ... 2nd Cdn Div[ision]" in correspondence from early August, after the punishing events of Operations ATLANTIC and SPRING.[77] Throughout the fighting in Normandy censors also mentioned how frequently Canadian soldiers proclaimed their superiority to the enemy. Much of this was bravado, perhaps putting on a brave face for friends and family at home, but since the censors also reported quite frankly on problems of morale and included remarks from letters that indicated troops were burning out and exhausted, there is little reason to think that the reports do not reasonably represent contemporary morale issues.[78] As in Italy, the weather also played a disproportionately important role in the fighting spirit of the soldiers. A July 1944 report from the Calgary Highlanders' "B" Company noted that, "The rain and mud were very detrimental to the men's spirits but it soon dried up and all was forgotten."[79]

With the previously established cautions in mind, the state of infantry morale in Normandy can also be examined through the lens of the disciplinary offence statistics. (Detailed offence statistics for the three Canadian divisions committed to Normandy, as compiled by CMHQ's Discipline & Pay Section, are reproduced as Appendix E.) All three divisions experienced "spikes" in offences just prior to their deployment to Normandy: 2nd Canadian Division had an astonishing 1,442 offences against it in June 1944, 722 from the infantry battalions alone – over twice as many as 1st Division experienced at any time during the Italian campaign. 3rd Division and 4th Armoured Division were not far behind.[80] Once the divisions were on the ground, however, the number of offences – and particularly the number of charges being laid against members of the infantry battalions – plummeted almost to zero, much lower than at any time during the Italian campaign (see chapters 3 and 4). The low numbers of offences could represent either an actual reduction in acts of indiscipline or a diminished intention on the part of provosts and COs to enforce the disciplinary code. Both were likely contributing factors. Few COs felt the need to "make an example" of troops in order to maintain discipline in Normandy, indicating that they were generally pleased with soldiers' conduct. There is also the consideration that in Normandy there was little opportunity for troops to go "on the loose," as an article in the *Canadian Army Training Memorandum* put it, and get into the sorts of trouble that contributed the lion's share of offences. By the end of August 1944, the Allies had landed two million men on the Normandy coast, 820,000 of them in the Anglo-Canadian zone, packed into a thin slice of a French province that itself was one-quarter the size of New Brunswick. There were few places to go in the beachhead that were not being directly used for military activity, and few opportunities were given for leave and recreation. The high-intensity operations in Normandy meant that even those soldiers who did go AWL were often treated with understanding. One company commander with Le Régiment de Maisonneuve contextualized the problem: "Fatigue was a serious problem with our unit due to the lack of rest. We had numerous cases of first-class soldiers going AWL for a few days. The reason given by them on their return was that the only way they could get any rest was by going AWL."[81] During the Normandy summer there were also only 95 suspected cases of self-inflicted wounds spread across three divisions.[82] By every measure prosecution rates among the Canadians were exceptionally low in Normandy, a possible indication that morale remained quite high, or at least that the prosecuting authorities remained content.

The number of Canadian infantrymen taken prisoner by the Germans in Normandy exceeded those of I Canadian Corps in Italy throughout

1944–45: the Consolidated Casualty Lists confirm 923 Canadian POWs from infantry battalions alone during that time span.[83] That amounted to over a battalion's worth of riflemen that had been captured, a distressing prospect given the perpetual shortage. These losses should, however, again be placed within the context of those of the Germans. The exact number of German prisoners taken by Canadians is not recorded, although most narratives mention vast numbers of prisoners and the large POW cages set up to temporarily house them in the beachhead. It is estimated that the Allies in Normandy took at least 200,000 Axis prisoners of war.[84] Early and late in the campaign, when circumstances were fluid and German positions were being consistently overrun, the number of Germans who gave up was tremendous. The Germans in Normandy are always credited with fighting hard, but they could also surrender in droves, particularly "foreign-born" troops serving the Nazi war machine. Lieutenant J.A.C. Auld of the Queen's Own Rifles, in giving an account of one of the actions in Normandy to an historical officer, described the behaviour of the Germans: "The numerous enemy [in Giberville] were not prepared for a desperate struggle. Even a small return of fire frightened them and any show of force against a position invariably resulted in some at least surrendering."[85] Some historians have claimed that German troops experienced virtually no neuropsychiatric casualties.[86] But the disparity in numbers of POW captures and the greater willingness of the Germans to surrender and desert (even when they half-expected to be shot) clearly represented a "way out" of an intolerable situation for them and should be explored as a phenomenon related to Allied neuropsychiatric casualties.[87] A much greater proportion of Canadian POWs were captured in combat and had surrendered only after all other alternatives had been exhausted.

Neuropsychiatric casualties were high in Normandy among the Canadians. The fighting was brutal and almost inescapable; from June through the middle of August most progress could only be measured in yards, and from the infantryman's perspective it was difficult to distinguish victory from defeat. The Canadian battles were particularly attritional, costly, and frustrating prior to the breakout, and even the junior officers were aware that their task (until August) was to draw German units from other parts of the front and to kill them.[88] A Second British Army psychiatric report for July 1944 estimated that while "exhaustion" casualties composed between 16 and 19 percent of all non-fatal casualties amongst the British I Corps, XXX Corps, and VIII Corps, 28 to 29 percent of II Canadian Corps' casualties over the same period of time were neuropsychatric.[89] The psychiatrist in question found that: "the greatest number of NP casualties occurred when the troops were very tired, very static, dug-in, and under heavy counterattack. Fully 80 percent of the NP casualties complained bitterly of mortar fire and 88mm artillery." Mirroring opinions from Italy, he also believed that many of the NP casualties were "untrained reinforcements" rather than longer-service troops.[90] Rather than being attributable to some inherent deficiency among Canadians, or to persistent morale problems, the higher Canadian NP casualty rates may have been due to the fact that the Canadian divisions spent considerably more time in combat in Normandy than did the British, and that most of that time was spent in largely static, frustrating, attritional warfare.[91] It did not help that the Canadians were ill-prepared to meet the mental health crisis in Normandy, and that the Canadian high command saw battle exhaustion as more of a matter for discipline and punishment than for medical treatment.[92]

Despite unprecedented casualties, brutal fighting, and high neuropsychiatric casualties sustained during the Battle of Normandy, Canadian morale appears to have held steady, and exploded into jubilation at the end of the summer when victory appeared close. The sense of purpose and tangible accomplishment, and soldiers' identification of their own roles within the Allied war machine, helped hold morale together throughout the fighting even while German morale disintegrated. Many soldiers were burned out and discontented, and at times entire units could be described as "looking worn out and very weary," as the Stormont, Dundas and Glengarry Highlanders were by their own war diarist at Tilly-la-Campagne.[93] But in aggregate, evidence indicates that collective spirits remained very high during these three bloody months.

Canadian veterans interviewed years after the end of the war almost unanimously express respect for their German opponents. Contemporary documents, however, indicate a complex interplay of feeling between the adversaries in Normandy. The well-documented murder of 156 Canadian prisoners of war by German soldiers of the 12th SS Panzer Division (Hitler Youth) is the best-known outcome of this interplay. The event became central to the way Canadians perceived their enemy and understood their task.[94] 3rd Canadian Division hit Juno Beach in Normandy without prior battle experience, but with well-established images of the Germans in mind. 2nd Division, arriving a month later, had lost 3,300 men in a day of fighting at Dieppe back in 1942, and many survivors were eager to exact some measure of revenge. The training the Canadians had received in Canada and England had promoted an aggressive style of fighting on the part of infantrymen and, according to some reports, had contained implicit and explicit exhortations toward ruthless behaviour against the enemy and cultivated a "take no prisoners" mentality.[95]

On D+1, the 3rd Division met local counterattacks by the 12th SS Panzer Division, a formation built around a cadre of Eastern Front Waffen-SS veterans and a great mass of fanatical young soldiers drawn from the Hitler Youth.[96] An appreciation by the 8th Canadian Infantry Brigade gave a Canadian perspective on them: "The 12th SS Division, with which we have been most concerned, was composed of young men 17 to 19 years of age, with old Officers and NCOs. The Private soldiers were fanatics, and had been convinced by their Officers that if caught they would be shot. They neither ran nor surrendered."[97] The Canadians ultimately defeated the 12th SS's counterattacks that the Hitler Youth had believed would wipe the invaders out or push them back into the English Channel, and despite their taking hundreds of Canadian prisoners and achieving some local successes, the young Germans' carefully cultivated aura of invincibility had been debunked.[98] Out of a mixture of fear, rage, adrenalin, contempt, an apocalyptic vision of the events unfolding in Normandy, and – in some cases – operating under orders to do so, SS troops began the mass killing of their Canadian prisoners.[99] Some Canadians were killed shortly after surrender; others were systematically executed behind the lines.[100]

Whatever the Germans' motivations and justifications, word spread quickly among the soldiers of the 3rd Canadian Division. Survivors of the massacre who evaded recapture brought back stories, such as one recounted by a sergeant writing home from hospital:

> I am in bed next to a lad who was taken prisoner by the Germans and then shot. He told me all about it and it makes me wonder how our boys keep their heads when they get the Jerries as prisoners. This lad and his chum were taken prisoner when the Huns

> overran the forward positions. After the Germans had taken them about 400 yards back the officer in charge took a machine gun and filled his chum with lead. Then he turned on this lad and shot him – luckily the first shot hit the lad in the leg and he went down. The officer fired several more shots but missed. The lad said the Jerries seemed all out of their minds and jumpy all the time.[101]

The Calgary Highlanders' Captain Ernest Teagle mentioned in a postwar interview: "[We] found about 50 Canadians buried there [on Verrières Ridge], hands wired behind their backs and shot in the head. And the word got out then very quickly."[102] On 1 August 1944, following the circulation of widespread rumours about the murders through II Canadian Corps, General H.D.G. Crerar gave the account to all commanders to be read to all troops in First Canadian Army. Although stating that revenge "must NOT under any circumstances take the form of retaliation in kind," Crerar nonetheless ordered: "Canadian anger must be converted into a steel-hard determination to destroy in battle."[103] Crerar's statement reflected official policy, and Terry Copp is right in asserting: "The reality is that there is no evidence, anecdotal or otherwise, pointing to the killing of [German] prisoners behind Allied lines in response to orders."[104]

Ambiguities, however, remain. "I never heard this myself," claimed Captain Teagle in his postwar interview, "but somebody else said that the Brigadier said that we would take no prisoners for a while."[105] Third-hand accounts do not constitute historical evidence that any orders or suggestions were issued to 2nd or 3rd Division soldiers not to take prisoners, but they reflect something of the ugly mentality in Normandy. One unnamed private, writing home from hospital in late July, was furious: "We found a bunch of our fellows in some of the other Units who were taken prisoner the first few days in France, and we found them all murdered. They were beside a fence and they were all riddled with machine gun bullets. They [the Germans] are not even soldiers but damn filthy beasts. Our boys say, and as far as I go, I will never take a prisoner if I can damn well help it."[106] "You hear all kinds of stories [from the Germans] of how the Allies don't always take prisoners," an officer writing around the same time was quoted by the censors, "or, if they do, take them behind a wall and shoot them. The Canadians apparently are notorious for this."[107]

Perhaps there was cause. The Calgary Highlanders' "B" Company, discussing the observed ruthlessness of the Germans in shooting at Red Cross personnel trying to evacuate casualties, mentioned: "At approximately 1530 hrs 25 July 1944 a large force of enemy, waving a white flag and carrying arms, appeared. Our tanks inflicted heavy casualties on them, the remnants disappearing over the hill."[108] An enthusiastic lance-corporal writing from No. 11 Canadian General Hospital described a mix of feelings: "I'd give anything if I could go back again because I really enjoyed it while I was there, even if it was hell." Referring to the Germans, he angrily wrote: "It's a pleasure to kill those black rats when you see how they have treated the people in France. It's hardly possible for a person to believe that a human being can be so cruel; therefore when we go into action, we were under the impression that the Germans are not human and so you can guess the rest."[109] An even more ominous comment, which speaks to a lasting hatred, was left in the Calgary Highlanders' War Diary at the end of August: "Four German prisoners were taken including two SS men. One is from the SS Panzer (Recce) ... They are a hateful arrogant bunch of heartless humanity and they are given no consideration when they are taken by us. The usual procedure is to have them dig slit trenches exactly to their own measurements."[110]

A cycle of hatred – if not tit-for-tat retaliation – was perpetuated in Normandy, fed by word of deed and propaganda, particularly on the part of the Germans. Many German units –particularly the SS – operated under the impression that they would be shot if captured by Canadians, something they were told in the Sicilian campaign too. Captain Teagle related one story from the Falaise Gap in August: "The prisoners we took going into the Falaise Gap, when we did take some of those SS youngsters, one of my carrier drivers spoke German, [and] I said to him, 'I'm awfully tired, why don't we get these characters to dig some slit trenches for us,' because we had some mortar fire coming in, and he did and these kids started to cry. They thought they were digging their own graves. They'd been told that we did this."[111] A 6th Brigade officer made note of a similar phenomenon in his letter home: "I saw some German prisoners about a week ago and their main question was whether we were Canadian or Poles. They add that they had been told by their Officers that if they should be captured by Canadians or Poles they would be shot, of course they were more than surprised when they discovered that we were Canadians, and that a Canadian doctor was attending to their wounds and fixing them up instead of having them shot."[112] Some [German] prisoners were terrified," confirmed a report written by the CO of the Calgary Highlanders. "In one case a Calgarian was attempting to sort POWs. He told them to line up against a wall. At once two or three were down on their knees praying, expecting that that would be the last wall they would stand against."[113] As in Sicily and Italy, acrimony was also engendered by the perceived "dirty tricks" of the Germans. Captain Teagle recalled something he had witnessed: "One of our officers being killed on the way up to Falaise ... by this kid, just jumped out of a hole in the field, a little slit trench hole in a field, and emptied a Schmeisser into him. And then threw the gun down and put his hands up ... he didn't get more than one pace and then the Bren gunner shot him."[114] And as one gunner would observe some years later, when dealing with the Hitler Youth, "We had a saying in Normandy, 'Take these guys to the beach and be back in ten minutes!'"[115]

Many Canadians fought for revenge, and the number of small, unauthorized atrocities that were exchanged, particularly between the Canadians and the 12th SS, can never be fully accounted for. One unnamed officer described how at least some of the Canadians viewed themselves after fighting in Normandy: "You hear great stories of the fighting qualities of the Canadians – apparently from impartial observers. On the attack they are the most ferocious, cruellest, dirtiest, foulest soldiers going who stop at nothing."[116] Evidently these were taken to be positive qualities.

COHESION AND MOTIVATION

The magnitude of the casualties suffered by infantry battalions in Normandy defined everything else about combat for the soldiers at the sharp end. Between June and September 1944, 3rd Division's battalions lost 5,803 other ranks and 335 officers; 2nd Division lost 5,504 other ranks and 336 officers; and 4th Armoured Division, committed to battle in August (and possessing fewer infantrymen), suffered 960 other ranks and 53 officer casualties.[117] Figure 5.1 shows the ratios of cumulative casualties to initial strengths, with distinctions between ranks.[118] In July and August 1944, the 2nd and 4th Divisions' battalions suffered a higher rate of casualties than any other Canadian formation at any other point in

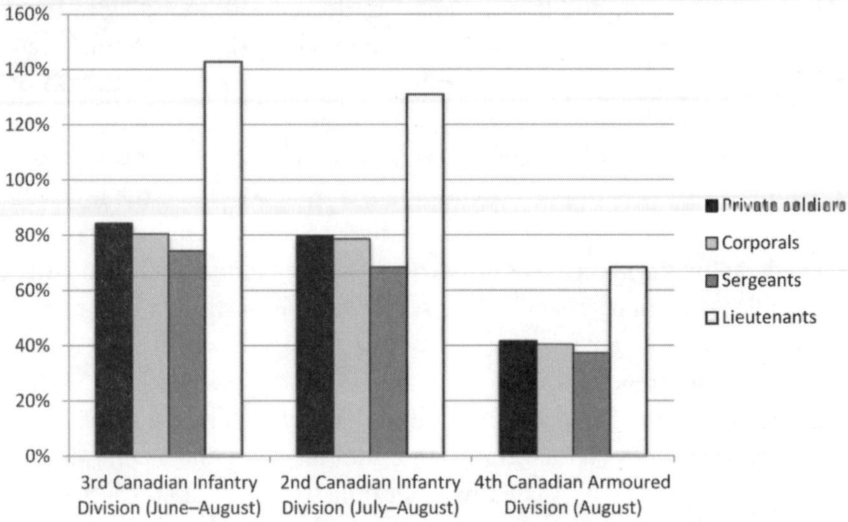

Figure 5.1: Cumulative infantry casualties, Normandy 1944, as percentage of battalion war establishments

the war, both losing close to half their war establishment of other ranks and well over half their battalion officers each month. Only 1st Canadian Division's battles on the Moro River and at Ortona in December 1943 came close to these monthly wastage rates. By way of comparison, the Gothic Line battles of August–September 1944 resulted in 34 percent of 1st Division's ORs becoming casualties, whereas in Normandy, over a similar stretch of time, 79 percent of 2nd Division's infantrymen were killed, wounded, or captured. The scale of the bloodletting was exceeded only by the casualties that the Canadians inflicted upon the Germans over the course of those months, which contributed to the wholesale destruction of several German divisions.[119] But for the infantry, every victory in Normandy was pyrrhic.

In his regimental history of the 4th Division's Lincoln and Welland Regiment, historian Geoff Hayes describes the staggering losses:

> If one views the Regiment as so many of its former members do – as a family – then the Regiment was perpetuated by no less than four generations of fighting troops during its time in Northwest

> Europe: the casualties sustained were about equal to the strength of its four rifle companies each being fully replaced four times over. This analogy is not completely satisfactory: some periods were more costly than others, some men survived all ten months of battle ... These men were witnesses to the changing face of the Regiment. These generations are almost (but not completely) distinct; they are bound by a common membership in the Lincoln and Welland Regiment.[120]

A similar statement could be made about any of the battalions deployed in Normandy, though one should include soldiers of platoons in the support company alongside those of the rifle companies, as they were in the thick of the fighting – and dying – too.[121] The men at the front were in constant rotation on account of casualties. With an average casualty rate of 80 percent across all battalions over three months of fighting, only a minority would have recognized one another as original members of the battalions. The experience of the long-service man fighting next to his close buddies and comrades under the familiar regimental colours was swiftly lost beneath the deluge of heavy casualties. Something else had to take its place.

How did cohesion and esprit de corps operate in this inimical combat environment? Censors' reports from Normandy give few indications about soldiers' identification with their senior leadership or formations. Only General Bernard Montgomery was noted as being the object of any specific affection on the part of Canadian troops. Even then the censors noted that most such comments came after the breakout and annihilation of the Germans in Normandy rather than during the hardest fighting. Comments such as, "We are still proud of [Montgomery] and love him very much too, as he is the greatest General ever met in any Army so far," and "[Montgomery's] Caen strategy was brilliant" were noted by the censors in the late summer.[122] But even Montgomery was not the same hands-on presence among the Canadians that he had been in Sicily and Italy. The censors made no mention of any significant references to Canadian senior officers in their reports. The two senior Canadians in Normandy were General H.D.G. Crerar and Lieutenant-General G.G. Simonds, and for all their qualities as administrative and tactical thinkers neither was a particularly inspiring leader of men.[123]

Personal connection and identification with higher formations on the part of soldiers is also difficult to gauge. No equivalent to 1st Division's outpouring of enthusiasm for joining Eighth Army in 1943 is evident in Normandy.[124] Some pride in the accomplishments of 3rd Division as a formation was notable in censors' reports immediately after D-Day; one unnamed rifleman in hospital reflected: "I was in the first wave ... now that I have come through it I wouldn't have missed it for worlds. I'm very proud of the 3rd Division."[125] But in Canada there were no peacetime divisions, and formations above the regiment were perhaps very abstract concepts for infantrymen. According to Harold Margolian: "The bond that the men had formed with their regiment tended to inhibit the growth of loyalties to the higher formations, like brigades or divisions ... Critics of the regimental tradition believed that it produced officers who found it difficult to effectively carry out military operations that had been planned on a brigade or divisional scale."[126]

Regimental identification played a role in combat motivation, although it was probably not as important as regimental histories imply. Censors commented that "magnificent pride of unit was evident" in soldiers' personal correspondence, and that "troops from every formation were confident of their superiority to the enemy."[127] Flagged by the censors as typical was the comment toward the end of August of a private from the North Nova Scotia Highlanders who had been part of a reinforcement draft but still found ways to connect to his regiment: "You can see I'm with the best Regiment in France. I have been with them ever since I've been in France."[128] Of course, these comments were from the end of the Battle of Normandy when the soldiers of First Canadian Army were flush with success and victory. Censors noted such outpourings of regimental spirit less commonly when the fighting was at its fiercest. The problem was that the "original veterans" and other long-standing members of the regiment quickly became casualties, and there was little time or space for reinforcements to become acquainted with the regiment's traditions, histories, or unique systems of meaning while the battle was still ongoing. There also were many fewer "original veterans" – men who had been issued their regimental numbers directly by their regiments at the start of the war – in Normandy with 2nd or 3rd Division than there had been with 1st Division in Sicily. In July–August 1943, 80 percent of

1st Division's infantry sergeants and corporals, and 60 percent of privates had been "originals." With 3rd Division, for whatever reason, less than 70 percent of sergeants, 50 percent of corporals, and 30 percent of privates were "originals." By the end of the fighting in Normandy, these numbers would decline to less than 45 percent of sergeants, and barely 10 percent of privates. When 2nd Division went into battle in July 1944, only 54 percent of sergeants, 42 percent of corporals, and 19 percent of privates among its ranks were still "original" soldiers, and this dropped down to 40 percent of sergeants, 37 percent of corporals, and 12 percent of privates in August.[129] 1st Division as a formation appears to have kept its "originals" together in a way that the other divisions did not.

Further, neither 2nd nor 3rd Division's regiments were as uniform in regional composition as 1st Division's had been when they landed in Sicily a year earlier. At the outset of operations in Normandy, on average 75 percent of the soldiers in any given infantry battalion were from the regiment's home Military District (it had been over 90 percent in 1st Division). And every regiment's regional distinctiveness declined precipitously between June and August 1944; by August the average among all Canadian battalions in Normandy had gone down to only 51 percent, meaning that half of all soldiers in all battalions were no longer from the same part of the country as their regiment.[130] The experience of the Calgary Highlanders was typical: they went from having 70 percent of their soldiers having enlisted in Alberta (having a regimental number beginning with "M," meaning it was issued at a depot in Alberta's Military District 13) in July 1944 to about 45 percent in August.[131] An 11 August War Diary entry from the Highlanders emphasized the changing face of the combat troops: "We are slowly coming up to strength and now we total 756. With the number of reinforcements coming up after the last three weeks fighting, the Battalion does not appear like the old one, with only a very small percentage of the original gang still about."[132] Regional homogeneity was not a necessary prerequisite for regimental pride and *esprit*, but the system was still intended to promote local distinctiveness as a core part of military identity. Successful units had to transcend narrow regional affiliations, because sooner or later a majority or substantial portion of a battalion's soldiers were going to come from outside their home region.

The effects of casualties can be viewed at an even lower level. Not only were the casualties grievous, but the replacement system had a difficult time keeping up with losses in Normandy and was always operating at a deficit; Canadian formations were perpetually understrength. By the end of August 1944, 2nd Canadian Division was operating at a deficiency of 2,612 other ranks (most of them riflemen), and at its high point that month had operated with a deficiency of "only" 1,216 other ranks. On August 31 the total from all three divisions in Normandy was a deficit of 4,318 other ranks below war establishment (the equivalent of about five full infantry battalions), with an average of 206 men lost per infantry battalion.[133] Battle experience questionnaires overwhelmingly indicated that infantry battalions, companies, platoons, and sections all went into battle understrength.[134] Sections often operated with only five or six men (out of twelve) in the middle of a battle. However, despite these losses, 51 percent of junior officers still indicated that even these reduced sections were adequate for close-quarters fighting in Normandy.[135] Depleted units had to find ways to continue functioning if any kind of meaningful success was to be put within reach in Normandy.[136]

Much has been made of the ability of the Germans to rally from defeat, rebuilding the remnants of shattered units into highly combat-effective, cobbled-together "battle groups" called *Kampfengruppen*. The term referred to any kind of battle group, but in 1944–45 they were more frequently ad hoc combined-arms formations and units that could range from an army corps to a single company, but were most commonly battalion-sized.[137] A 2nd Division intelligence report from late July described the Kampfgruppe forming from shattered German units, but warned its readers: "There must be no misconception, however, regarding the fighting effectiveness of such battle-groups. Mustering all they can from wherever they can they will contest our advance hill by hill, village by village."[138] Max Hastings has written: "It is striking to contrast the manner in which Allied units which suffered 40 or 50 per cent losses expected to be pulled out of the line, even disbanded, with their German counterparts who were merely reassembled into improvised battle groups – the *Kampfengruppen*."[139] But this is an inaccurate characterization, at least for the Canadians. Units and especially sub-units of the two Canadian infantry divisions in Normandy faced casualty rates in the 30–40 percent range (higher for the junior leadership) in the space of a single operation on numerous occasions. Canadian staff officers fought tooth and nail to ensure that no infantry field battalion was disbanded or broken up; no recombining of units occurred at the battalion level or higher. However, within battalions there was constant personnel turbulence at the section, platoon, and company level to ensure both that regiments were kept together and that the sub-units were kept up to strength as much as possible.

The process of putting together improvised "battle groups" within battalions was not as visible as was the creation of German *Kampfengruppen*, but from the perspective of the Canadian infantrymen on the ground the effect might have been similar. Men who became lost during the course of a confusing, high-intensity attack would trickle back into headquarters and then be grouped together as new platoons and dispatched to reinforce the companies still at the front.[140] "Readjusting" the battalion was common, particularly when reinforcements were not immediately available, and meant shuffling soldiers so that rifle sections and platoons were kept as close to 100 percent strength as possible (although even then there were always deficiencies). In his battle experience questionnaire Lieutenant-Colonel P.W. Bennett, CO of the Essex Scottish, mentioned: "The present [war establishment] of an infantry section fulfills all requirements. The difficulties arise when reinforcements are not available, but that is one of the problems of war solved only by compromise and by reorganizing two small sections into one normal one."[141] The handwritten "B" Company war diary of the Calgary Highlanders recalled platoons being shattered, scattering, rejoining as small groups of men, and then recombining with other units – including normally non-combat headquarters units – to achieve an objective or consolidate a position, all under their own initiative.[142] A captain in the RHLI reported similar norms: "The strength of a section would often be reduced so that you did not have enough riflemen to put in an attack. Sections had to be amalgamated so that [the] platoon had only two sections."[143] New companies sometimes had to be put together out of the remnants of decimated platoons. Fighting alongside unfamiliar faces and complete strangers quickly became standard operating procedure, with close "buddy" relationships quickly lost track of. The Left out of Battle (LOB) system provided continuity of leadership and provided a "welcome wagon" for reinforcements reaching a battalion.[144] The LOB system did not, however, change the equation: soldiers had to establish quick, cohesive connections with one another on the common basis of respect, reputation, and professional skill, under the guidance of the leadership, which the LOB system preserved.

Canadian soldiers in Normandy were grouped, regrouped, split off for patrols and ad hoc sub-units, organized into new sections, platoons, and companies, and re-integrated after being LOB. New faces continually replaced old ones until, by the end of August, almost all the faces were new. Units continued to function and fight hard on the basis of professional knowledge, thorough individual training, and a trust that the man beside you, even if you did not know him, was trained to a high standard and capable of holding up his end of the job. The battle-experienced groups and ad hoc units brought together by swift trust were sometimes more combat-effective than the inexperienced but highly socially cohesive groups that first went into battle.

Even under the best of circumstances the extraordinarily high casualty rate in Normandy changed the character of each infantry regiment, and after July 1944 most of the Canadian riflemen fighting in France were reinforcements or returned casualties. If "swift trust" bonds were formed among soldiers, the weak link in this process was the reinforcement soldier. Reinforcements were almost always going to be inexperienced, and each had to be taught how to survive and function in battle; their previous training and the crucible of shared experience formed a basis of professional trust. However, if those strangers were not able not live up to expectations of conduct, knowledge, skill, and behaviour, then problems could develop. "First reinforcements were good," wrote Major A.M. Hamilton on his questionnaire, "but became poorer with each new draft."[145] Two company commanders with the Black Watch were particularly scornful of reinforcements. Major William Ewing wrote that, "Weapon handling by reinforcements generally very bad," and "Reinforcements were <u>NOT</u> mentally prepared for battle. They worried generally in a very timid state of mind and had no desire to fight ... Very few reinforcements had the mental characteristics of fighting men and had rather little confidence in their own weapons."[146] Major A.H.M. Carmichael, on the other hand, did not doubt reinforcements' motivation but was skeptical of their skill: "Reinforcements that came to us in large numbers in August/September [1944] ... were willing – even determined – but they were *not* up to infantry standards in infantry work. In particular they were unfamiliar with the PIAT, inexpert with the Bren, in many cases afraid of grenades. We nearly liquidated the lot by marching them 60 to 70 miles."[147] These "inadequate" soldiers were explicitly blamed for many failures. Brigadier H.W. Foster, commanding the 7th Canadian Brigade on D-Day, recounted that, as early as 8 June, the Royal Winnipeg Rifles were overrun by the Waffen-SS, "owing to the fact that one assault company had been practically obliterated on the beach and the gaps in its ranks had had to be replaced by reinforcements of all sorts, some not even infantry."[148]

On the other hand, particularly vocal comments on the quality of infantry reinforcements were very few. Questionnaire responses on the topic of reinforcement efficiency from Normandy returned results similar to those from the Italian campaign: almost two-thirds (62 percent) of officers surveyed indicated that the reinforcements their units received had been of at least "moderate" efficiency, and only about 30 percent rated them as "poor."[149] As Captain W. Parker of the RHLI put it, his soldiers worried about the arrival of reinforcements, not because these men were ill-trained, but because reinforcements often did not show up at all: "[My men] don't mind being under strength so long as they know reinforcements will definitely arrive in the near future. But they never knew when they would come ... Lack of reinforcements was a constant topic with the men. They felt the risk of becoming a casualty was greater, because the strength of a platoon was less ... even poorly trained reinforcements were better for morale than no reinforcements at all."[150] As Appendix G shows, 10 percent of surveyed junior officers cited the lack of availability of reinforcements as a top factor in lowering morale, while only 4 percent cited reinforcements being untrained as lowering morale.[151] Without denying that problems with reinforcement training may have existed, the perception that reinforcements were not suitably trained nonetheless appears to have been a minority view. Most reinforcement infantrymen seemed to have filled the huge gaps left by the casualties quite well, and kept their units fighting at a high tempo. Such soldiers were inexperienced, but their training – and the desperate need for reinforcements – allowed them to integrate swiftly into new shattered and recombined sub-units.

It is accepted theory that untrained reinforcements threatened cohesion in the Canadian Army more than anything else, as they could undermine professionalism and trust in a way that simply having new faces in the line did not; and, further, that it was the perception that newcomers could not be trusted that poisoned "swift trust" and made units inoperable. However, there is evidence that this was not usually the case in Normandy. Officers usually rated reinforcements as satisfactory, and only a tiny percentage of questionnaire respondents reported that morale and effectiveness were adversely affected by low-quality men. Three times as many officer respondents rated receiving reinforcements as a top factor in raising morale as respondents who claimed that untrained reinforcements degraded morale.[152] In Normandy, units found ways to function and work together as teams despite being strangers, and despite the tremendous adversity they faced.

CONCLUSION: GROUNDS FOR SERIOUS RECONSIDERATION

C.P. Stacey, for all his skill as a historian, was not particularly fair to the Canadians who fought in Normandy. In *The Victory Campaign* he quoted a report by the 10th SS Panzer Division from late July 1944 claiming that: "The morale of the enemy infantry is not very high. It depends largely on artillery and air support. ... Whenever enemy is engaged with force, he usually retreats or surrenders." Despite the 10th SS having had little contact with the Canadians, Stacey applied these remarks to First Canadian Army as part of his "balance sheet" on the campaign.[153] But Stacey should have known better. The Germans' perceptions of Allied fighting abilities – which were heavily coloured by Nazi propaganda that portrayed Allied soldiers as unmotivated and having no reason to fight – bears no relationship to the truth in the Canadian case.[154] Historian Marc Milner's recent historiographical examination of the Normandy campaign has shown how incomplete work and biases against the Canadians have cast their performance in Normandy in a dubious light. Milner's latest book, *Stopping the Panzers* (2014), has shown that there are grounds for a serious reconsideration of how well and how successfully the Canadians fought during the Battle of Normandy.[155]

Canadian tactical performance (or perhaps senior leadership) in Normandy sometimes left something to be desired, and as mentioned, there were several instances during the summer of 1944 when attacks failed, orders were refused, leadership faltered, and the will to fight wavered. But the fighting in Normandy was carried out against an elite enemy, against whom there was no numerical superiority, who, after the initial counter-attacks, were defending in-depth. Setbacks and failures would have been expected. That they were so few in number is more remarkable. (Unfortunately, this book's source base does not permit a detailed study of morale and motivation in any given action: it can only speak to the larger aggregate over the timeframe of the entire campaign.) And overall, in Normandy, the Canadian infantry fought with tenacity and skill, remaining cohesive and efficient despite ruinously high casualty rates. Many units were shattered and rebuilt, sometimes on the fly, only to return to the fight combat-capable. Canadian morale may have wavered in the face of the frustrating, slow-moving combat against an enemy whose defence-in-depth was well prepared, but it never broke. In comparing the censors' reports to those from the Italian campaign, it is clear that the soldiers in Normandy, despite suffering casualty rates a dozen times higher, were in a far more positive mood than the troops of I Canadian Corps had been in the static winter lines of 1944 and 1945.

The spirit of the troops, as reflected in letters home, remained at a very high pitch throughout the Normandy summer. Rather than having "no real reason for fighting," Canadians, particularly in Normandy, identified closely with the Allied war effort and strove to locate their own individual efforts within its greater context. It was insufficient to be told to do something; Canadians wanted to know *why* a task should be done and what impact it would have on the war. In Normandy, the soldiers possessed a powerful sense of the monumental events they were involved in and could locate their role within the greater effort, though disasters such as befell 2nd and 3rd divisions during Operation SPRING could strain the will to fight. However, success, and the prospect of fighting the war in the decisive theatre, underwrote high morale, which in turn seems to have positively affected discipline. Canadian infantrymen fought for themselves and for those beside them, even if they did not know them personally, buoyed by the "swift trust" expectation that even strangers in arms would do everything they could to help protect one another under fire and with experience and leadership would contribute effectively to the team. In the face of casualties that could devastate the pre-existing bonds of social and regimental cohesion with which units first went into battle, the ultimate success of the campaign speaks to how strong new impromptu bonds could be. When the war in Northwest Europe turned from a victorious rout of the broken enemy into another frustrating, wearying, endless campaign against a tenacious foe, however, the motivation of Canadian soldiers would be put to its final and most challenging test.

6

The Canadians in Northwest Europe, 1944–1945

The victory in Normandy decided the ultimate outcome of the war in Europe, but protracted fighting over the next eight months demonstrated that Nazi Germany still intended to die by the sword. These months would see the soldiers of First Canadian Army, repurposed as the "long left flank" of the 21st Army Group advance across Northwest Europe, besieging the Channel Ports, opening the port of Antwerp, fighting across the Rhineland, liberating Holland, and directly engaging in the conquest of Germany.[1] The tasks of the Canadians were inglorious but necessary, and the logistical logjam that faced the over-extended Allied Expeditionary Forces in Europe in the autumn of 1944 could only be alleviated by First Canadian Army. Presented with some of the worst conditions and terrain imaginable, the Canadians fought a long, bloody struggle through a waist-deep, watery hell into the heart of the German Reich.

The campaign in Northwest Europe coincided with the height of the Conscription Crisis back in Canada. That the morale and motivation of the Canadian infantry was at a low point during this stage of the fighting is taken for granted in the historiography, but this chapter's exploration of the contemporary documents shows such appraisals to be overblown. All the Allied armies fighting in Northwest Europe experienced significant manpower shortfalls during 1944–45, and the British in particular took to breaking up entire divisions to serve as reinforcement fodder for others, as they had done in Italy.[2] Although the Canadian situation became desperate, they never had to dismantle formations in order to make good on deficits of riflemen, and First Canadian Army remained a capable and accomplished combat force throughout the last stage of the war in Europe.

Treating the Northwest Europe campaign as one continuous campaign is a narrative convenience for this study; in reality the fighting from September 1944 to May 1945 took on distinct stages, few of which had much in common in terms of terrain and opposition. Broadly speaking, the Canadians were involved in a logistical war in the autumn of 1944, and a battle to destroy Germany in 1945.

In September 1944, the German Army was in full retreat eastward across France, with the British 21st Army Group and the US 12th Army Group in pursuit. However, the Allies were operating near the end of their logistical tether. Two million Allied soldiers had been put ashore in Normandy between June and August 1944, plus a secondary force that landed in southern France, and there was no port on the English Channel big enough to be able to sustain their build-up. After Normandy, the rate of Allied advance outpaced the speed with which railway communications and supply maintenance areas could be established.[3] So while the rest of the 21st Army Group pushed across northern France, First Canadian Army was tasked with forcibly opening the Channel ports, investing and capturing key ports at Le Havre, Boulogne, and Calais. The Germans left behind garrisons to render these ports inoperable, and they needed to be captured by means of brutal siege warfare during September 1944 while the Canadians struggled with their own serious logistical and administrative difficulties.[4] But these were either small ports with their facilities damaged, or else they were assigned to the American logistical chain, like Le Havre.[5] What the Allies needed was Antwerp, Europe's second-largest port. The Belgian city fell without a fight in early September, but the approaches to the city along the Scheldt River, which had been one of the heavily fortified keystones of Hitler's *Atlantikwall* defences, were still in German hands. No water traffic could reach the city intact. The German Army Command in the West (*Oberbefehlshaber West*) had received orders on 5 September stressing the fact that the Führer regarded holding the Scheldt fortresses as the most important task on the entire western front.[6] It proved to be so. By October 1944, the Allied offensive was grinding to a halt for want of supplies, fuel, and reinforcements. First Canadian Army undertook the gruelling process of fighting across dykes and through the flooded fields of the Scheldt Estuary in order to open Antwerp as the new logistical nexus for the western front. The Germans were finally dislodged after a month of fighting in terrible conditions and terrain, and by mid-November the Allies' supply difficulties were easing.[7]

The Canadians were in the line for much of November and December, but they saw little sustained action and were in reserve during the Battle of the Bulge, although the 1st Canadian Parachute Battalion, operating as part of the British 6th Airborne Division, fought in the Ardennes. Major combat operations for First Canadian Army began again in February and March of 1945, when they participated in a concerted Allied assault on Germany's Rhineland, the last German redoubt before the Rhine River. First Canadian Army launched an offensive southeastward between the Rhine and Maas rivers, intending to meet a perpendicular American advance at Geldern, Germany. There has been criticism about the strategic decision making associated with the Rhineland campaign, in particular some of the delays that meant the offensive did not begin until the spring, from hard ground to mud and water.[8] The Americans were delayed by enemy-induced flooding along their section of the front, so the Germans managed to concentrate before the Canadians. German paratroopers fought hard to defend the Hochwald Forest, but the Canadians' advance was aggressive, and by the time the American offensive began two weeks later the German reserves were exhausted and on the verge of collapse. Following victory in the Rhineland, First Canadian Army was switched northward (and reunited with the soldiers of I Canadian Corps from Italy) to liberate the Netherlands and occupy northwest Germany as the war in Europe finally wound to a close.

The terrain and the weather defined the Canadian experience in Northwest Europe, and both created serious obstacles for operations. The dyke- and polder-country of Belgium and the Netherlands, and the forests and flooded fields of the Rhineland were as formidable a defensive ground as the mountains and rivers of Italy and the densely fortified plains and ridges of Normandy. The Canadian infantrymen slogging through the Scheldt Estuary in autumn 1944 were particularly adamant that they had never fought on worse ground: "This is the most God awful country I have ever had thrust on me. The damn place is 99% water and the other 1% is about to be or has just been. The only means of getting from point A to B is by the top of the so-called dykes."[9] But it was also a highly varied battlefield, and by the end of the campaign in the spring of 1945 the Canadians were fighting in spread-out, unflooded areas of Holland where they could manoeuvre properly and use armour to their full advantage.[10] Few generalizations can be made, except that the terrain they fought in usually acted as a force-multiplier for the German defenders.

FORCE STRUCTURE

First Canadian Army and the British Second Army constituted the key formations under the command of General Bernard Montgomery's 21st Army Group throughout 1944–45. First Canadian Army remained the principal Canadian formation in Northwest Europe, and during the campaign would also have significant British formations under its command (such as the British I and XXX Corps), as well as Polish and American divisions. By the end of the war in Europe all Canadian ground forces in Europe (save for the 1st Canadian Parachute Regiment, which, as mentioned, was part of the British airborne forces) would be united under General H.D.G. Crerar's First Canadian Army. In March–April 1945, I Canadian Corps and its two divisions, the 1st Canadian Infantry and the 5th Canadian Armoured (plus an independent armoured brigade) were removed from Eighth Army in Italy and reunited with the other Canadian formations in time for final combat operations in the Netherlands and Germany.[11] II Canadian Corps would continue to operate throughout Northwest Europe with the 2nd and 3rd Canadian Infantry Divisions, as well as the 4th Canadian Armoured Division, under its command.

BEHAVIOUR IN BATTLE

The eight months between September 1944 and April 1945 saw the Canadians always on the offensive, attempting to advance and either destroy or capture the enemy. At the tactical sharp end, however, they were often thrown onto the defensive, locally, in order to cope with the violent counterattacks that the Germans continued to rely upon. As Terry Copp and Roger Vogel outlined in their *Maple Leaf Route* series: "the German command … persisted in its by-now 'doctrinaire' policy of repeated local counterattacks … every German commander believed that the important thing in counterattacks was speed 'to strike the enemy before he can improve his position and prepare a defence in the areas he penetrated to.'"[12]

Counterattacks forced the Canadians back onto the tactical defensive as they struggled to consolidate new positions, and they usually represented the critical stage of the fighting. The battle experience questionnaires continued to reflect the necessity of planning to defeat German counterattacks in Northwest Europe: almost 70 percent of officer respondents reported having to organize "rapid defence against counter-attack" in their infantry units, a ratio virtually identical to its counterpart for Normandy.[13] "Possibly the most difficult phase of battle," wrote Major Froggett of the Royal Hamilton Light Infantry in a questionnaire annex, "is the consolidation and the repelling of enemy counter-attacks, especially if the enemy is supported by tanks." The major advised lots of grenades, a "tight company defence," the necessity of tolerating German infiltration of Canadian lines, and continuous fighting even when this created the impression of being surrounded; and he recommended that infantry commanders should not hesitate to call down an artillery strike on their own position if being overrun. "If his [company] is properly dug-in, his casualties will be light, but to the enemy [counter-attacking] above ground the reverse is apparent."[14] Anti-personnel land mines often had to be laid in front of new positions in order to keep the Germans from physically reaching them during counterattacks.[15] Artillery was of significant assistance as well, and throughout the Northwest Europe campaign the Germans had no answer for the Allied guns. A "lessons learned" document from late 1944 by the Highland Light Infantry's Major R.G. Hodgins indicated that his unit owed its success against enemy counterattacks to "the very great determination and initiative of our troops which can overcome the enemy's advantages, which include complete familiarity with the ... terrain; and the skilful employment of artillery. [Forward Observation Officers] were placed well forward with the infantry."[16]

While the Germans could gain local success with aggressive counterattack, and used it to prevent Canadian exploitation, it was a self-defeating tactic. By the end of the Second World War, the Canadians, British, and Americans were preparing countermeasures: rapid consolidation, lavish fire support, and a "bite and hold" style of seizing limited objectives and allowing the Germans to wipe themselves out counterattacking.[17] Even elite German parachute and armoured units could be guilty of doctrinal rigidity, pressing forward in repeated frontal assaults after the Canadians had gone over to the defensive, in spite of unsupportable heavy losses. Northwest Europe was a showcase for such behaviour.[18] The "bite and hold" manner of fighting was slow and methodical, and few commanders were pleased to be fighting in such a conservative manner, but it was more punishing to the Germans than it was to the Allies and it permitted the great Allied superiority in artillery to be brought to bear.[19] But it was still the infantry who had to win the fight at close quarters during the advance and consolidation. As Major Hodgins observed in the Breskens pocket, "Despite the enemy's frequent counterattacks, he very rarely recovered any ground."[20] And as an oblique comment from a 4th Canadian Armoured Division soldier put it, "At least [the Germans] are out in the open and it is always easier to kill a rat out of his hole than in it."[21]

The close country that the Canadians were fighting through in Northwest Europe, including the siege warfare of the Channel coasts, the dyke-and-polder areas of Belgium and Holland, and the flooded fields and thick woods of the Rhineland, placed a premium on infantry action. Armoured support remained important – and the great majority of questionnaire respondents reported having cooperated with tanks – but the ground frequently precluded the use of heavy vehicles.[22] A 4th Brigade "lessons learned" document from the fighting on Zuid Beveland emphasized: "Heavy armour is almost useless preceding infantry where movement is restricted solely to a few roads," as it is in dyke and polder country.[23] Even when the ground permitted the movement of heavy armour, infantry-tank cooperation was often a matter of continued struggle for Canadians. Infantry wanted the tanks to lead the advance or to be up among the infantry, covering the riflemen as closely as a suit of armour on a medieval knight, and lending their firepower and physical presence to the offensive.[24] Armoured corps officers, to the frustration of the infantry, imagined those roles in reverse, with the infantry protecting the tanks from the Germans' lethal and plentiful anti-tank guns, and the tanks lending the infantry the use of their firepower – from a safe distance to the rear.[25] Although they frequently cooperated to great effect, as late as the Northwest Europe campaign Canadian tanks and infantry still lacked a shared set of assumptions about combat, a deficiency in training and doctrine that in retrospect would dog them until the end of the war.[26]

The Canadian infantry division's main source of firepower came from its field artillery: three regiments each of 24 guns firing 25-pound shells. Officers fighting in Northwest Europe reported attacking under an artillery barrage much more frequently than had those in Normandy: about 82 percent versus 70 percent.[27] Not even half, however, indicated that their troops had received any kind of training in cooperating with the artillery before going into battle; to the end of the war this remained an apparent shortcoming in Anglo-Canadian infantry training.[28] It is a testament to the abilities of both the infantry and the supporting artillerymen that two-thirds of respondents still indicated that their troops had been able to effectively operate beneath the barrages.[29] Major J.G. Stothart of the Stormont, Dundas and Glengarry Highlanders had more specific comments to make on infantry-artillery cooperation: "It is my firm opinion that if the Artillery can register and even in some cases when they cannot, the closer the infantry can get to a stonk or a barrage the better the final result. The casualties they may suffer are not in proportion with those they may incur through hesitation or lack of speed in reaching the objective."[30] The true utility of artillery, as discussed in previous chapters, was in suppressing, rather than destroying the enemy, and in this sense it made an excellent adjunct to infantry fire-and-movement tactics. A 3rd Canadian Division study period in November 1944 concluded that the destructive or killing power of the field artillery was materially decreased in the soft, boggy ground of the Dutch polder country; since the main use of artillery there was in persuading the enemy to keep under cover, it was used entirely as an adjunct to infantry fire-and-movement and only erratic artillery fire had to be kept up until the infantry arrived on the spot.[31] The fact that shells were exploding overhead forced the Germans to stay huddled in their trenches and bunkers and caused untold psychological damage, but few fortified positions could be destroyed even by the densest artillery concentrations.[32]

But destructive fire could rarely be counted upon. In Northwest Europe the Canadian infantry most often had to operate with artillery as a supporting arm, calling in concentrations of fire to cover their own movement. And a key part of fire-and-movement remained the infantry's ability to move forward, whether with their own weapons or with supporting fire, in spite of obstacles and poor weather. Small-group actions were preferred. The essence of this manner of fighting, according to Lieutenant-

Colonel Lett, CO of the Queen's Own Rifles in November 1944, was "first to feel out the enemy's positions, then to infiltrate a small group, perhaps only a platoon or section, which can later be expanded into a full battalion."[33] "Large numbers of men are NOT required," reads a lessons learned report from the 10th Brigade from early 1945: "No more than a pl[atoon] can be employed at any one time [in dyke fighting] and not more than one sec[tion] [can] actually advance on the dyke itself. It would seem that a stripped section (5 or 6 men) would be ideal for this task."[34] Ranges were short; a report using aggregated data about weapon usage in Anglo-Canadian rifle companies suggested that the infantry never fought at ranges beyond 400 yards from the enemy, and usually closer than that; truly effective range for rifle fire was closer to 100 yards.[35]

Fire-and-movement tactics remained central to the Canadian way of war in Northwest Europe. Infantry officers who had served in Northwest Europe gave the highest response of any campaign – 84 percent affirmative – to questions about whether they put fire-and-movement and battle drill into practice in combat, and of these about two-thirds indicated using these tactics "often" or "fairly often," a frequency consistent with the Mediterranean campaigns.[36] Training instructions from 2nd Canadian Division HQ from early 1945 highlighted these requirements, stressing that companies had to "be prepared to carry out wide sweeps and outflanking manoeuvres without the [support] of heavy weapons ... Develop to the full the greatest potential that the infantry possesses – mobility – stressing the necessity of getting ahead with infantry weapons alone."[37] As a junior officer with the Highland Light Infantry wrote in April 1945, "We can hold off [the Germans'] best infantry, even his paratroopers, and man for man we can outfight him."[38]

Given the close ranges at which the fighting in Northwest Europe took place, hand-to-hand close combat did occur, perhaps more often in the dyke country and the heavily wooded areas of this campaign than in the open Normandy countryside. Over half of responding officers reported that bayonets had been used in combat in their units, and there are regimental accounts of how the fighting sometimes came down to a bloody melee at close quarters.[39] Despite all the appeals in the training literature to take "the King's steel" to the enemy with bayonet charges, no officer rated the bayonet as an "outstandingly effective" weapon. Neither did anyone rate it as "ineffective," which was interesting given that over 50 percent claimed their units used it in combat. Bayonets and bladed weapons were less frequently employed for close fighting than were grenades, which had wider killer power and possessed the supreme advantage of being usable from behind cover. The No. 36 "Mills Bomb" fragmentation grenade and the No. 77 phosphorus smoke grenade were probably the most common "hand-to-hand" weapons, but even they were rated as "outstandingly effective" by only a minority. The weapons that Canadian officers rated most highly were those that allowed their work to be done from safely behind cover, and from a distance.

Northwest Europe also saw a great expansion in the number of flame and incendiary weapons within infantry battalions. In terms of "clearing" German-held pillboxes, bunkers, trenches, houses, machine-gun nests, and other strongly held positions, flame weapons were found to be almost uniquely effective.[40] Carrier-mounted Wasp flamethrowers could project streams of burning petroleum almost 150 yards under the right conditions, and by aiming the flame projector at a high elevation, Wasps could also rain flaming fuel down over a wide area. The Saskatoon Light Infantry's Lieutenant George Bannerman, discussing the technique of flame throwing with a historical section officer, referred to this area-saturation as "Golden Rain": "The gun is fired at maximum elevation, in the direction of the enemy, with the result that the rod of fuel breaks up in midair into small, ignited blobs of fuel. Depending on the wind, this 'Golden Rain' will cover a very large area of ground. Under normal conditions the zone covered by the 'Golden Rain' extends from roughly 40 yards to 140 yards in front of the 'Wasp.'"[41] This technique was used to great effect during the Leopold Canal crossing. An operational research report indicated that in the later stages of the Northwest Europe campaign, area targets formed about half of all total uses of flame and were highly effective against German slit trenches in the open.[42] Canadian infantry battalions typically had six Wasps each, deployed with the support company, so they had the advantage of being under direct battalion command and were available as often as conditions permitted. Lifebuoy man-portable flamethrowers were also employed, though less frequently, as were Crocodile tank-mounted flamethrowers.[43]

As in Italy, flame weapons in Northwest Europe were equal parts terror and damaging effect. The effects of these weapons on the human body were terrible, and static positions offered defending troops almost no protection from them whatsoever; the burning phosphorus acted as a liquid and could seep into bunkers and covered trenches that could withstand shellfire. An operational research report on the effect of flame weapons on military personnel noted instances when German Waffen-SS troops had stood firm against multiple assaults, but "the sight of one of their number running about covered with flame and screaming was enough to make them [all] break and run."[44]

During the sieges of the Channel ports, Canadian company commanders "quickly discovered that Wasp and especially Crocodile flamethrowers were the most effective means of forcing the enemy to abandon fortified positions. The infantry learned that if they could protect flamethrowers while guiding them into position, a few bursts were usually enough to inspire an enemy surrender.[45] Writing about fighting in the polder country of the Scheldt Estuary, Lieutenant Bannerman reported: "with the enemy occupying positions on one side of a dyke and our own troops on the other, the only weapon which effectively winkled out the enemy was the 'Wasp.' The flame was fired over the dyke, and blobs of ignited fuel set fire to straw and wood-covered trenches. In almost every case, the enemy was driven out of his positions and was immediately cut down by the fire of supporting infantry or machine-guns mounted on the carriers themselves."[46] Flamethrowers were also used to burn away enemy positions in the Rhineland. As one North Shore Regiment soldier wrote in a letter home in early 1945: "We started in with eight flame throwers and only four of [them] got in, but that was enough for the Jerry as they dread that flame and I don't blame them."[47] During the final campaign in the Netherlands during April 1945, fanatical Nederlandsche SS troops had to be dislodged and defeated without employing the indiscriminate destruction of artillery or air power, and flamethrowers combined with infantry assaults were used to rout the enemy without undue harm to the civilian population.[48] Throughout the fighting in Northwest Europe, Canadian infantry were very happy to act as an adjunct to their supporting flame weapons, protecting them until the carriers were close enough to unleash their inferno upon the Germans.

While the flamethrowers could seem like miracle weapons, they had drawbacks. Wasp and Crocodile flame weapons faced limitations of terrain, and the man-portable Lifebuoy weapons were not popular, as they could be distinguished as targets for snipers.[49] Wasps could also be vulnerable to enemy fire and mines, and had to be closely protected by infantry and integrated into a fire plan as a best practice.[50] Flamethrower fuel ran out very quickly, and after a few "squirts" of flame the hose pressure dropped off. The Wasp was also found to be highly inaccurate when used on the move, due to the oscillations of the carrier and the difficulty of controlling the flame projector: the need to fire from a stationary position increased its inherent vulnerability, and made close support and protection by the infantry an absolute prerequisite for its use.[51]

The fighting in Northwest Europe marked some radical changes from the tactics of Sicily and Italy in 1943, but it also showed important continuities. By September 1944 the Allies possessed the full initiative on the ground, and they enjoyed material superiority with no substantive interference from enemy air forces. But while the Canadians held these clear material advantages over the Germans, the fighting was still infantry-intensive. Wherever possible, particularly toward the end of the fighting in 1945, Canadian infantry adopted risk-mitigation techniques. They favoured weapons and behaviours that supplied overwhelming firepower, nullified enemy advantages, and could allow them to do their job safely. Cooperation with air, armour, and artillery were eagerly sought, and were among the top contributors to morale in the Canadian Army. But the other arms boosted morale primarily because the tremendous advantages they conferred could help reduce infantry exposure and casualties. After Normandy, staying alive and unwounded was an increasingly difficult task for the infantry. They would take whatever risks were necessary, but their patterns of behaviour and weapons use indicate little relish for daring. Major Harvey Bailey of the Canadian Scottish Regiment recounted one example of pragmatic fighting in 1945: "[my company] was going to have to go over a forward slope again in broad daylight against a bunch of paratroops, and we'd just got started when we came under quite heavy fire … so nothing doing, I wasn't going to have a Charge of the Light Brigade."[52]

MORALE

In the immediate wake of the victory in Normandy, a sense of collective jubilation washed over First Canadian Army. "The entire mail was permeated with elation created by the rapid advance," noted the field censors in early September 1944. The victory had "raised morale to the highest possible pitch ... Weariness due to prolonged, continuous pursuit was discounted in the general decision to bring the enemy to battle. The Canadian Army, in brief, knows itself to be a victorious army."[53] But less than ninety days later the dreams of a swift victory over Germany were ashes and First Canadian Army's collective morale was supposedly so low that the forces teetered on the verge of disintegration. Much of the evidence used to discuss this moral collapse in the historiography is anecdotal, however, and contemporary documentation suggests that the Canadian Army's morale may not have been in so dire a state.

The uniquely detailed censorship report data gathered by Canadian Army Overseas (CAO) personnel attached to the 21st Army Group allows a look at the "big picture" of morale in Northwest Europe on an empirical level unavailable during the other campaigns.[54] It is worth looking at some of their results, shown in Figure 6.1. While there are limits to this data set (discussed in the introduction), it is still of great interest, since it is one of the only aggregate sources that give insight into soldiers' morale. Very few soldiers – the high was only 2.5 percent in a given period – expressed opinions interpreted by the censors to represent discontent and dissatisfaction. Only a minority at any time (except in late March 1945 when the number reached 50 percent) wrote letters that were interpreted as being clearly indicative of good morale, but this number was always much larger and fluctuated at interesting intervals. Throughout the fighting in the Scheldt Estuary and the Rhineland, the percentage of soldiers who indicated contentment actually increased, whereas it declined sharply over the winter months spent in static positions. The major dip in the number of troops optimistic about the progress of the war corresponded with bad weather and with the German *Ardennenoffensive* in December 1944 rather than with any particular Canadian action, and rebounded thereafter. Periods of heavy fighting were linked to an increased perception on the part of the censors that army morale was high and increasing.[55] Optimism regarding the progress of the war, although not identical to good morale, varied along similar lines. The number of letters explicitly expressing *pessimism* about the progress of the war was usually negligible.[56] If there was a significant decline in morale, it was brought on by the long winter spent in static positions, a pattern consistent with the experience of Italy.

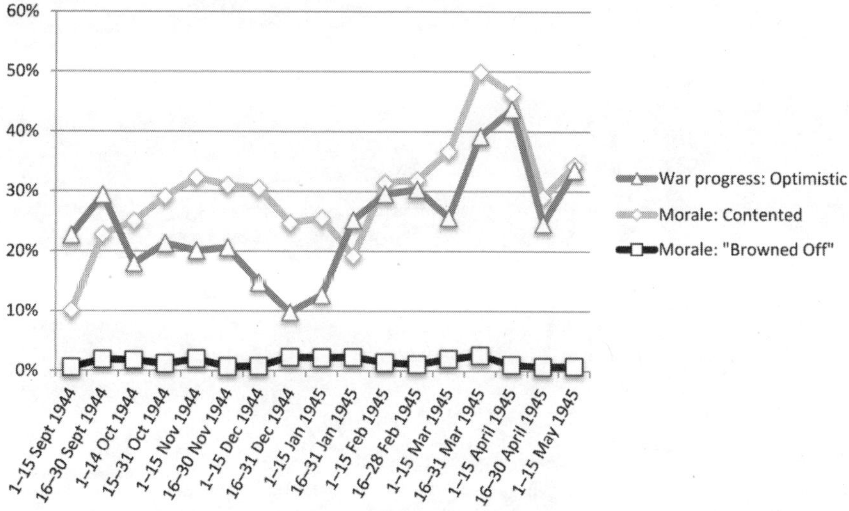

Figure 6.1: Censorship reports on morale, First Canadian Army, 1944–45

The field censors also reported on which letters (in their judgment) explicitly identified the senders as being "keen for action." The number of letters expressing that their authors were keen to get into the fight was always a small minority, fluctuating between a high of about 15 percent and a low of 3 percent. "Keenness for action" was lowest in September 1944 in the aftermath of Normandy and during the sieges of the Channel ports – at which time the war looked virtually over – and again in April and May of 1945, when the war was in fact coming to an end. Conversely, the high points in expressions of desire for action occurred during the Scheldt campaign in October–November, and again during the Rhineland campaign in the early months of 1945. If "fighting spirit" was something that could be captured in letters, its expression among the troops was at its highest during the periods of fiercest combat and highest casualty rates.

The censors' reports also reveal that Canadian soldiers believed their military service to be highly contingent. They accepted and invested themselves in the necessity of the job they had to do in Northwest Europe. However, the same soldiers who were willing to fight to the death against

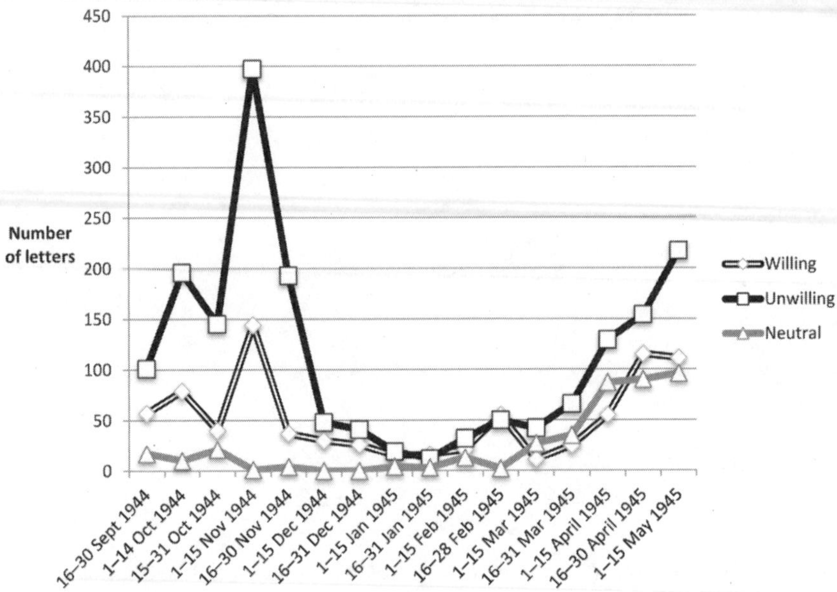

Figure 6.2: Censorship reports on Far East service, First Canadian Army, 1944–45

the Nazis were often bitterly opposed to the idea that their war was going to continue afterward, outside Europe. Beginning in September 1944 speculation in the mail was rife about whether the Canadian Army would be dispatched to the Pacific to fight the Japanese once Germany was defeated. The proximate cause for these rumblings was the OCTAGON (Second Quebec) Conference in early September between Britain, the United States, and Canada, during which Allied commitments to the Pacific War were renewed.[57] The censors tracked the number of letters indicating soldiers to be willing, unwilling, and neutral about being deployed for service in the Far East, as shown in Figure 6.2. In both autumn 1944 and spring 1945 the topic of Far East service became one of the most frequently recurring topics in the mail, and was watched closely by censors for signs of discontent. "There's some talk of us going to Japan," wrote a lance corporal with 2nd Canadian Division in October 1944. "Well that's what they think. I'll go to jail first and that's no fooling. All the boys here feel the same way, so I think they will have their hands full trying to send us."[58] However, once it became official policy that the Canadian

Pacific Force of one division was going to be an all-volunteer force (and that these would be men who specifically *re*-volunteered), attitudes toward service in the Far East improved considerably. And when fighting against Japan was contrasted with the available *non*-voluntary duty, namely serving in the postwar Army of Occupation in Germany, the prospect became more appealing, particularly since volunteering for the Pacific Force meant repatriation to Canada and home leave. The censors believed the younger, single men were willing to volunteer for service in the Far East, and that the older married men were unwilling to do so.[59] Overall, service against Germany was accepted as legitimate, but the thought of being sent to the Pacific provoked rancorous reactions. When given the free choice, however, many did indeed opt for further service.

The crisis of reinforcements in the Northwest Europe campaign, discussed in more detail ahead, ultimately sparked the political firestorm over conscription back in Canada, and resulted in 2,400 National Resources Mobilization Act "Zombie" conscripts being deployed as reinforcements for First Canadian Army in 1945.[60] Throughout late 1944 and into early 1945, while the conscription crisis raged in Ottawa, parallel outcries among the overseas volunteers regarding the "Zombie" conscripts were reflected in the censorship reports. Most of the remarks captured by the censors expressed hostility at the conscripts for failing to volunteer or at the government for not forcing them to deploy overseas. Many of the soldiers in First Canadian Army believed they would be better off remaining an all-volunteer force. One 4th Division soldier spoke of the conscripts as a "black stain" upon Canada's war effort, and fumed about "the farce of an army that even has the nerve to call themselves home-defence. If the Canadian Government doesn't get rid of those zombies some way or other, I'm afraid there is going to be trouble."[61] I will discuss the problem of the "zombie" reinforcements further later in this chapter, but the issue was a serious one for morale and was treated with gravity by the censors throughout the campaign.

The battle experience questionnaires also provide insight into our question of what issues determined high and low morale among Canadian infantry. (The complete data from Northwest Europe are reproduced in Appendix G.) As with the other campaigns, the more material aspects of service – good food, plenty of mail from home, the opportunity for rest, recreation, and cleanliness – were the key determinants of good morale mentioned by the greatest number of officers. The lack of such provisions correspondingly presented the greatest problems for morale. After the bloodletting in Normandy, "rest and recreation" and variations thereof understandably took on a much greater importance for soldiers. Over the space of the long 1944–45 campaign, on the other hand, "success in battle" seems to have diminished in importance as a perceived contributor to high morale. Most other factors remained roughly unchanged from Normandy, including, notably, the impact of deficiencies in the number of reinforcements.

The troops appear to have considered the efforts of First Canadian Army on behalf of its soldiers to attend to their "creature comfort" as exemplary. The censorship reports, which adopted an empirical approach in September 1944, also give a quantitative impression of what soldiers were thinking. In any given bi-weekly period only about 5 to 10 percent of soldiers' letters expressed an opinion that censors interpreted as being related to the "Work of Auxiliary Services," but of those the positive comments outweighed the negative ten to one. Comments on billets and on the quality of food were even more overwhelmingly positive, as seen in Figure 6.3. The spike in praise for the quality of the food in March 1945 aside, the data show that after September 1944 the quality of both lodgings and food was consistently high, and more significantly, elicited very few complaints. The same could not always be said of the postal services, which were subject to disruption both from enemy action and from sheer volume, particularly around Christmas time, as shown in Figure 6.4. Complaints about the mail service were far more frequent but were still usually in the minority. An exception occurred in January and February 1945, when the Canadian Postal Corps was dealing with a frustrating logjam of Christmas parcels that stretched into February. Otherwise, five or six positive reports on the mail were normally received for every one negative one in letters home. Overall, Canadian soldiers' material needs were well met.[62]

Here, as with other campaigns, offence statistics are another potential source of information on Canadian morale. (Unfortunately, there is a gap in the archives for the Discipline & Pay Section's statistics, and only those from September through December 1944 are presently available; these are reproduced in full as Appendix E, as are specific statistics on AWL and desertion charges.) After the Normandy campaign ended and the

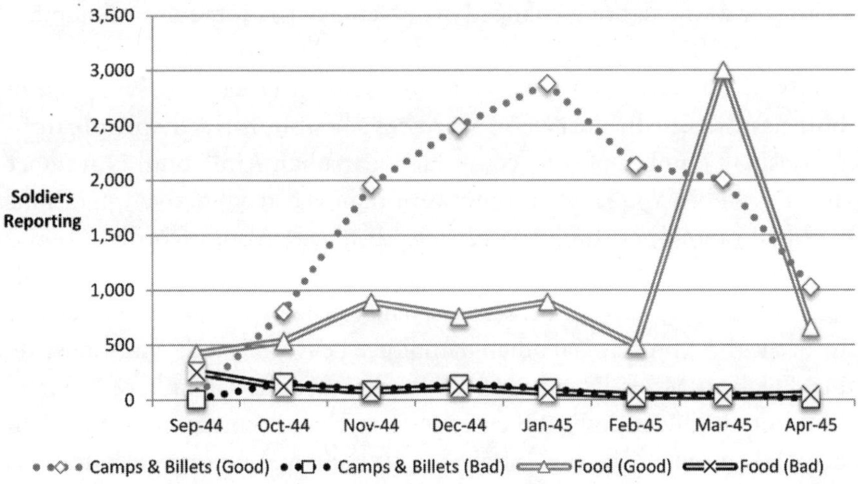

Figure 6.3: Censorship reports on billets and food, First Canadian Army, 1944–45

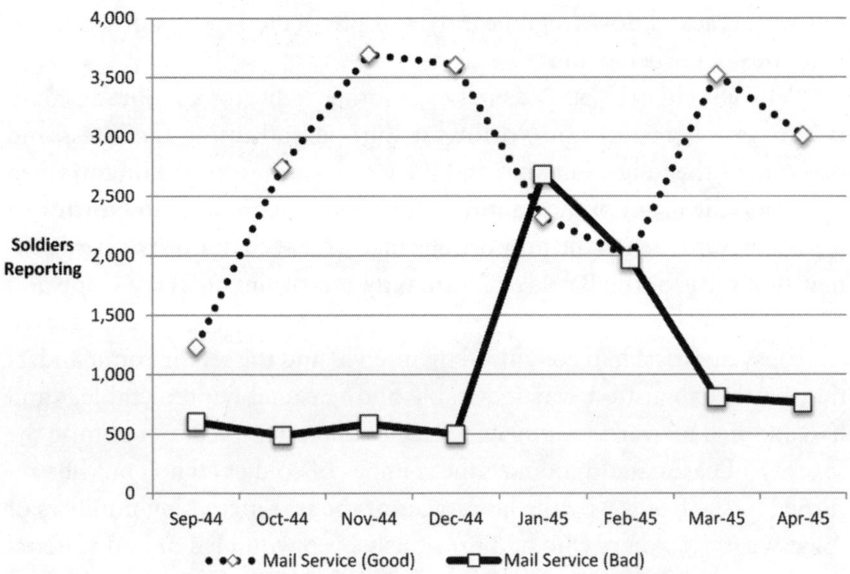

Figure 6.4: Censorship reports on mail service, First Canadian Army, 1944–45

character of the fighting changed in September 1944, the overall number of offences from each of 2nd, 3rd, and 4th Divisions increased significantly: there were usually twice as many offences as there had been in Normandy. But infantrymen were responsible for a disproportionately small number of offences in First Canadian Army until November and December 1944, when they were removed from active operations and had more opportunity to get into trouble.[63] Also, according to 2nd Echelon, over half the cases of desertion from Canadian infantry battalions in Northwest Europe between September 1944 and January 1945 came from the three French-Canadian battalions: Le Régiment de Maisonneuve, Les Fusiliers Mont-Royal, and Le Régiment de la Chaudière.[64] Many (but not all) of the desertion cases seem to have occurred after units had been taken out of the line. Similarly, AWL charges among all battalions were low in September (82 charges) and rose sharply in October (318 charges) before almost doubling in December 1944 (598 charges).[65] The increase in AWL during October 1944, at the height of the Scheldt campaign, may indicate wavering morale under the awful conditions in the river estuary – or at least the perception of wavering morale by authorities who cracked down significantly and prosecuted more infractions to deter future misbehaviour.

Neuropsychiatric (NP) casualties, another indicator of morale, could rise to very high rates in Northwest Europe, indicating the stress and pressure of the long campaign and the war-weariness of the infantrymen who took the brunt of the fighting. However, NP casualties in Northwest Europe never reached the proportions that were seen during the battle exhaustion crisis of the Battle of Normandy. According to Terry Copp and Mark Humphries in a recent study: "By the fall of 1944 ... Canadian neuropsychiatrists had convinced themselves and the senior commanders that battle exhaustion was inevitable and reasonably predictable," and had adopted forward-treatment strategies that attempted to minimize the severity of cases and maximize the number of soldiers who could be returned to the front.[66] By the late stages of the war increasing numbers of "war weary" soldiers who had previously been wounded or had suffered from exhaustion were again diagnosed with battle exhaustion. At least one-third of troops who had returned from being wounded or exhausted would be diagnosed with battle exhaustion, and the ratio was reportedly higher in 3rd Division. However, according to the II Canadian Corps neuropsychiatric specialist, the ratio of exhaustion to battle casualties during the Rhineland campaign did not reach that of previous heavy fighting, and overall was much lower than anticipated.[67]

The number of Canadian soldiers surrendering to the enemy, another potential gauge of morale, represented no serious problem in Northwest Europe. The consolidated casualty lists indicate that of the 17,289 total infantry casualties from Northwest Europe 1944–45, only 867 were taken prisoner by the Germans, approximately 3 percent, lower than in Italy.[68] The number of infantry casualties lost as prisoners in most Canadian campaigns was almost negligible, and was much less significant than sources of attrition like venereal disease, which took far more Canadian soldiers out of action than German POW cages did.[69] The number of Canadians taken prisoner also contrasts favourably with the rates among the Germans. Although soldiers from the elite and fanatical German formations often fought to the death, the Germans as a rule were much more inclined to give up, and freely used surrender as an escape mechanism in a way unthinkable to the Canadians. Between late July 1944 and May 1945 approximately 192,000 German soldiers were captured on First Canadian Army's front, a number not including the German dead and wounded.[70]

Discussion of Canadians' feelings toward the enemy is also necessary. The mass murder of Canadian prisoners that happened in Normandy does not appear to have occurred again, but real animosity remained. The fighting was fierce and brutal throughout, and censors' reports often cited soldiers characterizing the Germans as "lice," "vermin," and other pejoratives.[71] It was the discovery of German atrocities against civilians that produced the greatest revulsion among Canadians during 1944–45. Canadian soldiers of the 1st Parachute Battalion, deployed to the Ardennes to help stem the German offensive there in December 1944, were among the first in Northwest Europe to witness concrete evidence of the widespread murder of civilians by the enemy, particularly in the town of Bande, Belgium. "I was chosen yesterday from our Company to witness the exhuming of 34 civilian bodies, men and boys ranging from 14 to 30," wrote one paratrooper sergeant, "The Germans had brutally tortured and murdered these people ... It's a sight I'll never forget, and it's still hard to believe any human could do such a thing. The bodies were beaten and broken almost beyond recognition, then the 'brave' Germans shot them and pushed them into a hole." The sergeant finished by saying: "Needless to say no prisoners have been taken on this front, and no men of mine will bring in any."[72] On 12 April 1945 elements of the 2nd Canadian Division liberated Westerbork Transit Camp in the Netherlands, whence 107,000 Dutch Jews, political prisoners, and other "undesirables" had been sent by train to their deaths in the extermination camps; several hundred maltreated prisoners were rescued. Soldiers of the South Saskatchewan Regiment also reportedly discovered the bodies of four Canadian soldiers, "hands wired behind their backs and shot in the back of the head, a characteristic SS method of execution," although the documentation on this event remains sketchy.[73] The liberation of the Netherlands as a whole was a similarly grim experience. The Canadians were met by jubilant populations in large part because the Germans had attempted to starve out the Dutch population in retaliation for civilian railway strikes in September 1944. From this privation, in combination with a harsh winter, 18,000 Dutch civilians died of malnutrition, and, when First Canadian Army completed the liberation of the Netherlands in April–May 1945, they reported 150,000 cases of starvation edema in western Holland.[74]

At the end of April 1945, First Canadian Army divisions pushing into Germany's Lower Saxony region encountered smaller concentration camps and Gestapo police facilities. "I am not in the habit of telling what I see over here but this is something that should be told to everyone," wrote a private with 3rd Canadian Division, "It is about ten Dutch civilians that were murdered right close to where we are now in a concentration camp. One of them was buried alive. The others were all battered to pieces either with rifles or sticks. Some had their heads bashed in, some their ankles were broke or twisted, their chests bashed in. You should see some of the things that were used for torture." A corporal wrote about the same discovery: "Never have I seen butchery or mutilated mankind of that sort before."[75] These sorts of incidents hardened many Canadians toward the Germans. "We liberated a Concentration Camp yesterday, [and] some of the inmates were horrible to look at – just skin and bone – the expression on their faces was one of misery," wrote a lance corporal with 4th Division some months later – to which in the same letter he added, "They brought in some tough-looking [German POWs] today, but we soon took the toughness out of them."[76]

Informed by the freshly discovered atrocities, but also shaped by the new victorious role they found themselves in, a complex relationship with the enemy began to develop among the Canadians toward the end of the war. One unnamed soldier, writing home about the invasion of Germany in 1945, captured this shifting mentality: "We are no longer a liberating army now that we are in Germany. We come as conquerors."[77] A 4th Division officer had similar reflections on the change he witnessed in his countrymen: "Funny how Johnny Canuck changed when he crossed the [German] border – he is no longer the carefree, happy-to-luck, don't-give-a-damn bloke we have always known – by some strange alchemy he suddenly became a grim, hard, cold, fighting man – very stiff, very correct, very proper, very much the soldier; but the fun is gone, he is part of an army of conquest and retribution – his attitude shows it."[78] Enemy behaviour judged by Canadians to be illegitimate met with increasingly swift retaliation. A corporal from the South Saskatchewan Regiment wrote: "I was bringing four [Hitler Youth soldiers] over a hedge as prisoners and one ducked back and threw a grenade [at me]. I had to shoot two of them before the other two realised I meant business."[79] Germans firing at stretcher-bearers or Red Cross personnel became a death warrant for the shooter.[80] A signalman with 5th Armoured Division related one such incident: "One of our [sentries] was bayoneted 5 times in the face: the boys got rearing and went out and cleaned up the whole lot of Jerries, they finished every damn one of them. Our boys are not the easy-going lads they were."[81] Partisan activity by non-uniformed German military personnel or civilians – real or perceived – was met with draconian measures. In the town of Sögel in Lower Saxony, conquered by 4th Canadian Armoured Division in April 1945, according to several Canadian accounts, "the citizens of Sögel turned werewolf on us." The Canadians responded with extreme measures. One 4th Division officer mentioned: "So far only one [German] town has given us any trouble through civilians taking part in the shooting, and that town has paid the full price – there is no town there now."[82] Another wrote home: "I lost a very dear friend [in Sögel] ... They used dum-dum bullets, and nearly tore the chaps apart that they hit."[83] In retaliation, the Canadians deliberately and completely destroyed Sögel, although (marking the moral difference between the Canadians and their enemy) they evacuated the civilian population first and left them homeless. A similar fate befell the town of Friesoythe,

Germany, when the CO of the Argyll and Sutherland Highlanders, Lieutenant-Colonel F.E. Wigle, was reportedly killed by a German civilian "werewolf" irregular shooter. In retaliation and anger for the death of a friend, 4th Division's Major-General Christopher Vokes ordered the town to be completely destroyed and the rubble to be used to pave traversable roads for Canadian tanks.[84] First Canadian Army's GOC, General Crerar, refused to allow Canada's fallen soldiers to be buried on the unhallowed ground of German soil and had the dead from the Rhineland campaign taken back to cemeteries in the Netherlands.[85]

The conquerors of Germany did not always comport themselves well. During the early stages of the invasion of Germany, the Canadians were particularly prone to looting the (comparatively) rich, untouched German towns that they encountered. One unnamed soldier, for instance, wrote in a letter home, presumably to a female relative: "The first thing we do is to go looting in the houses. Of course we don't call it looting here, it's booty. I found a small piece of dress material yesterday, several yards of it. I'll try and bring it home with me." Another, cited in the same censorship report, remarked: "They haven't told us not to loot yet, and everybody is lifting everything in sight." Sometimes, however, this license could lead to tragic consequences: "Of course we can do all the looting we want to, and it is plenty of fun, if we don't meet up against any booby traps."[86] Far more serious were the sexual assaults that took place against German civilians, which were widespread despite prosecution by Canadian authorities.[87] Assessments of field general courts-martial (FGCM) indices from First Canadian Army show an enormous increase in charges laid against Canadian soldiers for rape, sexual assault, and gross indecency during the invasion of Germany between February and May 1945. Such charges were vanishingly rare throughout the campaigns in Italy, France, Belgium, and the Netherlands – they occurred infrequently and usually as individual incidents. Once in Germany, however, sexual assaults became far more frequent, far more violent, and far more organized, with gang rape being a common prosecuted offence. Forty-six FGCMs were held for Canadians accused of sexual violence against German women (and men) for incidents taking place between February and May 1945, representing 65 individual charges of rape, attempted rape, or indecent assault. Defendants were found guilty on 38 of the 65 charges. Sexual violence charges became so frequent that they constituted a significant minority of all Canadian courts-martial during May 1945. These acts of violence against German civilians are particularly notable because 86 percent of them involved men from combat units, including infantry regiments, and only 14 percent involved men from noncombat support units.[88] One corporal with 4th Division wrote home openly describing one incident: "One of the boys I joined up with ... and another fellow herded a couple of German Frauleins 'up the stairs' ahead of a Sten Gun. While one held the Sten Gun the other gave them a painless meat injection, now they are both up on a charge of rape, which isn't so good."[89]

The number of sexual assaults that occurred against German civilians will never be known. Even today rapes are among the most underreported of crimes, and during the 1940s even more so, on account of the "muted voice of women in general, and of female victims in particular."[90] Writing a decade after the Second World War, prominent Anglo-Polish criminologist Sir Leon Radzinowicz estimated that 95 percent of rapes went unreported.[91] Given the dire circumstances in occupied Germany in 1945, it would have taken courage for German civilians to report to the occupation authorities the sexual crimes committed against them by that authority's own soldiers. On the other hand, the number of rape charges implies a serious crackdown by the military justice system. We also cannot say with certainty that similar waves of sexual violence did not occur elsewhere. There is evidence of some Canadian soldiers engaging in gang rape during the Sicily campaign, but few courts martial were held. Sexual violence may have accompanied the Canadians in other campaigns, but simply gone unreported or been overlooked by authorities, who always had myriad competing priorities for the maintenance of discipline. Clearly there was a fear that soldiers would get out of control in their role as "conquerors" in Germany, so sexual violence offences (and violation of the non-fraternization orders) were punished swiftly and severely. All we can say is that, by any estimate, the Canadian invasion of Germany was accompanied by a wave of sexual violence, though the uniqueness of this phenomenon remains unknown. The Canadians were by no means exceptional in this regard. Without even discussing the sexual atrocities systematically carried out by the Soviets on the Eastern Front, similar behaviour took place among the Americans and the Free French during their own invasions of Germany in 1945.[92] As the Canadian censors noted in a summary of their late April 1945 report,

"The great majority of writers were definitely hostile towards German civilians."[93] Such attitudes would change – quickly – during the coming occupation of Germany, but ill will toward the German military and civilian populations prevailed at the time of operations.

COHESION AND MOTIVATION

At no time during the fighting in Northwest Europe did Canadian casualties reach the rate experienced in Normandy. However, these campaigns still resulted in horrifying losses, and cumulatively, from September 1944 to May 1945, exceeded those of Normandy. (Complete casualty statistics for the campaign are reproduced as Appendix F.) During each month of intense combat, the other ranks of infantry battalions lost 15 to 20 percent of their total strength, while officers lost between about 20 to 30 percent. A detailed breakdown is seen in figures 6.5 and 6.6. By the end of the war, infantry battalions fighting in Normandy and Northwest Europe had lost close to 175 percent of their starting strength to casualties, and platoon commander casualties in all three divisions totalled around 300 percent.[94] Many of these casualties were men wounded several times who kept returning to the fight, but the degree of overall turnover is still staggering to contemplate. Even the sergeants, who suffered the lowest rate of loss, approached 150 percent casualties over time. Only a lucky few infantrymen made it through both Normandy and Northwest Europe start-to-finish without becoming casualties. However, all these statistics must be placed in perspective. In Northwest Europe casualties to private soldiers occurred on an average of 25 percent in any single month, which meant that although units were frequently decimated (in the Roman sense of the word) through attrition, they were rarely outright destroyed. The heroic leadership of platoon commanders, on the other hand, meant that lieutenants were still suffering 40 to 50 percent casualties per month of intense combat in some battalions. NCOs continued to fulfill a much more stable, everyday leadership role within infantry units than did junior officers, who were rarely around for very long at the platoon and company levels. In First Canadian Army's censorship reports, specific note was made when troops made "good" or "adverse" comments on their officers. While the positive comments always outweighed the negative ones significantly, only a tiny handful of

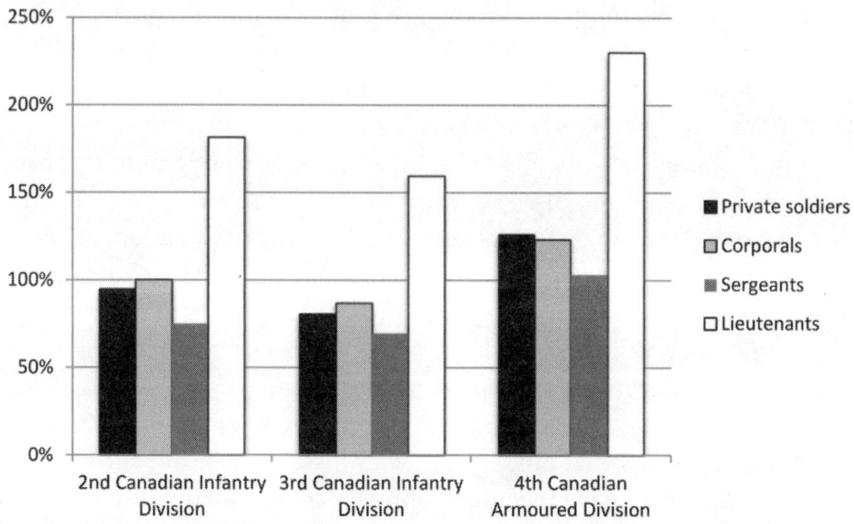

Figure 6.5: Infantry casualties, NW Europe, 1944–45, as percentage of battalion war establishment

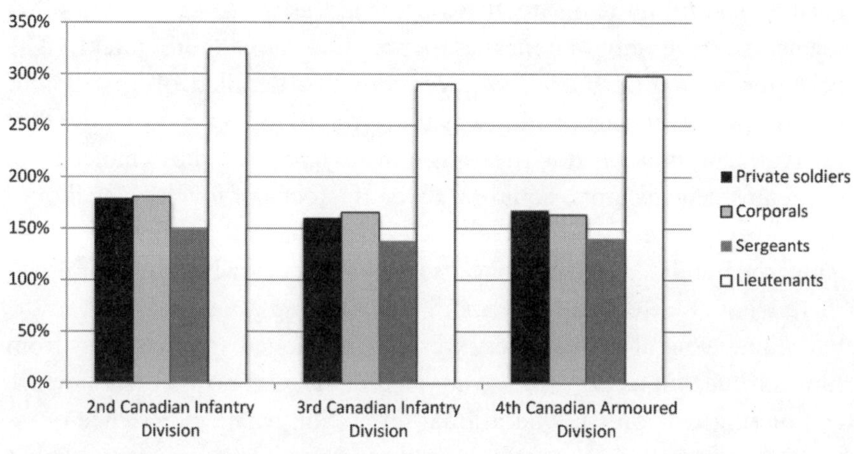

Figure 6.6: Cumulative infantry casualties, Normandy and NW Europe, 1944–45, as percentage of battalion war establishment

soldiers (no more than 200 in any given month, out of approximately 20,000 to 24,000 letters seen by censors) were commenting on their officers.[95] Particularly for the infantry, junior officers may have been seen as a more transitory source of leadership.

The accomplishments of the Canadian soldiers were significant, particularly in the autumn of 1944, when the lack of reinforcements due to the massive Allied logistical crisis meant that infantry battalions were well understrength. After November–December 1944 the logistical situation eased, and the Canadians went into battle in the Rhineland and in the Netherlands at full strength. In 1945 the deficiencies in strength for infantry battalions never exceeded 700 across five divisions in action, whereas in October and November the deficiencies across three divisions had reached 2,300 other ranks.[96] So, while losses were heavy throughout the campaign, they gave the impression of a crisis only in the autumn of 1944, when the logistical strain placed limits on the ability of reinforcements to get forward.

Esprit de corps and connections between soldiers and their higher formations had become severely eroded by this period. Terry Copp and Bill McAndrew have speculated on the reasons: "Few Canadian generals had made any attempt to win the affection of their men and fewer had tried to lead from the front. Division and Corps were vague entities that seemed to have only one message – press on, move more quickly. The brigadier was little more than a conduit for detailed orders. If unit morale was to be sustained it was up to the battalion commander. But the regiment, now filled with strangers who had arrived by chance from the reinforcement units, could rarely be the focus of loyalty it had once been."[97] Other evidence corroborates the erosion of esprit de corps. Amid the hundreds of pages of censorship reports for Northwest Europe there were no references to Canadian leadership above the level of the battalion. General Montgomery was still mentioned appreciatively from time to time, but as army group commander he was now a distant figure conducting war on the operational level. The battle experience questionnaires from Northwest Europe likewise indicate that most combat soldiers felt little or no attachment to higher formations, and that the sense of identity associated with higher formations was not a determinant of morale. Being part of First Canadian Army evinced few public (or private) displays of pride from soldiers in Northwest Europe. The number of "original veteran" soldiers, those who had enlisted directly with their regiments early in the war and were still with their regiments in Northwest Europe, continued to decline, especially in 2nd Division: by the end of the campaign, "original" sergeants were below 15 percent, corporals below 10 percent, and private soldiers below 5 percent.[98] By the end of the campaign, the "originals" were a small minority among the NCOs and virtually gone from the ranks of private soldiers.

Because the monthly casualties were not as great as those in Normandy, small-group cohesion based upon strong social bonds and personal knowledge of one's comrades may have had a greater chance to thrive in Northwest Europe than it had in Normandy. However, non-casualty personnel fluctuations meant that, even at very low levels – the company, platoon, and section – Canadian soldiers often had no pre-existing relationships with the men they were fighting beside, particularly during heavy fighting. Infantry small-group sections were always the first and hardest hit by casualties; when these could not be properly and promptly reinforced they were amalgamated with other sections, just as in Italy and Normandy. This was routine at the section level but happened among platoons and companies as well. "I was down to three stripped-down companies [instead of the standard four companies]," Lieutenant-Colonel Roger Rowley, CO of the Stormont, Dundas and Glengarry Highlanders reflected in a postwar interview: "We were damn short. Our platoons, which were supposed to be thirty-three to thirty-four men, were all down to about sixteen men. We were down to twenty-five at one point in a couple of companies."[99] Some officers found tactical flexibility in continuing to operate with smaller companies with amalgamated platoons, rather than breaking up an entire company to reinforce the others, but that decision was up to individual battalions.[100] Even convalesced veterans who were returning to the fight after being wounded stood only a chance of being returned to their specific sections, platoons, and companies. The War Diary of the Calgary Highlanders from mid-October 1944 mentioned that when reinforcements came down the pipeline the companies would be "putting in a bid for them," particularly for returning veterans who had previously been with the battalion.[101] Sometimes previously wounded veterans were not returned to the same regiment at all.

The Left out of Battle system continued to characterize infantry companies in Northwest Europe, with key personnel being left behind the front lines in rotation to serve as a nucleus around which to rebuild a company in case of disaster. Over 85 percent of respondents to battle experience questionnaires who had fought in Northwest Europe in 1944–45 reported detaching "LOB" personnel prior to engaging in an action.[102]

Complaints about the level of training, knowledge, and general "greenness" of incoming soldiers have loomed large in the Canadian Army's literature. As Lieutenant-Colonel (and future Brigadier-General) Denis Whitaker wrote in his influential postwar account of the Scheldt fighting: "The reinforcements were nearly all men who had been remustered from other arms of the service. It was evident that they had been shunted over to infantry units with only the most rudimentary training. Tragically, they did not know how to look after their weapons – or themselves. They didn't for example, know how to load or fire their weapons."[103] Such assessments do have some grounding in the primary sources of the time. An unnamed 2nd Division officer from outside the infantry corps wrote home to say:

> I've spoken to the infantry officers ... Reinforcements are not good. They are constantly taking gunners and sappers and slapping them in as infantry reinforcements with two weeks training or less. Gunners are literally afraid to go on sick parade for they know if they are struck off strength to hospital they'll be smack in the infantry when they get better. The reinforcements from Canada are shocking. The battalions are getting kids to take into action who were on civvy street two months ago. Talk about training, they barely know how to soldier, let alone how to fight. And two weeks later they are either dead or wounded.[104]

Another account, which is often quoted in the historiography, is the assessment made by Lieutenant W.J. Shea, then the intelligence officer of the Montreal-based Black Watch regiment, in a report on the battalion's action at Woensdrecht in October 1944:

> Reinforcements were mainly from the [Service Corps], had little or no infantry training, and exhibited poor morale. One reinforcement had never fired a Bren, another was not familiar with the No. 36 grenade. These men were received a matter of hours

> before an attack, and there was no time available to give them the requisite training. Furthermore, most of these reinforcements were not interested in infantry work to begin with, and did not want to fight. ... There were a considerable number of deserters among these reinforcements.[105]

The Black Watch were particularly hard hit during the fighting in the Scheldt, and the second-in-command of that regiment dispatched statistics to his brigade headquarters. These indicated that in the four rifle companies, 42 percent of soldiers claimed to have over three months training, 13 percent claimed two months or over, 34 percent claimed only one month, 8 percent claimed less than one month, and 3 percent claimed to have no infantry training at all.[106] The accuracy of these self-reported returns is questionable, and claims of no training whatsoever were probably hyperbolic.[107] However, they still add up to a portrait of an army perceiving itself to be in crisis, receiving reallocated men who they felt were unqualified as infantrymen.

It is interesting to note that although the censorship reports were filled with complaints about the quality of incoming reinforcements during the autumn of 1944, these seemed to have begun in volume only after the fanous Major Conn Smythe, who had fought in both World Wars, issued a diatribe on the reinforcement crisis that was published in the *Globe and Mail* on 19 September 1944.[108] Prior to Smythe's public statement, censors' reports gave no indication that there was any serious concern about reinforcements among the troops themselves; afterward, beginning with the early October report, they seemed to talk about little else. As one private soldier put it: "I see Conn Smythe has really started some talk about sending improperly trained lads over here; well I think he may be right in some respects, as I know some of the reinforcements are no more ready for action that the man in the moon. It is not only tough on themselves, but risky for the boys who have to fight with them. Of course some of them are alright."[109] In his *Globe and Mail* appeal Smythe also made specific reference to troops having "little or no knowledge of the Bren gun and ... most of them have never seen a PIAT anti-tank gun, let alone fired one."[110] These precise statements are echoed in many accounts thereafter. Perhaps this was due to the accuracy of Smythe's observations. But it also seems possible that Smythe's widely circulated remarks planted the idea in the minds of soldiers that the reinforcements they were receiving were of uniformly poor quality.

There are reasons for skepticism about the reinforcement situation being as terrible as indicated. Battle experience questionnaire responses paint a picture of difficulty with reinforcements, but not one of crisis bordering upon collapse. Chapter 4 showed that in Italy almost 70 percent of surveyed junior officers rated their reinforcements as being of "high" or "moderate" quality (and only 16 percent rated them as "low"), while chapter 5 showed that 62 percent of junior officers from Normandy rated their reinforcements as of "high" or "moderate" quality. The numbers indeed slipped slightly in Northwest Europe, for which, when queried about infantry reinforcements' "general standard of efficiency" 60 percent rated their quality as "high" or "moderate," and 33 percent rated them as "low."[111] That one-third of infantry officers indicated that their reinforcements were of low quality still represents a potentially serious problem on the ground, but this evidence does not bear out the proposition that the reinforcements being received were uniformly poor; quite the opposite, in fact. As brought out in the questionnaire data on morale in Appendix G, only 8 percent of respondents listed "poorly-trained reinforcements" as being detrimental to morale, the same percentage as those who thought that the absence of those reinforcements was most detrimental. And 13 percent thought that reinforcements were actually a top factor in *raising* morale.[112] Moreover, what constituted "poorly-trained" reinforcements was entirely a matter of conjecture. No amount of training will substitute for actual combat experience, and those veterans who had survived the killing fields of Normandy seem to have taken a dim view even of fully trained soldiers in Northwest Europe. As one reinforcement rifleman in 3rd Division remarked in a letter home in October 1944: "The sergeants don't think much of all the training we have had before we came to this inf[antry] unit, but it's too late to do anything about it now. They say that the only way to learn, and learn fast is, to get into it and then you learn fast enough, or else you got it."[113] Even fully trained reinforcements who had received the full battery of infantry training were considered "green" until they had proved themselves in battle.

At least one historian who has studied the reinforcement crisis has come to similar conclusions: that blaming the quality of reinforcements for tactical setbacks had the characteristics of a fad in the autumn of

1944, and that the actual deficiency of these replacement soldiers is not supported by the available evidence.[114] According to Terry Copp's study of the 5th Brigade:

> The Black Watch, by all accounts including their own, had fought with conspicuous success in early October at St. Leonard and Brecht, using reinforcements obtained in September ... The fighting at Hoogerheide, which was also successfully handled, produced 81 casualties, most of them in D company which under ordinary circumstances would have received the bulk of the 49 additional replacements who arrived after October 6th. It was normal practice to leave new men out of battle ... but if D company did take its reinforcements forward they must have shared in the considerable success achieved that day. Veterans will find this argument difficult to accept but it is supported by the available evidence from personnel files and may be more accurate than impressionistic evidence, even from those who were there.[115]

A letter home from a 3rd Division infantry officer during the fighting in the Scheldt made the same point: "We are in a rather tough show and have managed only now to get back behind the lines (within the shell fire, [though]) and reorganize. My platoon is composed of all raw men and they have much to learn, as I also! They have done a fine job nevertheless and stood up to one of the fiercest counter-attacks I ever hope to see, the night following our attack."[116] Copp undertakes a close study of the personnel records for infantrymen of the Black Watch killed during an action at the height of the reinforcement crisis: of fifteen ORs killed in action on 13 October 1944, the average length of service in the infantry was two years. Four had joined the army in 1944 and fourteen had been reallocated to the infantry during 1944 after undergoing an "intensive conversion course."[117] In other words, most of the men killed that day had been experienced, long-service infantrymen, and less than a third had been the maligned soldiers reallocated from other branches, who were reportedly dying as fast as they could reach the front. Copp's point – and it is a good one, supported by the evidence of this study – is that accounts such as Whitaker's, which suggest that most casualties were badly trained reinforcements, are inaccurate. Given the nature of the fighting, well-trained, long-service soldiers were very likely to become casualties, and the reinforcements that the Canadians received were usually quite acceptable, even the remustered men. It turned out that even the loathed "zombie" conscripts from the home defence units back in Canada proved to be efficient, effective, and highly disciplined reinforcements when they were finally sent into combat in Northwest Europe in 1945.[118] The censorship report for early April 1945 stated, with obvious satisfaction, that "men who had been conscripted for service in this theatre had apparently been accepted by the veteran troops without animosity, and were doing a creditable job of work."[119]

It seems likely that Whitaker and other writers who were present during the Second World War have searched for explanations for the horrible bloodletting they experienced in Northwest Europe, and latched on to the quality of the infantry reinforcements as a proximate cause or contributor to the misery. But to what degree did casualties and reinforcements really compromise the ability of the infantry to fight? Eighty-two percent of infantry officer respondents from Northwest Europe (and virtually all of those who commanded rifle companies) indicated in their questionnaires that they had gone into battle below strength, as would be expected given the casualty rates and the LOB system.[120] At times infantry sections operated with only five or six men in combat, prior to being reconsolidated. However, most respondents (60 percent) still believed that their infantry sections remained capable of close-quarters combat despite depletion by casualties, a rate that was actually much higher than the 51 percent who indicated as much during the Normandy campaign.[121] Major Graves of the North Nova Scotia Highlanders noted that, "the battle strength of 1 NCO and 5 other ranks proved sufficient in every case [of combat] except in village or street fighting, where as many men as possible are needed."[122] So there are strong indications that, even depleted by casualties and refilled and reorganized with reinforcements, the Canadian infantry units fighting in Northwest Europe normally fought very effectively.

In a postwar interview with writer Will Bird, Lieutenant Blake Oulton of the North Shore Regiment recalled what an achievement this had been: "[At the end of] our fighting in the Scheldt ... I wound up with ten men all told in my platoon. How did we accomplish so much with so few men? I do think that the tough fibres of the Canadian soldier carried him through the most difficult operation of the whole war, which combined the worst weather and the worst fighting ground imaginable."[123] To "tough fibres" might be added training regimes that drilled Canadians extensively on section-, platoon-, and company-level tactics and made them quite formidable as opponents even with the catastrophic casualty rates. And the combined deficiencies and personnel turmoil of the battalions meant that, once in battle, few of the infantrymen at the section- or platoon- level knew one another personally for any length of time. We return to "swift trust" among soldiers as the most compelling explanation for why the Canadians remained combat-effective throughout these periods. It also explains why some of the most vivid accounts and memories from Northwest Europe involved the supposedly untrained reinforcements. The fact that newcomers were strangers was not nearly as problematic as the perception that they could not be trusted to behave efficiently and effectively in combat, or to live up to professional standards and expectations. But it seems to have been a particularly vocal minority of soldiers who, casting about for explanations for failures, blamed the quality of the reinforcements. No doubt some of the replacement soldiers were short on infantry training; but, as was the case with the "reinforcement crisis" in the Italian campaign, the concerns appear to have been greatly exaggerated.

CONCLUSION: A REASON FOR SELF-CONFIDENCE

Canada's war in Northwest Europe was equal parts frustration and elation. The German Army's back had been broken in Normandy, but there would be no shortcuts to ending the war, and the battles in the fall, winter, and spring of 1944 and 1945 were savage and unrelenting. Even with new technology and weapons systems being deployed and material superiority that was, to quote Brigadier Robert Moncel, "extravagant to the point of immorality," it remained an infantryman's war to the end, fought under conditions chosen by the enemy to require immense sacrifice and bloodshed for every victory.[124] Morale fluctuated between the highs of the September breakout and the lows of the bitter German resistance that impeded the final march toward Berlin.

Accounts of Northwest Europe have tended to emphasize a low-level view of the savagery of the war and the moral desolation amid the mud and water of the 1944–45 autumn and winter. However, looking at some of the more broadly based sources, a number of alternative conclusions can be reached. Behaviour in combat saw adjustment and changes from previous campaigns but Canadian troops remained highly capable, and assessments of the ineffectiveness of reinforcements are unsubstantiated. Collectively, morale was not always at a high pitch, but even during periods of hard fighting there are few indications that morale was close to breaking. Offences against military discipline certainly increased during this campaign, which may reflect some disillusionment and declining morale, but the main problems in this regard came during the months that the Canadians spent in static positions enduring cold weather and little activity, with no end to the war in sight. From what the offence statistics and the censorship reports can tell us, the high-intensity combat periods appear to have had a buoying effect on morale rather than a depressive one and, in the view of the censors, the evidence showed that attitudes were more positive in the Canadian Army in the aftermath of heavy fighting, even despite serious casualties.

These observations may indicate the fundamental importance in military psychology of soldiers' having a reason for self-confidence: despite the punishing costs of combat in Northwest Europe, Canadian operations were almost invariably successful, always on the offensive, and always conveyed a sense of bringing the end of the war closer. These were the main priorities for all soldiers. There was a prevalent sense that the Germans needed to be punished for what they had done, both on a personal and a national level, which seems to have sometimes crossed the line into acts of criminality and violence against German civilians. In the end, Canadians managed to overcome not just casualties, but also the fact that their lowest-level units were constantly being merged, torn apart, and reorganized into ad hoc arrangements. In the face of these fluctuating structures, the influx of reinforcements, and the decimation of units by the enemy, stable social relationships were constantly in jeopardy during the heavy fighting, but do not appear to have greatly affected Canadian combat effectiveness.

Conclusion: Strangers in Arms

Both before and after he led I Canadian Corps into battle in the Liri Valley and the Gothic Line, Lieutenant-General E.L.M. "Tommy" Burns was a prolific author and military intellectual. Best known for his postwar study of Canadian Army manpower, during the interwar years Burns became one of the premier military contributors to *The American Mercury* magazine, whose pages he shared with literary titans like F. Scott Fitzgerald, William Faulkner, W.E.B. Du Bois, and Leon Trotsky. He wrote under his own name occasionally, but used the pen name "Arlington B. Conway" when writing what one historian describes as "more acerbic pieces that he no doubt worried would turn his permanent force career path into a cul-de-sac."[1] Burns had fought in the trenches as a junior officer in the First World War, and had a critical mind. In a 1924 *American Mercury* article entitled "The Training of the Soldier," Conway provided one of the more perceptive assessments of soldiers' morale and motivation ever written by a Canadian. "Good morale," he wrote, "is simply a feeling in the mind of the soldier that, on even terms, he can trounce his enemy. He may have had the worst of battle after battle, but if he is still able to make excuses for himself, and is willing to have another go, his morale is all right for practical purposes. But once troops admit that the enemy may have, man to man, some advantage over them ... they become unreliable in battle."[2] Unusually for this time period, Burns identified morale as an individual trait with a group component. In discussing how morale, the will to fight, was tied to the perception of success in battle, he wrote: "A man fights well simply because he feels a superiority in himself, and in the collective mass of those like him which he calls his nation, over his enemies – those who would deny that superiority."[3] Burns also underscored the importance of rest, rations, and material comforts for morale, and the role of the leader and the support services in providing for the troops, claiming that an army "fights on its stomach," and that "*Ersatz Kaffee* and *Kriegsbrot* probably had a good deal to do with the defeat of the Germans in 1918."[4] While patriotism and love of country were "popularly believed to ensure the warrior's steadfastness and eventual triumph," Burns discarded this notion as "moonshine": "The incantations and spells of orators, the flash and flare of flags and uniforms and the barbaric rhythm of martial music may work a man up to enthusiasm while his feet are yet on the asphalt, but let him spend five minutes in a trench listening to the blurred wailing of a comrade shot through the belly, and if he thinks of patriotism at all it will only be to curse it."[5]

This study has offered an exploration of many of the same themes that Burns raised in 1924, through a thematic examination of the Canadian infantry in the Mediterranean and Northwest Europe from 1943 to 1945. The interrelationships between morale, motivation, and behaviour are complex and intertwined, and it is always difficult to try and speak to collective experiences. However, having studied sources of aggregated information about the Canadian infantrymen at war, we can approach a number of general conclusions about their experiences in the Second World War.

Historian Richard Overy, in his excellent book *Why the Allies Won*, broadly characterizes the Allied fighting forces as coming from "democracies, whose populations were used to a high standard of living and amenity. They could not be regimented to the extent of Soviet [or German] citizens, or their armies terrorised to fight."[6] The Depression-era standard of living for the Canadians who fought in the Second World War varied widely but Overy's point is well taken. Coercive disciplinary mechanisms existed within the Canadian Army, but this was not a fighting force that was terrorized into fighting its country's battles. The Canadians executed only one of their soldiers overseas during the entire war: Private Pringle, a non-combat soldier in the Mediterranean who was sentenced to death in February 1945 for murder. Unlike the case of the First World War, no Canadians were executed for military crimes such as desertion or cowardice.

So what *did* motivate Canadian soldiers to fight? I began this study by assessing some of the determinants of morale: in simple terms, having a *goal*, a *role*, and a *reason for self-confidence*. In large part the Canadian infantrymen fought because they were asked to, told to, and ordered to, because they had been well trained to, and because the weight of behavioural expectations were heavy even in a relatively non-coercive military force.

There were, however, also observable ideals at work. If Russia collectively remembers the Second World War as the "Great Patriotic War," the same cannot be said of Canada. Very little patriotism was espoused during the fighting, even if it may have been involved in the original decision to join up.[7] "Canadian-ness" served a function as a unifying identity and as a factor in differentiation from the surrounding armies and troops to varying degrees, complicated by the dense network of British Empire symbols and power-structures that Canadians were enmeshed within overseas. Canadian nationalism was still nascent, and the British connection was very important. Given the distinctively pro-British leanings of the English-Canadian majority (and particularly the predominantly Anglican officer corps) it is difficult to make generalizations about nationalism and motivation. French-Canadian units experienced a greater sense of shared identity due to language and religious difference between themselves and English-Canadian units. But were Canadian soldiers "fighting for the mother country" or the "fatherland" the way that Soviet and German soldiers are sometimes portrayed? The scaffolding of Canadian nationalism was fragile in the 1940s and does not seem to have been an abstract concept that many soldiers clung to, particularly given the physical and psychological distance between themselves and their homes. There was also no real sense that Canada was particularly imperilled. Much like the First World War, Canada's Second World War was expeditionary and was also entered into because the empire was at war, though some soldiers had been told that, in the words of Les Fusiliers Mont-Royal's Arthur Fraser, "c'était toujours mieux de ... se battre ailleurs que dans son propre pays" – it was always better to fight somewhere that was not your own country.[8]

But precisely whose country were they fighting for? The greatest voluntary recruiting surges for the Canadian Army came in September of 1939 and during the summer of 1940, when it required little imagination to foresee Great Britain falling to Nazi Germany.[9] By the time they went into battle in 1943, many Canadians had been living in England for almost four years. By the end of 1946 approximately 36,000 men from the Canadian Army are known to have married British women, and between them had over 18,000 children, but these official numbers fail to capture the hundreds of thousands of intimate connections established by Canadians in Britain.[10] For years the Canadians served on coastal-defence duty for the protection of England, and then were integrated seamlessly with British forces when they took the fight back onto the continent in Sicily and Normandy. They raged at the Germans when bombing raids and rocket attacks struck London and killed their friends and loved ones. And when it came to Canada, they had little to say. When "their country" was mentioned in their correspondence as summarized in censorship reports or questionnaire results, it was almost invariably in the negative – how asinine government policies, incompetent politicians, and naïve people back home in Canada were deliberately or inadvertently disrupting the war effort and making their lives harder. It is doubtful whether national sentiment and patriotism added anything at all to Canadian combat motivation (though they provided a basis for shared identity and comradeship), but in whatever measure they did, it is possible that these "British subjects" (not "Canadian citizens," a legal concept that did not technically exist yet) in the Canadian infantry felt as much affinity for Britain as they did for Canada.[11] Much the same can be said of French-Canadian soldiers. Although their sense of identity and belonging was reinforced by the linguistic and religious distinctiveness of their regiments, the battle experience questionnaires and censorship reports reflecting the opinions of men from French-Canadian units reveal little sense of nationalism or patriotism, whether for Canada or for Quebec. The soldiers identified themselves as Canadian amidst a community of their fellows, but showed little identification with Canada itself. Indeed, as Burns wrote in a curious mixture of hindsight and prophecy, most soldiers only mention Canada in order to curse it.[12]

Similarly, there is virtually no evidence from any of the campaigns that religion played a significant role in motivating Canadian soldiers to fight. Religion and spiritualism were never once mentioned as factors underlying morale – good or bad – in any questionnaire, and only ever appeared at the periphery of the censorship reports, such as discussions of Christmas or as an element of French-Canadian distinctiveness. While there is no evidence at all of a "crusading" mentality with spiritual dimensions, chaplains and the religious institutions gave succour and stability to fighting soldiers, and this account should not be seen as trying to downplay their roles. A promise of Heaven provided solace, comfort, hope, and (perhaps above all) identity when they were in the line, but the motives that propelled Canadians into combat were far more earthly.

Canadians' ideals were more complex. As Richard Overy writes: "The real success of the Allies lay in their ability to win the moral high ground throughout the conflict by identifying their cause with progressive, post Enlightenment values."[13] More than any other belligerent in the Second World War, the Canadian state emphasized voluntarism and individualism, and until the very end resisted the idea of compulsory overseas military service. For political reasons, the Canadian ideal from 1939 to 1945 was the "sovereign individual" issuing a personal declaration of war by volunteering to fight Nazism overseas. Everyone who did not was, through a carefully constructed propaganda campaign, shown to be subhuman, a "zombie" of Haitian myth.[14]

Individual Canadian soldiers normally felt that they had an individual stake and a role to play in the conflict, even if that stake was not described in nationalist terms. Few could have articulated what Canada's international interests in fighting Germany were, or even what Britain's interests were. But during the European campaigns there was a prevalent sense among Canadian soldiers that a job needed to be done, and that the job was both legitimate and important, even though it was incredibly violent, distasteful, dangerous, and scarring. Canadian soldiers were generally convinced that the war against Germany was a necessary one, and if the existential question – "Why are we fighting this war?" – was being asked, it was seldom put in print at the time. The aim of destroying Nazi Germany quickly and efficiently, and with as little loss of Canadian life as possible, was widely accepted, bolstered by repugnance in both the Mediterranean and Northwest Europe theatres toward the atrocities of the enemy. Canadians' service was contingent upon that sense of necessity. The uproar against the possibility that Canadians would be involuntarily sent to the Pacific theatre to fight the Japanese after Germany's defeat is proof that not every war was equal in their minds. These men were not disinterested automatons; infantrymen were happiest when given the information and context necessary for them to locate their individual efforts not only within a battle but within the entire war effort.

And their morale suffered when authorities expected them to obey unthinkingly, "browned" them off by denying them sufficient information to do their jobs, or otherwise kept them "out of the picture." Once the fighting started, for many Canadians the war took on a very personal character that shaped motivation. They reacted fiercely and viciously against perceived Nazi atrocities and illegal behaviour, although they sometimes engaged in acts of brutality themselves. This paradox problematizes the heroic image of the Canadians, shows how violence in war can spiral out of control, and gives us an indication of the importance of the distinction between *liberator* and *conqueror* to the Canadians, as mentalities and behaviours seem to have differed in the two roles.

Along with the *goal* and the *role*, Canadian morale and willingness to fight hinged upon material considerations. Good and plentiful food, mail from home, and opportunities for rest, recreation, and leave were always the most popular answers to the question of morale throughout the Canadian campaigns. Studied in aggregate, the opinions in the battle experience questionnaires consistently ranked "creature comforts" as the greatest determinants of morale. Even success in battle was not as frequently cited as a positive contributor to morale as the prosaic elements of soldier life. Throughout the campaigns infantrymen praised the support services, particularly the Royal Canadian Army Service Corps and the Royal Canadian Ordnance Corps; they did not always function perfectly, but problems were usually of finite duration and swiftly corrected. Only the issue of leave – often denied to Canadians, especially in Italy – proved to be consistently irksome. There was a strong materialism among Canadians, and high-spirited combat service seemed conditional upon the unspoken bargain that the troops should be well supplied and well looked after by the army's ample support system if they were going to fight. This unwritten covenant demonstrated to troops both competence and caring on the part of the chain of command, and was a function of good, if subtle, leadership. Given the central importance of these support services to the morale of Canadian soldiers, the element of the historiography that condemns the "over-administration" of the Canadian Army may need to be rethought. The sense that they were part of a larger fighting force and enmeshed with a paternalistic relationship in which their needs were largely being met seems to have contributed to the durability of the Canadians in spite of their extended time in combat.

Throughout the campaigns infantry training contributed a sense of knowledge and self-confidence to soldiers. In hindsight the training that the Canadians carried out did not prepare them in every way for combat, especially in regard to combined-arms warfare, for which training was often demonstrably lacking. But training never fully prepares soldiers for combat, and what the Canadians received seems to have conditioned them quite well. Their battle drill training was quite effective in honing a tactical sense in relation to field craft, and junior officers consistently reported putting battle drill to work in combat. Despite how important creature comforts were for morale, Canadian infantrymen proved able to withstand considerable deprivation and physical hardship in the field as they fought up, down, and across some of the most difficult terrain that Europe has to offer in both the Mediterranean and Northwest Europe. Even reinforcement soldiers were generally considered to have been acceptably well trained, and data show that a only a vocal minority voiced complaints about the replacements. It is true that Canadians did not get everything they might have gained out of their training. Effective combined-arms cooperation was often dodgy and difficult to obtain.[15] But the infantry training and conditioning of Canadian soldiers, particularly longer-service soldiers, were highly effective and contributed to both a reason for self-confidence and a basis for professional trust.

The fact that the Canadians did not seem to have had any sense that the Germans were the superior force was an inestimable benefit. German military superiority is a staple of the postwar historiography and a regular feature in veterans' interviews carried out decades after the fighting. But the contemporary documents examined for this study give very little indication that Canadian infantrymen seriously believed at the time that the Germans were better or more capable soldiers than they were. Canadian soldiers afforded their adversaries respect and even admiration, but throughout the war the Canadians believed they consistently proved that, to use Burns's terms, man-for-man they were the superior force. This self-confidence underwrote their morale and their willingness to fight aggressively in awful conditions and despite terrible casualties.

I have also devoted considerable attention in this book to discussing cohesion in the Canadian infantry. Working from Gay Siebold's "standard model of cohesion," I have noted that cohesion has several different axes and dimensions, which play different roles in maintaining morale and inspiring teamwork. Canada continues to have a strong regimental tradition at the level of the infantry battalion, and vested interests still champion the primacy of regimental esprit de corps in combat motivation. However, much of the evidence from this study shows that organizational bonding at the level of the regiment, while certainly desirable, may be overstated as a source of morale. There is no doubt that regimental spirit and pride proved to be a motivator among the "original veterans" and long-service troops whose lives were imbricated within their infantry regiments. But these "originals" were a finite and expendable resource, and after several months of hard fighting most soldiers were reinforcements who had no prior connection to the regiment or even familiarity with its region of Canada. These newcomers nonetheless socialized swiftly, thanks to "swift trust" and the LOB system.

A similar process can be seen even in "primary-group cohesion." Much of the literature on combat motivation also indicates that soldiers fight for their buddies and comrades in the immediate small-group setting, but such an idea is problematized by the Canadian experience. The infantry took the majority of the casualties, and during the worst of the fighting (Ortona, the Liri Valley, Normandy, the Gothic Line), casualties could obliterate infantry rifle sections and platoons, the building blocks of primary-group cohesion. If battalions sustained 20–30 percent casualties per month during heavy fighting, that would likely translate into over 50 percent losses to their rifle sections, platoons, and companies. Even so, some measure of primary-group cohesion might have been possible to maintain. But as early as Sicily the infantry battalions in combat were constantly reorganizing and regrouping their sub-units to accommodate casualties, which meant ongoing personnel turbulence as sections, platoons, and companies were pulled apart and recombined. Special-purpose teams, from assault troops to improvised task forces to fighting patrols, were fashioned from existing resources and sub-units. Ad hoc sub-units were thrown together in emergency situations. Reinforcements were allocated to existing battalions on an individual basis rather than fed in as complete replacement units. These processes would be repeated throughout the war. The German Army receives credit for its ability to reconstitute improvised *Kampfgruppe* task forces out of shattered formations, but the Canadians were doing much the same thing at lower organizational levels. To the men on the ground, the effect would have been almost identical: when the fighting was intense, Canadian infantrymen were in situations where their lives were in the hands of strangers, not long-established "buddies." So part of the achievement of the Canadians came from their ability to adapt rapidly, socialize, and adjust to the reality of being strangers in arms who nonetheless needed to accomplish a task.

The "swift trust" understanding of primary-group cohesion is therefore extremely important. The 1st Canadian Infantry Division that landed in Sicily in 1943 was a battle-inexperienced but extremely cohesive formation, with strong and trusted leadership at the junior level, established networks of trust and mutual support among the soldiers, and for most, ties to their regiments that dated back to 1939, or even earlier. They achieved conspicuous success and suffered tragic failure, but fought ferociously and defeated a skilled enemy. So also did the Canadians at the Moro River and Ortona later in 1943, when they outfought some of the German Army's elite units in a Great War–style battle of attrition. During December 1943, losses were almost unsustainably high and reinforcements had constantly to be fed into the fighting line to keep the battle going. The cooperation of these strangers in arms throughout the infantry battalions made it possible for 1st Division to keep fighting, and the same can be said of any of the high-intensity actions fought by the Canadian Army during the war. Units were also being torn apart and put back together again so that even the veterans often did not know the men they were fighting beside very well. Cohesion, as Siebold points out, is not about close "buddy" relationships: it is about trust. Professional trust, common experience of training and doctrine, and institutional connections and knowledge provided the framework for "swift trust" and cooperation among strangers. And while reinforcement soldiers often felt socially out of place – and were scapegoated for failures – sufficient professional trust generally existed even between veteran combatants and inexperienced replacements to allow for combat operations to succeed. As Siebold stresses, personnel within the same military force who are apparent strangers are not random entities: "They share common goals, a common culture with norms and expectations, probably a generally common doctrine and training, shared practical knowledge, usually common secondary group cohesion, and similar past experiences." So in effect, "armed with these intellectual and social tools," even the strangers in arms of the Canadian Army could "quickly develop a relationship based on trust and teamwork, which [could] be soon refined and increased" and allow them to act together effectively and cohesively.[16]

Leading an infantry platoon was the most dangerous job in the world, and lieutenants were killed and maimed in numbers wildly out of proportion to their numbers within the battalion, both on account of their sense of "heroic leadership" and because of the frequency with which they had to have their heads raised out of a slit trench. While the example offered by officers may have provided much of the fighting impetus for the Canadians, leadership as an element in cohesion also came from the non-commissioned officers, who as a group did not suffer nearly the same casualty rate as junior officers, and had casualty rates even below those of private soldiers throughout most the fighting. As far as can be measured, at the end of the war 40 percent of sergeants in 1st Canadian Infantry Division were still "original veterans" who had joined their regiments directly in 1939–40, while less than 5 percent of private soldiers were still "originals" and the casualty rate for junior officers meant that they had been replaced several times over.[17] The concentration of combat-experienced, long-service soldiers was most pronounced among NCOs. Their long-term survival and leadership within the infantry battalions was central to continued effectiveness and cohesion.

During the most intensive fighting almost one-third of infantrymen in the field battalions were being killed, wounded, or captured each month. Infantry casualty rates were normally lower, but the Second World War in the West, like its Great War precursor, was a war of attrition. The consolidated casualty lists provide reams of raw data of a hauntingly intimate character; the names of the soldiers they list are echoed among the headstones of the Canadian war cemeteries throughout Europe. But the meaning and effect of such heavy casualties on the survivors should not be taken for granted. Throughout the fighting heavy casualties were rarely considered to be particularly detrimental to morale in battle experience questionnaires. And gauging by the censorship reports (which give evidence that is impressionistic but uniquely well informed) the Canadian Army's morale was more correlated with success, the weather, and the ability of the "tail" to keep the "teeth" functioning properly than it was with casualties. Victory, movement, and forward progress – all of which represented control over a situation for soldiers – always brought forward waves of enthusiasm in letters and what censors identified as "high morale" and a willingness to fight, even though these periods usually witnessed the worst fighting and the heaviest casualties. Poor weather, mud, static warfare, and lack of any kind of perceived progress or control over their own fates caused morale to plummet and representations in letters home to become grim and morose, even though these were periods when, relatively speaking, it was much safer to be infantrymen. Safety is not necessarily a condition that fosters morale, and the relationship between morale, effectiveness, and environmental conditions definitely demands further study in a historical context. E.L.M. Burns, having fought at Hill 70 and Passchendaele in 1917 and in Italy in 1944–45, was a keen observer of this phenomenon, naming his memoirs *General Mud* in recognition of his experience. And it was mud, static conditions, frustration, and lack of control that caused Canadian fighting spirit to deteriorate, not the sharp, violent actions of the mobile campaigns. Some of the latest psychiatric research has shown, for instance, that operational stress injuries and post-traumatic stress are not correlated with exposure to or participation in combat, but with feelings of helplessness, or guilt and responsibility.[18]

In 1924 Burns was feeling disillusioned. In his *American Mercury* article he recalled an incident in 1917 when he was told by his sergeant that he must "never kid the troops." "But that is really what we did," Burns morosely reflected, "and that's what we'll have to do in the next war. We'll kid them with the news that they are to die for the Glory of the Flag, for the defense of democracy, for their wives and firesides, to keep God's country inviolate."[19] However, during the Second World War, while the rhetoric and propaganda may have been used to "kid" people at home, the Canadian infantrymen had little time for the idea that they were fighting for high ideals of nationalism and politics, or for the protection of their country. They fought for themselves and for one another, because they believed their cause to be right (a claim none would deny in hindsight). At first, they fought as brothers-in-arms, but they quickly found themselves fighting as strangers in arms. They kept on fighting anyway, proficiently and aggressively, despite constantly being on the offensive, facing unfavourable ground and elite opposition. It is a feat of arms that historians have only just begun to truly appreciate.

Appendices

Appendix A

METHODS AND SOURCES

Given the range of sources used in the writing of this book, a few additional notes are worth including for the benefit of the interested reader.

First, a few points about what has been omitted, and why. Each of the "core" chapters of this book, three through six, discusses one phase of the major Canadian campaigns in the Second World War, on a thematic basis. Absent from these discussions are the more isolated Canadian actions at Hong Kong and Dieppe, as well as those of Canadians serving in the armed forces of other states. The decision to exclude Hong Kong and Dieppe in particular was difficult, but necessary. The Battle of Hong Kong in 1941 was fought in isolation from the rest of the Canadian Army, and the kinds of sources used to create this present study for the other campaigns simply do not exist or did not survive the doomed operations against the Japanese. The source base for Dieppe is richer, but is still not systematized in the way that it has been for later campaigns. Given the centrality of Dieppe to the Canadian imagination of the Second World War, combat motivation during Operation JUBILEE also warrants a separate study of its own.

There are many challenges in analyzing interpersonal phenomena such as cohesion, morale, and motivation through the historian's methodology, which typically involves documentary evidence. In this study I have taken the approach of examining aggregate data over the distinct phases of the Canadian campaigns in Europe, making the book more akin to a (limited) population study of Canadian infantrymen, their behaviour, and their opinions. Its inspiration, as noted in the introduction, has been *The*

American Soldier, the excellent volumes written during the Second World War by American social psychologist Samuel Stouffer and his team, who carried out extensive direct studies on the behaviour and motivation of combat soldiers. The authors did interviews, sent out questionnaires, and used other social science techniques to determine the attitudes of over half a million American GIs on a multitude of topics relating to their lives in and out of combat. No unified sociological surveys were done on Canadian soldiers at the time (at least not those in combat – more were carried out on troops stationed in Canada), but, using a variety of discrete sources, it is possible to develop an aggregate view of Canadian infantrymen's behaviour and motivations.

I have here focused upon what certain observed battlefield behaviours and expressed opinions can tell us about morale, cohesion, and motivation. Analysis in this book of soldiers' behaviour and opinions, in the aggregate, comes from several different sources. Despite their shortcomings, the Canadian Army's official histories provide the scaffolding for this discussion. They are supplemented by the trove of original reports (now held by the Directorate of History and Heritage) written by historical officers during the war, which contributed to the final shape of the official histories. Battalion, brigade, and divisional war diaries, intelligence reports, and operations logs are the basic tools that historians use to discern what happened on the ground, though these tools vary enormously in quality, depending upon their completeness in the archives and the ability, punctuality, personal gumption, and time-management skills of the intelligence officers who penned the war diaries and assembled them. During the fighting, official historian Colonel C.P. Stacey took the initiative in reading unit war diaries and other memoranda from combat units, and circulated extracts highlighting key experiences, successes, shortcomings, and lessons learned, for the benefit of future operations.[1] These extracts covered a vast range of tactical issues and problems, and, although they were filtered through Stacey's eyes, they were very popular among officers.[2] Given the rapid pace at which warfare changed during the Second World War, other "lessons learned" documents used here were the by-product of staff and combatant officers coming to grips with modern war.[3] Such documents are helpful in filling in details glossed over by more chronological battle narratives. The reports that historical officers often solicited from junior and mid-level officers during the fighting provide detailed tactical analyses of operations. Other "lessons learned" documents include official training and tactical instructions distributed by the War Office, Canadian Military Headquarters, and National Defence Headquarters, including the *Current Reports from Overseas* series, the *Canadian Army Training Memoranda*, the British Directorate of Infantry's "Infantry Progress Bulletin," and the like. Most of these were heavily edited or condensed, and represented the military's orthodox, though evolving, views on tactical issues and soldiers' behaviour. For historical purposes they provide snapshots of how the army wanted to improve.[4] Finally, a significant amount of information on combat behaviour has been derived from the battle experience questionnaires filled out by convalescing Canadian junior officers immediately after the fighting. Officers were queried on a great number of tactical and behavioural issues, and their answers offer us a fresh, systematized perspective on Canadian warfare at the level of the infantry section, platoon, and company. For this study statistics have been compiled from questionnaire returns, and the commentaries and accounts left by respondents as appendices to their questionnaires provide texture and detail.

A number of sources exist for studying morale: the attempt to measure and even quantify morale was a preoccupation of contemporary Allied military minds. The mail was one. For reasons of security it was determined in July 1941 that Canadian mail should be processed by British field censors, and that 15 percent of the hundreds of thousands of letters home each week should be opened and examined.[5] The field censors were assiduous not only in rifling through soldiers' correspondence to check for security leaks but in writing reports about the contents of the letters. Different sets of field censors attached to the Central Mediterranean Forces (CMF), the 21st Army Group, and the Canadian Army Overseas wrote bi-monthly reports analyzing patterns and trends in soldiers' attitudes, as revealed by their mail. The field censor reports from 21st Army Group in particular provide a mountain of empirical data, and give a unique perspective, even if it is second-hand, on the changing shape of morale and the pressing concerns of soldiers at the time. The data were filtered through the opinions and biases of the censorship branch, which categorized soldiers' views on particular issues, as expressed in their letters home. All the reports quote representative extracts from soldiers' letters extensively and anonymously.[6] With thousands of letters demanding assessment each week, there would have been little time for careful consideration of the nuances of each text. But while these reports have limitations as sources, they represent an aggregate collection of information that can never be recreated; letters home from Europe were briefly bottlenecked with the field censors, so the censors had access to a body of data that can never be reconstituted. We are, of course, hostage to the censors' eyes, and historian Bill McAndrew has described the field censors as "habitually optimistic."[7]

The battle experience questionnaires are also a source of valuable information on morale. Among the surveys' tactical discussions were questions directly related to morale: how various enemy weapons affected (or did not affect) the morale of Canadian soldiers, and which other factors were involved in the raising or lowering of morale. This information is still somewhat second-hand, since it reflects the opinions of junior infantry officers on what affected morale in their units rather than the opinions of the other ranks within those units – a key distinction. Nonetheless, historians are unlikely to find another source that offers such intimate immediacy on the issues of close combat, morale, and battlefield command during the Second World War, systematized for hundreds of junior officers.

I have also consulted evidence on army discipline for inferences about morale. The prevalence of indiscipline and punishment is a potential yardstick for studying morale, particularly if it is understood that good discipline in a military force is a function of high morale.[8] Although data on field and general courts martial and on summary field punishments for soldiers' offences are available, they are incomplete. Statistical data on courts martial exist in the army's Deputy Judge Advocate General files summarizing all general courts martial.[9] More detailed information on offences comes from statistics obtained from the Pay & Discipline Office of the Canadian Section, GHQ 2nd Echelon, which received monthly returns on offence data for every unit in the field force.[10] These data do not, however, give a clear indication of how many acts of indiscipline were occurring; rather, they represent the numbers of soldiers being caught and punished, a function of the priorities and determination of the units and provosts. Rises in the number of offences against the Army Act in a unit might well represent increases in indiscipline and a drop in morale, but could also represent intensification of the authorities' crack-downs, increased policing, and harsher sentencing, with soldiers who might normally have simply been fined or dealt with by summary proceedings being dragged before a court martial.[11] In most cases it is not possible to tell, and as a result statistics on disciplinary measures, while included in this study, do not constitute core evidence. Rather, they are used as a supplement to other discussions on morale.

Cohesion and motivation are the most elusive aspects to capture through documentary evidence, and lateral approaches are necessary for analyzing these qualities in a historical context. Fortunately, the (relatively) small size of the Canadian Army's infantry force allows for some degree of thoroughness. While this study does not pretend to ascribe motives to every Canadian soldier, it can at least describe some of the observable patterns and problems. An analysis of casualties is particularly important to assessing cohesion, because casualties shatter the primary-group social circle traditionally linked with combat effectiveness. For this project a database was built using Canadian Military Headquarters' Consolidated Casualty Lists (CCL), which listed (and amended) each unit's casualties as they were reported from the front, and gave details on the casualty's name, rank, unit, regimental number, nature of casualty (killed, wounded, prisoner, and, less reliably, psychiatric), and date of casualty.[12] This is the most complete information yet available on Canadian infantry casualties during the 1943–45 campaigns: the database contains 17,637 listings from Sicily and Italy, and 31,143 listings from Normandy and Northwest Europe. We cannot be absolutely certain of the accuracy of these lists. Since they were produced in-theatre by Canadian formations in combat and then transmitted to CMHQ in London, the lists were constantly amended with the most current statistics, and so were in flux. Much of the information, however, correlates with official knowledge on casualties. A random sampling of fifty soldiers listed as killed in the database, for instance, corresponded 100 percent with the dates of death given by the Commonwealth War Graves Commission, so this study presumes a fair degree of accuracy on the part of its casualty database, if not infallibility. The casualty reports from several days of the Italian campaign in September 1944 could not be located among the files, and unfortunately are not included in the data. In terms of the database's creation, raw information from the CCL were entered into a spreadsheet, allowing for the compiling of statistics and detailing of casualties on the basis of type of casualty, regiment, date, rank, and regimental number. Many soldiers were listed as "Died of Wounds," meaning they perished in hospital rather than being killed on the battlefield. Sometimes soldiers were listed as having Died of Wounds the same day they were wounded, but often it was some days or weeks later that they succumbed to their injuries. For the purposes of this study, every soldier listed as Died of Wounds was recorded as a "Wounded" casualty for the day they received their wounds, except those who died of wounds on the day they received their wounds – these were listed as "Killed" on that date, an arbitrary but, I believe, fair assessment. This means that the number of deaths in the statistics is under-represented, but that the overall casualty numbers and dates at which casualties occurred are as accurate as possible. Also, since neuropsychiatric casualties were variously listed as "Wounded" in some campaigns and "Psychiatric" in others, all soldiers listed as "Psychiatric" casualties in the CCL were categorized as Wounded for the sake of consistency, so unfortunately very few specific comments can be made on neuropsychiatric casualties from the CCL.

This casualty database provides a wealth of information on losses suffered by the infantry battalions during the fighting, and makes possible the assessment of casualties among officers and other ranks in every action of the campaigns. In combination with existing battle narratives and other sources, this level of detail provides a skeleton key for understanding the scale of the problems faced by regiments. In this study, these data are frequently paired with information on the standard War Establishment strength of Canadian battalions, thereby allowing the comparison of casualties as a function of normal unit strength.[13] While this is for abstract comparison only (units hardly ever went into battle at full strength),[14] it is nonetheless revealing to cast casualty rates in comparison with optimal strength, especially when, over time, the casualties exceed 100 percent of strength. Data on the soldiers' regimental numbers in the CCL also allow for the exploration of issues related to reinforcements, regionalism, and personnel turbulence. At enlistment Canadian soldiers were issued unique regimental numbers that served as their numeric identifier throughout their service. These numbers were assigned in blocks to specific regiments and units upon mobilization.[15] A letter prefix to every soldier's regimental number indicated the Military District of Canada in which they had been recruited.

Table A.1
Canadian military districts and regimental numbers

Military District	Location of Military District	Regimental Number Prefix
1	Southwest Ontario	A
2	Toronto and Central Ontario	B
3	Eastern Ontario and Gatineau	C
4	Montreal and SW Quebec	D
5	Quebec City and NE Quebec	E
6	Nova Scotia and Prince Edward Island	F
7	New Brunswick	G
10	Manitoba, NW Territories, Northern Ontario	H
11	British Columbia, Yukon Territories	K
12	Saskatchewan	L
13	Alberta and NW Territories	M
—	Permanent Force (PF)	P

The system of regimental numbers makes it possible to track, through this study's CCL database, how many casualties from each regiment hailed from (or at least were recruited in) particular Military Districts, allowing a glimpse of the force's regional composition. This information also shows how many soldiers in each combat battalion were "originals" who enlisted directly into their infantry regiment in 1939–40. This is important information since it speaks directly to the effectiveness of the Canadian regimental system, as discussed at some length in chapter 2 and afterward.

On the topic of the regimental system, few documentary or statistical sources exist that tell us about regimental identification and esprit de corps in a systematic way. The most vocal sources on *esprit* and regimental spirit are regimental and oral histories from the postwar years. These are potentially problematic; nothing is more predictable than a regimental history funded and published by a regimental association emphasizing the importance and role of that unique regiment in the lives of its soldiers.

Nonetheless, the individual character and traditions of the infantry regiments still play a part in this discussion of combat motivation, if only because it was a basic assumption at the time that regimental character would affect combat effectiveness.[16] One of the observable regimental distinctions was language. Four infantry regiments in the Canadian Army Overseas – the Régiment de la Chaudière, the Royal 22e Régiment, the Régiment de Maisonneuve, and the Fusiliers Mont-Royal – were French-speaking and contained close to 100 percent francophone other ranks, including many who spoke no English at all.[17] It would be hard to argue that regimental connection and identity were unimportant to these units; for French Canadians the regiments were islands of cultural familiarity in an Anglo-dominated institution.[18] The struggles, successes, and failures of the regiments in maintaining their unique identities for their members to connect with constitute an important consideration for combat motivation. Among the sources used for this study, the censorship reports and battle experience questionnaires provide the most systematic treatment of this topic.

In addition to the above sources, a number of personal papers, accounts, and transcripts from English- and French-language oral interviews with soldiers have been used. These are employed to add colour and corroboration to period documentary evidence, and do not constitute core evidence in and of themselves. I also consulted a large body of secondary literature relating to the campaigns in question in order to frame the study.

Appendix B

PULHEMS

Table B.1
PULHEMS

Physique (P)	
Grade 1	Fit after training for full strain and fatigue of combatant duty. A front line fighter.
Grade 2	Fit for all normal work or strain but unable to endure extreme degrees for long periods.
Grade 3	Fit to do ordinary general duty. Has not the stamina, even after training, to endure the strain and fatigue of full combatant duty. Will be used as storemen, batmen, clerks, certain trade branches, etc.
Grade 4	Specific diseases of internal organs, e.g. peptic ulcer, or certain surgical conditions, for which see details under "Systems."
Grade 5	Unsuitable for service anywhere in any capacity.
Factors to be considered	Age, build, strength, stamina, guts.

Upper Extremities (U)

Grade 1	Able to lift 50 lbs. up to head level. Can use rifle to shoot and for bayoneting. Can throw grenades, dig, and potentially able to drive heavy vehicles. Fit for hand to hand fighting.
Grade 2	Able to lift 50 lb. up to head level, use rifle and bayonet, throw grenades, dig, lift, push or drag strongly, drive heavy vehicles.
Grade 3	Able to lift 25 lbs at least to shoulder height. Is potentially able to drive light vehicles. In an emergency can fire a rifle or sub-machine gun.
Grade 4	Specific defects or defect which necessitate keeping the man in Canada, such as: serious interference with use of joints, muscles, spine, especially those with pain on use, or of a possible progressive character.
Grade 5	Unsuitable for service anywhere in any capacity.
Factors to considered	Strength, range of movement and general efficiency *be* of upper arm, shoulder girdle, and back.

Locomotion (L)

Grade 1	Able to march 20 miles per day after having completed training. No disabilities of feet or legs which would hamper the man in standing, running, climbing, or digging.
Grade 2	Able to march 5 miles per day after having completed training. Must have no difficulty in standing, running, climbing or digging.
Grade 3	Able to walk 5 miles per day and do limited standing but not able to do continuous standing for long periods (e.g. guard duty).
Grade 4	Specific defects or defect which necessitate keeping the man in Canada.
Grade 5	Unsuitable for service anywhere in any capacity.
Factors to considered	Strength, range of movement and efficiency of feet, *be* legs, pelvic girdle and lower back.

Hearing (H)

Grade 1	Able to hear normal spoken voice at 15 feet distant in one ear and 10 feet distant in other ear.
Grade 2	C.V. one ear 20 feet, other 0 feet. C.V. one ear 10 feet, other 10 feet. C.V. one ear 15 feet, other 5 feet.
Grade 3	Completely deaf in one ear, but able to hear spoken voice at 15 feet distant with other ear, or C.V. at 10 feet in one ear and 5 feet in other ear.
Grade 4	Specific defect or defects which necessitate keeping the man in Canada (e.g. more deaf than grade 3 but can hear spoken voice at least 5 feet away).
Grade 5	Unsuitable for service anywhere in any capacity.
Factors to be considered	Auditory acuity.

Eyesight (E)

Grade 1	Able to see to shoot using right eye without glasses 20/40 right eye, 20/100 left eye. If with glasses must have better than 20/100 both eyes correctible to 20/40 in both eyes. Have binoculars (stereoscopic) vision sufficient for driving and use of binocular instruments.
Grade 2	Must have 20/120 right eye, 20/200 left, correctible with glasses to 20/40 in both eyes. No stereoscopic vision required. Not dependent on glasses.
Grade 3	Must have 20/200 or better in both eyes, correctible with glasses up to 20/40 in both eyes. No stereoscopic vision required. Dependent on glasses.
Grade 4	Specific defect or defects which necessitate keeping the man in Canada (e.g. 20/400 in both eyes correctible to 20/40).
Grade 5	Unsuitable for service anywhere in any capacity.
Factors to be considered	Visual acuity.

Mental (M)	
Grade 1	Intelligence sufficient for full combatant duty and training including appropriate tradesman or specialist training.
Grade 2	Intelligence sufficient for non-tradesmen or non-specialist combatant duties or for trades requiring experience rather than ability.
Grade 3	*Blank.*
Grade 4	Specific defect or defects e.g. slight mental retardation. Useful only in Works Companies, Pioneer Companies, etc.
Grade 5	Unsuitable for service anywhere in any capacity
Factors to be considered	Intelligence.

Stability (S)	
Grade 1	Emotionally stable – no signs of psychoneurosis, or any serious divergence from the normal in autonomic nervous system function or stability.
Grade 2	Same as No. 1.
Grade 3	Have evidence of some instability but is being used overseas.
Grade 4	Some evidence of emotional instability; no sufficient disability to preclude useful work in Army. Grade 4 in both "M" and "S" should preclude enlistment or warrant discharge of a serving soldier.
Grade 5	Unsuitable for service anywhere in the country.
Factors to be considered	Emotional stability. Personality.

From: CMHQ, "Physical Standards and Instructions: for the Medical Examination of serving soldiers and recruits for the Canadian Army" (Ottawa: 4 May 1943). (LAC RG 24, vol. 12642, 11/STANDARDS/2.)

Appendix C

DIRECTORATE OF PERSONNEL SELECTION'S MEAN "M" SCORE FOR POPULATION

Table C.1
Mean "M" score for population

Military Districts	Average School Grade	Percent over Grade 8	Mean "M" Test Score
11 (British Columbia)	8.98	48.53	146.10
13 (Alberta)	8.29	37.84	133.75
12 (Saskatchewan)	8.15	34.63	130.40
10 (Manitoba)	8.17	38.42	130.55
1 (S. Ontario)	8.68	43.82	139.25
2 (Toronto)	8.69	46.29	136.95
3 (E. Ontario)	8.75	43.80	131.50
4 (W. Quebec)	7.68	35.69	126.35
5 (E. Quebec)	6.47	20.76	107.05
6 (Nova Scotia)	7.25	25.63	115.15
7 (New Brunswick)	7.61	30.31	118.85
AVERAGE	8.17	36.70	130.50

From: Major H.S.M. Carver, "Personnel Selection in the Canadian Army: A Descriptive Study" (Ottawa: Directorate of Personnel Selection, 1945), 251–2. (DHH 86/71 File 8.)

Appendix D

CANADIAN ARMY INFANTRY ORGANIZATION

A word about the actual organization of the infantry will be helpful here. In the Commonwealth, infantry divisions were composed of nine infantry battalions, which were triangularly brigaded (three battalions per brigade). The division itself also included in its war establishment a supporting machine gun battalion, the divisional artillery, Royal Canadian Engineer field companies, medical personnel and field ambulances, reconnaissance, signals, ordnance, service, electrical and mechanical engineers, pay, postal, dental, and provost corps. There were no tanks permanently attached to the infantry division; when needed, they were temporarily attached from armoured brigades.[1] Armoured divisions, of which there were two in the Canadian Army, had tanks organically attached as part of their structure. At full war establishment, the division would have 915 officers and 17,176 other ranks; of these, only 400 officers and 7,600 other ranks were in the nine infantry rifle battalions.[2] As a proportion of its total strength, the Canadian division contained fewer fighting men than did those of other countries, particularly Germany, although the Canadian division was numerically much larger.[3]

Almost all the actual fighting was done by the division's infantry, machine-guns, artillery, and engineers, and the overwhelming majority of casualties were sustained by the infantry battalions. The world of the rifleman lay within the organization of his battalion. A battalion, or unit, at full war establishment consisted of 812 other ranks and 38 officers, and included a headquarters company for the commanding officer (a lieutenant-colonel) and his staff, four rifle companies, a support company containing troop carriers and heavier infantry weapons such as mortars and anti-tank weapons, and a "B" Echelon for signals, supplies, and pay.[4] Each rifle company was supposed to contain 120 infantrymen at full strength, and was commanded by a captain or a major – these were the largest tactical sub-units that contained infantrymen exclusively. Each company consisted of four platoons of about thirty men, commanded by a subaltern (a lieutenant) with a senior non-commissioned officer (a sergeant) as second-in-command. Every platoon was in turn composed of three sections, each of eight to ten soldiers apiece, commanded by a junior NCO (a corporal).[5] Battalions had an array of weapons available to them, but the heavy support that was often most useful to the infantry – the artillery, tanks, and air power – was external to their structure.

Most Canadian infantrymen (604 out of the battalion's 850) were armed with the Lee-Enfield rifle and grenades, and there was one Bren light machine gun per section for fire support (63 Bren guns per battalion). Every man was supposed to carry 50–100 rounds of .303 rifle ammunition on bandoleers, two hand grenades, plus spare magazine clips for the Bren even if someone else was carrying the machine gun itself.[6] What with weapons, entrenching tool, water, ground-sheet, tins of food, hard tack, cigarettes, mess tins, and a few personal items, every other rank infantryman was typically carrying no fewer than sixty pounds on his back, although particularly in the raging heat of southern Italy in 1943 many elected to unburden themselves with or without authorization.[7] Each NCO and officer, and sometimes designated other ranks, carried a sub-machine gun – in the Mediterranean these were the excellent American-made Thompson Sub-Machine Guns (TSMG), and in Normandy these were the more dubious British-made Sten Guns. Each section also carried a PIAT (Projector, Infantry Anti-Tank) bomb-thrower; 160 sub-machine guns and 23 PIATs were the established strength per battalion. Each battalion's support company also included 26 two-inch mortars, six three-inch mortars, and half a dozen six-pounder anti-tank guns for added fire-support.[8] Specialty weapons such as flamethrowers would be added to the war establishment in 1944. The Canadian infantry divisions were also completely motorized, at least on paper. Each infantry battalion had 38 tracked armoured carriers organically attached, as well as 57 assorted cars, trucks, lorries, and tractors; the division as a whole contained some 3,371 of these vehicles, almost one for every two men in the infantry battalions.[9] It required an enormous amount of fuel and maintenance, but the infantry division on the move could go very fast. In theory troops would go into battle dismounted, but would have motor transport to expedite them and their gear most of the way there. The realities of war meant that in practice the infantry often had to operate as their pre-Fordist forerunners had across country: on foot. But infantry training had involved such intensive ground pounding that cross-country work became a real strength of the Canadians.

The 4th and the 5th Canadian Armoured Divisions were organized slightly differently. In an armoured division there were only two brigades: one armoured brigade consisting of three tank regiments and a motorized regiment; and one infantry brigade of three battalions. An armoured division in 1943–44 contained 14,964 men all ranks, with only about 3,400 in the rifle companies of the three infantry battalions.[10] The armour was intended to operate organically with the infantry battalions, part of the renewed emphasis upon the development of armoured formations after the 1940 campaigns in France and Belgium. The armoured divisions were meant to be fast and hard-hitting, for pursuit and breakthroughs, but in practice, for technical and institutional reasons, the infantry-armour relationship could sometimes become very strained.[11] The development of the armoured division in British interwar doctrine also resulted in formations based too heavily upon tanks, and not enough on infantry; historian David French has assessed that they were not particularly effective instruments of all-arms cooperation.[12]

Appendix E

DISCIPLINE AND OFFENCE STATISTICS

Table E.1
Infantry offences, 1st Canadian Division, Italy 1943–44

Month and Year	1st Canadian Division Offences		
	Div. Total	Infantry	% Infantry
July 1943	317	173	54.6
August 1943	362	91	25.1
September 1943	498	197	39.6
October 1943	397	189	47.6
November 1943	390	197	50.5
December 1943	285	84	29.5
February 1944	441	231	52.4
March 1944	579	318	54.9
April 1944	517	280	54.2
May 1944	559	291	52.1
June 1944	448	259	57.8
July 1944	608	266	43.8
August 1944	460	282	61.3
September 1944	268	109	40.7
October 1944	335	244	72.8

Table E.1 (continued)

Month and Year	1st Canadian Division Offences		
	Div. Total	Infantry	% Infantry
November 1944	363	268	73.8
December 1944	309	172	55.7
TOTALS	7,136	3,651	51.2

Source: Discipline & Pay Section – Canadian Section GHQ, *2nd Echelon, Summary of Offences (by Formations) for Canadian Army in the Field,* LAC RG 24, *vols.* 10118–19.

Table E.2

Infantry offences, Normandy and NW Europe, 1944

Month / Year	3rd Canadian Division offences			2nd Canadian Division offences		
	Div. Total	Infantry	% Infantry	Div. Total	Infantry	% Infantry
June 1944	960	447	46.6	1,442	722	50.1
July 1944	217	29	13.4	367	194	52.9
August 1944	219	49	22.4	185	18	9.7
September 1944	426	157	36.9	394	78	19.8
October 1944	452	142	31.4	696	207	29.7
November 1944	524	224	42.7	581	186	32.0
December 1944	721	415	57.6	550	316	57.5
TOTALS	3,519	1,463	41.6	4,215	1,721	40.8

Source: Discipline & Pay Section – Canadian Section GHQ, *2nd Echelon, Summary of Offences (by Formations) for Canadian Army in the Field,* LAC RG 24, *vol.* 10117.

Table E.3
Absence without leave and desertion, NW Europe, autumn 1944

Battalion	AWL charges, September to December 1944	Reported deserters, September 1944 to January 1945
Royal Regiment of Canada	74	17
Royal Hamilton Light Infantry	85	6
Essex Scottish Regiment	57	7
Black Watch (Royal Highlanders)	52	7
Le Régiment de Maisonneuve	114	35
Calgary Highlanders	21	1
Les Fusiliers Mont-Royal	65	45
Queen's Own Cameron Highlanders	18	15
South Saskatchewan Regiment	55	2
Royal Winnipeg Rifles	10	6
Regina Rifle Regiment	49	6
Canadian Scottish Regiment	37	4
Queen's Own Rifles	50	3
Le Régiment de la Chaudière	178	35
North Shore (N.B.) Regiment	41	2
Highland Light Infantry of Canada	94	6
Stormont, Dundas & Glengarry Highlanders	72	9
North Nova Scotia Highlanders	75	1
Algonquin Regiment	43	—
Argyll & Sutherland Highlanders	35	4
Lincoln & Welland Regiment	36	5
Lake Superior Regiment	80	5
TOTALS	1,341	221

Source: Desertion statistics are from Crerar Papers (LAC MG 30, E157, vol. 4), AWL statistics are from Summary of Offences (by Formations) for Canadian Army in the Field (LAC RG 24, vol. 10117, 22/OFFENCE/1/6).

Appendix F

COMPARATIVE CASUALTY DATA

Table F.1
Infantry battalion casualties, Italy 1943, totals, and as approximate percentage of war establishment

Time period	1st Canadian Division	
	Officer casualties	Other ranks casualties
July–August 1943	84 (21%)	1,154 (15%)
September–October 1943	50 (17%)	759 (11%)
December 1943	164 (55%)	2,329 (33%)
Cumulative	298 (93%)	4,242 (59%)

Source: *CMHQ Records Office – Consolidated Casualty Statistics – CMF (LAC RG 24 vols. 12697–8, RG 24 vol. 18576, file 133.065(D18D).)*

Table F.2

Infantry battalion casualties, Italy 1944, totals, and as approximate percentage of war establishment

Time Period	1st Canadian Division		5th Canadian Division	
	Officer casualties	Other ranks casualties	Officer casualties	Other ranks casualties
January–April 1944	74 (25%)	1,147 (16%)	21 (21%)	456 (20%)
May–June 1944	73 (25%)	1,593 (23%)	20 (20%)	417 (18%)
August–September 1944	125 (42%)	2,335 (34%)	84 (44%)	1,407 (31%)
October 1944	38 (13%)	561 (8%)	12 (6%)	190 (4%)
December 1944	88 (30%)	1,287 (19%)	38 (19%)	1,012 (22%)
Cumulative	398 (135%)	6,923 (100%)	175 (110%)	3,482 (95%)

Source: CMHQ *Records Office – Consolidated Casualty Statistics* – CMF (LAC RG 24 *vols.* 12697–8, RG 24, *vol.* 18576 *file* 133.065(D18D).)

Table F.3: Infantry battalion casualties, Normandy 1944, totals, and as approximate percentage of war establishment

Time Period	2nd Division		3rd Division		4th Division	
	Officer casualties	Other ranks casualties	Officer casualties	Other ranks casualties	Officer casualties	Other ranks casualties
June 1944	0	0	108 (38%)	2,079 (30%)	0	0
July 1944	150 (52%)	2,884 (42%)	136 (47%)	2,344 (34%)	0	0
August 1944	186 (65%)	2,620 (38%)	91 (32%)	1,380 (20%)	53 (55%)	960 (41%)
Cumulative	336 (117%)	5,504 (80%)	335 (117%)	5,803 (84%)	53 (55%)	960 (41%)

Source: CMHQ *Records Office – Consolidated Casualty Statistics –* AEF *(*LAC RG *24 vols. 12695–6,* RG *24, vol. 18576 file 133.065(D18D).)*

Table F.4
Infantry battalion casualties, NW Europe 1944–45, totals, and as approximate percentage of war establishment

Time Period	2nd Division		3rd Division		4th Division	
	Officer casualties	Other ranks casualties	Officer casualties	Other ranks casualties	Officer casualties	Other ranks casualties
Sept. 1944	59 (21%)	1,024 (15%)	62 (22%)	860 (12%)	32 (33%)	476 (21%)
Oct. 1944	102 (35%)	1,939 (28%)	96 (33%)	1,721 (25%)	29 (30%)	577 (25%)
Nov. 1944	18 (6%)	298 (4%)	12 (4%)	166 (2%)	13 (14%)	160 (7%)
Dec. 1944	26 (7%)	271 (4%)	5 (2%)	116 (2%)	0	36 (2%)
Jan. 1945	10 (4%)	144 (2%)	6 (2%)	94 (1%)	23 (24%)	229 (10%)
Feb. 1945	61 (21%)	953 (14%)	55 (19%)	862 (12%)	16 (17%)	270 (12%)
March 1945	65 (23%)	1,043 (15%)	55 (19%)	835 (12%)	22 (23%)	420 (18%)
April 1945	61 (21%)	943 (14%)	61 (21%)	955 (14%)	33 (34%)	720 (31%)
Cumulative	402 (138%)	6,651 (95%)	352 (122%)	5,609 (81%)	168 (175%)	2,888 (124%)

Source: CMHQ *Records Office – Consolidated Casualty Statistics –* AEF (LAC RG 24, *vols.* 12695–6, RG 24, *vol.* 18576 *file* 133.065(D18D).)

Table F.5
Infantry battalion casualties, cumulative 1943–45, totals, and as approximate percentage of war establishment

Formation	Officer casualties	Other ranks casualties
1st Cdn Infantry Division*	696 (228%)	11,165 (159%)
2nd Cdn Infantry Division	738 (255%)	12,155 (175%)
3rd Cdn Infantry Division	687 (239%)	11,412 (165%)
4th Cdn Armoured Division	221 (230%)	3,848 (165%)
5th Cdn Armoured Division*	175 (110%)	3,482 (95%)
Cumulative	2,517	42,064

*Not including casualties from Northwest Europe
Source: CMHQ *Records Office – Consolidated Casualty Statistics –* CMF *and* AEF *(*LAC RG *24, vols. 12695–8).*

Appendix G

MORALE STATISTICS

Table G.1
Top factors involved in morale, Italy 1944–45

Factors involved in raising morale	Officers indicating
Rations / good food	24 (55%)
Mail / timely delivery of mail	22 (50%)
Action / success in battle	16 (36%)
Good leadership	15 (34%)
Artillery support	11 (25%)
Being kept "in the picture"	8 (18%)
Leave	7 (16%)
Tank Support	5 (11%)
Factors involved in lowering morale	**Officers indicating**
Bad information / kept "out of the picture"	15 (34%)
Bad leadership / absence of officers	14 (32%)
Poor rations or lack thereof	13 (30%)
Lack of mail delivery	12 (27%)
Inaction / static positions	10 (23%)
Unnecessary moving about	10 (23%)
No relief or reinforcements	10 (23%)
Weather	7 (16%)

Heavy casualties	7 (16%)
Failure	6 (14%)
Lack of artillery support	6 (14%)
Uncleanliness	5 (11%)

Source: Battle Experience Questionnaires, LAC RG 24, vol. 10450.

Table G.2
Top factors involved in morale, Normandy 1944

Factors involved in raising morale	Officers indicating
Mail and Parcels	48 (53%)
Food and Rations	47 (52%)
Allied Air Support	38 (42%)
Hot showers / cleanliness	30 (33%)
Rest and Sleep	27 (30%)
Artillery Support	27 (30%)
Success in action / Aggressive action	27 (30%)
Being kept "in the picture"	22 (24%)
Tank Support	21 (23%)
Good Leadership	15 (17%)
News from other fronts	15 (17%)
Leave	13 (14%)
Receiving reinforcements	10 (11%)
Factors involved in lowering morale	**Officers indicating**
Bad information / kept "out of the picture"	26 (29%)
Lack of food or rations	23 (25%)
Lack of rest	17 (19%)
Lack of mail	17 (19%)
Inaction / static positions	14 (15%)
Bombing own troops / friendly fire	11 (12%)
Heavy casualties	11 (12%)
Poor leadership	11 (12%)
Bad weather	10 (11%)
Lack of tank support	10 (11%)
Failure in battle	9 (10%)
Lack of cleanliness	9 (10%)
Lack of reinforcements	9 (10%)
Untrained reinforcements	4 (4%)

Source: Battle Experience Questionnaires, LAC RG 24, vol. 10450.

Table G.3
Top factors involved in morale, NW Europe, 1944–45

Factors involved in raising morale	Officers indicating
Rations and food	33 (54%)
Mail	32 (53%)
Rest and recreation	31 (51%)
Air support (in combat)	24 (39%)
Baths and cleanliness	20 (33%)
Artillery support (in combat)	14 (23%)
Tank support (in combat)	14 (23%
Good information / kept "in the picture"	13 (21%)
Leadership	12 (20%)
Success in battle	11 (18%)
Leave	11 (18%)
Reinforcements	8 (13%)

Factors involved in lowering morale	Officers indicating
Shortage of rations	20 (33%)
No opportunity for rest or leave	19 (31%)
Bad information / kept "out of picture"	14 (23%)
Lack of mail	12 (20%)
Lack of leadership	11 (18%)
Fighting in static positions	10 (16%)
Bad weather / terrain / environment	8 (13%)
Heavy casualties	8 (13%)
Lack of tank support	8 (13%)
Friendly fire	7 (12%)
Failure in the attack	6 (10%)
False rumours about the end of the war	6 (10%)
Lack of reinforcements	5 (8%)
Poorly trained reinforcements	5 (8%)

Source: Battle Experience Questionnaires, LAC RG 24, vol. 10450.

Notes

INTRODUCTION

1 Novel notes, 14 July 1952, McDougall Papers, Box III file 2, McGill University Rare Books Library (MURBL).
2 Notebook 1953–56, McDougall Papers, Box I file 6, MURBL.
3 See Clark, *A Keen Soldier*.
4 Notebook 1953–56, 16 March 1953, McDougall Papers, Box I file 6, MURBL.
5 PPCLI War Diary, Jan. 1945, LAC RG 24, vol. 15158.
6 DSO Citation for Major Colin Malcolm McDougall, 19 Jan. 1945, TNA WO 373/13/124; LAC Reference 2004-01505-5, item 79986. Major McDougall had previously been "Mentioned in Despatches" in January 1945.
7 Consolidated casualty lists, CMF, LAC RG 24, vol. 12695 and 12696.
8 Novel Notes, 4 April 1953, McDougall Papers, Box III file 2, MURBL.
9 McDougall, *Execution*, 108–9.
10 McDougall, *Execution*, 107.
11 Novel Notes, 4 April 1953, McDougall Papers, Box III file 2, MURBL.
12 Farley Mowat to Colin McDougall, 29 Jan. 1960, McDougall Papers, Box I file 4, MURBL.
13 PPCLI War Diary, Jan. 1945, LAC RG 24, vol. 15158.
14 For more on the background to the questionnaires, see Engen, *Canadians Under Fire*, 28–48.
15 Completed Battle Experience Questionnaires file, LAC RG 24, vol. 9879.
16 Notebook 1953–56, 16 March 1953, McDougall Papers Box I file 6, MURBL.
17 Major Colin McDougall, PPCLI, BEQ 255, LAC RG 25, vol. 10450, form "A."
18 Major Colin McDougall, PPCLI, BEQ 255, LAC RG 25, vol. 10450, form "H."

19 Major Colin McDougall, PPCLI, BEQ 255, LAC RG 25, vol. 10450, annexure.
20 Novel notes, 10 Sept. 1954, McDougall Papers, Box III file 2, MURBL.
21 Major Colin McDougall, PPCLI, BEQ 255, LAC RG 25, vol. 10450, form "A" and annexure.
22 Due to the nature of the sources employed, the brief actions at Hong Kong in December 1941 and Dieppe in August 1942 have been omitted from this study, as have the experiences of Canadians serving in the military forces of Allied nations.
23 Marshall, *Men Against Fire*, 50–63.
24 Engen, *Canadians Under Fire*. I have been particularly critical of Dave Grossman's work on "killology." See Grossman, *On Killing*; Engen, "Killing for Their Country."
25 A small sampling of the postwar published accounts consulted for this book: Barris, *Days of Victory*; Cederberg, *Long Road Home*; Chatillon, *Carnets de guerre*; Frost, *Once a Patricia*; Kipp, *Because We Are Canadians*; Martin, *Battle Diary*; Mowat, *And No Birds Sang*; Munro, *Gauntlet to Overlord*; Wilmot, *Through the Hitler Line*.
26 War Diary, 29 June 1944, Queen's University Archives, William Eric Craven Harrison Fonds, Box 10, File 15.
27 Stacey, *A Date with History*, 230. Emphasis in original.
28 Spiller, "S.L.A. Marshall," 64–9.
29 Cook, *Clio's Warriors*, 111.
30 A partial list of the regimental histories consulted for this book: Beattie, *Dileas*; Bercuson, *Battalion of Heroes*; Bernier, *The Royal 22e Regiment*; Bird, *North Shore (New Brunswick) Regiment*; Hayes, *The Lincs*; Morrison and Slaney, *The Breed of Manly Men*; Mowat, *The Regiment*; Roy, *Seaforth Highlanders*; Stevens, *A City Goes to War*; Tascana, *The Little Black Devils*; Tooley, *Invicta*. For the definitive historiographical analysis, see Cook, *Clio's Warriors*, 200–52.
31 Kellett, *Combat Motivation*, xv.
32 Copp and McAndrew, *Battle Exhaustion*, especially 44–148.
33 Margolian, *Conduct Unbecoming*.
34 Delaney, *The Soldiers' General*, especially 20–70 for the purposes of this discussion.
35 Copp, *Fields of Fire*; Copp, *Cinderella Army*.
36 Copp, *The Brigade*.
37 For the interested, a detailed discussion of methods and sources in this book can be found in Appendix A.
38 Fennell, *Combat and Morale in the North African Campaign*.
39 Stouffer, *The American Soldier*. For a recent analysis, see Joseph Ryan, *Samuel Stouffer and the GI Survey*.

40 Kellett, *Combat Motivation*, 6.
41 Shalit, *The Psychology of Conflict and Combat*, 6–7.
42 Watson, *War on the Mind*, 53.
43 Quoted in Kellett, *Combat Motivation*, 3.
44 "Morale," discussion with VCIGS–DTI, 6 Sept. 1945, Laurier Centre for Military, Strategic, and Disarmament Studies Archives, RG 1, File 00023.
45 Bartlett, *Psychology and the Fighting Man*, 152.
46 National Research Council, *Psychology for the Fighting Man*, 289.
47 Baynes, *Morale*, 92.
48 Stewart, *Mates & Muchachos*, 28–9.
49 Laurence and Matthews, *Oxford Handbook of Military Psychology*, 3.
50 War Office, *Field Service Regulations 1935, Vol.* 2, 7.
51 For a more thorough discussion of doctrine as it relates to the different services and to the *Field Service Regulations*, the best book is French, *Raising Churchill's Army*, chap. 1.
52 Shalit, *Psychology of Conflict and Combat*, 35–6, 135.
53 Manning, "Morale, Cohesion and Esprit de Corps," 455.
54 Ibid., 460. Emphasis mine.
55 For variations on many of these themes that are semantically different but essentially making the same points, see Hauser, "The Will to Fight," 186–207.
56 Possony and Mantoux, "Du Picq and Foch," 25–6.
57 Shils and Janowitz, "Cohesion and Disintegration," 280–315.
58 Henderson, *Cohesion*, 4.
59 A good, concise academic overview can be found in Stewart, *Mates & Muchachos*, 11–30.
60 Siebold, "Essence of Military Cohesion," 287.
61 Ibid., 288–92.
62 See, for instance, Winslow, "Rites of Passage and Group Bonding," 429–57. Another relevant example is the case of the Salerno Mutiny in 1943, which saw a group of experienced combat veterans refuse to fight because they had, in their minds, been unjustly separated from their long-time units. See David, *Mutiny at Salerno*.
63 Siebold, "Essence of Military Cohesion," 289.
64 For organizational imperatives, the example most frequently cited is the US Army's one-year rotation policy for individual soldiers during the Vietnam War. See Moskos, *American Enlisted Man*, 142.
65 For discussion, see Bercuson, *The Fighting Canadians*, 1–21.
66 For a recent example, see Reid, *No Holding Back*, 370–1.
67 Ben Shalom, "Cohesion During Military Operations," 66–70. For more, see Lester and Vogelgesang, "Swift Trust in Ad Hoc Military Organizations," 176–86.

68 Ben-Shalom, "Cohesion During Military Operations," 74–6.
69 Shurkin, "France's War in Mali," 28–9, 45–6.

CHAPTER ONE

1 In Canada this has frequently taken the form of the "militia myth." For an in-depth treatment, see Wood, *Militia Myths*.
2 Biddle and Long, "Democracy and Military Effectiveness," 541.
3 For exploration, see McKay and Swift, *Warrior Nation*, 5–27.
4 See Rodgers, "Billy Yank and G.I. Joe," 93–121. For further discussion of the relationship between the state and the will to fight, see Coker, *Waging War Without Warriors?*, 1–59.
5 Bousfield and Toffoli, *Royal Observations*, 152.
6 Margaret Young, "Canadian *Citizenship Act* and Current Issues," Aug. 1998, retrieved 14 March 2014 from: http://publications.gc.ca/collections/Collection-R/LoPBdP/BP/bp445-e.htm
7 Chief Plebiscite Officer for Canada, *Canadian Service Voter Plebiscite Regulations*, 7.
8 McKay, "Canada as a Long Liberal Revolution," 399.
9 Mills, "When Democratic Socialists Discovered Democracy," 53–81.
10 For an effective discussion, see Walker, "The Revolt of the Canadian Generals."
11 For the most recent work on the Mac-Paps, see Petrou, *Renegades*.
12 For a discussion of "character" as an understanding of liberal individualism, see McKay and Bates, *In the Province of History*, 145–8. For a more detailed analysis of dynamics of voluntarism and conscription in Canada in the Second World War, see Engen, "The Zombies' War," paper presented at Society for Military History, AGM 2013.
13 Enlistments and appointments in Canadian Army, LAC RG 24, vol. 18826, 133.065 (D697).
14 Memo, ADAG (A), "Canadian Army Population Statistics, Racial Groups by Military District," 13 Oct. 1944, LAC RG 24, vol. 10262, 52/SURVEYS/3.
15 Lackenbauer, *History of Aboriginal Peoples in the Canadian Military*, 135–50.
16 Tremblay, *Volontaires*, 17.
17 For more on this, see Durflinger, *Fighting from Home*.
18 Gravel (ed.), *Le Québec et la guerre*, 87.
19 Language Stats – CA (A), 1939–1945, LAC RG 24, vol. 18715, 133.056 (D366). Additionally, a further 78.887 (10.8%) were classified as "Others," typically speaking English and a non-French foreign language.
20 Dominion Bureau of Statistics, *Eighth Census of Canada, 1941, Volume*

1, 255. For some critiques of the idea of the census in Canadian history, see Curtis, *The Politics of Population.*

21 Durflinger, "City at War," 82.

22 Morton, *When Your Number's Up*, 17; Dominion Bureau of Statistics, *Eighth Census of Canada 1941*, 164.

23 Cook, *At the Sharp End*, 29.

24 Enlistments and appointments in Canadian Army, LAC RG 24, vol. 18826, 133.065 (D697); Dominion Bureau of Statistics, *Eighth Census of Canada 1941*, 163.

25 Compiled from: Dominion Statistics Bureau, *Eighth Census of Canada 1941*, 288; LAC RG 24 vol. 18824, 133.065 (d710), War Service Records stats on Cdn Army Enlistment Sept. 1939 by Profession, religion, place of birth.

26 LAC RG 24, vol. 18826, 133.065(d710).

27 Hayes, *Anglicans in Canada*, 69.

28 Ibid., 4–5, 77–9.

29 Granatstein, *Canada's Army*, 188.

30 Burns, *Manpower in the Canadian Army*, 6, 92.

31 Walker, "The Revolt of the Canadian Generals, 1944," 55–97.

32 DGMS (AMD2) Statistics Canada, LAC RG 24, vol. 18826, 133.065 (D665). The statistics here are extracted from the consolidated returns of Unit and Corps strengths prepared by A.G. Stats after the war. Includes personnel taken POW and those on extended leaves of absence.

33 Cohen, *Citizens and Soldiers*; Reid, *No Holding Back*, 24.

34 Stacey, *Six Years of War*, 34–5.

35 Granatstein, *Canada's Army*, 179. On the cadre system see Cohen, *Citizens and Soldiers*, 23, 60–86.

36 Consolidated casualty lists, LAC RG 24, vol. 12695 to 12698.

37 War Service Records stats on Canadian Army Enlistments, Sept. 1939 (Nov. 1948), LAC RG 24, vol. 18826, 133.045 (D710).

38 Seventeen hundred Canadians volunteered to fight in the Spanish Civil War in the International Brigade's Mackenzie-Papineau Battalion and survived the experience; many would attempt to join the Canadian Army for a second chance to fight fascism, though the exact numbers remain unknown, since volunteers for Spain were under blanket RCMP investigation for pro-communist activities upon their return and were initially barred from service. Some men found ways around this and brought combat experience to the Canadian Army. See Petrou, *Renegades*, 174–5.

39 Stats on Canadian Army intakes by civil profession, 1939–45, supplied by War Service Records (March 1954), LAC RG 24, vol. 18826, 133.065 (D678).

40 Stats on Canadian Army intakes by civil profession, 1939–45, supplied

by War Service Records (March 1954), LAC RG 24, vol. 18826, 133.065 (D678).

41 Douglas and Greenhous, *Out of the Shadows*, 36.

42 Keshen, *Saints, Sinners, and Soldiers*, 12–13; Miller, "Toronto's Response to the Outbreak of War, 1939," 7–21; Durflinger, "City at War," 66–7.

43 DHH 86/71, File 8; Carver, "Personnel Selection in the Canadian Army: A Descriptive Study" (Ottawa: DPS, 1945), 252.

44 Dominion Bureau of Statistics, *Eighth Census of Canada 1941 vol. 1*, 27–8.

45 AAG (SP) Memo, "CAO (Other Ranks Only) Statistics on Education, Age, and 'M' Score," 14 Nov. 1944, LAC RG 24, vol. 10262, 52/ SURVEYS /3.

46 DHH 86/71, Carver, "Personnel Selection in the Canadian Army," 250.

47 AAG (S) Memo, "Statistics – Revised Examination 'M'," 21 August 1944, LAC RG 24, vol. 10262, 52/ SURVEYS /3.

48 Lackenbauer, *History of Aboriginal People in the Canadian Military*, 136.

49 Hayes, "The Development of the Canadian Army Officer Corps," 140–3.

50 Ibid., 224.

51 LAC RG 24, vol. 2466, Major-General E.L.M. Burns, memorandum to Committee on Provision of Officers for the Canadian Army, "Recruiting and Training of Officers for Canadian Army Permanent Cadre."

52 Dominion Bureau of Statistics, *Survey of Higher Education, Part II*. Admittedly the wartime number of university enrolments may not have been generally representative.

53 Stacey, *Six Years of War*, 130; Hayes, "Canadian Army Officer Corps," 142.

54 AAG (SP) Memo, "CAO (Other Ranks Only) Statistics on Education, Age, and 'M' Score," 14 Nov. 1944, LAC RG 24, vol. 10262, 52/ SURVEYS/3.

55 Queen's University Archives online exhibit, "Queen's Remembers," http://archives.queensu.ca/Exhibits/queensremembers.html (accessed 4 April 2014).

56 DHH 86/71, Army Examiners Circular Letter No. 279, "Recommendations of Officer Candidates," 1 Dec. 1942. Emphasis in original. Other "basic attributes of a leader" included resourcefulness, adventurousness, self-control under stress, moral character, personal magnetism, initiative and decisiveness, articulateness, reserve, and consideration for subordinates.

57 Hayes, "Canadian Army Officer Corps," 201–3.

58 Horn, "Warrior/Scholar," 2–9.

59 Wakelam, "Try and Try Again," 43.

60 LAC RG 24, vol. 12695 and 12696, CMHQ Records Office, Consolidated Casualty Lists.

61 Vance. *Maple Leaf Empire*, 143–6.
62 Granatstein, *Canada's Army*, 178.
63 Numbers taken from: WSR stats on Cdn Army Enlistment Sept. 1939, LAC RG 24, vol. 18826, 133.065 (d710); Stacey, *Six Years of War*, 33–5.
64 Cdn Army Enlistments 1939–1943, LAC RG 24, vol. 18826, 133.065 (d577).
65 Horn, *The Dirty Thirties*, 78–81.
66 Weintraub, *City Unique*, 27.
67 For an innovative study on this, see Jackson, *One of the Boys*.
68 Quoted in Broadfoot, *Ten Lost Years*, 373.
69 Collins, *You Had to Be There*, 59.
70 Granatstein, *Canada's Army*, 178.
71 Quoted in Collins, *You Had to Be There*, 56.
72 DHH 86/71, File 8, Carver, *Personnel Selection in the Canadian Army*, 51–7.
73 Directorate of Special Services, "Preferred Arms of the Service (Army)," 30 June 1943, LAC Reel C-5290, HQS 8719-3-7. Unit Morale Reports based upon data from recruitment depots indicated that it was the Royal Canadian Ordnance Corps (RCOC) and the Royal Canadian Army Service Corps (RCASC) that were the overwhelmingly preferred branches of service for new army recruits; the armoured corps and artillery were sometimes preferred by "mechanically minded" men, but the infantry were specifically listed as "non-desired" on 74 percent of the morale reports and in no instance was it ever listed as the "preferred" branch. Most soldiers put the infantry on the "not-desired" list on account of its reputation as "The Marching Unit" (94 percent of reporters hated the idea of long route marches) and of course because of the danger – the common soldiers may have realized better than high command that the "PBI [poor bloody infantry] are for it again" and would incur heavy casualties.
74 RIS Special Report No. 174, "Attitude of Men Towards Service in Infantry," 1945, LAC Reel C-5290, HQS 8719-3-7.
75 From a *Globe and Mail* editorial in February 1942: "The fact is indisputable that the young men who volunteer for action in the fighting zones are the cream of the country, for the most part seized with the importance of the task in hand, loyal to principles as well as their homes. They are the best we have." Editorial, *Globe and Mail*, 12 Feb. 1942.
76 Vance, *Death So Noble*, 259–60.
77 Thompson and Seager, *Canada 1922–1939*, 326.
78 Quoted in Stacey, *Arms, Men and Governments*, 398.
79 In the 1942 plebiscite held to release the government from its prior pledge about not sending conscripts to fight overseas, Quebec voted solidly "*non*," registering 72.9 percent opposed to the measure (with six

heavily French-speaking constituencies outside the province doing the same), while English Canada voted "yes" by a margin of 80 percent. See Granatstein, *Broken Promises*, 171–2. The 1942 plebiscite was clearly split along French-English lines perhaps most clearly in Montreal, where French ridings voted overwhelmingly "*non*" and the English ridings voted solidly in favour. See Weintraub, *City Unique*, 50.

80 For part of this literature, see Dawson, *The Conscription Crisis of 1944*; Stevenson, *Canada's Greatest Wartime Muddle*; Granatstein, *Conscription in the Second World War*; Gibson, *Ottawa at War*.

81 Dawson, *Conscription Crisis of 1944*, 12.

82 Wood, *Militia Myths*. For excellent assessments of why the English military system developed this way, see Brewer, *Sinews of Power*; Beckett, *The Amateur Military Tradition*.

83 Wood, *Militia Myths*, 5.

84 Ibid., 254.

85 For more on this see Granatstein, *Broken Promises*; Engen, "The Zombies' War."

86 Burns, *Manpower in the Canadian Army*, 105.

87 Ibid., 106.

88 Complaints against recruiting techniques such as these were found to be a serious drain on morale for the army in Canada. See: Memorandum – Comparison of Conditions Detrimental to Morale in Operational Units and Training Centres, 1943, LAC Reel C-5290, HQS 8719-3-7.

89 Service file, Corporal Charles Daniel Lloyd, LAC RG 24, vol. 26383.

90 Correspondence between author and Paul Cory, Corporal Lloyd's nephew, January 2014.

91 Service file, Corporal Charles Daniel Lloyd, LAC RG 24, vol. 26383.

92 Correspondence between author and Paul Cory, Corporal Lloyd's nephew, January 2014.

93 Service file, William Lloyd, LAC RG 150, Accession 1992-93/166, Box 5695–62.

94 Canadian Army (Active) Computation of Service, Service file, Corporal Charles Daniel Lloyd, LAC RG 24, vol. 26383.

95 See the account by Lord Tweedsmuir, British officer and son of the Canadian Governor-General John Buchan: IWM 91/8/1, Private Papers of Lord Tweedsmuir.

96 Bradford, *Decorations and Awards*.

CHAPTER TWO

1 See Stacey, *Six Years of War*, 253; Stacey, *The Victory Campaign*, 270–8; English, *Canadian Army in Normandy*, 107. Also see transcript of inter-

view with Bill McAndrew, J.L. Granatstein Collection, RMC Cavalry House Archives.

2 Hastings, *Overlord*; French, *Raising Churchill's Army*, especially chapters 2 and 4; Place, *Military Training in the British Army*.

3 Kellett, *Combat Motivation*, 112.

4 Ibid., 47.

5 Ibid., 48.

6 Bercuson, *The Fighting Canadians*, 16.

7 Ibid., 9.

8 For details, see Stacey, *Six Years of War*, 110–15.

9 Personal letter, Crerar to Brigadier A.W. Beament, 3 Nov. 1943, quoted in CMHQ Historical Section Report No. 166, "Administrative Aspects of the Operations of 1 Cdn Inf Div in Italy, December 1943" (29 Nov. 1946), 6.

10 CMHQ Records Office – Consolidated Casualty Lists – CMF, LAC RG 24, vols. 12697 and 12698.

11 CMHQ Records Office – Consolidated Casualty Lists – AEF, LAC RG 24, vols. 12695 and 12696.

12 Harris, *Canadian Brass*, 210.

13 For McAndrew's comments, see transcript of interview with William McAndrew, 20 Feb. 1991, RMC Cavalry House Archives, J.L. Granatstein Interview Collection.

14 According to regimental numbers lists provided by Law, *Regimental Numbers of the Canadian Army*; CMHQ Records – Consolidated Casualty Statistics – CMF, LAC RG 24, vol. 12697 and 12698.

15 Durflinger, "French Canada and Recruitment During the First World War," Canadian War Museum online exhibit, http://www.warmuseum.ca/education/online-educational-resources/dispatches/french-canada-and-recruitment-during-the-first-world-war/ (accessed 28 Sept. 2013).

16 French Canadian Personnel Overseas, January 1942, LAC RG 24, vol. 5812, file 8841 vol. 2. It should also be noted that several non-combat units contained a majority of French-Canadians, including 18th Canadian Field Ambulance RCAMC. The Cameron Highlanders of Ottawa, the machine-gun battalion for 3rd Division, had 25% French-Canadian personnel in 1942, although none who did not speak English. The Carleton and York Regiment was 19% French-Canadian, the Stormont, Dundas and Glengarry Highlanders, 15%, and the Royal Canadian Regiment 13%, but in all of those battalions bilingualism was necessary.

17 French Canadian Personnel Overseas, January 1942, LAC RG 24, vol. 5812, file 8841 vol. 2.

18 Kellett, *Combat Motivation*, 46–7.

19 Judges 7: 5–7, KJV.

20 Directorate of Tactical Investigation Battle Study No. 2 – The Standard of Soldier Required for Infantry, TNA WO 32/17726.

21 The institutional history of the DPS has been written and needs only minimal reiteration here for the sake of clarity. See Carver, *Personnel Selection in the Canadian Army*, 29–39; Copp and McAndrew, *Battle Exhaustion*, 27–43; Feasby, *Clinical Problems*, chap. 6; J.M. Hitsman, *The Problem of Selection and Reallocation of Personnel in the Canadian Army Overseas*, CMHQ Report No. 164, DHH. For more on personnel selection in the British Army, see Ahrenfeldt, *Psychiatry in the British Army*, 29–50.

22 Carver, *Personnel Selection in the Canadian Army*, 57–70.

23 Feasby, *Canadian Medical Services, Vol.* 2, 495.

24 For a complete listing of PULHEMS codes for each job description in the army, see Canadian Military Headquarters, *Physical Standards and Instructions for the Medical Examination of serving Soldiers and Recruits for the Canadian Army, Section IV: Classification of Types of Army Duties* (London: CMHQ, 4 May 1943), LAC RG 24, vol. 12642, 11/STANDARDS /2.

25 Carver, *Personnel Selection in the Canadian Army*, 105.

26 Ibid., 88.

27 Copp and McAndrew, *Battle Exhaustion*, 40–1; Carver, *Personnel Selection in the Canadian Army*, 49. The idea that personnel could be arbitrarily reallocated out of a unit where they had long been assigned on the basis of mechanical test scores was deeply offensive to the regimental traditions of the Anglo-Canadian armies, and did nothing to improve morale and cohesion in units so affected.

28 Carver, *Personnel Selection in the Canadian Army*, 137–8.

29 Ibid., 138–40.

30 Canadian Job Analysis, A.G.4 / CMHQ, July 1942, 92, LAC RG 24, vol. 10258, 52/REPORTS /1.

31 Von Nostrand to Dr J. Cohen, "Classification by Categories," 18 March 1943, TNA CAB 21/921. A2 personnel could have slight defects of locomotion.

32 Directorate of Tactical Investigation Battle Study No. 2, TNA WO 32/17726.

33 Feasby, *Campaigns*, 501.

34 As an aside, although it was emphasized that a soldier's PULHEMS "M" grade should not be determined solely on the basis of their "M" Test score, it was decided that a good "rule of thumb" was that an "M" Test score above 115 would receive an M1 PULHEMS rating, and below 115 would receive an M2. That was for the English-language "M" Tests; for French-language "M" Tests a score of above 100 would receive an M1,

and below 100 would receive an M2. These differences will be discussed later. See Army Examiners Circular Letter No. 453, "PULHEMS M and S Grades," 2 Dec. 1943, DHH DPS Fonds, 86/71, File 3; Draft directive to all SPOs, "PULHEMS 'M' and 'S' Gradings," 7 July 1944, LAC RG 24, vol. 10253, 52/PSYCHIATRY/1.

35 CMHQ, *Physical Standards and Instructions – Active and Reserve 1943*, May 1943, 1, 25, LAC RG 24, vol. 12642, 11/STANDARDS/2. The full PULHEMS classification chart is included as Appendix B.

36 Feasby, *Medical Services*, vol. 1, 502.

37 Army Examiners Circular Letter 550, PULHEMS Profiles – Suitability for Allocation, 25 July 1944, DHH DPS Fonds, 86/71, File 3.

38 The Committee on Standards of Selection comprised top officers in charge of training, selection, organization, and medical services at NDHQ in Ottawa. See: Committee on Standards of Selection, minutes of 21st meeting, 14 Nov. 1944, LAC RG 24, vol. 10244, 52/CONFERENCE/4.

39 Carver, *Personnel Selection in the Canadian Army*, 9.

40 AE circular letter 246, Education status and intelligence of recruits, 9 Oct. 1942, DHH 86/71.

41 Carver, *Personnel Selection in the Canadian Army*, 10. For a devastating critique, see Gould, *The Mismeasure of Man*.

42 Carver, *Personnel Selection in the Canadian Army*, 11–12.

43 AE circular letter 246, Education status and intelligence of recruits, 9 Oct. 1942, DHH 86/71.

44 AE Circular Letter 439, Selection of Officer Candidates, 10 Nov. 1943, DHH 86/71.

45 Carver, *Personnel Selection in the Canadian Army*, 13–14.

46 Memo to DAG: "Utilization of Man Power, Canadian Army Overseas," 11 March 1943, LAC RG 24, vol. 10258, 52/REPORTS /1. Also see "M" Score means by regiment, AG4 memorandum, 18 May 1942, LAC RG 24 vol. 10258, 52/ REPORTS /2.

47 Canadian Army Overseas (other ranks only) statistics on education, age, and "M" score, 25 Nov 1944, LAC RG, vol. 10262, 52/SURVEYS /3.

48 AG4 Memo, "Report of Results of Revised Examination 'M' in Canadian Reinforcement Units," 24 April 1942, LAC RG 24, vol. 10262, 52/ SURVEYS/3. In this memo it was mentioned that due to drastically lower scores on the French "M" Test across the board, "an arbitrary figure of something like 15 should be added where the French test has been used."

49 "Study of Records of Men Scoring 200 or over on M-Test," March 1944, LAC RG 24, vol. 10262, 52/TESTS/1.

50 Memo to DAG: "Utilization of Man Power, Canadian Army Overseas," 11 March 1943, LAC RG 24, vol. 10258, 52/REPORTS/1.

51 Carver, *Personnel Selection in the Canadian Army*, 252–6.

52 Copp and Humphries, *Combat Stress in the 20th Century*, 8.
53 Brigade Training, 1st Canadian Division, Imber Trench Warfare Training & Experimental Centre, Salisbury Plain, 13 April 1940, LAC RG 24, vol. 10856, file 232C1.(d36).
54 Stacey, *The Victory Campaign*, 28–30.
55 *Visiting Forces (British Commonwealth) Act 1933*, (Regnal. 23_and_24_Geo_5) sec 4 http://www.legislation.gov.uk/ukpga/Geo5/23-24/6/section/4 (27 Sept. 2013); Dickson, *A Thoroughly Canadian General*, 126–7.
56 See, for example "Editorial: Infantry Re-Organization," *Canadian Defence Quarterly* 13, 3 (April 1936); "*Field Service Regulations* vol. II and III, 1935," *Canadian Defence Quarterly* 13, 4 (July 1936); "Editorial: Tactical Change," *Canadian Defence Quarterly* 15, 1 (Oct. 1937).
57 Stacey, *Six Years of War*, 132–4, 141–2, 230; Dickson, *A Thoroughly Canadian General,* 159; War Office, *Small Arms Training Vol. No. 1: Weapons Training*, 5–6.
58 Stacey, *Six Years of War*, 203–4, 230; Dickson, *A Thoroughly Canadian General*, 185; Policy of Training Reinforcements – UK and Theatres of Operations, 20 Dec. 1944, LAC RG 24 vol. 9880, 2/TL REP/12/1.
59 English, *Canadian Army and Normandy*, 116–17.
60 NDHQ, *Standard Syllabus 1942*, 4. By the autumn of 1941 there were 27 Basic Training Centres and 32 Advanced Training Centres in Canada, 9 of which were specifically Infantry Training Centres. See Stacey, *Six Years of War*, 532–3.
61 NDHQ, *Canadian Infantry Training Centre Syllabus*, 5–28.
62 Stacey, *Six Years of War*, 135; War Diary, Demonstration Company, HQ #1 Training Brigade Group, Camp Debert, April 1944, LAC RG 24, vol. 17459.
63 Stacey, *Six Years of War*, 230–53.
64 French, *Raising Churchill's Army*, 204. Such was Alexander's impression. In reality the Germans suffered many of the same problems at the sharp end. The British counterattack at Arras on 18 May 1940 threw German infantrymen into a similar panic. See May, *Strange Victory*, 442–3.
65 Bercuson, *Battalion of Heroes,* 35; French, *Raising Churchill's Army*, 204.
66 War Office, *Infantry Training 1937 Supplement: Tactical Notes for Platoon Commanders* (1941), 1.
67 CMHQ Report No. 123, 2–3; Place, *Military Training in the British Army*, 54–5.
68 CMHQ Historical Section Report No. 123, "Battle Drill Training," 9; J. English, *Canadian Army and Normandy*, 112; Canadian Battle Drill School, *Battle Drill*, CWM 58C 3 22.3.

69 NDHQ, *Canadian Infantry Training Centre – Standard Syllabus 1942*, 28–9.
70 Montague was referring specifically to the doctrines laid out in: War Office, *Infantry Training Part VIII – Fieldcraft, Battle Drill, Section and Platoon Tactics 1944* (reprinted in Canada Feb. 1944), Chap. 4, "The Battle Drills for Attack."
71 CMHQ Historical Section Report No. 123, "Battle Drill Training," 1.
72 War Office, *Infantry Training Supplement* 1937, 2; Place, *Military Training in the British Army*, 67.
73 Canadian Battle Drill School, Battle Drill, 5th Edition, 11 April 1943, 70, CWM 58C 3 22.3.
74 Canadian Battle Drill School, *Battle Drill Manual*, 70–2, 185. These tactics are modern staples of infantry tactics and variations were still taught in the 1970s. See MacGregor, "In Defence of Battledrill," 24–9.
75 Canadian Battle Drill School, *Battle Drill*, 77–80, 136–42.
76 War Office, *Infantry Training 1944 Part VIII*, 59. Also see CGS Circular, 31 Dec. 1941, LAC RG 24 vol. 9764, 2/BATTLE SCH/1; MacGregor, "In Defence of Battledrill," 24–9. For the idea that formal drill and discipline are connected to battle discipline, and a potent critique of this assumption, see Shalit, *The Psychology of Combat and Conflict* (New York: Praeger, 1988), 124–35.
77 War Office, *Infantry Training 1944 Part VIII*, "Method of Teaching the Battle Drills," 50.
78 CMHQ Historical Report 123, 7–8.
79 Place, *Military Training in the British Army*, 56.
80 For examples, see "Every Man a Marksman," *CATM* 42 (Sept. 1944); "Shoot to Kill," *CATM* 34 (Oct. 1943); "Passing It On! Sten Battle Ranges," *CATM* 44 (Nov. 1944). Training centres in Canada also experimented with wiring clay pigeons to targets so that a successful hit would shatter the clay and give instant feedback on the shooter's accuracy. See "Passing It On! Realism in Training," *CATM* 42 (Sept. 1944).
81 English, *Canadian Army in Normandy*, 107.
82 Place, *Military Training in the British Army, 1940–1944*, 63–75.
83 English, *Canadian Army in Normandy*, 116.
84 Canadian Battle Drill School, *Battle Drill*, 72.
85 Dickson, *A Thoroughly Canadian General*, 194.
86 Copp, *Fields of Fire*, 27–9.
87 Transcript of interview with Lt J.S. Edmonson, DHH 79/567, file 032.
88 Liaison Visit of SD&T to School of Infantry, 5 Dec. 1944, LAC RG 24, vol. 9880, 2/TL/REP/14/1.
89 Place, *Military Training in the British Army*, 62.

90 Engen, *Canadians Under Fire*, 178.
91 Transcript of interview with G.G. Buchanan, DHH 79/567, file 016.
92 French, *Raising Churchill's Army*, 45.
93 Canadian Battle Drill School, *Battle Drill*, 70. For more on German infiltration tactics, see Gudmundsson, *Stormtroop Tactics*.
94 Canadian Battle Drill School, *Battle Drill*, 173–81.
95 Ibid., 70.
96 Quoted in: CMHQ Report No. 123, 2. This exact quotation from the manual provoked a Geneva Convention complaint from Nazi Germany.
97 War Office, *Small Arms Training Vol. 1, Pamphlet 12: Bayonet* (10 June 1942, reprinted in Canada August 1942), 14–15. This was put into action at the Battle Inoculation Range for assault practice at Camp Debert. See War Diary – No. 1 Infantry Training Battalion, November 1943, "Training Brigade Group Narrative – Battle Inoculation Range, 17 Nov. 1943," LAC RG 24, vol. 17459.
98 Corum, *Roots of Blitzkrieg*, 7–8.
99 French, *Raising Churchill's Army*, 24–5.
100 Brown, "Not Glamorous, But Effective," 421–4.
101 For another perspective, see Copp, *Fields of Fire*, 39–40.
102 French, *Raising Churchill's Army*, 223–4.
103 Doubler, *Closing with the Enemy*, 39–61.

CHAPTER THREE

1 The American division landed to the immediate left of the Canadians, the US 45th Infantry Division was similarly "fresh off the boat" and was the only US formation invading Sicily that had not had combat experience. See Garland and Smyth, *Sicily and the Surrender of Italy*, 100.
2 One of the key Combined Operations lessons from Operations HUSKY and AVALANCHE was: "The assaulting force must land with sufficient weapons to be able to neutralise early enemy counter-attacks. The follow-up formations must have further supporting arms to be able to deal with more elaborate counter-attacks. Anti-tank weapons of all calibres must have high priority in landing." Combined Ops Lessons Learnt in the Mediterranean, 1943, LAC RG 24, vol. 20339, 952.013(D31A).
3 1 Canadian Division Operation Order No. 1, 7 June 1943, War Diary General Staff 1st Canadian Infantry Division, LAC Microfilm Reel T-1876; Account by Captain R.W. Potts, PPCLI, given to Historical Officers, LAC RG 24, vol. 10481, file 263C2.011(01).
4 Nicholson, *The Canadians in Italy*, 51; Extracts from War Diaries – Series 2, 27 Sept. 1943, LAC RG 24, vol. 12748, 24/ DIARIES /8.
5 "It is the intention of *Oberbefehlshaber Sud* [OBS Field-Marshal Albert

Kesselring] to withdraw 15 Pz Grd Div in general line Bonpietro-Leonforte and to defend this line." Reports of OBS, 18 July 1943, quoted and translated in: Canadian Army Headquarters Historical Report No. 14, "The Sicilian Campaign – Information from German Sources" (Ottawa: Army Headquarters, 15 April 1947), 12–13.

6 Windsor, "The Eyes of All Fixed on Sicily," 4–34.

7 Historians have been critical of the BAYTOWN/AVALANCHE plan, possibly misunderstanding that they were never meant to support one another. Robin Neillands, for instance, has criticized the plan for not abiding by Montgomery's cherished concentration of force. Neillands, *Eighth Army,* 239–43.

8 1 Cdn Inf Div Planning Intelligence Summary 2, 25 Aug. 1943, LAC Microfilm Reel T-1876; 1st Cdn Inf Div Embarkation Tables – Operation BAYTOWN, 30 Aug. 1943, LAC Microfilm Reel T-1876. D-Day embarkation across the Straits included infantry, RCE, the divisional HQ, artillery, RCAMC, and, overlapping with D+1, elements of the lead 12th Canadian Armoured Regiment. In contrast with HUSKY, engineers, infantry, and motor vehicles deployed early, while anti-aircraft and anti-tank elements deployed later.

9 Porch, *The Path to Victory,* 486–505.

10 Windsor, "'Boforce,'" 51–60; Nicholson, *The Canadians in Italy*, 224–9. As Farley Mowat wrote in his regimental history of the Hastings & Prince Edward Regiment, "The men who actually took part in that 400-mile race know, as do their comrades who waited at Salerno, that the dash up the northern spine of Italy was as remarkable a feat of arms as any roaring victory on the battlefield." Mowat, *The Regiment*, 109.

11 1st Cdn Inf Div G.S. Branch War Diary, 29 Sept. 1943, LAC Microfilm Reel T-1876.

12 Stacey, *The Canadian Army, 1939–45,* 110. One exception to this was the battle of Termoli, which was a fully developed German counterattack against British troops and elements of 1st Canadian Armoured Brigade. See Canadian Army Headquarters Historical Section Report No. 18, "The Campaign in Southern Italy (Sept.–Dec. 1943): Information from German Military Documents" (Ottawa: AHQ, 1 Nov. 1947).

13 Linklater, *The Campaign in Italy*, 106.

14 The British official history: Molony, *Mediterranean and the Middle East, Vol. V*, 429–521.

15 For discussion, see Brown, "The Rock of Accomplishment," 10–23; Atkinson, *The Day of Battle*, 297–306; Greenhous, "Would it not have been better to bypass Ortona completely...?" 51–5.

16 Nicholson, *The Canadians in Italy*, 20–9.

17 Stacey, *Six Years of War,* 51–2.

18 MacFarlane, *Triquet's Cross*, 32.
19 Stacey, *Six Years of War*, 72, 112–14. For some exceptions, see Galloway, *A Regiment at War*, 25.
20 Feasby, *Official History of the Canadian Medical Services, Vol.* 2, 100–8.
21 CMHQ Records – Consolidated Casualty Statistics – CMF, LAC RG 24, vol. 12697 and 12698.
22 Account of Lt.-Colonel I.S. Johnston, given at Campobasso 22 Oct. 1943, *War Diary Extracts* (Series 6), 29 Nov. 1943, LAC RG 24, vol. 12748, 24/DIARIES/8.
23 H.D.G. Crerar, Address on the principles of effective fire support in the 'break-in' battle, 11 Feb. 1944, LAC RG 24, vol. 10785, 224C1.036(D3).
24 Maj-Gen. G.G. Simonds, memo to all commands and COs, 1st Cdn Division, 15 May 1943, RMC Cavalry House, Delaney Collection.
25 AFHQ Report, "German Tactics in Italy No. 1: From Salerno to Anzio," 28 May 1944, LAC RG 24, vol. 10785, file 224C1.036(d3).
26 AFHQ, German Tactics in Italy, No. 1 – Salerno to Anzio, 28 May 1944, LAC RG 24, vol. 10785, 224C1.036(D3). Also see US Army Military Intelligence Division, "German Doctrine of the Stabilized Front" (Washington, DC.: War Department, Aug. 1943).
27 Extract from "Crossing of the Moro and Capture of Ortona," narrative by Maj-Gen. C. Vokes, Extracts from Memoranda – Series 13, 19 April 1944, LAC RG 24, vol. 12748, 24/DIARIES/8.
28 Of the 29 questionnaires from the 1943 campaigns, on question 8(a), 22 answered "Yes" in response to this question, 3 answered "No," and 4 gave no answer. BEQS, LAC RG 24, vol. 10450.
29 Captain Charles E. Levesque (Royal 22e Régiment), BEQ 259; Major C.M. McDougall (PPCLI), BEQ 255, LAC RG 24, vol. 10450.
30 "Notes on Lessons on Recent Fighting," issued by 2nd Canadian Infantry Brigade, 30 July 1943, LAC RG 24, vol. 10981, file 263C2.011(01); Canadian Operations in Sicily – Extracts from War Diaries, Series 2, 27 Sept. 1943, LAC RG 24, vol. 12748, 24/ DIARIES /8; "Canadian Tactical Lessons from Sicily," *Canadian Army Training Memorandum* 34 (Jan. 1944), LAC RG 24, 2003-00441-6, Box 1.
31 Beattie, *Dileas*, 294. Emphasis in original.
32 Question 12(a): "Did your unit carry out an attack under an artillery barrage?": "Yes," 20; "No," 2; no answer, 7. Question 12(b): "If so, did they have preliminary training?": "Yes," 10; "No," 10. Question 12(c): "Did they keep up with the barrage effectively?": "Yes," 15; "No," 3; no answer, 2. BEQS, LAC RG 24, vol. 10450.
33 *Canadian Battle Drill Manual*, 11 April 1943, 209–10, CWM, 58C 3 22.3.
34 Phrasing is from Lee Windsor, "'Boforce,'" 51. Also see McAndrew, "Fire or Movement?"

35 Brown, "Rock of Accomplishment," 10–23.
36 Various battle experience questionnaires, LAC RG 24, vol. 10450.
37 15th Pz Grd Div "Experience report for the Campaign in Sicily," 7 Sept. 1943, translation quoted in Army Headquarters Historical Section Report No. 14, "The Sicilian Campaign (July–Aug. 1943): Information from German Sources" (15 April 1947).
38 Question 11: "Were you able to put the tactical principles of fire and movement, taught as battle drill before going overseas, into practice?": "Yes," 25; "No," 1; no answer, 3. "Often, fairly often, or seldom?": Often," 8; "Fairly often," 11; "Seldom," 5; no answer, 1. BEQS, LAC RG 24, vol. 10450.
39 Extracts from account by Captain C.H. Pritchard, Canadian Operations in Sicily – Extracts from War Diaries and Memoranda, Series 3, 5 Oct. 1943, LAC RG 24, vol. 12748, 24/DIARIES/8. This is corroborated by the diary of Major Sesia, which says almost exactly the same thing: Major A.T. Sesia, Personal Notes and Observations – Sicily, 19 July 1943, LAC RG 24, vol. 10878, file 233C1.011(5).
40 Many also noted, however, that this was infrequent and usually temporary: the robust Allied logistical network normally came through for ammunition. See Question 14(a): "Was your unit ever short of ammunition in battle?": "Yes," 15; "No," 12; no answer, 2. BEQS, LAC RG 24, vol. 10450.
41 General Bernard Montgomery, quoted in CMHQ Historical Section Report No. 166, "Administrative Aspects of the Operations of 1st Canadian Infantry Division in Italy, December 1943" (29 Nov. 1946).
42 Major H. Tellier, BEQ 242, LAC RG 24, vol. 10450.
43 "Lessons from the Sicilian Campaign," Allied Forces Headquarters Training Memorandum No. 50, 20 Nov. 1943, TNA WO 204/1906.
44 For a broader discussion, see Engen, *Canadians Under Fire*, 133–49.
45 Personal notes and observations – Sicily, Major A.T. Sesia, 24 July 1943, LAC RG 24, vol. 10878, file 233C1.011(5).
46 Major Thompson, Saskatoon Light Infantry (MG), BEQ 273, LAC RG 24, vol. 10450.
47 CMF Appreciation & Censorship Report No. 35, for period 16–31 Dec. 1943, Part B – Canadian Expeditionary Force, TNA WO 204/10381.
48 School of Military Neuropsychiatry, "John Steinbeck Tells of Soldiers' Letters," 9 Aug. 1943, LAC RG 24, vol. 63, file HQ 650-99-86.
49 BEQS, LAC RG 24, vol. 10450.
50 CMF Appreciation & Censorship Report No. 36, for period 1–15 Jan. 1944 inclusive, Part B – Canadian Expeditionary Force, TNA WO 204/10381.
51 CMF Appreciation & Censorship Report No. 37, for period 16–31 Jan.

1944 inclusive, Part B – Canadian Expeditionary Force, TNA WO 204/10381. One soldier in the PPCLI wrote: "Personally I don't think the war will be much longer. My only fear now is that we might have to go and fight Japan before we get a chance to get home."

52 For more on the relationship of discipline and morale, see Shalit, *The Psychology of Conflict and Combat*, 135–46.

53 Madsen, *Another Kind of Justice*, 81–5. Also see Tooley, "Appearance or Reality? Variations in Infantry Courts Martial – 1st Canadian Division: 1940–1945," 40.

54 Standard Canadian Infantry Division – Summary of Personnel & Vehicles, LAC RG 24, vol. 18576, file 133.065(D18D); Account by Major N. Cooper, RCMP, Provost, in Extracts from Memoranda (Series 7), 27 Dec. 1943, LAC RG 24, vol. 12478, 24/DIARIES/8.

55 Discipline & Pay Section – Canadian Section GHQ, 2nd Echelon, Summary of Offences (by Formations) for Canadian Army in the Field, LAC RG 24, vol. 10118, 10119; Standard Canadian Infantry Division – Summary of Personnel and Vehicles, LAC RG 24, vol. 18576, file 133.065 (D18D); "An Infantry Battalion," GO 466/43, II/233/2, 27 April 1943.

56 A.A.40 was a catch-all category that included a number of diverse offences otherwise unspecified under other sections of the Army Act, including credit and cheque fraud, improper use of vehicles for private purposes, borrowing money from subordinates, producing false documentation, negligently wounding or injuring self, and improperly obtaining railway warrants, among others. See War Office, *Manual of Military Law 1929*, 459.

57 Tooley, "Appearance or Reality," 45.

58 See comments to that effect made in: Preliminary Survey of Sicilian Casualties Admitted to Tripoli District, August 1943, LCMSDS RG 1, file 00063. The "ideal demoralisation index" that the paper proposes is a function of: ((Total war neuroses) + (Absentees) / Total Surgical Injured).

59 LAC RG 24, vol. 10118, 10119.

60 Copp and McAndrew, *Battle Exhaustion*, 44–62.

61 Major A. Manning Doyle, RCAMC, Neuropsychiatrist 1 Cdn Div, Summary Report – Neuropsychiatrist 1 Cdn Division, 10 July–10 Nov. 1943, RMC Cavalry House Archives, McAndrew Papers. A study by Professor S. Zuckerman of casualties from 8th Army admitted to hospitals in Tripoli during the Sicilian campaign, though filled with interesting details, ultimately concluded that admissions for "war neuroses" "have not been on anything like the scale of those from the Mareth fighting." Zuckerman, Preliminary Survey of Sicilian Casualties Admitted to Tripoli District, Aug. 1943, LCMSDS RG 1, file 00063.

62 Copp and McAndrew, *Battle Exhaustion*, 53–62. For an account, see Dancocks, *D-Day Dodgers*, 154–74.

63 Canadian Neuropsychiatric Base, No. 14 Cdn General Hospital, RCAMC, Neuropsychiatric Report, 15 Feb. 1944, RMC Cavalry House Archives, McAndrew Collection, Box 10 Folder 8.

64 For the first few months of their deployment to the UK, tensions between the 1st Canadian Division soldiers and the English civilian population were quite strained. However, during the Blitz, new respect was found for them: "When in the late summer heavy air attacks on England began, there was no doubt that the Canadian troops found good reason to admire the manner in which the civilian population of England confronted this new menace. The courage of the British civilian under the bombs has certainly been an important element in winning for him the regard of the Canadian soldier. This fact is amply demonstrated in the Field Censors' reports." Historical Officer CMHQ, Report No. 119, "Canadian Relations with the People of the United Kingdom, and General Problems of Morale, 1939–44," 30 June 1944. For a description of an air raid on a Canadian camp, see intercepted letter, "Beau" to Marge Carswell, 27 May 1943, Intercepted Mail Received from Censorship, LAC Microfilm Reel T-17922, 4/CENSOR REPS/4/12.

65 Personal notes and observations, 19 July 1943, Major A.T. Sesia, LAC RG 24, vol. 10878, file 233C1.011(5)

66 Major A.T. Sesia, 21–22 July 1943.

67 Pond, *Sicily*, 172. For the Edmontons' account of the fighting, see Stevens, *A City Goes to War*, 236–40.

68 Captain A.H. MacLean, West Nova Scotia Regiment, BEQ 62, LAC RG 24, vol. 10450.

69 Field Censors (Home) – CAO – Notes on mail examined 21 Aug.–5 Sept. 1943, LAC Microfilm Reel T-17924, 4/CENSOR REPS/1/2.

70 Brig.-General C. Vokes, comments and impressions on the Sicilian campaign, 17 Aug. 1943, LAC RG 24, vol. 10981, file 263C2.011(01).

71 For comments on this in the US Army, see Stouffer, *The American Soldier Vol.* 2, 156.

72 CMF Appreciation & Censorship Report No. 37, for period 16–31 Jan. 1944 inclusive, Part B – Canadian Expeditionary Force, TNA WO 204/10381.

73 Roy, *Seaforth Highlanders*, 271.

74 Ibid., 272.

75 Wedemayer, *Wedemayer Reports!*, 226.

76 D'Este, *Bitter Victory*, 317–18, 612–13.

77 Cook, "The Politics of Surrender," 663.

78 Atkinson, *The Day of Battle*, 243.
79 Field Censors (Home) – CAO – Notes on mail examined 21 Sept.–5 Oct. 1943, LAC Microfilm Reel T-17924, 4/CENSOR REPS/1/2.
80 Montgomery was an inspired trainer and made an impression on the Canadians for his desire to whip them into shape as soldiers. He was also responsible for mounting some of the first large-scale military exercises and manoeuvres. See English, *Canadian Army in Normandy Campaign*, 125–42.
81 Field Censors (Home) – CAO – notes on mail examined 21 May–5 June 1943, LAC Microfilm Reel T-17924, 4/CENSOR REPS/1/2.
82 Field Censors (Home) – H.M. Transports – report on mail received from the Sicilian invasion force, LAC Microfilm Reel T-17294, 4/ CENSOR REPS /1/2.
83 Extract from Middle East Field Censorship Summary No. 69, 28 July–10 Aug. 1943, LAC Microfilm Reel T-17924, 4/CENSOR REPS/1/2.
84 Mowat, *The Regiment*, 67.
85 Ibid., 53. For similar views from a different regimental history, see Beattie, *Dileas*, 235.
86 Battle experience questionnaires, 59, 62, 67, 169, 207, 245, 272, 281, LAC RG 24, vol. 10450.
87 Battle experience questionnaires, LAC RG 24, vol. 10450.
88 CMF Appreciation & Censorship Report No. 37, for period 16–31 Jan. 1944 inclusive, Part B – Canadian Expeditionary Force, NA WO 204/10381.
89 MacFarlane, *Triquet's Cross*, 32.
90 CMHQ Records Office – Consolidated Casualty Lists – CMF, LAC RG 24, vols. 12697 and 12698.
91 Consolidated Casualty Lists, LAC RG 24, vols. 12697 and 12698; "Standard Canadian Infantry Division – Summary of Personnel and Vehicles," LAC RG 24, vol. 18576, file 133.065(D18D). These numbers include only casualties in the nine infantry battalions and do not include casualties in any other arm such as armour, artillery, or engineers.
92 Major H. Tellier, Royal 22e Régiment, BEQ 242, LAC RG 24, vol. 10450.
93 Major F.J. Hammond, Hastings & Prince Edward Regiment, BEQ 59, LAC RG 24, vol. 10450.
94 Questionnaire responses from junior officers indicate tremendous fluctuations in the "average number of ORs in the section" due to combat casualties.
95 Stevens, *A City Goes to War*, 279.
96 Nicholson, *The Canadians in Italy*, 104–5.
97 Bernier, *Royal 22e Regiment*, 135.
98 According to both doctrine and practice. War Office, *Infantry Section Leading 1938*; Experiences of a Fighting Patrol, extract from account

by Captain E.H. Pritchard, Loyal Edmonton Regiment, 31 July 1943, War Diary Extracts Series 1 – 3 Sept. 1943, LAC RG 24, vol. 12748, 24/DIARIES/8.

99 Major M.B. John, Royal Canadian Regiment, BEQ 151; Captain Charles E. Levesque, Royal 22e Regiment, BEQ 259, LAC RG 24, vol. 10450.

100 CMHQ Historical Section Report No. 166, "Administrative Aspects of the Operations of 1st Canadian Infantry Division in Italy, December 1943" (29 Nov. 1946).

101 Major-General C. Vokes to GOC 5 Corps, 3 Jan. 1944, quoted in CMHQ Historical Section Report No. 166, "Administrative Aspects of the Operations of 1st Canadian Infantry Division in Italy, December 1943" (29 Nov. 1946). It is also worth noting that the reinforcements who reached 1st Division in late December had been allowed no rest after their journey across the Mediterranean and through the Apennines to the Adriatic Coast, before being put into the line. They were likely exhausted before they ever reached the front.

102 Question 10(f): "Was [the reinforcements'] general standard of efficiency high, moderate, or low?": "High," 3; "Moderate," 14; "Low," 5; no answer, 7. BEQS, LAC RG 24, vol. 10450.

103 For an excellent study on the quality of reinforcements, see Brown, "New Men in the Line," 35–47.

104 Tooley, *Invicta*, 199. On the eve of the December battles, 1st Canadian Division had already been experiencing a shortage of about 50 officers and 600 other ranks, most of them infantry.

105 Stevens, *A City Goes to War*, 276; Brown, "The Rock of Accomplishment," 18.

106 Account by Brig. D.C. Spry, in *Extract from Memoranda* (Series 12), 24 March 1944, LAC RG 24, vol. 12478, 24/DIARIES/8.

107 Copp and McAndrew, *Battle Exhaustion*, 53–62.

108 According to Reginald Roy, at the start of the fight for Ortona: "Neither battalion was at full strength, and indeed platoons with only half their complements available were asked to take on tasks which would be difficult if sections were up to full strength. To make matters worse, the reinforcements stream seemed to be drying up to a trickle, and with the constant daily casualties suffered by the rifle companies especially, the man at the front was frequently doing double duty." Roy, *The Seaforth Highlanders of Canada,* 262.

109 Personal letter Vokes to GOC 5 Corps, 3 Jan. 1944, reproduced in: CMHQ Historical Section, Report No. 166, "Administrative Aspects of the Operations of 1 Cdn Inf Div in Italy, December 1943," (29 Nov. 1946).

110 Transcript of interview with Captain Felix Carriere, UVic Oral History Collection, Record ID 000024.

111 Ibid.

112 CMF Appreciation & Censorship Report No. 36, for period 1–15 Jan. 1944, Part B – Canadian Expeditionary Force, TNA WO 204/10381.
113 For discussion in the censorship reports, see CMF Appreciation & Censorship Report No. 34, for period 16 Nov.–15 Dec. 1943 inclusive, Part B – Canadian Expeditionary Force, TNA WO 204/10381.
114 BEQS, LAC RG 24, vol. 10450.
115 Engen, *Canadians Under Fire*, 67–8.
116 Transcript of interview with Major John Alpine Dougan, UVic Military Oral History Collection, Record ID 0000058.
117 Transcript of interview with Captain Felix Carriere, UVic Oral History Collection, Record ID 000024.
118 Ops – 1 Cdn Inf Brigade – Discussions on Lessons of December battles, 11 Jan. 1944, LAC RG 24, vol. 10982, file 264C1.033(D1). Emphasis mine.
119 CMHQ Records Office – Consolidated Casualty Lists – CMF, LAC RG 24, vols. 12697 and 12698; "Standard Canadian Infantry Division – Summary of Personnel and Vehicles," LAC RG 24, vol. 18576, file 133.065(D18D). These numbers reflect casualty data for all battalion officers holding the rank of "lieutenant," "captain," "major," and "lieutenant-colonel," including for those who held those positions in an "acting" rank at the time of their injury. For most of August and November 1943, 1st Canadian Infantry Division had been pulled out of the line.
120 LAC RG 24, vols. 12697 and 12698; "Standard Canadian Infantry Division – Summary of Personnel and Vehicles," LAC RG 24, vol. 18576, file 133.065(D18D).
121 Consolidated Casualty Statistics – CMF, LAC RG 24, vols. 12697 and 12698.
122 Tooley, *Invicta*, 14.
123 Kitching, *Mud and Green Fields*, 163.
124 Transcript of interview with Maj.-General M.P. Bogert, 8 Sept. 1991, RMC Cavalry House Archives, J.L. Granatstein Interview Collection.
125 For comments, see Transcript of interview with Brigadier H.P. Bell-Irving, 4 March 1992, RMC Cavalry House Archives, J.L. Granatstein Interview Collection.
126 Discipline & Pay Section – Canadian Section GHQ, 2nd Echelon, Summary of Offences (by Formations) for Canadian Army in the Field, LAC RG 24, vol. 10118, 10119.

CHAPTER FOUR

1 McAndrew, *Canadians and the Italian Campaign*, 158.
2 Porch, *The Path to Victory*, 656.

3 Kesselring, *The Memoirs of Field-Marshal Kesselring*, 222.
4 For a detailed study, see Behrens, *Merchant Shipping and the Demands of War.*
5 Jackson, *The Mediterranean and Middle East, Vol. VI, Part* 2, 302.
6 Ellis, *Cassino*, 445; Windsor, "Overlord's Long Right Flank," 219–38.
7 For a good description of the breakthrough process in the Second World War, see Burns, *General Mud*, 164.
8 Porch, *The Path to Victory*, 546–50; Dancocks, *The D-Day Dodgers*, 238.
9 "The 'Set-Piece' Attack: Lessons from the Breakthrough of the Hitler Line (from HQ 1 Cdn Corps)," *Extracts from Memoranda* (Series 21), 31 July 1944, LAC RG 24, vol. 12748, 24/DIARIES/8/2.
10 Ellis, *Cassino*, 444; McAvity, *Lord Strathcona's Horse.*
11 Leese to Maj.-General J.N. Kennedy, 8 June 1944, quoted in Delaney, *The Soldiers' General*, 153.
12 Roy, *The Seaforth Highlanders of Canada*, 321.
13 Morton, *A Military History of Canada*, 217.
14 Stevens, *The Royal Canadian Regiment*, vol. 2, 173.
15 For a good description, see Delaney, "Knowing Enough Not to Interfere," 317–33.
16 See Cessford, "Crack Canadian Troops," 34–43. In the official history, see Nicholson, *The Canadians in Italy*, 646–51.
17 I Canadian Corps had additional units permanently and temporarily under its command starting in September 1944, including the New Zealand Division, but its normal composition was just 1st Canadian Division and 5th Canadian Armoured Division. In May 1944 Eighth Army had four corps commanding ten divisions, a very inefficient ratio owed mostly to the Canadians and the Poles. For more see Burns, *Manpower in the Canadian Army*, 29–30.
18 Stacey, *Six Years of War*, 88–93.
19 Nicholson, *The Canadians in Italy*, 342.
20 Dancocks, *D-Day Dodgers*, 293.
21 According to Corps Commander Lt-General E.L.M. Burns's postwar analysis, of all the Canadian soldiers in Italy only 53% were in the fighting services, and only 25% were in the infantry; 12.5%, fully half the total number of infantrymen, were tied up in headquarters units. The British contribution to the Allied Armies in Italy, by comparison, was 65.3% fighting troops and only 6.2% headquarters. See Burns, *Manpower in the Canadian Army*, 22.
22 Jackson, *Mediterranean and Middle East, Vol. VI, Part* 3, 352.
23 Memorandum by Major-General C. Vokes, Appendix to W.D., G.S. Branch 1 CID HQ, July 1944. Quoted in: Extracts from War Diaries and

Memoranda (Series 27), July–Sept. 1944, LAC RG 24, vol. 12748, 24/DIARIES/8/3.

24 Of the 44 questionnaires from the 1944–45 Italian campaigns, on question 8(a) 30 answered "Yes" in response to the question about organizing rapid defence against counterattack, 10 answered "No," and 4 gave no answer. In the 1943 campaign it had been: "Yes," 22; "No," 3, no answer, 4. BEQS, LAC RG 24, vol. 10450.

25 Memorandum on Training Conference held at 1 Cdn Corps, 16 June 1944, RMC Cavalry House, Delaney Collection. For greater context, see Delaney, *The Soldiers' General*, 159.

26 1st Canadian Infantry Division in the Liri Valley Battle, 31 July 1944, LAC RG 24, vol. 12303, 3/LESSONS OPS/1.

27 Question 12(a): "Did your unit carry out an attack under an artillery barrage?": "Yes," 36; "no," 2; no answer, 6. BEQS, LAC RG 24, vol. 10450.

28 CMF Appreciation & Censorship Report No. 47, 16–30 June 1944, TNA WO 204/10381.

29 Question 12(b): "Did they have preliminary training?": "Yes," 17; "No," 20; no answer, 5. BEQS, LAC RG 24, vol. 10450.

30 Delaney, *The Soldiers' General*, 129. As discussed in previous chapters, it was a common shortcoming of Canadian training that it tended to focus on too low a level of operations.

31 Question 12(c): "Did they keep up with the barrage effectively?": "Yes," 29; "No," 6; no answer, 7. BEQS, LAC RG 24, vol. 10450.

32 Question 11: "Were you able to put the tactical principles of fire and movement, taught as battle drill before going overseas, into practice?": "Yes," 30; "No," 10; no answer, 4. "Often, fairly often, or seldom?": "Often," 5; "Fairly often," 9; "Seldom," 11. BEQS, LAC RG 24, vol. 10450.

33 For detailed discussions from an operational research perspective, see LCMSDS RG 1, file 00023.

34 "Report, Hitler Line Defences, by G.S. 1 Cdn Inf Div," Extracts from War Diaries and Memoranda (Series 25), June 1944, LAC RG 24, vol. 12748, 24/ DIARIES /8/2.

35 Question 15(a): "Have you ever co-operated with Infantry Tanks?": "Yes," 30; "No," 10; no answer, 4. BEQS, LAC RG 24, vol. 10450.

36 Question 15(b): "Did you move in front of, behind or amongst the tanks?": "In front," 12; "Behind," 2; "Amongst," 2; "All of the above," 14. BEQS, LAC RG 24, vol. 10450.

37 Memorandum by Major-General C. Vokes, Appendix to W.D., G.S. Branch 1 CID HQ, July 1944. Quoted in: Extracts from War Diaries and Memoranda (Series 27), July–Sept. 1944, LAC RG 24, vol. 12748, 24/DIARIES/8/3.

38 Nicholson, *The Canadians in Italy*, 607.
39 "Wasp Flame Thrower – Use in Defence," notes prepared by G(CW) Eighth Army, 12 Jan. 1945, LAC RG 24, vol. 10785, 224C1.033(D1).
40 "The capture of 'BULGARIA,' 13–14 Oct. 1944, by Hastings & P.E.R.," Extracts from War Diaries and Memoranda (Series 30), 16 Jan. 1945, LAC RG 24, vol. 12748, 24/DIARIES/8/3.
41 12 Cdn Inf Bde Memorandum No. 1, 19 July 1944, appendix to W.D., 12 Cdn Inf Bde July 1944, LAC Microfilm reel T-12397.
42 Mowat, *The Regiment*, 164.
43 Jackson, *Mediterranean and Middle East, Vol. VI, Part* 2, 105–10.
44 Air Operations on the GOTHIC Line – extracts from report on Air Operations issued by 1 Cdn Corps, 4 Oct. 1944, LAC RG 24, vol. 10672.
45 Question 7(a) "Did you receive Direct Air Support?": "Yes," 27; "No," 12; no answer, 4. Question 7(c): "Was the support effective?": "Yes," 26; "No," one. BEQS, LAC RG 24, vol. 10450.
46 BEQS, LAC RG 24, vol. 10450.
47 LAC RG 24, vol. 10450. The BEQS studied for these tables represent all Canadian officers with experience in 1944–45, including some of those who also fought in 1943, as long as they had more than two months of combat experience in the 1944–45 period.
48 Transcript of interview with Honorary Captain (Rev. Bishop) Robert Lowder Seaborn, UVic Military Oral History Collection #00000129.
49 Wilmot, *Through the Hitler Line*, 13–26.
50 CMF Appreciation & Censorship Report No. 38, for period 1–15 Feb. 1944, TNA WO 204/10381. Although these reports are part of consolidated Allied censorship reports, only the sections specifically pertaining to the Canadians in Eighth Army are referred to in this chapter.
51 CMF Appreciation & Censorship Report No. 40, for period 1–15 March 1944, TNA WO 204/10381.
52 The specific example of a high-morale regiment in March 1944 was the Royal 22e, where morale was at a "new high-level after announcement of the award of the Victoria Cross to Major Paul Triquet." CMF Appreciation & Censorship Report No. 41, for period 16–31 March 1944, TNA WO 204/10381.
53 CMF Appreciation & Censorship Report No. 42, for period 1–15 April 1944, TNA WO 204/10381.
54 CMF Appreciation & Censorship Report No. 44, for period 1–15 May 1944, TNA WO 204/10381.
55 CMF Appreciation & Censorship Report No. 45, for period 16–31 May 1944, TNA WO 204/10381.
56 CMF Appreciation & Censorship Report No. 46, for period 1–15 June 1944, TNA WO 204/10381.

57 CMF Appreciation & Censorship Report No. 48, for period 1–15 July 1944, TNA WO 204/10381.
58 CMF Appreciation & Censorship Report No. 52, for period 1–15 Sept. 1944, TNA WO 204/10381.
59 Windsor, "Overlord's Long Right Flank," 219–38.
60 CMF Appreciation & Censorship Report No. 53, for period 16–30 Sept. 1944, TNA WO 204/10381.
61 CMF Appreciation & Censorship Report No. 54, for period 1–15 Oct. 1944, TNA WO 204/10381.
62 CMF Appreciation & Censorship Report No. 56, for period 1–15 Nov. 1944, TNA WO 204/10381.
63 CMF Appreciation & Censorship Report No. 59, for period 16–31 Dec. 1944, TNA WO 204/10381.
64 CMF Appreciation & Censorship Report No. 60, for period 1–15 Jan. 1944, TNA WO 204/10381.
65 CMF Appreciation & Censorship Report No. 62, for period 1–14 Feb. 1945, TNA WO 204/10381.
66 A/Major T.M. Lowe, Cape Breton Highlanders, BEQ 129, LAC RG 24, vol. 10450.
67 One reinforcement officer with No. 4 Battalion, 1 CBRD wrote: "Frankly we are all tired of being reinforcement officers and I personally will welcome the day I am taken on strength of the regiment even if it does mean getting right into action." CMF Appreciation & Censorship Report No. 39, for period 16–29 Feb. 1944, TNA WO 204/10381.
68 In all likelihood the discussion of weather in the morale reports is the result of an overrepresentation of the weather in soldiers' letters home. The weather was generally a "safe" topic to get past censors, affected everyone while being beyond the control of anyone, and was easily discussed with correspondents back home. But at the same time, it had a profound effect upon soldiers' moods, attitudes, and motivations.
69 CMF Appreciation & Censorship Report No. 55, for period 16–31 Oct. 1944, TNA WO 204/10381.
70 Burns, *General Mud*, 73.
71 BEQS, LAC RG 24, vol. 10450. For more on the environment as it affects warfare, see Cyr, "Elemental Pursuits of Survival," especially chap. 6.
72 CMF Appreciation & Censorship Report No. 51, for period 16–31 Aug. 1944, TNA WO 204/10381.
73 Standard Canadian Infantry Division – Summary of Personnel and Vehicles, LAC RG 24, vol. 18576, file 133.065(D18D); "An Infantry Battalion," GO 466/43, II/233/2, 27 April 1943.
74 Discipline & Pay Section – Canadian Section GHQ, 2nd Echelon, Sum-

mary of Offences (by Formation) for Canadian Army in the Field, LAC RG 24, vol. 10118 and 10119.

75 Jackson, *Mediterranean and Middle East, Vol. VI, Part* 2, 374; Discipline & Pay Section – Canadian Section GHQ, 2nd Echelon, Summary of Offences (by Formations) for Canadian Army in the Field, LAC RG 24, vol. 10118, 10119.

76 Nicholson, *The Canadians in Italy*, 681; CMHQ Records Office – Consolidated Casualty Lists – CMF, LAC RG 24, vol. 12697, 12698.

77 Jackson, *Mediterranean and Middle East, Vol. VI, Part III*, 163.

78 AHQ Historical Section, "The Italian Campaign (4 Jan. 44–4 June 44): Information from German Sources," Report No. 20 (19 July 1948), 7.

79 General Statistics on 1 Cdn Corps front for first week in January 1945, LAC RG 24, vol. 10785, file 224C1.023(D15); CMHQ Records office – Consolidated Casualty Statistics – CMF, LAC RG 24, vols. 12697 and 12698.

80 Including those captured by the Americans, Free French, and Poles, the number is over 110,000. These numbers do not include the 200,000 surviving soldiers of Army Group "C" who surrendered in the last month of the Italian campaign during the final German collapse. Enemy POW captures reported by HQ 15th Army Group. Casualty Stats – Italian Campaign – Sept. 1943 to May 1945, LAC RG 24, vol. 18824, file 133.065(D597).

81 Jackson, *Mediterranean and the Middle East, Vol. VI, Part 3*, 399–400. For an interesting treatise on German desertion, see Lt-Colonel H.V. Hicks, "The German Deserter: A Psychological Study" (May 1944), LAC RG 24, vol. 10717, 215C1.98(D405).

82 Molony, *Mediterranean and Middle East, Vol. VI, Part* 1, 409–59.

83 CMHQ Records Office – Consolidated Casualty Statistics – CMF, LAC RG 24, vols. 12697 and 12698; "Standard Canadian Infantry Division – Summary of Personnel and Vehicles," LAC RG 24, vol. 18576, file 133.065(D18D).

84 "Notes from V Corps (after the break into the GOTHIC Line)," 9 Oct. 1944, TNA WO 204/7559.

85 "Standard Canadian Infantry Division – Summary of Personnel and Vehicles," LAC RG 24, vol. 18576, file 133.065(D18D).

86 Throughout most of the fighting, however, the casualties were still (barely) within the parameters calculated for the wastage rate by the Canadian Army Overseas' statisticians. See CMHQ Historical Section, "Historical Sketch, Rates of Wastage of Personnel, Canadian Army Overseas, 1939–1945," Report No. 134 (5 April 1945), DHH.

87 The British 46th Infantry Division had been part of Eighth Army during

Operation HUSKY, but the 46th had been the floating reserve and had not in fact gone ashore.

88 CMF Appreciation & Censorship Report No. 47, for period 16–30 June 1944, TNA WO 204/10381.

89 Mowat, *The Regiment*, 251.

90 Ibid., 174.

91 CMF Appreciation & Censorship Report No. 58, for period 1–15 Dec. 1944, TNA WO 204/10381.

92 CMF Appreciation & Censorship Report No. 63, for period 15–28 Feb. 1945, TNA WO 204/10381.

93 Comment from an officer of the Royal 22e Régiment, CMF Appreciation & Censorship Report No. 58, for period 1–15 Dec. 1944, TNA WO 204/10381.

94 Bernier, *The Royal 22e Regiment*, 153.

95 CMF Appreciation & Censorship Report No. 54, for period 1–15 Oct. 1944, TNA WO 204/10381.

96 Discipline & Pay Section – Cdn Section GHQ 2nd Echelon, Summary of Offences (by Formations) for Canadian Army in the Field, LAC RG 24, vol. 10118, 10119. Also see Tooley, "Appearance or Reality?" 40.

97 Consolidated Casualty Lists – CMF, LAC RG 24, vol. 12697, 12698. Based on regimental numbers.

98 12 Canadian Infantry Brigade Memorandum No. 23, "Reinforcement Reception Drill," 11 Aug. 1944, LAC Microfilm Reel T-12397.

99 Mowat, *The Regiment*, 177.

100 LAC RG 24, vols. 12697, 12698. These numbers only take into account other ranks (privates and NCOs), as officers were not given regimental numbers.

101 In fairness, only two officers rated their efficiency as being "High." Question 10(f): "Was [casualty replacements'] standard of efficiency high, moderate or low?" "High," 2 (5%); "Moderate," 28 (64%); "Low," 7 (16%); No reply, 7 (16%). BEQS, LAC RG 24, vol. 10450.

102 Captain Arthur Kendall Gale of the Cape Breton Highlanders listed "unit casualties among section and platoon commanders" as being detrimental to morale, and his was the only period questionnaire that came close to touching upon the issue. See BEQ 294, LAC RG 24, vol. 10450.

103 Jackson, *The Mediterranean and Middle East, Vol. VI, Part 1*, 447–50.

104 CMF Appreciation & Censorship Report No. 38, for period 1–15 Feb. 1944, UK TNA, WO 204/10381.

105 Mowat, *The Regiment*, 291.

106 12 Canadian Infantry Brigade Memorandum No. 6, "Training Policy," 21 July 1944, LAC Microfilm Reel T-12397.

107 References to "XII Canadian Light Brigade" and emphasis are found in:

12 Canadian Infantry Brigade War Diary, 19 Aug. 1944, LAC Microfilm Reel T-12397; Oldfield, *The Westminsters' War Diary*, 105. The nickname "slaughterhouse battalion" is mentioned in Dancocks, *D-Day Dodgers*, 293.

108 HQ 12 Cdn Inf Bde, Report on Operations, Period 22 Sept. 44–27 Sept. 44, appendix to 12 Cdn Inf Bde W.D. September 1944, LAC Microfilm Reel T-12397.

109 Memo from TAC Eighth Army to 12 Cdn Inf Bde, appendix to 12 Cdn Inf Bde W.D. September 1944, LAC Microfilm Reel T-12397.

110 BEQS, LAC RG 24, vol. 10450. Question 10(g): "Did you detach 'Left out of Battle' personnel before going into action?" "Yes," 40; "No," 1; no reply, 3.

111 Roy, *Seaforth Highlanders of Canada*, 274.

112 12 Cdn Inf Bde Memorandum No. 10, "Extracts from 5 Cdn Armd Div Op Instrs for distribution down to companies," 27 July 1944, appendix to W.D. 12 Cdn Inf Bde, July 1944, LAC Microfilm Reel T-12397.

113 Roy, *Seaforth Highlanders of Canada*, 312.

114 Mowat, *The Regiment*, 286.

115 Roy, *Seaforth Highlanders of Canada*, 349.

116 Major John C. Clarke, 48th Highlanders, BEQ 178, LAC RG 24, vol. 10450.

117 Jackson, *Mediterranean and Middle East, Vol. VI, Part 3*, 207.

118 Battle experience questionnaire responses were unanimous on the point of sections going into battle beneath their approved strength. Question 10(a): "Did your section go into battle under WE strength?": "Yes," 37; "No," 5; no reply, 3. BEQS, LAC RG 24, vol. 10450.

119 Question 10(b): "What was the average number of O.R.s in the section?" "3," one respondent; "4," four respondents; "5," ten respondents; "6," thirteen respondents; "7," four respondents; "8," three respondents; no answer, nine respondents. BEQS, LAC RG 24, vol. 10450.

120 Question 10(d): "Did your sections at that strength prove adequate for close quarter fighting?" "Yes," 25; "No," 12; no reply, 7.

121 Question 10(e): "Did they prove adequate for carrying sufficient ammunition for platoon weapons into battle?": "Yes," 18; "No," 16;, no reply, 9. BEQS, LAC RG 24, vol. 10450.

122 See Appendix G. BEQS, LAC RG 24, vol. 10450.

123 CMHQ Records Office – Consolidated Casualty Statistics – CMF, LAC RG 24, vols. 12697, 12698; "Standard Canadian Infantry Division – Summary of Personnel and Vehicles," LAC RG 24, vol. 18576, file 133.065(D18D).

124 Beattie, *Dileas*, 513.

125 For more, see Brown, "New Men in the Line," 35–47.

CHAPTER FIVE

1 For some comparative statistics, see: Casualties – World War I and World War II, LAC RG 24, vol. 18715, 133.065(D369).
2 Canadian Special Interrogation Report, *Brigadefuhrer* Kurt Meyer, 1946, TNA CAB 146/473.
3 Copp, *Fields of Fire*, 35–57.
4 Lorelli, *To Foreign Shores*.
5 Milner, *Stopping the Panzers*, 58–60.
6 Copp, *Fields of Fire*, 256–8.
7 Milner, "No Ambush, No Defeat," 335–65.
8 D'Este, *Decision in Normandy*; Beevor, *D-Day*; Wieviorka, *Normandy*.
9 For a balanced scholarly critique, see Reid, *No Holding Back*.
10 Whitaker, *Victory at Falaise*, 294–5.
11 Stacey, *The Victory Campaign*, 34.
12 Callahan, "Two Armies in Normandy," 271.
13 Although there were a few changes to the infantry battalion war establishment between 1943 and 1944, they were almost entirely administrative. See: War Establishments for a Canadian Infantry Battalion, II/233/3 (5 Aug. 1943), II/233/4 (15 Aug. 1944).
14 Stacey, *Six Years of War*, 389.
15 Vance, *Maple Leaf Empire*, 188–90.
16 Quoted in CMHQ Historical Report No. 109, "Operation JUBILEE: The Raid on Dieppe, 19 Aug. 1942, Part III: Some Special Aspects," (CMHQ, 17 Dec. 1943), 28.
17 Delaney, *Corps Commanders*, 76–7.
18 Ibid., 77–8.
19 The evidence seems to indicate that this conception of the campaign's operational plan existed at least a month before D-Day and was generally followed through by Montgomery. Although Montgomery was fully prepared (and hopeful) for the Anglo-Canadian forces to produce a breakthrough and breakout, his intention from start to finish seems to have been that the major rupture should be made on First US Army's front. See Stacey, *The Victory Campaign*, 83, 144; Copp, *Fields of Fire*, 84–5. For the major critique, see D'Este, *Decision in Normandy*.
20 For more discussion, particularly of the critical early phase of the plan as to where the counterattacks would need to be defeated, see Milner, *Stopping the Panzers*, 299–315.
21 According to Gregory Liedtke, "Far from being as decimated or as weak as some sources have indicated, the German formations opposing the Canadians throughout their breakout efforts still retained a very considerable portion of their original strength, and in some cases were com-

pletely fresh." Liedtke, "Canadian Offensive Operations in Normandy Revisited," 67.

22 English, *Canadian Army and the Normandy Campaign*, 204.
23 Feasby, *Clinical Subjects*, 425.
24 Montgomery, *Memoirs*, 232.
25 Operational Policy – II Canadian Corps HQ, 17 February 1945, LAC RG 24, vol. 10799, 225c2.012(D8). Simonds released further operational policy instructions on the basis of lessons learned closer to the actual deployment of II Canadian Corps to Normandy, and said much the same thing. See "Lessons Learned from Ops during War," memorandum by Lt-General G.G. Simonds, 1 July 1944, LAC RG 24, vol. 10799, 225c2.012(D8).
26 Address by Lt-General H.D.G. Crerar to Senior Officers, First Canadian Army, 14 May 1944, LAC RG 24, vol. 10586, 215c1.(D286).
27 Question 8(a) "Did you ever have to organize rapid defence against counter-attack?": "Yes," 68 (71%); "No," 22 (23%); "Not Known," 3 (3%); no answer, 3 (3%).
28 A/Major G.E. Colgate, South Saskatchewan Regiment, BEQ 116, LAC RG 24, vol. 10450.
29 Major Froggett, Royal Hamilton Light Infantry, BEQ 290, LAC RG 24, vol. 10450.
30 A/Captain Sinkewicz, Division Intelligence Officer, BEQ 48, LAC RG 24, vol. 10450.
31 Question 11: "Were you able to put the tactical principles of fire and movement, taught as battle drill before going overseas, into practice?": "Yes," 79 (82%); "No," 9 (9%); "Not Known" 5 (5%); no answer, 3 (3%); "Often, fairly often, or seldom?": "Often," 23 (28%); "Fairly often," 27 (33%); "Seldom," 29 (36%); "Not Known," 2 (3%).
32 A/Major C.K. Crummer, Lincoln and Welland Regiment, BEQ 29; Major R.D. Medland, Queen's Own Rifles, BEQ 271, LAC RG 24, vol. 10450.
33 Regina Rifle Regiment – Combat Lessons, 3 Aug. 1944, LAC RG 24, vol. 10924, 239c3.(D13).
34 Lessons Learned – Stormont, Dundas and Glengarry Highlanders, 14 July 1944, LAC RG 24, vol. 10924, 239c3.(D13).
35 Account by Sgt. Benson, Black Watch, of the attack on May-sur-Orne, 25 July 1944, in: Canadian Operations in North-West Europe, Extracts from War Diaries and Memoranda (Series 5), July 1944, LAC RG 24, vol. 12748, 24/DIARIES/8/3.
36 Account by Lt. J.A.C. Auld, Queen's Own Rifles, in: Canadian Operations in North-West Europe, Extracts from Memoranda (Series 4), 30 Aug. 1944, LAC RG 24, vol. 12748, 24/DIARIES/8/3.
37 A/Major C.K. Crummer, Lincoln and Welland Regiment, BEQ 29, LAC

RG 24, vol. 10450. Sometimes the same tendencies were observed in the Germans. A 6th Canadian Brigade intelligence report from early August 1944 described the German forward lines "shooting [machine-gun] and rifle fire rather wildly" when their suspicions were aroused." 6 Cdn Inf Bde INTREP, 5 Aug. 1944, appended to Les Fusiliers Mont-Royal W.D., LAC RG 24, vol. 15065.

38 Captain F.W. Grafton, Algonquin Regiment, BEQ 145, LAC RG 24, vol. 10450.

39 Question 12(a): "Did your unit carry out an attack under an artillery barrage?": "Yes," 69 (72%); "No," 15 (16%); "Not Known," 5 (5%); no answer, 7 (7%). BEQS, LAC RG 24, vol. 10450.

40 Question 12(b): "If so, did they have preliminary training?": "Yes," 39 (55%); "No," 27 (38%), "Not Known," 1 (1%); no answer, 4 (6%). Question 12(c): "Did they keep up with the barrage effectively?": "Yes," 58 (83%); "No," 6 (8.5%); no answer, 6 (8.5%). BEQS, LAC RG 24, vol. 10450.

41 8th Canadian Infantry Brigade, "Barrage in the Attack," 3 Aug. 1944, LAC RG 24, vol. 10986, 265c8.013(D3).

42 Combat Lessons – 7th Canadian Infantry Brigade, LAC RG 24, vol. 10986, 265c7.013(D1).

43 "Lessons Learned from Ops during War," memorandum by Lt-General G.G. Simonds, 1 July 1944, LAC RG 24, vol. 10799, 225c2.012(D8).

44 Captain F.T. Rea, Black Watch (Royal Highlanders), BEQ 69, LAC RG 24, vol. 10450.

45 On "soul-shattering" artillery, see Fritz, *Frontsoldaten*, 63.

46 Army Operational Research Group Report No. 292, "Comparison of British and American Areas in Normandy in terms of Fire Support and its Effects," LAC RG 24, vol. 20339, 952.013(D37).

47 Copp, *Fields of Fire*, 258–9.

48 Ellis, *Victory in the West*, 490.

49 Stacey, *The Victory Campaign*, 274.

50 Although, as Copp has demonstrated, the campaign that the air forces wanted to fight was not the same one that the armies on the ground were fighting. Copp, *Fields of Fire*, 260.

51 Question 7(a): "Did you ever receive Direct Air Support?": "Yes," 64; "No," 22; "Not Known," or no answer, 10. BEQS, LAC RG 24, vol. 10450.

52 Question 7(b): "Was the support effective?": "Yes," 62; "No," 1; "Not Known," 27. BEQS, LAC RG 24, vol. 10450.

53 Question 3: "Please list in order of importance factors which, in your unit, appeared to have the effect of raising morale." BEQS, LAC RG 24, vol. 10450.

54 Operation Research Report No. 4, "Air Attacks on Enemy Tanks and Motor Transport in the Mortain Area, August 1944," LAC RG 24, vol. 10553, 215a21.093(D2).

55 No. 2 Operational Research Section, 21st Army Group and Operational Research Section, 2nd Tactical Air Force, Joint Report No. 3, "Rocket-Firing Typhoons in Close Support of Military Operations," LAC RG 24, vol. 10553, 215a21.093(D2).

56 Regina Rifle Regiment – Combat Lessons, 3 August 1944, LAC RG 24, vol. 10924, 239c3.(D13).

57 Question 15(a): "Have you ever co-operated with Infantry Tanks?" "Yes," 72; "No," 16; "Not Known," 2; no answer, 5. BEQS, LAC RG 24, vol. 10450.

58 Question 15(b): "Did you move in front of, behind, or amongst the tanks?" "in front of," 48; "behind," 24; "amongst," 27; no answer, 9. Officers making multiple selections were put down for each category they indicated, so the number of responses to this question is higher than the total number of respondents. BEQS, LAC RG 24, vol. 10450.

59 J. English, *Canadian Army and the Normandy Campaign*, 204; Combat Lessons – 7th Canadian Infantry Brigade, LAC RG 24, vol. 10986, 265c7.013(D1).

60 Captain Harry C. Blanshard, Fort Garry Horse, BEQ 144, LAC RG 24, vol. 10450.

61 Major John Wesley Burgess, Essex Scottish, BEQ 131; A/Captain Thomas D. Murray, Queen's Own Cameron Highlanders, BEQ 161; Major R.A. Cottrill, Queen's Own Rifles, BEQ 177; Major J.W. Ostiguy, Regiment de Maisonneuve, BEQ 192, LAC RG 24, vol. 10450.

62 Major David Durward, Highland Light Infantry, BEQ 130, LAC RG 24, vol. 10450. For more on the problems of armour facing the Allies in Normandy, see Reid, *No Holding Back*, 367; Zaloga, *Armored Thunderbolt*, 233–41.

63 21st Army Group Interim Report on Equipment in the Early Stages of Operation OVERLORD, 10 Aug. 1944, LAC RG 24, vol. 10581-A, 215c1.(D173).

64 Captain Reginald Harvey Smith, BEQ 146, LAC RG 24, vol. 10450.

65 Captain M.D. Guy Levesque, BEQ 149, LAC RG 24, vol. 10450.

66 See: A/Major Harrison, Calgary Highlanders, BEQ 191, LAC RG 24, vol. 10450.

67 Report on Wask Mk II (Canadian) by Lt.-Colonel R. Rowley, S.D.&G. Highlanders, in: Canadian Operations in North-West Europe, Extracts from Memoranda (Series 7), Aug. 1944, LAC RG 24, vol. 12748, 24/DIARIES/8/3. Emphasis in original. This report was circulated, in an edited form, to all Commonwealth armies: "Notes on the Tactical Handling of

Wasps and a Drill for their Use," *Current Reports from Overseas* 60 (25 Oct. 1944).

68 "Crocodiles in co-operation with Infantry: the attack on May-sur-Orne," 8 Aug. 1944, account by Major Brochu and Captain Lamothe, Fusiliers Mont-Royal, in: Canadian Operations in Northwest Europe, Extracts from War Diaries and Memoranda (Series 9), 16 Oct. 1944, LAC RG 24, vol. 12748, 24/DIARIES/8/3.

69 BEQS, LAC RG 24, vol. 10450.

70 Comments by Brigadier K.G. Blackader, 8 CIB in the assault, in: Canadian Operations in North-West Europe, Extracts from Memoranda (Series 1), 12 July 1944, LAC RG 24, vol. 12748, 24/DIARIES/8/2.

71 Reid, *No Holding Back*, 371. Also see Margolian, *Conduct Unbecoming*, 18–29; English, *Canadian Army and Normandy*, xiv.

72 Combat Lessons – 7th Canadian Infantry Brigade, August 1944, LAC RG 24, vol. 10986, 265c7.013(D1).

73 Calgary Highlanders W.D. 13 July 1944, LAC RG 24, vol. 15020.

74 Censorship Report – Canadian Mail, for period 1–15 June 1944, LAC Microfilm Reel T-17925.

75 Field Censors (Home) – Canadian Army Overseas – 6–20 June 1944, LAC Reel T-17925.

76 Censorship Report – Canadian Army Overseas, for period 16–31 July 1944, LAC Reel T-17925.

77 Censorship Report – Canadian Army Overseas, for period 1–15 Aug. 1944, LAC Reel T-17925.

78 For one example, a soldier in the Royal Regiment of Canada wrote that: "There's not much to tell in this letter apart from the battlefield blues. Things are still quite hot for us over here and we are all pretty tired and worn to a nervous state. I'm speaking of the majority of the new boys and myself." Censorship Report – Canadian Army Overseas, for period 1–15 Aug. 1944, LAC Reel T-17925.

79 Calgary Highlanders W.D. appendix, LAC RG 24, vol. 15020.

80 Discipline & Pay Section – Canadian Section GHQ, 2nd Echelon – Summary of Offences (by Formations) for Canadian Army in the Field, LAC RG 24, vol. 10117.

81 Lt.-Colonel E.T. Jacques, Le Régiment de Maisonneuve, BEQ186, LAC RG 24, vol. 10450.

82 Copp and McAndrew, *Battle Exhaustion*, 135

83 Consolidated Casualty Statistics – AEF, LAC RG 24, vol. 12695 and 12696.

84 Stacey, *The Victory Campaign*, 270.

85 Account by Lt J.A.C. Auld, Queen's Own Rifles, in: Canadian Operations

in Northwest Europe, Extracts from Memoranda (Series 4), 30 Aug. 1944, LAC RG 24, vol. 12748, 24/ DIARIES /8/3.

86 Transcript of interview with Major-General Bert Hoffmeister by B. Greenhous and Bill McAndrew, 71, RMC Cavalry House Archives.

87 The high rate of German desertion and POW captures was tentatively viewed this way by contemporary Allied psychologists who were exploring the issues. See Lt-Colonel H.V. Dicks, "The German Deserter: A Psychological Study," May 1944, LAC RG 24, vol. 10717, 215C1.98(D405).

88 Calgary Highlanders W.D., July 1944, LAC RG 24, vol. 15020.

89 Report by Major D.J. Watterson to DDMS, Rear HQ 2nd Army, LAC RG 24, vol. 12631, file 11/PSYCHIATRY/4.

90 Quoted in Copp and McAndrew, *Battle Exhaustion*, 113.

91 Copp and Humphries, *Combat Stress in the 20th Century*, 245; Terry Copp, "To the Last Canadian? Casualties in 21 Army Group," paper.

92 Copp and McAndrew, *Battle Exhaustion*, 126, 128–35. As Copp and McAndrew point out, these attitudes were not shared in the rifle companies or among divisional psychiatrists.

93 Quoted in Copp, *Fields of Fire*, 178.

94 By far the best and most completely documented account is Margolian, *Conduct Unbecoming*.

95 Captain John Rickard, conversation with author at Fort Frontenac, 20 March 2013.

96 Mitcham, *Hitler's Legions*, 454.

97 "Enemy Tactics" (Lessons of War, No. 1), Extracts from War Diary, 8th Canadian Infantry Brigade, 12 July 1944, in: Canadian Operations in North-West Europe, Extracts from War Diaries and Memoranda (Series 5), July 1944, LAC RG 24, vol. 12748, 24/DIARIES/8/3.

98 Margolian, *Conduct Unbecoming*, 43–58.

99 Nowhere can the apocalyptic overtones of the Normandy fighting be seen as clearly as in the person of SS Major-General Kurt Meyer, commander of the 12th SS Panzer Division for part of the Battle of Normandy. As his Allied interrogators noted during debriefing in 1945: "To [Meyer] the battle of Caen-Falaise was magnificent in the best Wagnerian tradition. As he described his actions and those of his men, it seemed as though he liked to consider himself as Siegfried leading his warriors to their death. When he described how he came out of the Falaise Gap with sixty men, it is likely that the familiar strains of 'Twilight of the Gods' were echoing in his ears." Special Interrogation Report – Brigadefuhrer Kurt Meyer, comd 12 SS Pz Div "Hitler Jugend," TNA CAB 146/473.

100 After the war Major Ronald Shawcross offered the hypothesis that on 6–7 June the 12th SS retook ground briefly occupied by the Canadians

the day before and found the graves of a number of Germans killed near Carpiquet Airfield, who had been shot from a high angle of trajectory, and whom they might have assumed had been executed. Transcript of interview with Major Ronald Shawcross, UVic Oral History Collection Record 0132.

101 Field Censors (Home) – Canadian Army Overseas, 16–31 July 1944, LAC Microfilm Reel T-17925. This report suggests that operational stress injuries may have been a contributing factor to the Germans' behaviour.

102 Transcript of interview with Captain Ernest Edmund Teagle, UVic Oral History Collection, Record 0140.

103 Dickson, *A Thoroughly Canadian General*, 298. The reading out of this account is mentioned in many unit war diaries. For example, see War Diary, South Saskatchewan Regiment, 1 Aug. 1944, LAC RG 24, vol. 15263.

104 Copp, *Fields of Fire*, 71.

105 Transcript of interview with Captain Ernest Edmund Teagle, UVic Oral History Collection, Record 0140.

106 Field Censors (Home) – Canadian Army Overseas, 16–31 July 1944, LAC Microfilm Reel T-17925.

107 Field Censors (Home) – Canadian Army Overseas, 16–31 July 1944, LAC Microfilm Reel T-17925.

108 Calgary Highlanders W.D. appendix, July 1944, LAC RG 24, vol. 15020.

109 Field Censors (Home) – Canadian Army Overseas – Special Report on Mail from Canadian Military Hospitals on the Invasion of France, 1–15 Sept. 1944, LAC Reel T-17925.

110 Calgary Highlanders War Diary, 24 Aug. 1944, LAC RG 24, vol. 15020.

111 Transcript of interview with Captain Ernest Edmund Teagle, UVic Oral History Collection Record 0140.

112 Censorship Report – Canadian Army Overseas, for period 1–15 Sept. 1944, LAC Microfilm Reel T-17925.

113 Account of the attack by Calgary Highlanders on May-sur-Orne, 25 July 1944, given by Lt-Colonel D.G. MacLaughlan in: Canadian Operations in North-West Europe, Extracts from War Diaries and Memoranda (Series 5), July 1944, LAC RG 24, vol. 12748, 24/DIARIES/8/3.

114 Transcript of interview with Captain Ernest Edmund Teagle, UVic Oral History Collection Record 0140.

115 Quoted in Milner, *Stopping the Panzers*, 285.

116 Field Censors (Home) – Canadian Army Overseas – Special Report on Mail from Canadian Hospitals on the Invasion of France, 16–31 July 1944, LAC Reel T-17925.

117 CMHQ Records Office – Consolidated Casualty Statistics – AEF, LAC RG

24, vols. 12695 and 12696; "Standard Canadian Infantry Division – Summary of Personnel and Vehicles," LAC RG 24 vol. 18576, file 133.065(D18D).

118 LAC RG 24, vols. 12695 and 12696; "Standard Canadian Infantry Division – Summary of Personnel and Vehicles," LAC RG 24 vol. 18576, file 133.065(D18D).

119 For example, the 12th SS Panzer Division, which was mostly in the line against Canadian forces from June through August 1944, had a strength of 20,000 men and 150 tanks on 6 June, and on 22–23 August the German Army Group "B" reported the 12th SS's strength as being 300 men, ten tanks, and no artillery. Proportionate casualties had been inflicted on all eight of the German panzer divisions in Normandy. See: Army Headquarters Historical Section, Report No. 50, "The Campaign in North-West Europe – Information from German Sources, Part II: Invasion and Battle of Normandy, 6 June–22 August 1944" (Ottawa: AHQ, 14 Oct. 1952), 134.

120 Hayes, *The Lincs*, 4.

121 As Lt-Colonel Lawrence Henderson was to remark in a postwar interview, "The support company was strictly action ... carrier platoon, anti-tank platoon, mortar platoon ... anti-aircraft platoon, so everything was pretty much covered that a CO would need." Transcript of interview with Lt-Colonel Lawrence S. Henderson, UVic Oral History Collection Record 064. Also see Barnard, *The Queen's Own Rifles of Canada*, 209.

122 See: Censorship Reports – Canadian Army Overseas, for period 16–31 Aug. 1944 and for period 1–15 Sept. 1944, LAC Reel T-17925.

123 For more specific comments, see Granatstein, *The Generals*.

124 The British Second Army, which was the parent formation in which the Canadian divisions were operating until the end of the Normandy campaign when First Canadian Army was activated, had only been created in 1943 and had not seen action prior to 6 June 1944. See Ellis, *Victory in the West*.

125 Field Censors (Home) – Canadian Army Overseas – Special Report on Mail from Canadian Hospitals on the Invasion of France, 16–31 July 1944, LAC Reel T-17925.

126 Margolian, *Conduct Unbecoming*, 26.

127 Censorship Report – Canadian Army Overseas, for period 1–15 Aug. 1944, LAC Reel T-17925.

128 Censorship Report – Canadian Army Overseas, for period 16–31 Aug. 1944, LAC Reel T-17925.

129 CMHQ Records Office – Consolidated Casualty Statistics – AEF, LAC RG 24, vols. 12695 and 12696.

130 Consolidated casualty statistics, AEF, LAC RG 24, vols. 12695 and 12696.
131 Law, *Regimental Numbers of the Canadian Army*; Consolidated casualty statistics, AEF, LAC RG 24, vols. 12695 and 12696.
132 Calgary Highlanders W.D., 11 Aug. 1944, LAC RG 24, vol. 15020.
133 Deficiencies and Holdings of Canadian Infantry Other Ranks, North-West Europe, 9 June 1944–28 April 1945, LAC RG 24, vol. 10669, 215C1.065(D4).
134 Question 10(a): "Did your section go into battle under WE strength?": "Yes," 75 (78%); "No," 16 (17%); no answer, 4. BEQS, LAC RG 24, vol. 10450.
135 Question 10(b): "What was the average number of ORS in the section?" Average of all responses (excluding 14 "No Answer" or "Not Known") was 5.69; median of all responses was 6. Question 10(d): "Was this strength adequate for close quarters fighting?": "Yes," 47 (51%); "No," 29 (32%); "Not Known," 17%; no answer, 4. BEQS, LAC RG 24, vol. 10450. This was a smaller ratio than the 60 percent who so indicated in Italy, a difference obviously attributable to the higher casualty rate in Normandy.
136 A much higher ratio of officers than in Italy also agreed that even with casualties their sections were adequate for carrying ammunition for platoon weapons, likely reflecting the fact that the terrain in northern France did not hinder communications and logistics the way that the Italian landscape did. See Question 10(e): "Did they prove adequate for carrying sufficient ammunition for platoon weapons into battle?": "Yes," 45 (47%); "No," 33 (34%), "Not Known," 4 (4%), no answer, 14 (15%). BEQS, LAC RG 24, vol. 10450.
137 German military documents on the Battle of Normandy captured and studied by the Canadian Army after the fighting are replete with discussions of "battle groups" throughout the campaign. See: Canadian Army Headquarters Historical Section, Report No. 50, "The Campaign in North-West Europe: Information from German Sources, Part II: Invasion and Battle of Normandy (6 June–22 August 1944)" (Ottawa: Army Headquarters, 14 October 1952).
138 2 Cdn Inf Div Intelligence Summary No. 4, 22 July 1944, Les Fusiliers Mont-Royal W.D., July 1944, appendix, LAC RG 24, vol. 15065.
139 Hastings, *Overlord*, 183.
140 Calgary Highlanders W.D., 1 Aug. 1944, LAC RG 24, vol. 15020.
141 Lt.-Colonel P.W. Bennett, Essex Scottish Regiment, BEQ 81, LAC RG 24, vol. 10450.
142 Calgary Highlanders W.D. July 1944 appendix, LAC RG 24, vol. 15020.
143 Captain W. Parker, Royal Hamilton Light Infantry, BEQ 17, LAC RG 24, vol. 10450.

144 Question 10(g): "Did you detach 'Left out of Battle' personnel before going into action?": "Yes," 81 (84%); "No," 7 (7%); no answer, 8 (9%). Compare with Italy 1944–45: 90% responded with "Yes." BEQS, LAC RG 24, vol. 10450.
145 Major A.M. Hamilton, Stormont, Dundas & Glengarry Highlanders, BEQ 35, LAC RG 24, vol. 10450.
146 A/Major William Ewing, Black Watch (Royal Highlanders), BEQ 176, LAC RG 24, vol. 10450.
147 A/Major A.H.M. Carmichael, Black Watch (Royal Highlanders), BEQ 86, LAC RG 24, vol. 10450.
148 Memorandum of interview with Brigadier H.W. Foster, 22 June 1944, LAC RG 24, vol. 10986, 265C7.011(D1).
149 Question 10(f): "Was [reinforcements'] standard of efficiency high, moderate or low?": "High," 4 (4%); "Moderate," 53 (58%); "Low," 26 (28%); no answer, 9 (10%). BEQS, LAC RG 24, vol. 10450.
150 Captain W. Parker, Royal Hamilton Light Infantry, BEQ 17, LAC RG 24, vol. 10450.
151 LAC RG 24, vol. 10450. The BEQS studied for these tables represent all Canadian infantry officers with experience in Normandy in 1944, 90 officers.
152 BEQS, LAC RG 24, vol. 10450.
153 Quoted in Stacey, *The Victory Campaign*, 274.
154 On German propaganda views of the Allies, see SHAEF Intelligence Notes No. 39, 9 Dec. 1944, LAC RG 24, vol. 10717, 215C1.98(D407).
155 For more, see Milner, *Stopping the Panzers*, 5–25.

CHAPTER SIX

1 The expression is borrowed from Williams, *The Long Left Flank*.
2 Ellis, *Victory in the West*, vol. 2, 158–9. The British had to break up the 59th Division for reinforcements in August 1944, and during the fall determined that they also needed to disperse the 50th Division.
3 Advanced Warfighting Studies Program, "Case Study: Operation Overlord"; Ellis, *Victory in the West*, vol. 2, 2–3, 16–8.
4 Copp, *Cinderella Army*, 82–3.
5 Ellis, *Victory in the West*, vol. 2, 135–6.
6 Canadian Army Historical Section, The Campaign in North-West Europe – Information from German Sources Part III – German Defence Operations in the Sphere of First Canadian Army (23 Aug. – 8 Nov. 1944), Report No. 69 (30 July 1954), 26.
7 21st Army Group, Report on Clearing of the Scheldt Estuary, Oct.–Nov. 1944, LAC RG 24, vol. 10535, 215A21.013.

8 Whitaker, *Rhineland*, 347.
9 Comment from soldier of the 4th Canadian Armoured Division, in Canadian Army Overseas – 21st Army Group, Censorship Report for period 16–30 Nov. 1944, LAC Microfilm Reel T-17925.
10 Delaney, *The Soldiers' General*, 206.
11 Dancocks, *The D-Day Dodgers*, 423–5.
12 Copp and Vogel, *Maple Leaf Route: Victory*, 35, 46.
13 Question 8(a): "Did you ever have to organize rapid defence against counter-attack?": "Yes," 42 (69%); "No," 17 (28%); "Not Known," 1; no answer, 1. LAC RG 24, vol. 10450, BEQS. Compare with Question 8(a) from chapter 6: "Yes," 68 (71%); "No," 22 (23%); "Not Known," 3 (3%); no answer, 3 (3%).
14 Major Froggett, Royal Hamilton Light Infantry, LAC RG 24, vol. 10450, BEQ 290.
15 Question 5(a): "Has your unit undertaken mine laying?": "Yes," 37 (61%); "No," 14 (23%); "Not Known," 5 (8%); no answer, 5 (8%); LAC RG 24, vol. 10450, BEQS.
16 Dyke Warfare (account by Major R.G. Hodgins, 2i/c Highland Light Infantry, given to historical officer 26 Oct. 1944), in: Canadian Operations – Northwest Europe – Extracts from War Diaries and Memoranda Series 14, 15 Dec. 1944, LAC RG 24, vol. 12748, 24/DIARIES/8/3.
17 Engen, *Canadians Under Fire*, 105–11.
18 Copp, *Cinderella Army*, 136–7, 219–20.
19 Copp and Vogel, *Maple Leaf Route: Victory*, 76.
20 Dyke Warfare (account by Major R.G. Hodgins, 2i/c Highland Light Infantry, given to historical officer 26 October 1944), in: Canadian Operations – Northwest Europe – Extracts from War Diaries and Memoranda Series 14, 15 Dec. 1944, LAC RG 24, vol. 12748, 24/ DIARIES /8/3.
21 Canadian Army Overseas – 21st Army Group, Censorship Report for period 16–31 Dec. 1944, LAC Microfilm Reel T-17925.
22 Question 15(a): "Have you ever co-operated with Infantry Tanks?": "Yes," 53 (87%); "No," 5 (8%); no answer, 3 (5%). LAC RG 24, vol. 10450, BEQS.
23 Lessons Learned during Operations on Zuid Beveland, account by Brigadier F.N. Cabeldu, 4 Cdn Inf Bde, given to historical officer 14 Nov. 1944, in: Canadian Operations, Northwest Europe – Extracts from War Diaries and Memoranda (Series 16), 10 Jan. 1945, LAC RG 24, vol. 12748, 24/DIARIES/8/3.
24 Lt.-Colonel E.T. Jacques, Le *Régiment de Maisonneuve*, LAC RG 24, vol. 10450, BEQ 186.
25 Report on Ops by 2 Cdn Armoured Brigade, Operation BLOCKBUSTER, n.d., LAC RG 24, vol. 12303, 3/LESSONS OPS/1.

26 Copp, *Cinderella Army*, 217.
27 Question 12(a): "Did your unit carry out an attack under an artillery barrage?": "Yes," 50 (82%); "No," 9 (15%); "Not Known," 2 (3%). LAC RG 24, vol. 10450, BEQS.
28 Question 12(b): "If so, did they have preliminary training?": "Yes," 25 (41%), "No," 23 (38%), no answer, 13 (21%). LAC RG 24, vol. 10450, BEQS.
29 Question 12(c): "Did they keep up with the barrage effectively?": "Yes," 42 (69%), "No," 2 (3%); no answer, 17 (28%). LAC RG 24, vol. 10450, BEQS. There was a relative decline of about 15 percent in officers answering "Yes" to this question between Normandy and Northwest Europe (see chapter 6), but this decline was due to many more officers not answering the question than answering "No." The number of "No" responses declined by 5 percent as well.
30 Major J.G. Stothart, Stormont, Dundas and Glengarry Highlanders, LAC RG 24, vol. 10450, BEQ 205. A "stonk" is a sudden concentration of artillery fire on a specific target, whereas a barrage is a more linear firing pattern. The stonk was intended to suppress or destroy a target, while the barrage was more generally put down to discourage counterattack.
31 Notes on Dyke and Polder Fighting – 3rd Cdn Inf Division Study Period, account by historical officer November 1944, in: Canadian Operations – Northwest Europe – Extracts from Memoranda (Series 15), 20 Dec. 1944, LAC RG 24, vol. 12748, 24/DIARIES/8/3.
32 An operational research report during Operation VERITABLE indicated that, while a density of 650–1,300 field and medium artillery shells falling per square kilometre succeeded in cutting all the line communications to the enemy's forward position, which was certainly useful, Allied casualties were not significantly reduced by weights of artillery fire over 100 tons per square kilometre. See: No. 2 Operational Research Section Report No. 26, "Fire Support in Operation Veritable: Effect on Forward Defensive Positions," 26 May 1945, LAC RG 24, vol. 20338, 952.013(d27).
33 Polder Fighting, account given by Lt-Colonel S.M. Lett, to historical officer 3 Nov. 1944, in: Canadian Operations – Northwest Europe – Extracts from Memoranda (Series 15), 20 Dec. 1944, LAC RG 24, vol. 12748, 24/DIARIES /8/3.
34 HQ 10th Cdn Inf Brigade, Lessons from Operation Elephant, 7 Feb. 1945, LAC RG 24, vol. 10944, 249C4.(d29).
35 Weapons Technical Staff Field Force, Report on Small Arms Weapons, 24 May 1945, LAC RG 24, vol. 10974, 260C6.009(d13).
36 Question 11: "Were you able to put the tactical principles of fire and movement, taught as battle drill before going overseas, into practice?": "Yes," 51 (84%); "No," 51 (10%); "Not Known," 2 (3%); no answer,

2 (3%); "Often, fairly often, or seldom?": "Often," 22 (36%); "Fairly often," 17 (28%); "seldom," 12 (20%); "Not Known," 1 (2%); no answer, 7 (12%).

37 Memo, 2 Cdn Inf Div HQ to all formation/unit commanders, 16 March 1945, LAC RG 24, vol. 10974, 260c6.009(d13).

38 Canadian Army Overseas – 21st Army Group, Censorship Report for period 16–31 March 1945, LAC Microfilm Reel T-17925

39 See, for instance, Bird, *North Shore (New Brunswick) Regiment*, 471.

40 Many reports to this effect were made in the Battle Experience Questionnaires. For a few, see: LAC RG 24, vol. 10450, BEQS 224, 229, 243, 246, 257, 270.

41 Some Aspects of the Technique of Flame Throwing: "Wasp" and "Lifebuoy," account by Lt George Bannerman, Saskatoon Light Infantry, in: Canadian Operations – Northwest Europe – Extracts from War Diaries and Memoranda Series 17, 24 Jan. 1945, LAC RG 24, vol. 12748, 24/DIARIES /8/3. The etymological link between the "Golden Rain" referred to here and the nickname for the sexual act of urolagnia is unknown, but highly suggestive.

42 Operational Research Group (Weapons & Equipment) Report No. 332, "The Effect of Flame Throwers on Military Personnel (A General Review)," TNA WO 291/308.

43 The Crocodile, which was under armoured and not infantry command, was less vulnerable than the Wasp to enemy fire and carried more fuel for the flame gun, but was less manoeuvrable and obstructed the crews' view. See: First Canadian Army, Notes on Wood and Village Fighting, 23 January 1945; Report – Operation VERITABLE, 30 June 1945, LAC RG 24, vol. 10581, 215c1.(d169).

44 Operational Research Group (Weapons & Equipment) Report No. 332, "The Effect of Flame Throwers on Military Personnel (A General Review)," TNA WO 291/308; Employment of Wasps, Extract taken from war diary of a unit in Northwest Europe, in: Progress Bulletin (Infantry) No. 17, 22 Dec. 1944, TNA WO 165/94.

45 Copp, "Canadian Operational Art," 47.

46 Some Aspects of the Technique of Flame Throwing: "Wasp" and "Lifebuoy," account by Lt George Bannerman, Saskatoon Light Infantry, in: Canadian Operations – Northwest Europe – Extracts from War Diaries and Memoranda Series 17, 24 Jan. 1945, LAC RG 24, vol. 12748, 24/DIARIES/8/3. For similar remarks, including the observation that the only drawback to flamethrowers was that there were not enough of them, see "Dyke Warfare," account by Major R.G. Hodgins, Highland Light Infantry, given to historical officer, 26 Oct. 1944, in: Canadian

Operations – Northwest Europe – Extracts from War Diaries and Memoranda (Series 14), 15 Dec. 1944, LAC RG 24, vol. 12748, 24/DIARIES/8/3.

47 Canadian Army Overseas – 21st Army Group, Censorship Report for period 16–31 March 1945, LAC Microfilm Reel T-17925.

48 Dykstra, "The Liberation of Groningen," 52.

49 HQ 10th Canadian Infantry Brigade, lessons from Operation ELEPHANT, 7 Feb. 1945, LAC RG 24, vol. 10944, 249c4.(d29).

50 Recounting an episode from the Battle of the Scheldt in his regimental history of the North Shore Regiment, Will Bird wrote, "Flame-throwing carriers had been allotted for the job but they had come to a fiery twisted end on mines, so steel and spirit had to take over." Bird, *North Shore (N.B.) Regiment*, 444.

51 Army Operational Research Group Memorandum No. 341, "An Investigation of the Accuracy of Aiming with the Wasp Flame Thrower Mark II," LAC RG 24, vol. 20339, 952.013(d34). Also see "Flame Throwers in Action," War Office, *Current Reports from Overseas* 70, 3 Jan. 1945, LAC RG 24, vol. 20348, 952.013(d71).

52 Transcript of interview with Major Harvey F. Bailey, UVic Military Oral History Collection, record 0006.

53 Canadian Army Overseas – 21st Army Group, Censorship Report for period 1–15 Sept. 1944, LAC Microfilm Reel T-17925.

54 LAC Microfilm Reel T-17925.

55 One criticism might be that during periods of heavy fighting the infantry were less likely to be writing letters home than support troops and that the state of morale might be even less representative of the infantry. While it is acknowledged that there is ultimately no way to control for this variable, in their more detailed annexes the censorship reports attribute specific remarks according to the soldier's unit, and comments from infantry battalions are cited heavily throughout 1944–45. At the very least the distinct impression is given that infantrymen continued to write home given any opportunity, even during the heaviest fighting.

56 Censorship Reports for periods 1–15 Nov. and 16–30 Nov. 1944, LAC Microfilm Reel T–17925.

57 Churchill arrived at OCTAGON determined that the British Empire should "play our full and equal part" against Japan, and that it "had to regain on the field of battle our rightful possessions in the Far East, and not have them handed back to us at the peace table." Churchill, *Triumph and Tragedy*, 146–7.

58 Canadian Army Overseas – 21st Army Group, Censorship Report for period 1–15 Oct. 1944, LAC Microfilm Reel T-17925.

59 Canadian Army Overseas – 21st Army Group, Censorship Report for period 16–31 May 1945, LAC Microfilm Reel T-17925.
60 Granatstein, *Broken Promises*; Walker, "The Revolt of the Canadian Generals, 1944"; Dawson, *The Conscription Crisis of 1944*; Bothwell, *Canada and Quebec*.
61 Censorship Report – Canadian Army Overseas, for period 16–30 Sept. 1944, LAC Reel T-17925.
62 Censorship Reports – First Canadian Army, 1 Sept. 1944–30 April 1945, LAC Microfilm Reel T-17925.
63 Standard Canadian Infantry Division – Summary of Personnel and Vehicles, LAC RG 24, vol. 18576, file 133.065(D18D); "An Infantry Battalion," GO 466/43, II/233/2, 27 April 1943.
64 Desertion statistics are from: Crerar Papers, LAC RG 30, E157, Vol. 4. AWL statistics are from: Summary of Offences (by Formations) for Canadian Army in the Field, LAC RG 24, vol. 10117, 22/OFFENCE/1/6.
65 Summary of Offences (by Formations) for Canadian Army in the Field, LAC RG 24, vol. 10117, 22/OFFENCE/1/6.
66 Copp and Humphries, *Combat Stress in the 20th Century*, 154.
67 B.H. McNeel, "Quarterly Report of N.P. specialist attached to DDMS Office 2 Cdn Corps, for the quarter 1 Jan 45 to 31 Mar 45 inclusive," LAC RG 24, vol. 12631, file 11/PSYCHIATRY/4.
68 CMHQ Records Office – Consolidated Casualty Statistics, LAC RG 24, vols. 12695 and 12696.
69 In April 1945 the VD rates of Canadian soldiers were again on the rise, and in First Canadian Army in Northwest Europe the rates reached 54.6 per 1,000 strength per month. See Feasby, *Clinical Subjects*, 442–4.
70 *First Canadian Army Intelligence Periodical*, 1, 14 May 1945, quoted in Stacey, *The Victory Campaign*, 641–2.
71 For comments about the Germans being "lice," see Canadian Army Overseas – 21st Army Group, Censorship Report for period 1–15 Nov. 1944, LAC Microfilm Reel T-17925.
72 Canadian Army Overseas – 21st Army Group, Censorship Report for period 16–31 Jan. 1945, LAC Microfilm Reel T-17925. For greater context on the killing of civilians during the Battle of the Bulge, see Schrijvers, *The Unknown Dead*. The German winter offensive did not fall upon First Canadian Army, and the soldiers of 1st Canadian Parachute Battalion, then attached to the British 6th Airborne Division, were among the only Canadians directly involved. See Horn and Wyczynski, *Paras Versus the Reich*, 183–4. For a contemporary video clip: http://www.criticalpast.com/video/65675036158
73 Law, *Westerbork*, 57.
74 Kennedy, *The Shock of War*, 102.

75 Canadian Army Overseas – 21st army Group, Censorship Report for period 16–30 April 1945, LAC Microfilm Reel T-17925.
76 Canadian Army Overseas – 21st army Group, Censorship Report for period 16–30 April 1945, LAC Microfilm Reel T-17925.
77 Canadian Army Overseas – 21st Army Group, Censorship Report for period 16–28 Feb. 1945, LAC Microfilm Reel T-17925.
78 Canadian Army Overseas – 21st Army Group, Censorship Report for period 1–15 March 1945, LAC Microfilm reel T-17925.
79 Canadian Army Overseas – 21st Army Group, Censorship Report for period 16–30 April 1945, LAC Microfilm Reel T-17925.
80 Mowat, *The Regiment*, 304.
81 Canadian Army Overseas – 21st Army Group, Censorship Report for period 16–30 April 1945, LAC Microfilm Reel T-17925.
82 Canadian Army Overseas – 21st Army Group, Censorship Report for period 16–30 April 1945, LAC Microfilm Reel T-17925.
83 Canadian Army Overseas – 21st Army Group, Censorship Report for period 16–30 April 1945, LAC Microfilm Reel T-17925. For a bit more context on the battle at Sögel, see Stacey, *The Victory Campaign*, 558. For more on the destruction of Sögel and the Nazi partisan movement, see Biddiscombe, *Werewolf!*, 258.
84 Granatstein, "The End of Darkness." Wigle's death was later discovered to have been the work of regular German troops who had been bypassed during the rapid German advance, but Vokes remained unrepentant.
85 Vance, *Maple Leaf Empire*, 209.
86 Canadian Army Overseas – 21st Army Group, Censorship Report for period 1–15 March 1945, LAC Microfilm reel T-17925.
87 The widespread sexual assaults on the Eastern Front are well known and on a much larger scale, but sexual violence against German civilians happened on the Western Front as well in 1945, and the story has not been as well told. Paul Jackson is one of the only Canadian historians to discuss this topic even tangentially. See Jackson, *One of the Boys*; Lilly, *Taken by Force*, 109–52; Beevor, *The Fall of Berlin 1945*.
88 See Claire Cookson-Hills, Robert Engen, and Allan English, "Addressing the Problem of Sexual Harassment and Sexual Assault in the CAF: The Canadian Invasion of Germany in 1945 as an Historical Case Study," podium presentation, Canadian Institute for Military and Veterans Health Research Forum 2015, November 2015, Quebec City. Thank you to Dr Claire Cookson-Hills for collaborating on this material with me, and to Dr Jonathan Fennell, who originally found these sources and gave permission for Dr Cookson-Hills to use and share them.
89 Canadian Army Overseas – 21st Army Group, Censorship Report for period 16–30 April 1945, LAC Microfilm Reel T-17925.

90 Lilly, *Taken by Force*, 11.
91 Radzinowicz, *Sexual Offences*, xv.
92 Lilly, *Taken by Force*, 117–18.
93 Canadian Army Overseas – 21st Army Group, Censorship Report for period 16–30 April 1945, LAC Microfilm Reel T-17925.
94 CMHQ Records Office – Consolidated Casualty Statistics – AEF, LAC RG 24, vols. 12695 and 12696; "Standard Canadian Infantry Division – Summary of Personnel and Vehicles," LAC RG 24 vol. 18576, file 133.065(D18D).
95 Censorship Reports – First Canadian Army, 1 Sept. 1944–30 April 1945, LAC Microfilm Reel T-17925.
96 Deficiencies and holdings of Canadian infantry, other ranks: Northwest Europe, Aug. 1944–April 1945, LAC RG 24, vol. 10699. For context, there were 7,600 infantry other ranks in the battalions of an infantry division, and about 2,500 in an armoured division.
97 Copp and McAndrew, *Battle Exhaustion*, 145.
98 CMHQ Records Office – Consolidated Casualty Statistics – AEF, LAC RG 24, vols. 12695 and 12696; "Standard Canadian Infantry Division – Summary of Personnel and Vehicles," LAC RG 24 vol. 18576, file 133.065(D18D).
99 Postwar interview, quoted in Whitaker, *Tug of War*, 224.
100 Notes from 6th Cdn Infantry Brigade Conference, 16 Sept. 1944, LAC RG 24, vol. 10986, 265c6.033(d1).
101 Calgary Highlanders W.D., 12 Oct. 1944, LAC RG 24, vol. 15020.
102 Question 10(g): "Did you detach Left out of Battle personnel?": "Yes," 52 (85%); "No," 4 (7%); no answer, 4 (7%). LAC RG 24, vol. 10450, BEQS.
103 Whitaker, *Tug of War*, 218.
104 Canadian Army Overseas – 21st Army Group, Censorship Report for period 15–30 Nov. 1944, LAC Microfilm Reel T-17925.
105 Extract from a report on the action at Woensdrecht, account by Lt. W.J. Shea, I/O Black Watch (RHC) given to historical officer, 15 Oct. 1944, LAC RG 24, vol. 10669, 215c1.065(d4).
106 Extracts from 1st Battalion, The Black Watch (RHR) of Canada War Diaries, LAC RG 24, vol. 10669, 215c1.065(d4).
107 D'Amour, "Reassessment of a Crisis," 72–89.
108 "Untrained Troops Hazard at Front, Smythe Complains," *Globe and Mail* (19 Sept. 1944), front page.
109 Canadian Army Overseas – 221st Army Group, Censorship Report for period 1–15 Oct. 1944, LAC Microfilm Reel T-17925.
110 "Untrained Troops Hazard at Front, Smythe Complains," *Globe and Mail* (19 Sept. 1944), front page.

111 Question 10(f): "Was [reinforcements'] standard of efficiency high, moderate or low?": "High," 4 (6%); "Moderate," 37 (54%); "Low," 23 (33%); no answer, 5 (7%). LAC RG 24, vol. 10450, BEQS. Several officers responded with answers of "Moderate to Low," in which case they were recorded for both answers, so the total overall respondents are higher for this question.

112 LAC RG 24, vol. 10450. The BEQS studied for these tables represent all Canadian infantry officers with experience fighting in Northwest Europe between October 1944 and April 1945. Sixty-one BEQS were used for this data.

113 Canadian Army Overseas – 221st Army Group, Censorship Report for period 15–31 Oct. 1944, LAC Microfilm Reel T-17925.

114 Copp, *Cinderella Army*, 144.

115 Copp, *The Brigade*, 150.

116 Canadian Army Overseas – 21st Army Group, Censorship Report for period 15–31 Oct. 1944, LAC Microfilm Reel T-17925.

117 Copp, *The Brigade*, 166, n56.

118 Dickson, *A Thoroughly Canadian General*, 370; Engen, "The Zombies' War," presentation at the Society for Military History AGM, March 2013.

119 Canadian Army Overseas – 21st Army Group, Censorship Report for period 1–15 April 1945, LAC Microfilm Reel T-17925.

120 Question 10(a): "Did your section go into battle under WE strength?": "Yes," 50 (82%); "No," 8 (13%); "Not Known," 1; no answer, 2. LAC RG 24, vol. 10450, BEQS.

121 Question 10(d): "Was this strength adequate for close quarters fighting?": "Yes," 36 (59%); "No," 18 (30%); "Not Known," 1; no answer, 6. LAC RG 24, vol. 10450, BEQS.

122 Major R.C. Graves, North Nova Scotia Highlanders, LAC RG 24, vol. 10450, BEQ 280.

123 Bird, *North Shore (New Brunswick) Regiment*, 464.

124 Transcript of interview with Lt-General Robert Moncel, 6 Oct. 1991, RMC Cavalry House Archives, J.L. Granatstein collection.

CONCLUSION

1 McKay and Swift, *Warrior Nation*, 81.

2 Conway, "Training of the Soldier," 210.

3 Ibid., 211.

4 "Replacement coffee" and "war bread."

5 Conway, "Training of the Soldier," 211.

6 Overy, *Why the Allies Won*, 361.

7 Vance, *Maple Leaf Empire*, 149–50.

8 Transcript of interview with Arthur Fraser, Les Fusiliers Mont-Royal, DHH 96/11 file 06, interview by Béatrice Richard.
9 Stacey, *Six Years of War*, 526.
10 Resume of Marriages and Births, of known marriages and births for servicemen married while serving outside Canada to 31 December 1946, Canadian War Brides, accessed 23 March 2014: http://www.canadianwarbrides.com/marriagesstats.asp.
11 When asked why he joined the army in 1939, Jean Poulin of the Royal 22e answered that, aside from adventure, he had been chosen to represent his university's cadet contingent at the coronation of King George VI in London in 1937. Transcript of interview with Jean G. Poulin, Royal 22e Regiment, DHH 96/11 file 06, interview by Béatrice Richard.
12 Conway, "Training of the Soldier," 211.
13 Overy, *Why the Allies Won*, 351.
14 Engen, "The Zombies' War."
15 Yves Tremblay argues that this was due to a command "tactical culture" that did not make the most of its own lessons learned. See Tremblay, "La culture tactique canadienne," 308.
16 Siebold, "Key Questions," 448–68.
17 CMHQ Records – Consolidated Casualty Statistics – CMF, LAC RG 24, vol. 12697 and 12698.
18 Kimberley Watkins, "Association between Combat Experiences and Post-Deployment Mental Health Problems among CAF Members Deployed in Support of the Mission in Afghanistan"; Mark Zamorski, "Recent Suicide Ideation and Combat Exposure in CAF Members Deployed to Afghanistan Between 2009 and 2011," both papers presented at the Canadian Institute for Military and Veterans Health Research, Forum 2014, Toronto, 24–26 Nov. 2014.
19 Conway, "The Training of the Soldier," 214.

APPENDIX A

1 War Diary Extracts, Mediterranean Area and North West Europe, LAC RG 24, vol. 12748, 24/DIARIES/8/.
2 For some background on the Extracts from War Diaries and Memoranda, see Stacey, *A Date with History*, 127–30; Cook, *Clio's Warriors*, 103–4.
3 See account by W.E.C. Harrison of the search for lessons after the Hitler Line: War Diary, June 1944 Summary, QUA, Eric Harrison Fonds, Box 10 File 15.
4 Tremblay, "La culture tactique canadienne," 269–316.
5 Beauregard, *Guerre et censure au Canada,* 113–19.

6 For a similar use of censorship reports in a different Allied formation, the British Eighth Army in North Africa, see Fennell, *Combat and Morale.*
7 McAndrew, *Canadians and the Italian Campaign*, 16.
8 Shalit, *Psychology of Conflict and Combat*, 120.
9 Offence Statistics, 1943–45, LAC RG 24, vol. 12770 and 12771, 29/STATISTICS.
10 Summary of Offences (by Formation), LAC RG 24, vol. 10118 and 10119, 22/OFFENCE/3/.
11 Tooley, "Appearance or Reality?" 40.
12 Casualty Lists – Canadian Formations in AEF [Allied Expeditionary Forces] and Casualty Lists – CMF [Central Mediterranean Forces], LAC RG 24, vols. 12695, 12696, 12697, 12698.
13 "Standard Canadian Infantry Division – Summary of Personnel and Vehicles," LAC RG 24 vol. 18576, file 133.065(D18D).
14 Copp, *Cinderella Army*, 297.
15 DND, *Mobilization Instructions for the Canadian Militia*, 42–4.
16 Personal letter Crerar to Brigadier A.W. Beament, 3 Nov. 1943, quoted in: CMHQ Historical Section Report No. 166, "Administrative Aspects of the Operations of 1 Cdn Inf Div in Italy, December 1943" (29 Nov. 1946), 6.
17 French Canadian Personnel Overseas – Tables, Jan. 1942, LAC RG 24, vol. 5812, HQS 8841 vol. 2.
18 Bernier, *The Royal 22e Regiment*; Tremblay, *Volontaires.*

APPENDIX D

1 For a discussion of the relative merits and demerits of this organizational structure, see English, *The Canadians in Normandy*; French, *Raising Churchill's Army.*
2 Infantry division numbers are from "Standard Canadian Infantry Division – Summary of Personnel and Vehicles," LAC RG 24 vol. 18576, file 133.065(D18D).
3 As historian David Bercuson points out: "That imbalance would later prove a source of great difficulty in combat and would hamper the Canadian Army in its efforts to keep its front-line units up to proper fighting strength. Put bluntly, the Canadian Army contained too many cooks and bottle-washers and too few riflemen." Bercuson, *Maple Leaf Against the Axis*, 18–19.
4 "Standard Canadian Infantry Division"; Bernier, *The Royal 22e Regiment*, 117.
5 Thomas H. Raddall, *West Novas: A History of the West Nova Scotia Regiment* (self-published, 1986, c1947), 83.

6 Kitching, *Mud and Green Fields*, 134. Stats on numbers within the battalion are from "Standard Canadian Infantry Division."
7 Farley Mowat, *And No Birds Sang*, 90.
8 Raddall, *West Novas*, 83; "Standard Canadian Infantry Division." Infantry sections would often go to some lengths to increase their organic firepower by picking up additional, unauthorized automatic weapons outside of their unit's war establishment. See Engen, *Canadians Under Fire*, 133–43.
9 "Standard Canadian Infantry Division."
10 H.F. Joslen, *Orders of Battle: Second World War, 1939–1945* (Uckfield, UK: Naval and Military Press, 2003), 129.
11 For more on the "tactical culture" and some of the problems thereof, see Tremblay, "La culture tactique canadienne," 269–316.
12 French, *Raising Churchill's Army*, 42.

Bibliography

ARCHIVAL SOURCES, CANADA

Canadian Forces Directorate of History and Heritage (DHH), Ottawa, Ontario

CMHQ Historical Reports, 1940–48.
AHQ Historical Reports, 1948–59.
CMHQ Historical Reports, 1960–80.
Collection 79/567, McCartney-Filgate & Whitehead Fonds.
Collection 86/71, Directorate of Personnel Selection Fonds.
Collection 96/11, Fonds Béatrice Richard.
Collection 96/23, Fonds Patrick Capolupo.
Directorate of History Cardex Files.

Canadian War Museum (CWM), Ottawa, Ontario

Manuscript Group 58C 3 22.3, Battle Drill Manual.
Canadian War Museum Oral History Project.
"French Canada and Recruitment during the First World War," online exhibit.
Thomas Edward Charbonneau papers.

Laurier Centre for Military, Strategic, and Disarmament Studies (LCMSDS) Archives, Waterloo, Ontario

Dr. Max Stewart Collection.
Record Group 1 – Ronald Shepherd Operational Research Collection.

Library and Archives Canada (LAC), Ottawa, Ontario

Manuscript Group 28 I161, Canadian Psychological Association.
Manuscript Group 30 E157, Crerar Papers.
Microfilm reels.
Record Group 24, Department of National Defence.
Record Group 150, Military Records.

McGill University Rare Books Library (MURBL), Montreal, Quebec
Colin McDougall Papers.

National Research Council of Canada (NRC), Ottawa, Ontario
C-Series files.
Miscellaneous files.

Queen's University Archives (QUA), Kingston, Ontario
Charles Gavan "Chubby" Power fonds.
"Queen's Remembers" online exhibit.
William Eric Craven Harrison fonds.

Royal Military College of Canada (RMCC) Cavalry House Archives, Kingston, Ontario
Delaney Collection.
Granatstein Collection.
McAndrews Collection.

University of Victoria (UVic), Victoria, British Columbia
Reginald Roy Military Oral History Collection.

ARCHIVAL SOURCES, UNITED KINGDOM

Imperial War Museum (IWM), London
Manuscript Group 91/8/1, private papers of Lord Tweedsmuir.
Manuscript Group 99/2/1, private papers of Major W.H. Pope.
Manuscript Group 216 (3120), Robert Neilland files.

The National Archives (TNA), Kew, London
Records of the Cabinet Office (CAB).
Records of the War Office (WO).

Wellcome Library and Archives (WLA), London
Service Psychiatry Monographs, 1939 to 1945.

PUBLISHED PRIMARY SOURCES

Canada, Department of National Defence. *Mobilization Instructions for the Canadian Militia*. Ottawa: King's Printer, 1937.

Canada, Dominion Bureau of Statistics. *Eighth Census of Canada, 1941, Volume 1: General Review and Summary Tables*. Ottawa: Edmond Cloutier, 1950.

Canada, Department of National Defence. *"Shoot-to-live": Presenting the Johnson Method of Musketry Coaching as adopted by the Canadian Army*. Ottawa: Edmond Cloutier, 1945.

Canada, National Defence Headquarters. *Canadian Infantry Training Centre – Standard Syllabus 1942*. Ottawa: Edmond Cloutier, November 1942.

Conway, Arlington. "The Training of the Soldier." *American Mercury* 2 (May–Aug. 1924).

de Bloch, Jean. "The Wars of the Future." *Contemporary Review* 80 (July/Dec. 1901): 305–32.

Editorial. "Field Service Regulations vol. II and III, 1935." *Canadian Defence Quarterly* 13, 4 (July 1936): 395–403.

Editorial. "Infantry Re-Organization." *Canadian Defence Quarterly* 13, 3 (April 1936): 251–61.

Editorial. "Tactical Change." *Canadian Defence Quarterly* 15, 1 (Oct. 1937): 1–12.

Montgomery, Bernard L. "The Problem of the Encounter Battle as Affected by Modern British War Establishment." *Canadian Defence Quarterly* 15, 1 (Oct. 1937): 13–25.

Olliver, Maurice (ed.). *The Colonial and Imperial Conferences from 1887 to 1937, vol. 1*. Ottawa: Edmond Cloutier, 1954.

United Kingdom, War Office. *Field Service Regulations 1935, Vol. 2: Operations – General*. Ottawa: Edmond Cloutier, 1941.

United Kingdom, War Office. *Infantry Training 1937 Supplement: Tactical Notes for Platoon Commanders*. London, 1941.

United Kingdom, War Office. *Infantry Training 1944 Part VIII – Fieldcraft, Battle Drill, Section and Platoon Tactics*. Canadian printing. Ottawa: February 1944.

United Kingdom, War Office. *Manual of Military Law 1929*. London: His Majesty's Stationery Office, 1940.

United Kingdom, War Office. *Operations – Part 1 – General Principles, Fighting Troops and their Characteristics 1939*. Military Training Pamphlet No. 23. Ottawa: reprinted in Canada, February 1941.

United Kingdom, War Office. *Section Leading 1938*. London: His Majesty's Stationery Office, 1938.

United Kingdom, War Office. *Small Arms Training (SAT) Vol. 1 Pamphlet No. 1: Weapons Training*. London: His Majesty's Stationery Office, 1942, reprinted in Canada, January 1943.

United Kingdom, War Office. Statistical *Report on the Health of the Army, 1943–45*. London: His Majesty's Stationery Office, 1948.

United Kingdom, War Office. *Training and Manoeuvre Regulations 1923*. London: His Majesty's Stationery Office, 1923.

United States Army, Military Intelligence Division. "German Doctrine of the Stabilized Front." Washington, DC: War Department, August 1943.

United States National Research Council. *Psychology for the Fighting Man*. Washington: Penguin Books, 1943.

van der Berg, J.W.C.H. "The Future of Machine Guns in the Attack." *Canadian Defence Quarterly* 14, 1 (Oct. 1936): 45–8.

SECONDARY SOURCES

Advanced Warfighting Studies Program. "Case Study: Operation Overlord." Carlisle Barracks, PA: United States Army War College Department of Military Strategy, Planning, and Operations, 1991.

Ahrenfeldt, Robert H. *Psychiatry in the British Army in the Second World War*. London: Routledge & Kegan Paul, 1958.

Alexander, Harold. "The Conquest of Sicily from 10th July 1943 to 17th August 1943." *London Gazette* (10 Feb. 1948): 1009–25.

Atkinson, Rick. *The Day of Battle: The War in Sicily and Italy, 1943–44*. New York: Henry Holt and Company, 2007.

Barnard, W.T. *The Queen's Own Rifles of Canada, 1860–1960: One Hundred Years of Canada*. Don Mills: Ontario Publishing Company, 1960.

Barris, Ted. *Days of Victory: Canadians Remember, 1939–1945*. Toronto: Macmillan Canada, 1995.

Bartlett, F.C. *Psychology and the Fighting Man*. Cambridge: Cambridge University Press, 1927.

Baynes, John. *Morale – A Study of Men and Courage: The Second Scottish Rifles at the Battle of Neuve Chapelle, 1915*. London: Cassell, 1967.

Beauregard, Claude. *Guerre et censure au Canada, 1939–1945*. Sillery: Septentrion, 1998.

Beattie, Kim. *Dileas: History of the 48th Highlanders of Canada*. Toronto: 48th Highlanders, 1957.

Beckett, Ian F. *The Amateur Military Tradition, 1558–1945*. Manchester: Manchester University Press, 1991.

Beevor, Anthony. *D-Day: The Battle for Normandy*. New York: Penguin Books, 2010.

– *The Fall of Berlin 1945*. New York: Penguin Books, 2003.

Behind Memory's Door: A Collection of Wartime Memories from Science '39, '40, '41 and '42. Kingston: Queen's University, Faculty of Applied Science, 2000.

Ben-Shalom, Uzi, et al. "Cohesion During Military Operations: A Field Study on Combat Units in the Al-Aqsa Intifada." *Armed Forces and Society* 32, 1 (Oct. 2005): 63–79.

Bercuson, David. *The Fighting Canadians: Our Regimental History from New France to Afghanistan*. Toronto: HarperCollins, 2008.

Bernier, Serge. *The Royal 22e Regiment, 1914–1999*. Charles Phillips (trans.). Montreal: Art Global, 2000.

Biddiscombe, Perry. *Werewolf!: The History of the National Socialist Guerrilla Movement, 1944–1946*. Toronto: University of Toronto Press, 1998

Biddle, Stephen and Stephen Long. "Democracy and Military Effectiveness: A Deeper Look." *The Journal of Conflict Resolution* 48, 4 (Aug. 2004): 525–41.

Bird, Will. *North Shore (New Brunswick) Regiment*. Fredericton: Brunswick Press, 1963.

Blumenson, Martin. *Official History of the US Army in World War 2 – The Mediterranean Theater: Salerno to Cassino*. Washington, DC: US Army Center for Military History, 1993, c1969.

Bousfield, Arthur and Garry Toffoli. *Royal Observations: Canadians and Royalty*. Toronto: Dundurn Press, 1991.

Bradford, R.D. *Decorations and Awards Received During World War II 1939–1945 by the Hastings and Prince Edward Regiment*. Belleville, ON: The Regimental Senate, 1986.

Brewer, John. *Sinews of Power: War, Money, and the English State, 1688-1783*. London: Unwin Hyman, 1989.

Broadfoot, Barry. *Ten Lost Years, 1929–1939: Memories of Canadians Who Survived the Depression*. Markham: PaperJacks, 1975.

Brown, Andrew. "New Men in the Line: An Assessment of Reinforcements to the 48th Highlanders in Italy, January–October 1944." *Canadian Military History* 21, 3 (summer 2012): 35–47.

Brown, Ian M. "Not Glamorous, But Effective: The Canadian Corps and the Set-Piece Attack, 1917–1918." *The Journal of Military History* 58, 3 (July 1994): 421–44.

Brown, Shaun R.G. "'The Rock of Accomplishment': The Loyal Edmonton Regiment at Ortona." *Canadian Military History* 2, 2 (autumn 1993).

Burns, E.L.M. *General Mud: Memoirs of Two World Wars*. Toronto: Clarke, Irwin & Co., 1970.

– *Manpower in the Canadian Army, 1939–1945*. Toronto: Clarke Irwin, 1956.

Buckley, John. *Monty's Men: The British Army and the Liberation of Europe*. New Haven: Yale University Press, 2013.

Callahan, Raymond. "Two Armies in Normandy: Weighing British and Canadian Military Performance." In Theodore A. Wilson, ed., *D-Day 1944*. Abilene: University Press of Kansas, 1994.

Carver, H.S.M. *Personnel Selection in the Canadian Army: A Descriptive Study*. Ottawa: Directorate of Personnel Selection NDHQ, 1945.

Cederberg, Fred. *Long Road Home: The Autobiography of a Canadian Soldier in Italy in World War II*. Don Mills, ON: General Publishing, 1984.

Cessford, Mike. "'Crack Canadian Troops': Clearing the South Bank of the Valli Di Commachio, 2–6 January 1945." *Army Training and Doctrine Bulletin* 1, 1 (summer 1998): 34–43.

Chatillon, Claude. *Carnets de guerre: Ottawa-Casa Berardi, 1941–1944*. Ottawa: Editions du Vermillon, 1987.

Churchill, Winston. *The Second World War, Vol. 6: Triumph and Tragedy.* Boston: Houghton Mifflin, 1948.

Cohen, Eliot. *Citizens and Soldiers: The Dilemmas of Military Service*. Ithaca: Cornell University Press, 1985.

Coker, Christopher. *Waging War Without Warriors? The Changing Culture of Military Conflict*. London: Lynne Rienner, 2002.

Collins, Robert. *You Had to Be There: An Intimate Portrait of the Generation that Survived a Depression, Won World War II, and Re-invented Canada.* Toronto: McClelland & Stewart, 1997.

Comeau, Paul-André, et al. *La Democratie en veilleuse: rapport des censeurs, 1939–1945*. Montreal: Editions Québec/Amérique, 1995.

Cook, Tim. *At the Sharp End: Canadians Fighting the Great War, 1914–1916.* Toronto: Viking Canada, 2007.

– *Clio's Warriors: Canadian Historians and the Writing of the World Wars*. Vancouver: UBC Press, 2006.

– "The Politics of Surrender: Canadian Soldiers and the Killing of Prisoners in the Great War." *Journal of Military History* 70, 3 (July 2006): 637–65.

Copp, Terry. "Canadian Operational Art: The Siege of Boulogne and Calais." *Canadian Army Journal* 9, 1 (spring 2006).

– *Cinderella Army: The Canadians in Northwest Europe, 1944–45*. Toronto: University of Toronto Press, 2006.

– *Fields of Fire: The Canadians in Normandy*. Toronto: University of Toronto Press, 2003.

– and Bill McAndrew. *Battle Exhaustion: Soldiers and Psychiatrists in the Canadian Army, 1939–1945*. Montreal & Kingston: McGill-Queen's University Press, 1990.

– and Mark Humphries (eds.). *Combat Stress in the 20th Century: The Commonwealth Perspective*. Kingston: Canadian Defence Academy Press, 2010.

– and Robert Vogel. *Maple Leaf Route: Victory.* Alma: Maple Leaf Route, 1988.

Corum, James. *The Roots of Blitzkrieg: Hans Von Seeckt and the German Military Reform*. Lawrence: University Press of Kansas, 1992.

Curtis, Bruce. *The Politics of Population: State Formation, Statistics, and the Census of Canada, 1840–1875*. Toronto: University of Toronto Press, 2001.

D'Amours, Caroline. "Reassessment of a Crisis: Canadian Infantry Reinforcements during the Second World War." *Canadian Army Journal* 14, 2 (2012): 72–89.

Dancocks, Daniel. *The D-Day Dodgers: The Canadians in Italy, 1943–1945*. Toronto: McClelland & Stewart, 1991.

David, Saul. *Mutiny at Salerno: An Injustice Exposed*. London: Conway Maritime Press, 2005.

Dawson, Robert MacGregor. *The Conscription Crisis of 1944*. Toronto: University of Toronto Press, 1961.

Delaney, Douglas. "Knowing Enough Not to Interfere: Lieutenant-General Charles Foulkes at the Lamone River, December 1944." In Geoffrey Hayes (ed.). *Canada and the Second World War: Essays in Honour of Terry Copp*. Waterloo, ON: Wilfrid Laurier University, 2013.

– *The Soldiers' General: Bert Hoffmeister at War*. Vancouver: UBC Press, 2005.

D'Este, Carlo. *Bitter Victory: The Battle for Sicily, 1943*. New York: Harper Perennial, 2008, c1991.

– *Decision in Normandy*. New York: Koencky, 2001.

Dickson, Paul. *A Thoroughly Canadian General: A Biography of General H.D.G. Crerar*. Toronto: University of Toronto Press, 2007.

Doubler, Michael. *Closing with the Enemy: How GIs fought the War in Europe, 1944–1945*. Lawrence: University of Kansas Press, 1994.

Douglas, W.A.B. and Brereton Greenhous. *Out of the Shadows*. Toronto: Oxford University Press, 1977.

Dupuy, Trevor. *Numbers, Prediction, and War: Using History to Evaluate Combat Factors and Predict the Outcome of Battles*. New York: Bobbs-Merrill, 1979.

Durflinger, Serge. "City at War: The Effects of the Second World War on Verdun, Quebec." PhD Dissertation, McGill University, 1997.

– *Fighting from Home: The Second World War in Verdun, Quebec*. Vancouver: UBC Press, 2006.

Dykstra, Ralph. "The Liberation of Groningen – An Urban Battlefield." *Army Doctrine and Training Bulletin* 5, 3 (fall 2002).

Ellis, John. *Brute Force: Allied Strategy and Tactics in the Second World War*. London: A. Deutsch, 1990.

– *Cassino: The Hollow Victory – the Battle for Rome, January–June 1944*. New York: McGraw-Hill, 1984.

Ellis, Lionel F. *Victory in the West, Vol. 1: The Battle of Normandy*. London: Her Majesty's Stationery Office, 1962.

– *Victory in the West, Vol. 2: The Defeat of Germany*. London: Her Majesty's Stationery Office, 1968.

Engen, Robert. *Canadians Under Fire: Infantry Effectiveness in the Second World War*. Montreal & Kingston: McGill-Queen's University Press, 2009.

– "The Zombies' War: Conscripts and Volunteers in the Canadian Army." Unpublished paper presented at the Society for Military History AGM, 2013.

English, John A. *The Canadian Army in Normandy: A Study of Failure in High Command*. Praeger: New York, 1991.

Feasby, W.R. *Official History of the Canadian Medical Services 1939–1945, Vol. 1: Campaigns*. Ottawa: Edmond Cloutier, 1956.

– *Official History of the Canadian Medical Services 1939–1945, Vol. 2: Clinical Problems*. Ottawa: Edmond Cloutier, 1953.

Fennell, Jonathan. *Combat and Morale in the North African Campaign: The Eighth Army and the Path to Alamein*. Cambridge: Cambridge University Press, 2011.

French, David. *Raising Churchill's Army: The British Army and the War against Germany, 1919–1945*. Oxford: Oxford University Press, 2000.

Frost, C. Sydney. *Once a Patricia: Memoirs of a Junior Infantry Officer in World War II*. St Catharines, ON: Vanwell Publishing, 1988.

Galloway, Strome. *A Regiment at War: The Story of the Royal Canadian Regiment, 1939–1945*. 1979.

Garland, Albert N. and Howard McGaw Smyth. *The United States Army in World War 2: Mediterranean Theater of Operations – Sicily and the Surrender of Italy*. Washington, DC: US Army Center for Military History, 1965.

Gibson, Frederick W. (ed.). *Ottawa at War: The Grant Dexter Memoranda, 1939–45*. Winnipeg: Manitoba Record Society, 1994.

Gould, Stephen Jay. *The Mismeasure of Man*. New York: Norton, 1996.

Granatstein, J.L. *Broken Promises: A History of Conscription in Canada*. Toronto: Oxford University Press, 1977.

– *Canada's Army: Waging War and Keeping the Peace*. Toronto: University of Toronto Press, 2002.

– *Conscription in the Second World War, 1939–45: A Study in Political Management*. Toronto: Ryerson Press, 1969.

– "The End of Darkness." *Legion Magazine* (1 May 2005).

– *The Generals: The Canadian Army's Senior Commanders in the Second World War*. Calgary: University of Calgary Press, 2005.

Gravel, Jean-Yves (ed.). *Le Québec et la guerre*. Montreal: Boréal Express, 1974.

Greenhous, Brereton. "'Would It Not Have Been Better to Bypass Ortona Completely...?': A Canadian Christmas, 1943." *Canadian Defence Quarterly* 18, 5 (April 1989): 51–5.

Harris, Stephen. *Canadian Brass: The Making of a Professional Army, 1860–1939*. Toronto: University of Toronto Press, 1988.

Hastings, Max. *Overlord: D-Day and the Battle for Normandy*. New York: Macmillan, 1993.

Hauser, William L. "The Will to Fight." In Sam Sarkesian (ed.). *Combat Effectiveness: Cohesion, Stress, and the Volunteer Military*. London: Sage Publications, 1980.

Hayes, Allan J. *Anglicans in Canada: Controversies and Identity in Historical Perspective*. Urbana and Chicago: University of Illinois Press, 2004.

Hayes, Geoffrey. "The Development of the Canadian Army Officer Corps, 1939–1945." PhD dissertation: University of Western Ontario, 1992.

Hayes, Geoffrey. *The Lincs: A History of the Lincoln and Welland Regiment at War*. Alma, ON: Maple Leaf Route, 1986.

Hayes, Geoffrey, Mike Bechtoldt and Matt Symes (eds.). *Canada and the Second World War: Essays in Honour of Terry Copp*. Waterloo, ON: Wilfrid Laurier University, 2013.

Henderson, William Darryl. *Cohesion: The Human Element in Combat*. Washington, DC: National Defence University Press, 1985.

Horn, Bernd. "Warrior / Scholar: A Critical Union in the Contemporary Operating Environment." In Bernd Horn and Jeff Stouffer (eds.). *Educating the Leader and Leading the Educated: The Defence Learning, Education and Training Handbook*. Kingston: CDA Press, 2012.

Horn, Bernd and Michel Wyczynski. *Paras Versus the Reich: Canada's Paratroopers at War, 1942–45*. Toronto: Dundurn Group, 2003.

Horn, Michiel (ed.). *The Dirty Thirties: Canadians in the Great Depression*. Toronto: Copp Clark, 1972.

Humphries, Mark. "War's Long Shadow: Masculinity, Medicine, and the Gendered Politics of Trauma, 1914–1939." *Canadian Historical Review* 91, 3 (Sept. 2010): 504–32.

Jackson, Paul. *One of the Boys: Homosexuality in the Military during World War II*. Montreal and Kingston: McGill-Queen's University Press, 2010.

Jackson, William. *The Mediterranean and Middle East, Vol. VI, Part 1 – Victory in the Mediterranean: 1 April to 4 June 1944*. London: Her Majesty's Stationery Office, 1984.

– *The Mediterranean and Middle East, Vol. VI, Part 2 – Victory in the Mediterranean, June to October 1944*. London: Her Majesty's Stationery Office, 1987.

– *The Mediterranean and Middle East, Vol. VI, Part 3 – Victory in the Mediterranean, November 1944 to May 1945*. London: Her Majesty's Stationery Office, 1987.

Kellett, Anthony. *Combat Motivation: The Behavior of Soldiers in Battle*. Boston: Kluwer-Nijhoff Publishing, 1984, c1982.

Kennedy, Sean. *The Shock of War: Civilian Experiences 1937–1945*. Toronto: University of Toronto Press, 2011.

Keshen, Jeffrey. *Saints, Sinners, and Soldiers: Canada's Second World War*. Vancouver: UBC Press, 2004.

Kesselring, Albert. *The Memoirs of Field-Marshal Kesselring*. London: William Kimer, 1974, c1953.

Kipp, Charles Disbrowe. *Because We Are Canadians: A Battlefield Memoir*. Vancouver: Douglas & McIntyre, 2003.

Kitching, George. *Mud and Green Fields: The Memoirs of Major-General George Kitching*. Langley, BC: Battleline Books, 1986.

Lackenbauer, P. Whitney. *A Commemorative History of Aboriginal Peoples in the Canadian Military*. Ottawa: Directorate of History and Heritage, 2010.

Laurence, Jance H. and Michael D. Matthew (eds.). *The Oxford Handbook of Military Psychology*. Oxford: Oxford University Press, 2012.

Law, Cecil. *Westerbork: Transit Camp to Eternity*. Clementsport, NS.: Canadian Peacekeeping Press, 2000.

Law, Clive. *Regimental Numbers of the Canadian Army, 1939–1960*. Ottawa: Service Publications, 2000.

Liedtke, Gregory. "Canadian Offensive Operations in Normandy Revisited." *Canadian Military Journal* 8, 2 (summer 2007): 60–8.

Lilly, J. Robert. *Taken by Force: Rape and American GIs in Europe during World War II*. New York: Palgrave Macmillan, 2007.

Linklater, Eric. *The Campaign in Italy*. London: His Majesty's Stationery Office, 1951.

Lorelli, John. *To Foreign Shores: U.S. Amphibious Operations in World War II*. Annapolis: Naval Institute Press, 1995.

MacFarlane, John. *Triquet's Cross: A Story of Military Heroism*. Montreal and Kingston: McGill-Queen's University Press, 2009.

MacGregor, E.M.K. "In Defence of Battledrill." *Canadian Defence Quarterly* 4 (spring 1972): 24-9.

Madsen, Chris. *Another Kind of Justice: Canadian Military Law from Confederation to Somalia*. Vancouver: UBC Press, 1999.

Manning, Frederick. "Morale, Cohesion and Esprit de Corps." In Reuven Gal and A. David Mangelsdorff (eds.). *Handbook of Military Psychology*. Chichester: John Wiley, 1991.

Margolian, Harold. *Conduct Unbecoming: The Story of the Murder of Canadian Prisoners of War in Normandy*. Toronto: University of Toronto Press, 1998.

Marshall, S.L.A. *Men Against Fire: The Problem of Battle Command in Future War*. New York: William Morrow and Company, 1968.

Martin, Charles Cromwell. *Battle Diary: from D-Day and Normandy to the Zuider Zee and VE*. Toronto: Dundurn Press, 1994.

May, Ernest. *Strange Victory: Hitler's Conquest of France*. New York: Hill and Wang, 2000.
McAndrew, William. *Canadians and the Italian Campaign, 1943–1945*. Montreal: Art Global, 1995.
– "Fire or Movement? Canadian Tactical Doctrine, Sicily – 1943." *Military Affairs* 51, 3 (July 1987): 140–5.
McKay, Ian. "Canada as a Long Liberal Revolution: On Writing the History of Actually Existing Canadian Liberalisms, 1840s–1940s." In Jean-François Constant and Michel Ducharme (eds.), *Liberalism and Hegemony: Debating the Canadian Liberal Revolution*. Toronto: University of Toronto Press, 2009.
– and Robin Bates. *In the Province of History: The Making of the Public Past in Twentieth-Century Nova Scotia*. Montreal and Kingston: McGill-Queen's University Press, 2010.
– and Jamie Swift. *Warrior Nation: Rebranding Canada in an Age of Anxiety.* Toronto: Between the Lines, 2012.
Miller, Ian. "Toronto's Response to the Outbreak of War, 1939." *Canadian Military History* 11, 1 (2002): 7–21.
Milner, Marc. *Stopping the Panzers: The Untold Story of D-Day.* Lawrence: University Press of Kansas, 2014.
Mitcham, Samuel. *Hitler's Legions: The German Order of Battle, World War II*. New York: Henry Holt, 1985.
Molony, C.J.C. *The Mediterranean and the Middle East, Vol. 5: The Campaign in Sicily 1943 and the Campaign in Italy 1943–1944*. London: Her Majesty's Stationery Office, 1973.
Montgomery, Bernard L. *The Memoirs of Field-Marshal the Viscount Montgomery of Alamein, K.G.* Cleveland and New York: World Publishing Company, 1958.
Morton, Desmond. *A Military History of Canada*. Toronto: McClelland & Stewart, 2007.
– *When Your Number's Up: The Canadian Soldier in the First World War*. Toronto: Random House, 1993.
Moskos, C.C. *The American Enlisted Man*. New York: Russell Sage Foundation, 1970.
Mowat, Farley. *And No Birds sang*. Toronto: McClelland & Stewart, 1979.
– *The Regiment*. Toronto: McClelland & Stewart, 1955.
Munro, Ross. *Gauntlet to Overlord*. Toronto: Macmillan, 1946.
National Research Council, United States. *Psychology for the Fighting Man*. Washington, DC: Penguin Books, 1943.
Neillands, Robin. *Eighth Army: The Triumphant Desert Army That Held the Axis at Bay from North Africa to the Alps, 1939–45*. New York: Overlook Press, 2004.

Nicholson, G.W.L. *Official History of the Canadian Army in the Second World War, Vol. 2 – The Canadians in Italy, 1943–1945*. Ottawa: Edmond Cloutier, 1956.

O'Keefe, David. "With Blinders On: The Black Watch and the Battle for Spycker, September 12–14 1944." *Canadian Army Journal* 11, 1 (spring 2008): 98–109.

Oldfield, J.E. *The Westminsters' War Diary: An Unofficial History of the Westminster Regiment (Motor) in World War II*. Vancouver: Mitchell Press, 1964.

Overy, Richard. *Why the Allies Won*. London: Pimlico, 2006.

Petrou, Michael. *Renegades: Canadians in the Spanish Civil War*. Vancouver: UBC Press, 2008.

Place, Timothy Harrison. *Military Training in the British Army, 1940–1944: From Dunkirk to D-Day*. London: Routledge, 2000.

Pond, Hugh. *Sicily*. London, 1962.

Porch, Douglas. *The Path to Victory: The Mediterranean Theater in World War 2*. New York: Farrar, Straus and Giroux, 2004.

Possony, Stefan and Etienne Mantoux. "Du Picq and Foch: The French School." In Edward Mead Earle, ed., *Makers of Modern Strategy: Military Thought from Machiavelli to Hitler*. New York: Atheneum, 1967.

Radzinowicz, Leon. *Sexual Offences: A Report of the Cambridge Department of Criminal Science*. London: Macmillan, 1957.

Reid, Brian A. *No Holding Back: Operation Totalize, Normandy, August 1944*. Toronto: Robin Brass, 2005.

Rodgers, Thomas E. "Billy Yank and G.I. Joe: An Exploratory Essay on the Sociopolitical Dimensions of Soldier Motivation." *Journal of Military History* 69, 1 (Jan. 2005): 93–121.

Roy, Reginald. *The Seaforth Highlanders of Canada, 1919–1965*. Vancouver: Evergreen Press, 1969.

Ryan, Joseph. *Samuel Stouffer and the GI Survey: Sociologists and Soldiers during the Second World War*. Knoxville: University of Tennessee Press, 2013.

Sarkesian, Sam (ed.). *Combat Effectiveness: Cohesion, Stress, and the Volunteer Military*. London: Sage Publications, 1980.

Shalit, Ben. *The Psychology of Conflict and Combat*. New York: Praeger, 1988.

Shils, Edgar and Morris Janowitz. "Cohesion and Disintegration in the Wehrmacht in World War II." *Public Opinion Quarterly* 12 (1948): 280–315.

Shurkin, Michael. "France's War in Mali: Lessons for an Expeditionary Army." Santa Monica, CA: RAND Corporation, 2014.

Siebold, Guy. "The Essence of Military Cohesion." *Armed Forces and Society* 33, 2 (Jan. 2007): 286–95.

Smelser, Ronald and Edward J. Davies II. *The Myth of the Eastern Front: The Nazi-Soviet War in American Popular Culture*. Cambridge: Cambridge University Press, 2007.

Spiller, Roger J. "S.L.A. Marshall and the Ratio of Fire." *RUSI Journal*, 133 (1988).

Stacey, Charles P. *A Date with History: Memoirs of a Canadian Historian*. Toronto: Deneau, 1983.

– *Arms, Men and Governments: The War Policies of Canada, 1939–1945*. Ottawa: Queen's Printer, 1970.

– *Official History of the Canadian Army in the Second World War, Vol. 1 – Six Years of War: The Army in Canada, Britain and the Pacific*. Ottawa: Edmond Cloutier, 1955.

– *Official History of the Canadian Army in the Second World War, Vol. 3 – The Victory Campaign: Operations in North-West Europe, 1944–1945*. Ottawa: Edmond Cloutier, 1960.

– *The Canadian Army, 1939–45: An Official Historical Summary*. Ottawa: Edmond Cloutier, 1948.

– "The Life and Hard Times of an Official Historian." *Canadian Historical Review* 51, 1 (1970): 21–47.

Stevens, G.R. *A City Goes to War*. Brampton: Charters Publishing, 1967.

– *The Royal Canadian Regiment, Vol. 2: 1933–1966*. London, ON: London Printing, 1967.

Stevenson, Michael. *Canada's Greatest Wartime Muddle: National Selection and the Mobilization of Human Resources during World War II*. Montreal & Kingston: McGill-Queen's University Press, 2001.

Stouffer, Samuel A. et al. *The American Soldier, Volume 2: Combat and Its Aftermath*. Princeton: Princeton University Press, 1949.

Thompson, John Herd and Allen Seager. *Canada 1922–1939: Decades of Discord*. Toronto: McClelland & Stewart, 1985.

Tooley, Robert. "Appearance or Reality? Variations in Infantry Courts Martial – 1st Canadian Division: 1940–1945." *Canadian Defence Quarterly* 22 (1992): 33–40.

– *Invicta: The Carleton and York Regiment in the Second World War*. Fredericton, NB: New Ireland Press, 1989.

Tremblay, Yves. "La culture tactique canadienne: le cas de l'opération Chesterfield, 23 mai 1944." In Geoffrey Hayes, et al. (eds.). *Canada and the Second World War: Essays in Honour of Terry Copp*. Waterloo, ON: Wilfrid Laurier University Press, 2013.

– *Volontaires: Des Québécois en guerre, 1939–1945*. Outremont: Athéna éditions, 2006.

Vance, Jonathan. *Death So Noble: Memory, Meaning, and the First World War*. Vancouver: UBC Press, 1997.

– *Maple Leaf Empire: Canada, Britain, and Two World Wars*. Oxford: Oxford University Press, 2012.

Wakelam, Randall. "Try and Try Again: Defining and Implementing Effective Professional Education in the Canadian Forces." In Bernd Horn and Jeff Stouffer, eds., *Educating the Leader and Leading the Educated: The Defence Learning, Education and Training Handbook*. Kingston: CDA Press, 2012.

Walker, Richard J. "The Revolt of the Canadian Generals, 1944: The Case for the Prosecution." In Howard G. Coombs, ed., *The Insubordinate and the Noncompliant: Case Studies of Canadian Mutiny and Disobedience, 1920 to Present*. Kingston: CDA Press, 2007.

Watson, Peter. *War on the Mind: The Military Uses and Abuses of Psychology*. New York: Basic Books, 1978.

Wedemayer, Albert C. *Wedemayer Reports!* New York, 1958.

Weintraub, William. *City Unique: Montreal Days and Nights in the 1940s and '50s*. Toronto: McClelland & Stewart, 1996.

Whitaker, W. Denis. *Tug of War: Eisenhower's Lost Opportunity*. New York: Beaufort Books, 1984.

Whitaker, Denis and Shelagh Whitaker, with Terry Copp. *Victory at Falaise: The Soldiers' Story*. Toronto: HarperCollins, 2000.

Wieviorka, Olivier. *Normandy: The Landings to the Liberation of Paris*. M.B. DeBevoise (trans.). Cambridge, MA: Belknap Press of Harvard University Press, 2008.

Williams, Jeffery. *The Long Left Flank: The Hard-Fought Way to the Reich, 1944–45*. Toronto: Stoddart, 1988.

Wilmot, Laurence F. *Through the Hitler Line: Memoirs of an Infantry Chaplain*. Waterloo, ON: Wilfrid Laurier University Press, 2003.

Windsor, Lee. "Overlord's Long Right Flank: The Battles for Cassino and Anzio, January-June 1944." In Geoffrey Hayes (ed.). *Canada and the Second World War: Essays in Honour of Terry Copp*. Waterloo, ON: Wilfrid Laurier University Press, 2013.

Windsor, Lee. "'The Eyes of All Fixed on Sicily': Canada's Unexpected Victory, 1943." *Canadian Military History* 22, 3 (summer 2013): 4–34.

– "'Boforce': 1st Canadian Infantry Division Operations in Support of the Salerno Bridgehead, Italy, 1943." *Canadian Military History* 4, 2 (autumn 1995): 51–60.

Winslow, Donna. "Rites of Passage and Group Bonding in the Canadian Airborne." *Armed Forces and Society* 25 (1999): 429–57.

Wood, James. *Militia Myths: Ideas of the Canadian Citizen Soldier, 1896–1921*. Vancouver: UBC Press, 2010.

Zaloga, Steven. *Armored Thunderbolt: The U.S. Army Sherman in World War II*. Mechanicsburg, PA: Stackpole Books, 2008.

Index